# EUROPEAN PENOLOGY?

Is there something distinctive about penology in Europe? Do Europeans think about punishment and penal policy in a different way to people in other parts of the globe? If so, why is this the case and how does it work in practice? This book addresses some major and pressing issues that have been emerging in recent years in the interdisciplinary field of 'European penology', that is, a space where legal scholarship, criminology, sociology and political science meet—or should meet—in order to make sense of punishment in Europe. The chapters in *European Penology*? have been written by leading scholars in the field and focus in particular on the interaction of European academic penology and national practice, with European policies as developed by the Council of Europe and, increasingly, by the European Union.

Oñati International Series in Law and Society

A SERIES PUBLISHED FOR THE OÑATI INSTITUTE FOR THE SOCIOLOGY OF LAW



**Recent titles in this series**

Challenging Gender Inequality in Tax Policy Making: Comparative Perspectives
edited by Kim Brooks, Åsa Gunnarson, Lisa Philipps and Maria Wersig

Emotions, Crime and Justice
edited by Susanne Karstedt, Ian Loader and Heather Strang

Mediation in Political Conflicts
Soft Power or Counter Culture?
edited by Jacques Faget

Criminological and Legal Consequences of Climate Change
edited by Stephen Farrall, Tawhida Ahmed and Duncan French

Shooting to Kill: Socio-Legal Perspectives on the Use of Lethal Force
edited by Simon Bronitt, Miriam Gani and Saskia Hufnagel

Managing Family Justice in Diverse Societies
edited by Mavis Maclean and John Eekelaar

Making Human Rights Intelligible
Towards a Sociology of Human Rights
edited by Mikael Rask Madsen and Gert Verschraegen

**For the complete list of titles in this series, see 'Oñati International Series in Law and Society' link at www.hartpub.co.uk/books/series.asp**

# European Penology?

Edited by

Tom Daems
Dirk van Zyl Smit
and
Sonja Snacken

Oñati International Series in Law and Society

A SERIES PUBLISHED FOR THE OÑATI INSTITUTE
FOR THE SOCIOLOGY OF LAW

•HART•
PUBLISHING
OXFORD AND PORTLAND, OREGON
2017

**Hart Publishing**
An imprint of Bloomsbury Publishing Plc

Hart Publishing Ltd
Kemp House
Chawley Park
Cumnor Hill
Oxford OX2 9PH
UK

Bloomsbury Publishing Plc
50 Bedford Square
London
WC1B 3DP
UK

**www.hartpub.co.uk**
**www.bloomsbury.com**

Published in North America (US and Canada) by
Hart Publishing
c/o International Specialized Book Services
920 NE 58th Avenue, Suite 300
Portland, OR 97213-3786
USA

**www.isbs.com**

**HART PUBLISHING, the Hart/Stag logo, BLOOMSBURY and the Diana logo are trademarks of Bloomsbury Publishing Plc**

First published in hardback, 2013
Paperback edition, 2017



**British Library Cataloguing-in-Publication Data**
A catalogue record for this book is available from the British Library.

ISBN: HB: 978-1-84946-233-4
PB: 978-1-50991-450-0

Typeset by Compuscript Ltd, Shannon
Printed and bound in Great Britain by
Lightning Source UK Ltd

# *Preface*

The question mark in the short title of this book, *European Penology?*, should alert the reader to two important but difficult questions that troubled us as editors as we began to conceive of this book as a means of understanding what was happening in the sphere of punishment in one part of the globe. What do we mean by 'penology'? And, how is what we mean by penology modified by the adjective, 'European'? Neither question can be answered satisfactorily by dictionary definitions, for the meaning of the words depends on the context of their usage. In the papers collected in this book this context is approached in several ways, which, we believe, collectively provide some answers that have hitherto been lacking to these questions.

In **Part One,** the underlying questions relating to **concepts and institutions** are addressed most directly: in Chapter 1 two editors, Sonja Snacken and Dirk van Zyl Smit, tackle the definitional issue head-on by pointing out that even within Europe, definitions of 'penology' vary greatly. They proceed to argue that an understanding of European penology is better reached by focusing on the specific European institutional context: the existence and roles of two pan-European organisations, the Council of Europe and the European Union, which are involved in intergovernmental and supranational penal policy-making and penological standard setting. Snacken and van Zyl Smit focus in particular on the Council of Europe which, as a result of the recommendations of its Committee of Ministers, the judgments of the European Court of Human Rights and the standards developed by the European Committee for the Prevention of Torture (CPT), has long been the leading European body in the penological field. They also seek to demonstrate that insights into the core of the collective meaning of penology for Europeans emerge from an examination of how European institutions, which act on behalf of European states jointly, intervene in penological issues, such as the death penalty, when they arise outside Europe.

The third editor, Tom Daems, addresses the meaning of 'European' in Chapter 2, by asking how notions of what Europe is have impacted on the overall approach to penology. Daems relies particularly on Ulrich Beck's idea of a 'cosmopolitan Europe' to ground his conception of Europe as an area which, while remaining open to the world, allows particular normative values to triumph. In Chapter 3 the theoretical discussion of the meaning and normative content of both 'penology' and 'European' are taken further by Ian Loader and Richard Sparks, who argue that the policy values that they identified in their earlier work as being inherent in 'public criminology', should apply on the European penological stage also.

The discussion of the European institutional context is developed further in Chapters 4 and 5 by Estella Baker and Roland Miklau respectively. Both focus on the European Union. Baker in her chapter considers how an increasing role has been carved out for the EU in penological matters and emphasises that, while the EU has a great deal of power that it can and increasingly does exercise in matters of penological concern, it also has a commitment, similar if not identical to that of the Council of Europe, to human right values that impact on the penological sphere. Baker's chapter is complemented by that of Miklau, which concentrates on attempts to approximate sanctions across the member states of the EU. Miklau warns that efficiency and necessary severity are often the primary concerns of the EU, and contrasts this unfavourably with the emphasis on proportionality and minimum intervention in the sentencing recommendations of the Council of Europe.

**Part Two** of the book groups together chapters that address a range of **cross-cutting issues** that arise in all European states and which can benefit from being studied at a European level. Prominent amongst these is immigation, which has placed pressures on European penal systems of a kind they have not experienced before. In Chapter 6, Dario Melossi argues strongly that a different pan-European approach is required to this issue. This approach would involve a dialogue, which has not been conducted hitherto, about fundamental 'European' values and their application to immigrants. Chapter 7 by Frieder Dünkel is more optimistic. On the basis of his comparative research, Dünkel discerns youth justice in Europe as being 'relatively invulnerable' to wider punitive tendencies and, while recognising that much more needs to be done at the national level, emphasises the important role that European and international human rights standards play in protecting young people against the worst excesses of the penal system. There is some cautious optimism too in Fergus McNeill's account of community sanctions and their place in European penology in Chapter 8. While McNeill recognises the danger of community sanctions increasingly becoming part of a culture of control that is imbued, particularly in Anglo-American jurisdictions, with a 'new punitiveness', he sees significant countervailing tendencies in the continued and even growing consensus at the pan-European level on social justice and on working with offenders in the community to foster their social inclusion.

Although in law remand detention should never be used as a punishment, it can increase the penal impact of the criminal justice system: certainly as it is perceived by the detained offender. In Chapter 9 Christine Morgenstern outlines national and European measures that are taken to prevent this abuse. Alison Liebling in Chapter 10 addresses the question of privatisation of (aspects of) imprisonment. Liebling points out that, although prison privatisation is primarily associated with common-law jurisdictions within and outside Europe, the reality is that all European states have to purchase some goods and services from private sector providers. More attention should therefore be paid, at the European level too, to how this is done and what impact privatisation, whether full or partial, will have both on penal policy and on prison conditions.

In **Part Three** the focus moves to **nationally based perspectives** for, as David Nelken has emphasised, all efforts to develop Europe-wide standards must face the challenges of ingrained differences in practice in national jurisdictions. In Chapter 11 Nelken illustrates this truth by describing the intricate debates about prosecutorial independence in Italy and the complexity of the impact that reliance on European standards can have in these debates—with further unintended consequences for offenders caught up in the system. Chapter 12 by Kristel Beyens, Sonja Snacken and Dirk van Zyl Smit also refers to unintended, or at least hidden, consequences of oversimplification. Surely, one may ask ironically, everyone should favour truth in sentencing, if its opposite would be dishonesty? However, by focusing on how complex the interaction between the decision to impose a sentence and the manner of its implementation is in Belgium and elsewhere, Beyens, Snacken and van Zyl Smit expose the shallowness of a slogan such as 'truth in sentencing', which tends to focus only on the formal imposition of a sentence and ignores the rest of the penal process of which it forms part. Complexity is also the keynote issue underlying the conviction-based employment discrimination that is described by Elena Larrauri and James B Jacobs in Chapter 13. Larrauri and Jacobs point out that whether there is such discrimination has not been studied systematically in Spain or elsewhere in Europe, and they speculate that this might be because criminal records are not made public in European jurisdictions in the same way they are in the United States. However, as they point out, this is not a guarantee that there is no such discrimination, for in Spain, as in other European countries, some positions may not be filled by persons who have a criminal record, and there may be discrimination for other, less legally acceptable reasons too.

Finally, Part Three concludes with two chapters dealing with the complexities of the impact of punitive tendencies in different parts of Europe. In Chapter 14 Krzysztof Krajewski reflects on the changes in penal policies in Poland and other Eastern European countries, where the impact of European policies and the desire to be 'European' played a very important part in the years immediately after the collapse of the Soviet Union. Krajewski finds that, while there was such an impact, it does not fully explain the changes that took place immediately after the political changes and certainly does not account for the subsequent changes where punitive policies have emerged in new guises. In Chapter 15 René van Swaaningen addresses a particularly complex issue: the fluctuations in penal policy in the Netherlands. In this jurisdiction, when imprisonment rates rose in the last decades of the twentieth century, this was seen as being directly related to the wave of popular punitivism sweeping Europe and the western world generally. However, in recent years incarceration rates have declined somewhat. This cannot be explained as easily, and van Swaaningen highlights the importance of looking closely at local factors to explain this partial reversal of the trend, while warning that it might not reflect a move away from underlying punitivism at all.

Taken as a whole, this book on European penology is therefore a combination of a search for a European identity in penal policies and research, a discussion of European institutional developments in penal policies, an overview of comparative research on specific topics in Europe, and a cautious attempt to highlight the differences between European countries, when European-level explanations provide only partial answers. Certainly, the book does not purport to provide definitive answers to our initial questions. Much more can be said about European penology, and much more certainly will be. Nonetheless, we believe that, taken together, the chapters in this volume and the broad range of themes they touch upon, illustrate why publishing a regionally focused book, such as this one, is so urgently necessary at this particular juncture of European (penal) history. We hope, therefore, that the contributions in this book will not merely introduce readers to the particular details of an emerging and fascinating European world of punishment, but also offer them inspiration and food for thought for future research and debate on the intricate analytic and normative questions that surround the topic of punishment and Europe—questions that have come to the fore only recently but will undoubtedly grow in significance in the years to come.

***

The idea for this book grew out of a workshop that we as editors organised at the Oñati International Institute for the Sociology of Law (IISL). The workshop was originally planned for April 2010, but the volcanic ash-cloud that was interfering with flights over Europe at that time put paid to that, as most participants were unable to travel. We are very grateful to the IISL for welcoming the idea of our workshop and for enabling us to reschedule it for 22 and 23 July 2010. In Oñati the IISL provided us with logistical and administrative support and made our stay in the Basque country a very pleasant experience. We would like to mention in particular its coordinator, Malen Gordoa Mendizabal, and its then director, Sol Picciotto.

A follow-up meeting with about half of the authors, including most of those who could not attend the rescheduled Oñati seminar, took place on 22 September 2011 in the Law Institute of Lithuania on the occasion of the 11th annual meeting of the European Society of Criminology (ESC). We would like to express our gratitude to Skirmantas Bikelis, Algimantas

Cepas and Aleksandras Dobryninas for their hospitality and help in hosting our meeting in Vilnius.

Our thanks go to the team at Hart Publishing, and in particular to Rachel Turner, for their professionalism, help and patience throughout this project.

Finally, we wish to thank our contributing authors who stuck with us through the long gestation process of this book. We hope that they share our satisfaction in having contributed to the understanding and, in the process, to the development of European penology.

*Tom Daems, Dirk van Zyl Smit and Sonja Snacken*
Ghent, New York and Brussels
16 October 2012

# Contents

# *Contributors*

**Estella Baker** is Professor of European Criminal Law and Justice at De Montfort University, Leicester and a member of the European Commission's Expert Group on EU Criminal Policy.

**Kristel Beyens** is Professor of Penology at the Vrije Universiteit Brussel.

**Tom Daems** is Lecturer in Criminology and Sociology of Law at Ghent University.

**Frieder Dünkel** is Professor of Criminology at the University of Greifswald.

**James B Jacobs** is Chief Justice Warren E Burger Professor of Law at New York University.

**Krzysztof Krajewski** is Professor of Criminology at Jagiellonian University.

**Elena Larrauri** is Professor of Criminal Law and Criminology at Universitat Pompeu Fabra.

**Alison Liebling** is Professor of Criminology at the University of Cambridge.

**Ian Loader** is Professor of Criminology at the University of Oxford.

**Fergus McNeill** is Professor of Criminology and Social Work at the University of Glasgow.

**Dario Melossi** is Professor of Criminology at the University of Bologna.

**Roland Miklau** is Chairman of the Austrian Section of the International Commission of Jurists (ICJ) and Former Director General for Penal Legislation at the Austrian Ministry of Justice.

**David Nelken** is Distinguished Professor of Sociology at the University of Macerata, Distinguished Research Professor of Law at Cardiff University and Visiting Professor of Criminology at the University of Oxford.

**Christine Morgenstern** is Senior Researcher at the University of Greifswald.

**Sonja Snacken** is Professor of Criminology, Penology and Sociology of Law at the Vrije Universiteit Brussel.

**Richard Sparks** is Professor of Criminology at the University of Edinburgh.

**René van Swaaningen** is Professor of International and Comparative Criminology at Erasmus University Rotterdam.

**Dirk van Zyl Smit** is Professor of Comparative and International Penal Law at the University of Nottingham and Global Visiting Professor of Law at the New York University School of Law.

# Part One

# Concepts and Institutions

# 1

# *Distinctive Features of European Penology and Penal Policy-Making*

SONJA SNACKEN AND DIRK VAN ZYL SMIT

**In Dutch:** 'Penologie is de wetenschap die zich bezighoudt met het onderzoeken van de effectiviteit van formele straffen'[1]

**In German:** 'Die Pönologie ist die Wissenschaft von den Strafen und Sanktionen. Den Kern der Pönologie bildet die Erforschung von Freiheitsstrafen und freiheitsentziehenden Maßregeln. Pönologie im engeren Sinne kann also mit der Gefängnisforschung gleichgesetzt werden'[2]

**In French:** 'La pénologie est la science sociale qui rend compte sociologiquement des pratiques pénales et qui inclut tous les travaux qui conçoivent la pénalité comme un phénomène social et qui tentent d'identifier les fonctions sociales de l'institution pénale'[3]

## I. EUROPEAN PENOLOGY AND PENAL POLICY-MAKING

A RELATIVELY NEUTRAL view of 'penology' is that it refers to the scientific study of punishment and is therefore an academic discipline. However, many different definitions of, and orientations towards, penology can be distinguished, reflecting varying aims and emphases.

The *Wikipedia* definitions of 'penology' quoted above vary quite considerably in the different language versions of this online encyclopedia: the Dutch definition reduces penology to a kind of administrative or

[1] 'Penology is the science that concerns itself with investigations of the effectiveness of formal sanctions.'

[2] 'Penology is the science of the penalties and sanctions. The essence of penology is the study of imprisonment and custodial measures. Penology in the strict sense can be equated with prison research.'

[3] 'Penology is the social science that analyses penal practices sociologically and includes all studies conceiving penality as a social phenomenon and attempting to identify the social functions of the penal institution.'

governmental criminology, where penologists-technicians assist the administration of sanctions by evaluating policies and practices and by proposing or developing instruments and techniques in order to make the practice more 'effective' (for example, risk assessment instruments). The German definition reduces penology even further to prison studies. The French definition emphasises a wider sociological approach, which is of course very important, but which, in our view, is not the only source of penological knowledge.

Academic literature has a similar range of definitions of penology, although the definitions do not necessarily follow the same national or linguistic patterns as those quoted above.[4] Perhaps the most jaundiced definition of penology is that implicit in the work of the moral philosopher CS Lewis, who wrote sarcastically:

> Only the expert 'penologist' (let barbarous things have barbarous names) can tell us what is likely to deter; only the psychotherapist can tell what is likely to cure.
>
> (Lewis 1953: 226)

A close reading of Lewis's polemic reveals that his conception of penology was extremely narrow. He saw penology as a deterministic social science that was concerned solely with the prediction of behaviour, to the exclusion of all concerns about justice or ethics.

It is true, historically, that many scholars have adopted a narrow view of penology that has largely limited it to a study of the reduction of recidivism. However, more sophisticated penologists, such as Nigel Walker (1987), made only modest claims for this form of penology, and recognised that there were larger ethical questions about the implementation of punishment, which traditional penology did not purport to answer but which, nevertheless, were of considerable importance (Moerings 2003).

In the early 1980s there was an argument that penology should be replaced by something different, the study of 'penality', which, like the French definition quoted above, referred mostly to the social analysis of the complex phenomenon of punishment (Garland and Young 1983). To some extent this dispute was merely terminological. It does not matter so much what one calls the subject, but what one does with it. This was recognised by David Garland, one of the initial protagonists of the idea of penality, for in his inaugural lecture in 1995 as Professor of Penology at the University of Edinburgh, he made the case for penology to encompass a much wider field, 'the study of the social processes of punishment and penal control,

[4] It does seem to be largely true in German, where, in academic discourse, '*Pönologie*' is largely limited to empirical studies of imprisonment, in terms both of its efficacy in reducing recidivism and, more rarely, of the effects of imprisonment (Müller-Dietz 1978).

which is to say of the whole complex of laws, ideas and institutions which regulate criminal conduct' (Garland 1997: 181; Daems 2008).

Like Garland, we do not think that the concept of penology should be abandoned, but would rather argue that it should be given much wider interpretation. We would describe penology as a field where law, sociology, political, economic and philosophical analyses, as well as history, ethics, psychology, psychiatry, anthropology and perhaps even medicine meet. Penology therefore reflects the same variations as criminology: etiological penology or penology of social reactions to deviance, administrative or critical penology: probably even a 'penology of the other' versus a 'penology of the self'.

When we called the seminar on which this volume is based 'European penology?', the question mark referred to the issue of whether there is something specific about penology as it is exercised or applied in Europe compared to other places. In our 2009 book *Principles of European Prison Law and Policy—Penology and Human Rights* (van Zyl Smit and Snacken 2009), we integrated penological evidence about the many aspects of imprisonment with a human rights approach that recognises prisoners as '*rechtsburgers*', or 'citizens with legal rights' (Kelk 2000). Prisoners continue to enjoy the protection of their fundamental human rights against state authorities, which, in the wake of increased public insecurity about crime, may feel pressured to resort to 'penal populism'. Our penological approach would probably fit Barbara Hudson's (2004) definition of 'critical penology' as a penology that tries to understand the present in order to strive for a better and more just future, by studying factors of liberation or domination, by analysing political choices and describing their detrimental consequences, and by indicating alternative possibilities.

Critical penology, which, of course, encompasses all forms of punishment and not only imprisonment, considers the links between its objects of study and inequalities of all sorts: social, economic, political, structural, or at the level of micro power relations. It is this critical penology that has offered evidence of the detrimental psychosocial consequences of deprivation of liberty, of the interaction between criminal justice and social justice, or between punishment and the selectivity of the criminal justice system (see also Snacken 2011).

This penological approach is obviously not uniquely European: it has also been strongly influenced by American scholars. However, what may be typically European is its continued legitimacy, not only within academia but also with penal policy-makers—although arguably to varying degrees in different European countries and different European institutions.

Our book on European prisons focused mainly on the human rights standards for the treatment of prisoners developed through the instruments of the Council of Europe—the judgments of the European Court of Human Rights (ECtHR), the reports of the Committee for the Prevention of Torture

(CPT), the recommendations of the Committee of Ministers—and their interaction with penological evidence. In this volume we want to explore further broader issues of penal policies in different European countries, and also at the level of the European Union, which is becoming increasingly active in fields that were traditionally covered by the Council of Europe. In this chapter we set the scene by considering, first, the interactions between penological evidence and human rights in penal policy-making by the European institutions and, subsequently, the place of a specifically European approach to penology in the relationship between Europe as a whole and the rest of the world.

## II. COMBINING HUMAN RIGHTS AND PENOLOGICAL EVIDENCE: A DISTINCTIVE FEATURE OF EUROPEAN PENOLOGY?

### A. Punishment, Penology and Human Rights

Traditionally, human rights have been perceived as a bulwark against criminalisation and over-penalisation. Criminal law and its sanctions make deep inroads into the rights and freedom of citizens. Criminal law in liberal or constitutional democracies should therefore be minimal and marginal, and must meet a number of strict constitutional and human rights related conditions and standards. National constitutional courts and international human rights courts, such as the ECtHR, play an essential role in setting these conditions and standards.

However, criminal law and punishment are also viewed as instruments of crime control and enhanced security. For example, it is no accident that the international human rights community supported the establishment of the International Criminal Tribunal for the former Yugoslavia and subsequently the permanent International Criminal Court, while arguing strongly at the same time that they should not be able to impose the death penalty or irreducible life sentences.

The balance between crime control and due process is an important factor in understanding different punishment levels and trends (Tonry 2001: 519). Several authors have argued (Tonry 2001; Kurki 2001; Morgan 2001) that, while American courts and legislators from the 1950s through to the 1970s emphasized due process values more than was the case in the inquisitorially oriented criminal justice processes in Western Europe, at the beginning of the twenty-first century that is no longer true. The American balance is now clearly in favour of crime control values, while European emphasis on due process and human rights has increased greatly under the influence of the ECHR and its interpretation by the ECtHR.

There is, however, also a more recent tendency, even within the ECtHR, in which criminalisation is seen as a necessary instrument for the protection of the human rights of victims of crime, by their fellow citizens or by the state. Human rights are therefore related to different aspects of punitiveness. Human rights of offenders relate to the acceptability of different forms of punishment (death penalty, corporal punishment), to the qualitative treatment of offenders and prisoners, and to the severity of sentences. Human rights of victims raise the question of the desirability of using criminal law and punishment as a necessary means of showing respect for their victimisation.

## B. European Institutions: 'Human Rights, Democracy and the Rule of Law'

European institutions stand for the promotion and defence of the basic principles of human rights, democracy and the rule of law. The interaction of these principles with penal policies in the Council of Europe and the European Union, however, differs.

### *i. Council of Europe*

The main instruments in the area of penology and penal policies are the ECtHR, CPT and the recommendations of the Committee of Ministers. Although the influence of human rights principles and penological evidence varies between these instruments, there is an obvious and increasing element of mutual reinforcement between them.

Human rights have by definition always been at the centre of the case law of the ECtHR. However, a clear evolution can be ascertained with regard to the Court's attitude towards penal issues and the increasing influence of penological evidence. We will briefly discuss four issues: the death penalty, the treatment of offenders and prisoners, the level of punitiveness in penal policies, and victims' rights.

The abolition of the death penalty in Europe has been described as both the result of a shared set of European values, and an instrument in creating a distinct European consciousness, a 'European community of sentiment' (Girling 2006). Both the Council of Europe and the European Union have over recent years elaborated a clear abolitionist policy, based primarily on defining the death penalty as a fundamental human rights violation (Council of Europe 2001: 12–13). This is a clear departure from the ECHR itself, which came into force in 1950 and which permitted the death penalty in its Article 2 as an exception to the right to life. The gradual abolition of capital punishment was fostered by Protocol 6 (1980) to the ECHR, which proposed abolition in peacetime, and Protocol 13 (2002), which imposed total abolition, including in wartime. The political pressure to abolish the death penalty was most obvious when central and eastern European countries wanted to join the Council of Europe (and eventually the European Union) in the 1990s. Conditions for joining were ratification of the ECHR and acceptance of the individual complaint procedure before the ECtHR, ratification of the European Convention for the Prevention of Torture and Inhuman and Degrading Treatment or Punishment (ECPT), an immediate moratorium on executions, and the obligation to abolish the death penalty within two years. This indicates that at the political level, allegiance to human rights protection and abolition of the death penalty were seen as essential values in a 'European identity' and preconditions for acquiring 'European' membership (Snacken 2006). This is also illustrated by the EU Charter of Fundamental Rights (2000), where prohibition of the death penalty is found under Title 1 Dignity, Article II-2: Right to life: 'No one shall be condemned to the death penalty, or executed.' The death penalty is contrary to human dignity and therefore unacceptable, full stop. This shift in the overall European approach has allowed the Grand Chamber of the ECtHR to declare in the case of *Öcalan v Turkey* (2005) that, in view of the general abolition of the death penalty in Europe, this form of punishment is now regarded as unacceptable and as inhuman and degrading treatment contrary to Article 3 of the ECHR. It is significant that the ECtHR did not find it necessary to balance this conclusion with a discussion of the effectiveness of the penalty or the support of public opinion. This can be contrasted with the prominent role that these issues continue to play in the US, even in case such as in *Roper v Simmons* (2005) where the US Supreme Court held that the death penalty was unconstitutional if imposed on a child under the age of 18 years at the time of the commission of the offence (Hood and Hoyle 2008).

As far as the qualitative treatment of offenders and prisoners is concerned, the ECtHR has strengthened its protection of offenders and prisoners against violations of their fundamental human rights over the last 30 years, and more specifically in the last 10 years (for a more extensive analysis, see van Zyl Smit and Snacken 2009). With regard to the absolute prohibition of torture and inhuman and degrading treatment (Article 3 of the ECHR), its case law used to be fairly restricted, due largely to the fact that the Court would only consider violation of Article 3 arising from deliberate acts, thus excluding prison conditions such as overcrowding. Moreover, the Court accepts that 'all punishment has an inherent element of suffering or humiliation', and therefore requires a certain threshold to be reached before constituting a violation of Article 3. Since 2001, however, Article 3 has been interpreted more broadly, and intention on the part of the authorities is not a precondition for a finding that prison conditions infringe its provisions (*Dougoz v Greece* 2001, concerning prison overcrowding). This approach has been confirmed in other judgments which have held that 'impoverished regimes' can infringe Article 3 (*Alver v Estonia* 2005).

This change of approach by the ECtHR is testimony to the increased influence of the CPT, which through its visits to places of detention all over Europe often fulfils the role as 'fact finding instrument' of the Court (Myjer 2010). Restrictions on penal excesses have also been imposed by the Court in cases concerning arbitrary strip searches in a special security unit (*Van der Ven v the Netherlands* 2003) or the disproportionate use of solitary confinement for a violent and uncooperative prisoner (*Mathew v the Netherlands* 2005). Its jurisprudence on high security units and solitary confinement clearly indicates that forms of total isolation as imposed in some 'supermax' prisons or units in the US would be considered inhuman and degrading treatment in Europe (*Messina v Italy (no 2)* 2000; *Ramirez Sanchez v France* 2006), as were the US's death rows (*Soering v UK* 1989). With regard to torture, the Court has explicitly reinforced its protection of suspects and prisoners (*Selmouni v France* 1999).

As far as the other fundamental civil and political rights protected by the ECHR are concerned, such as the right to family life, freedom of conscience and religion, freedom of expression and freedom of association (Articles 8–11), which can be restricted 'in the interest of national security, public safety or the economic well-being of the country, for the prevention of disorder or crime, for the protection of health or morals, or for the protection of the rights and freedoms of others', in 1975 the Court abandoned the previously held 'theory of inherent limitations' (*Golder v UK* 1975). Instead it recognised that prisoners retain their fundamental human rights, which may only be restricted if the interference is in accordance with the law, pursues a legitimate aim and is absolutely necessary (proportionate) in a democratic society. While the 'prevention of disorder or crime' and 'the protection of rights of others' have been accepted by the Court as legitimate aims in a democratic society, restrictions imposed on prisoners by national authorities have increasingly been found to be disproportionate. Over the last 10 years, various major cases have thus reaffirmed prisoners' rights: to marry (*Hamer v UK* 1979); to found a family (*Dickson v UK* [GC] 2007); to maintain parental rights where possible (*Sabou and Pircalab v Romania* 2004); to family visits (*Messina v Italy (no 2)* 2000; *Ostrovar v Moldova* 2005); against undue restriction of physical contact (*Ciorap v Moldova* 2007); to correspondence (*Cotlet v Romania* 2003); to liberty of expression (*Yankov v Bulgaria* 2003: even if it includes criticisms of the prison system and its staff); and to vote (*Hirst v United Kingdom (no 2)* [GC] 2005: total prohibition is contrary to Article 3 of Protocol 1 to ECHR). This brings prisoners in Europe closer to realising their status as rights-bearing citizens (Kelk 2000).[5]

[5] This concept of legal citizenship does not refer to citizenship of a national state, but to the ability of prisoners to participate in legal matters, on the basis that legal principles and values must be applied to them.

It is interesting to note that throughout this case law, the Court refers on several occasions to the increasing importance of 'rehabilitation' or 'reintegration' as a legitimate aim of imprisonment (*Messina v Italy (no 2)* 2000; *Mastromatteo v Italy* 2002 para 72; *Kafkaris v Cyprus* 2006; *Dickson v UK* [GC] 2007). In the last case, this aim was also used by the Court to counter the British government's argument that public confidence in the penal system requires that imprisonment should have a punitive element, thus justifying the restriction of prisoners' rights (*Dickson v UK* [GC] 2007 para 28). This use of 'public opinion' as an argument for punitive policies has been criticised on several occasions by the Court (*Stafford v UK* [GC] 2002 on parole; *Hirst v United Kingdom (no 2)* [GC] 2005 on the right to vote).

Even national legislation, adopted by democratic vote in national Parliaments, has in some instances been found to violate the ECHR for not being in accordance with the rule of law, for example, because it was too vaguely formulated or left too much arbitrary power to prison staff (*Petra v Romania* 1998; *Dankevich v Ukraine* 2003; *Čiapas v Lithuania* 2006; *Frerot v France* 2007).

So far, the ECtHR seems willing to exercise a moderating influence on penal excesses in Europe. However, the Court is more reluctant to interfere in *penal policies* concerning the choice and the length of sanctions imposed, except in some extreme cases. Thus, judicial corporal punishment was found to be contrary to Article 3 (*Tyrer v UK* 1978), but life imprisonment is not, if imposed for very serious offences (*Sawoniuk v UK* 2001). 'Life without parole' though, would 'raise an issue under Article 3', both for juveniles (*V v UK* 1999) and for adults (*Kafkaris v Cyprus* [GC] 2008). Although there has been no conclusive decision so far, the Court declared in *Kafkaris* that Article 3 requires 'that a life sentence is *de jure* and *de facto* reducible' (*Kafkaris v Cyprus* [GC] 2008 para 98; see also *Vinter and Others v UK* 2012).

As far as imprisonment is concerned, Article 5 of the ECHR guarantees the right to freedom and security, but also provides for lawful forms of deprivation of liberty, such as remand custody, imprisonment after conviction by a competent court, and detention of mentally ill offenders or illegal aliens. Article 5 protects individuals against undue or arbitrary restrictions of their liberty. The right to liberty is the norm and restrictions are the exceptions which must meet strict requirements of legality, legitimacy and proportionality (Smaers 2000). 'Arbitrary and disproportionate' punishment is therefore contrary to Article 5 of the ECHR (*Winterwerp v the Netherlands* 1979). In order to be legitimate, there must be a relation between the purpose and the place and regime of the detention (*Ashingdane v UK* 1985; *Bouamar v Belgium* 1988; *Aerts v Belgium* 1998). Nevertheless, the fact that the detention must be legitimate does not necessarily mean that the sentence must be appropriate. Grossly disproportionate sentences could amount to inhuman punishment contrary to Article 3, but this would depend on the sex, age and state of health of the defendant (*Ireland v UK* 1978, 1999). Such sentencing could also conflict with Articles 8 to 11 of the ECHR (van Zyl Smit and Ashworth 2004). But in general, the ECtHR has stated that Article 5(1) does not allow it to control the appropriateness of a sentence imposed by a trial judge (*Weeks v United Kingdom* 1987 para 50).

Although this view can be understood in view of the great variation in penal trends and policies in Europe,[6] we have argued elsewhere that it is illogical for the Court to apply a stricter subsidiarity and proportionality principle to sanctions imposed under Articles 8 to 11 than to those under Article 5 (Snacken 2006; van Zyl Smit and Snacken 2009). Under Articles 8 to 11, the Court requires the choice between different types of punishment or measures to be the result of a balancing of their relative severity with regard to interference with fundamental rights, and requires states 'to minimise, as far as possible, the interference with these rights, by trying to find alternative solutions and by generally seeking to achieve their aims in the least onerous way as regards human rights' (*Hatton and others v United Kingdom* 2001 para 87).[7] But this balancing is not required by the Court when deciding on penal sanctions or measures under Article 5 (*Bouchet v France* 2001). This is strange, as imprisonment is the most severe interference with the rights and freedoms of suspects and convicts by state authorities in Europe. This is not altered by the evolution of the case law of the ECtHR concerning prisoners' rights. Deprivation of liberty remains a severe restriction of 'normal' life and inevitably hampers the full enjoyment of other rights and freedoms, such as the right to private and family life, and freedom of association and expression. Research has consistently shown that most detrimental effects of imprisonment increase with the length of the detention (van Zyl Smit and Snacken 2009: 47–54). Other penalties, such as fines or community sanctions and measures, may also restrict rights and freedoms, but are usually less invasive than imprisonment. Applying the principle of proportionality, as interpreted for Articles 8 to 11, to imprisonment would then mean that, throughout the processes of criminalisation, prosecution, sentencing and implementation of sentences, only the least invasive decision could be considered legitimate and proportionate. In every sentencing or early release case, the choice of sanction should be the object of a debate, in which it is up to the prosecutor to demonstrate that

[6] To give one illustration, in a survey organised for the Council of Europe on the application of 'long term prison sentences', the definition in Member States of such sentences ranged from 18 months in Norway, to 10 years in most central and eastern European countries (Snacken 1999).

[7] The initial judgment in *Hatton* was overturned by a majority of the Grand Chamber, but this did not undermine the fundamental approach adopted by the initial chamber of the ECtHR towards the duty to minimise infringements of human rights (*Hatton and others v United Kingdom* [GC] 2003).

a prison sentence is necessary. It should no longer be up to the offenders to prove that they 'deserve' a non-custodial sanction, as is often the case now. The ECtHR could then evaluate the procedures to decide whether such a balancing exercise had taken place and whether, substantively, it had led to the imposition of the least invasive sanction or measure as regards human rights. This lack of consistency in the Court's case law could be interpreted as a lack of a coherent penological framework for the interpretation of penal issues.

The same could be said for the Court's ambivalent attitude towards forms of early release (*Kafkaris v Cyprus* 2008) and conjugal visits (*Aliev v Ukraine* 2003), which is not consistent with the penological evidence on these issues. The increasing frequency of references by the Court to CPT reports and recommendations of the Committee of Ministers as the 'legal instruments' of the Council of Europe could help to change this ambivalence.

Lastly, critics have commented that the relationship between criminal law and human rights is changing, even in the case law of the ECtHR itself. While human rights have traditionally been seen as a bulwark against overreaching criminal law, in some recent instances the Court has promoted the use of criminal law as protection against violations of human rights (De Hert et al 2007). Thus, for example, in *MC v Bulgaria* (2003), offenders suspected of rape had not been prosecuted because of the lack of evidence of physical resistance by the victim. The Court criticised Bulgaria for having failed to safeguard the physical and mental integrity of the victim, protected by Article 3 of the ECHR, and her right to autonomy as part of the right to respect for her privacy, protected by Article 8. The Court emphasized that in cases of sexual violence the state had a positive duty to prosecute whenever there was an absence of consent, and added that criminalisation was the most effective means of preventing such offences. Some members of the Court are aware of the dangers posed by this tendency and have sought to limit its impact. Judge Tulkens, in para 2 of the concurring opinion in *MC v Bulgaria*, emphasised that, although one could understand why criminal law and penalties could be used for this type of offence, this should remain, in theory as in practice, the *ultimum remedium*, a subsidiary intervention which should be applied with 'restraint'. Judge Tulkens challenged the idea that, as a general rule, the application of the criminal law offered the only or even the best mode of preventing undesirable behaviour or of acknowledging the suffering of victims (see also Tulkens 2012).

The CPT, with its multidisciplinary composition (lawyers, medical doctors, psychiatrists, criminologists), is more expert-based, and many of its standards have clearly been influenced not only by human rights considerations but also by penological evidence (see, for example, the 11th General Report (2001) 16 for standards concerning life sentence and long-term prisoners, high-security units, and relationships between prisoners and staff). However, its competence is limited to the prevention of torture and inhuman or degrading treatment or punishment, and does not extend to all aspects of penal policies in general. So, although the CPT has on occasions expressed views on aspects of penal policies, most notably supporting the reductionist penal policy advocated by Recommendation (1999) 22 to tackle prison overcrowding, it cannot function as an overall beacon for penal policy reforms.

Penal policy issues are mostly dealt with through the recommendations of the Committee of Ministers. These recommendations are also fairly 'expert'-based, as they are prepared by advisory bodies to the Committee for Crime Problems (CDPC) with the systematic and explicit involvement of criminological, penological or other experts. However, there have also been some developments here. Topics for recommendations used to be suggested by the Council for Penological Cooperation (PCCP), but prepared and drafted by 'expert committees' composed by a selection of national representatives (usually civil servants) and two or three experts. This system was replaced, for budgetary reasons, by the preparation and drafting of recommendations by the PCCP itself, which has nine members who have been elected by the CDPC, but who are more experts than national representatives. The increased reference by the ECtHR to these recommendations has changed their status from pure 'soft law' to influential standards. There seems to be now an increasing (political) pressure through the CDPC to get more control of the drafting process by the PCCP, inter alia, through more frequent reporting to the CDPC and the closer involvement of more national representatives in the work of the PCCP.

### *ii. European Union*

As far as the European Union is concerned, the elaboration of its Third Pillar on 'An area of Freedom, Justice and Security' (Treaty of Amsterdam, 1 May 1999) has been criticised for placing crime control above civil liberties, although not in a manner that necessarily fits into the 'new punitiveness' mould (Baker and Roberts 2005; Baker 2010).[8] The attachment of an EU Charter of Fundamental Human Rights to the Treaty of Nice in December 2000 was seen by other scholars as an illustration of its growing interest in human rights (Ashworth 2002). The Treaty of Lisbon, which came into force on 1 December 2009, explicitly refers in its Preamble to:

> Drawing inspiration from the cultural, religious and humanist inheritance of Europe, from which have developed the universal values of the inviolable and inalienable rights of the human person, freedom, democracy equality and the rule of law.

[8] See also the chapters by Baker and by Miklau in this volume.

In practice, the principle of mutual recognition of decisions as the cornerstone of judicial cooperation in civil and criminal matters (Tampere Conclusions 1999) and the introduction of the European Arrest Warrant in 2002 have strengthened the need for European states to have roughly similar prison conditions, and the European Commission has sponsored a myriad of educative programmes in prisons. Several recent Council Framework Decisions have aimed at facilitating the implementation of sanctions in the country of origin of an offender by applying the principle of mutual recognition to criminal matters imposing custodial sentences or measures (Council Framework Decision 2008/909/JHA), to supervision of probation measures and alternative sanctions (Council Framework Decision 2008/947/JHA) and to supervision measures as alternatives to provisional detention (Council Framework Decision 2009/829/JHA). These Framework Decisions are meant 'to enhance the social rehabilitation of sentenced persons' (Article 9 Council Framework Decision 2008/909/JHA), to monitor 'a defendants' movements in the light of the overriding objective of protecting the general public', to 'enhance the right to liberty and the presumption of innocence', and 'to promote where appropriate the use of non-custodial measures' (Articles 3 and 4 Council Framework Decision 2009/829/JHA).

However, the penal policy of the European Union, with its strong emphasis on 'increased security for all',[9] may have the opposite effect. There is also the danger that efforts to achieve uniformity may put pressure on countries to use imprisonment more readily and to impose longer prison sentences than they have done hitherto. Thus, for example, the 2005 Framework Decision laying down minimum provisions on the constituent elements of the criminal acts and penalties in the field of illicit drug trafficking requires that 'penalties provided for by the Member States shall be effective, proportionate and dissuasive, and include custodial sanctions'.[10]

Other critics have pointed out European Union policies towards immigration and terrorism as forces of increased repression. Loïc Wacquant (2006a) argues that, in the wake of the transnational neo-liberal revolution, welfare states are increasingly becoming 'penal states'. Collective socio-economic rights are being replaced by individual responsibility in employment, education, health and social security. Individual failure then results in poverty, marginality and exclusion, which increasingly are dealt with through repression and imprisonment. While this trend is most obvious in the United States of America, Wacquant (2006b) notes that

[9] This is one of the bases on which the Treaty of Lisbon was advocated by the EU: see http://europa.eu/lisbon_treaty/glance/index_en.htm.

[10] At § 5 of the Council Framework Decision 2004/757/JHA of 25 October 2004 laying down minimum provisions on the constituent elements of criminal acts and penalties in the field of illicit drug trafficking [2004] OJ L335/8.

this can also be observed in Europe, where the politics of 'fortress Europe' result in the increasing incarceration of high numbers of foreigners and ethnic minorities, especially from former colonies. The overrepresentation of these populations is even claimed to surpass that of African Americans in US prisons. Wacquant (2006a: 285–86) finds other instances of this movement towards 'penal states' in the increasing imprisonment rates in most Western European countries, prison overcrowding, and the emphasis on incapacitation rather than the reintegration of prisoners.

Gus Hossein (2005) also argues that, since the attacks of 11 September 2001, anti-terrorist measures have proliferated on both sides of the Atlantic, providing a 'turbo-motor' for penalisation in Europe and in the United States. He claims that some European measures, such as interception of communications, data retention, data profiling and data mining, the introduction of biometric identification, and the European Arrest Warrant, interfere even more with human rights than those taken in the US. In European Union initiatives, such as the Framework Decision of 13 June 2002 concerning the fight against terrorism[11] and the Hague Programme concerning Freedom, Security and Justice,[12] a remarkable grouping of problems of terrorism and serious crime with concerns about immigration may be discerned (Dumortier et al 2012).

Both these critiques point to several mechanisms in European Union and also national policies which could lead to an enhanced use of imprisonment, and deserve close scrutiny. Nevertheless, some important differences between the EU and the US should be highlighted. As far as Wacquant's comparison of the overrepresentation of foreigners and ethnic minorities as proof of the demise of the welfare state is concerned, the position of African Americans in the US, of which they are legal citizens and clients of the welfare system, cannot be equated with that of 'foreigners' in European prisons, who are much more heterogeneous: a significant proportion of them are designated 'illegal aliens' and therefore routinely excluded from welfare provisions, while others are transborder or transnational offenders with no ties in the country in which they are detained.[13] As far as Hossein's analysis is concerned, a major difference still remains between the degree of acceptance in the US, for a period prior to 2009 at least, of techniques of torture and extradition to countries where torture may occur, and secret places of detention or prisons that are meant to be outside the reach of judicial supervision, and the increased European protection against torture and

[11] Council Framework Decision 2002/475/JHA of 13 June 2002 on Combating Terrorism [2002] OJ L164/3.

[12] European Council 'The Hague Programme: Strengthening Freedom, Security and Justice in the European Union' [2005] OJ C53/1.

[13] For a detailed critique of Wacquant's writing in this regard, see Daems 2008: ch 5.

the enhanced supervision by the ECtHR and the CPT of the daily dealings with prisoners in European prisons.[14]

## III. EXTERNAL BOUNDARIES OF EUROPEAN PENOLOGY

A further dimension, which cannot be ignored, is the role of a 'European' penology based on human rights standards and penological evidence when 'Europe' interacts with the penal systems of other, non-European countries. This interaction can take a number of forms. The clearest of these arises in the case of the death penalty. As mentioned above, when the ECHR was adopted in 1950, it made clear provision for countries that retained the death penalty to continue to impose it without being accused of infringing the right to life guaranteed by Article 2. However, in the face of what were initially largely national movements for the abolition of the death penalty, the European position changed. Protocols were attached to the ECHR outlawing the death penalty, first in times of peace and then even in wartime. And this view was projected to the outside: not only to the states of central and eastern Europe who wished to join the Council of Europe in the early 1990s, but also outside of Europe. Opposition to the death penalty, a penal policy after all, has thus been recognised as a key element of modern European culture, and has become part of the way the pan-European elite defines itself in relation to others (Zimring 2003; Girling 2006). Even Tony Blair (2004), in a speech in 2004 dedicated to defending US foreign policy and the role of the United Kingdom as a bridge between the US and the rest of Europe, was moved to remark:

> I'm not saying America does not make mistakes; does not in its insularity of thinking sometimes seem obstinate to the concerns of the rest of the world. American political culture, for example on the death penalty, is different from European culture, and in Britain, in this respect at least, our culture is more European.

Both the Council of Europe and the European Union have indeed sought to present a united front in supporting abolition of the death penalty worldwide, and have taken a range of initiatives in this regard. These include, in the case of the EU states in particular, joint diplomatic initiatives and even briefing of counsel to argue against the retention of the death penalty before the US Supreme Court,[15] while the Council of Europe has focused its attention on retentionist countries, such as Japan and the US, which

[14] See for example FIDH-Fédération Internationale des ligues des Droits de l'Homme, *Counter-Terrorism versus Human Rights: the Key to Compatibility* (Report no. 429/2, October 2005) available online at www.fidh.org/IMG/pdf/counterterrorism429a.pdf#search=%22%22counter-terrorism%20versus%20human%20rights%22%22.

[15] See, for example, *Roper v Simmons* 543 US 551 (2005) where the US Supreme Court abolished the death penalty for offenders under the age of 18 years.

have observer status with the Council (Council of Europe 2004). They have also ensured that the death penalty is not a sentencing option available to international tribunals such as the International Criminal Tribunal for the former Yugoslavia (ICTY) and the International Criminal Tribunal for Rwanda (ICTR) and also the International Criminal Court (ICC).

The jurisprudence of the ECtHR, in cases where countries outside Europe are involved directly or indirectly, has come to play a key part in this development. In the landmark 1989 case of *Soering v United Kingdom* (1989), it refused to allow the extradition of Jens Soering to face the death penalty in the US, on the grounds that the potential delay in executing such a sentence could amount to a form of inhuman and degrading punishment in contravention of Article 3 of the ECHR. Since then European human rights law has evolved further. There is increasing recognition that the exception for the death penalty in Article 2 has been supplanted by the abolition of the death penalty through the two protocols.[16]

This was made clear by the ECtHR in the recent case of *Al-Saadoon and Mufdhi v United Kingdom* (2010), when it took as its explicit 'starting point ... the right not to be subjected to the death penalty'.[17] It did so when holding that the British government had a duty not to hand over, following the withdrawal of its own forces from Iraq, two Iraqi citizens that it had captured, for trial by Iraqi courts where they would face the possibly of being sentenced to death for the crimes they had allegedly committed. This case is significant too for the fact that the ECtHR, unlike domestic UK courts, was prepared to hold the UK bound by the ECHR also for actions taken outside its territory and involving nationals of a country which it initially occupied, but in which, at the time, legally speaking, it was active at the invitation of the national government.

The ECtHR has been similarly robust in cases involving corporal punishment beyond the geographical boundaries of its jurisdiction. It has prevented in at least two cases the expulsion to Iran of women who did not otherwise qualify to remain legally in Turkey, on the grounds that such expulsion would expose them to degrading treatment as they faced corporal punishment in their home country (*Jabari v Turkey* (2000); *D and others v Turkey* (2006)).

The same robustness is not applicable to all areas of penal policy, however. On a number of occasions, the ECtHR has stressed that it is bears in mind the importance of combating crime in a globalising world. Ironically, given the importance of *Soering*'s case for its recognition of the place of human rights concerns in extradition law, the key limiting dictum in this

[16] See above, in particular *Öcalan v Turkey* [GC] (2005).

[17] Para 115. *In casu* only a contradiction of Article 3 was again found—the court deeming it unnecessary to consider whether there had been a contravention of Article 2 as well—but the tendency is clear, nevertheless.

regard also comes from the judgment in *Soering*'s case. In the words of the unanimous Court:

> What amounts to 'inhuman or degrading treatment or punishment' depends on all the circumstances of the case ... Furthermore, inherent in the whole of the Convention is a search for a fair balance between the demands of the general interest of the community and the requirements of the protection of the individual's fundamental rights. As movement about the world becomes easier and crime takes on a larger international dimension, it is increasingly in the interest of all nations that suspected offenders who flee abroad should be brought to justice. Conversely, the establishment of safe havens for fugitives would not only result in danger for the State obliged to harbour the protected person but also tend to undermine the foundations of extradition. These considerations must also be included among the factors to be taken into account in the interpretation and application of the notions of inhuman and degrading treatment or punishment in extradition cases.
>
> (Para 89.)

This passage seems to suggest that in cases of extradition or expulsion there is generally an element of relativity about the meaning of inhuman or degrading punishment or treatment, if not about out-and-out torture. In subsequent cases, such as *Chahal v United Kingdom* (1996), however, the ECtHR repudiated this suggestion by holding that the risk posed by the person who is to be expelled or deported, may not be balanced against the treatment that he is likely to face on expulsion. This was most clearly stated by the Grand Chamber of the ECtHR in *Saadi v Italy* (2008):

> The Court considers that the argument based on the balancing of the risk of harm if the person is sent back against the dangerousness he or she represents to the community if not sent back is misconceived. The concepts of 'risk' and 'dangerousness' in this context do not lend themselves to a balancing test because they are notions that can only be assessed independently of each other. Either the evidence adduced before the Court reveals that there is a substantial risk if the person is sent back or it does not. The prospect that he may pose a serious threat to the community if not returned does not reduce in any way the degree of risk of ill treatment that the person may be subject to on return. For that reason it would be incorrect to require a higher standard of proof, as submitted by the intervener, where the person is considered to represent a serious danger to the community, since assessment of the level of risk is independent of such a test.
>
> With regard to the second ... [argument], to the effect that where an applicant presents a threat to national security, stronger evidence must be adduced to prove that there is a risk of ill-treatment, the Court observes that such an approach is not compatible with the absolute nature of the protection afforded by Article 3 either. It amounts to asserting that, in the absence of evidence meeting a higher standard, protection of national security justifies accepting more readily a risk of ill-treatment for the individual. The Court therefore sees no reason to modify the relevant standard of proof, as suggested by the third-party intervener [the

government of the United Kingdom], by requiring in cases like the present that it be proved that subjection to ill-treatment is 'more likely than not'. On the contrary, it reaffirms that for a planned forcible expulsion to be in breach of the Convention it is necessary—and sufficient—for substantial grounds to have been shown for believing that there is a real risk that the person concerned will be subjected in the receiving country to treatment prohibited by Article 3.

(Para 139.)

Even this strong dictum, however, has not ensured that courts in Europe do not continue to apply different standards to determining *whether* treatment which at home they might regard as inhuman or degrading is necessarily to be regarded in the same way when it takes place in another jurisdiction. Thus in *Wellington,*[18] three judges out of five in the House of Lords held that, even if an American who on extradition to the US faced a sentence of life imprisonment without the prospect of parole, which arguably might[19] be regarded as an inhuman or degrading punishment if imposed in Europe, it had to be judged differently if it was to be implemented in the US, and therefore should not be regarded as inhuman or degrading in that context. This example is complicated by the facts of *Wellington*'s case, but the reasoning is made more transparent in a hypothetical example put forward by Lord Hoffmann, in whose judgment the majority concurred:

A relativist approach to the scope of Article 3 seems to me essential if extradition is to continue to function. For example, the Court of Session has decided in *Napier v Scottish Ministers* 2005 SC 229 that in Scotland the practice of 'slopping out' (requiring a prisoner to use a chamber pot in his cell and empty it in the morning) may cause an infringement of Article 3 … [If] it were applied in the context of extradition, it would prevent anyone being extradited to many countries poorer than Scotland, where people who are not in prison often have to make do without flush lavatories.[20]

In 2012 the ECtHR has itself had to decide on two cases arising in the United Kingdom and involving extradition of offenders to face charges that could lead to life sentences without the prospect of parole in the US (*Harkins and Edward v UK* (2012); *Babar Ahmad and others v UK* (2012)). In both these cases the European Court rejected the interpretation given by Lord Hoffmann and others in the House of Lords to its earlier jurisprudence, that extradition cases should be treated differently, and held definitively that Article 3 should be applied without distinction between

[18] *R (on the application of Wellington) v Secretary of State for the Home Department* [2008] UKHL 72; [2009] 1 AC 335, HL.

[19] In the light of the somewhat ambiguous decision of the Grand Chamber of the EctHR in *Kafkaris v Cyprus* (2008). See above, and van Zyl Smit (2010a).

[20] Lord Hoffmann was clearly sceptical of the outcome in *Napier*. As he commented pointedly: 'Whether, even in a domestic context, [slopping out] attains the necessary level of severity is a point on which I would wish to reserve my opinion.'

the various forms of ill-treatment that that article prohibits. Nevertheless, the ECtHR has sought to give itself some room to manoeuvre, by citing the importance of not imposing Convention standards on non-European states and the difficulties of knowing prospectively what effect sentences that may be imposed abroad may have in practice.

A similar tension can be seen at the European level with regard to the expulsion of the seriously ill. Although in the case of *D v United Kingdom* (1997) the ECtHR prevented the expulsion at the end of his sentence of D, who had entered the UK illegally to deal in drugs, on the grounds that he was suffering from full-blown AIDS, was close to death and would not be able to obtain treatment in St Kitts, where he would have been sent, this was, as the Court recognised, a 'wholly exceptional' case. It is the only example of where the ECtHR has upheld the argument that the Article 3 rights of someone who is seriously ill would be infringed by their expulsion. If anything, the ECtHR has become stricter in this regard. In *N v United Kingdom* (2008) the Grand Chamber of the ECtHR upheld the expulsion of an HIV-positive woman to Uganda and explicitly reasserted the 'fair balance test' developed in *Soering* in determining whether the limited treatment she was likely to receive in Uganda would infringe Article 3. As the Court explained:

> While it is necessary, given the fundamental importance of Article 3 in the Convention system, for the Court to retain a degree of flexibility to prevent expulsion in very exceptional cases, Article 3 does not place an obligation on the Contracting State to alleviate such disparities through the provision of free and unlimited health care to all aliens without a right to stay within its jurisdiction. A finding to the contrary would place too great a burden on the Contracting States.
>
> (Para 44.)

Whatever the substantive justification—and a minority of three of the 17 judges was highly critical of it[21]—the reality is that the Court was prepared to allow for the applicant to be exposed, by the United Kingdom who sought to deport her to Uganda, to treatment abroad of a kind that the Court would not tolerate in Europe as compatible with the 'absolute' rights recognised by Article 3, or even Article 2, of the ECHR.

Offenders facing expulsion have also sought to rely on qualified rights, such as the right to a private or family life under Article 8 of the ECHR, in their bids to remain in European countries. States in turn have relied on the grounds for interfering with these rights contained in Article 8(2)—that

[21] The majority judgment was heavily criticised by three of the 17 judges. In a joint dissenting opinion Judges Tulkens, Bonello and Spielmann not only disagreed on the facts but attacked the majority judgment for diminishing the scope of Article 3 generally.

is, interference that is 'in accordance with the law and is necessary in a democratic society in the interests of national security, public safety or the economic well-being of the country, for the prevention of disorder or crime, for the protection of health or morals, or for the protection of the rights and freedoms of others'. The record has been mixed. In *Moustaquim v Belgium* (1991) the expulsion of a young offender with a long criminal record was prohibited by the ECtHR, although it was in accordance with law and for a legitimate purpose, preventing disorder. However, the Court held that it was not 'necessary in a democratic society' because of the 'special feature' of the applicant's close family ties in Belgium.

The evaluation of such family ties varies, however, from case to case. In *El Boujaïdi v France* (1997), in which the strength of the ties seems to be largely similar to those in *Moustaquim,* the ECtHR was prepared to enforce a permanent exclusion order against a young offender, while in *Radovanovic v Austria* (2004) the ECtHR regarded a permanent exclusion order as too severe, but gave a strong indication that it would have upheld some form of temporary expulsion. Jurisprudential niceties aside, the conclusion is that, in Article 8 cases too, the ECtHR is prepared to countenance restrictions to rights of offenders that it would not tolerate for offenders who are not subject to being forced to leave a European country against their will.

The jurisprudence outlined above should not be regarded as conclusive evidence of Europe-wide cynicism about penal standards, other than the death penalty, adopted in the rest of the world. There is a range of counter-examples of active European involvement to propagate its own standards globally. This involvement is not limited to governments and intergovernmental organisations. European-based, international non-governmental organisations, such as Amnesty International, Penal Reform International and the Association for the Prevention of Torture, have made a major contribution to the recognition of the human rights of offenders worldwide. There are also forms of co-operation between agencies that have a role in developing and enforcing penal policies for Europe and their international equivalents. An example is the supportive role that the CPT, the primary European body charged with inspecting places of detention in Europe in order to ensure that detainees are not tortured or treated in an inhumane or degrading way, has played as forerunner of and now partner to the SPT, the new international body charged with the prevention of torture and cruel inhuman or degrading treatment of detainees worldwide.[22]

Finally one cannot avoid the large topic of development aid and European penal ideals. Some aid for penal reform in non-European countries is genuinely idealistic and relates to a wider foreign policy thrust underpinned by

[22] For details, see van Zyl Smit (2010b).

human rights concerns. In many developing countries individual EU states and the European Union's own development arm combine around a common set of human rights goals for penal reform.

There are examples, however, of development aid that are more self-serving. The British government, for example, is spending money improving prison conditions in both Nigeria and in Jamaica. There is much that can be done in this regard for sound human rights reasons. However, a report in *The Times* of 12 July 2009 reveals what is really at stake:

> A new prison to hold hundreds of Nigerians currently in jail in England and Wales is to be funded by the British Government. Under the deal at least 400 Nigerians could be transferred home to serve the remainder of their sentence in the new jail, which Britain will give Nigeria millions of pounds to build. Officials are negotiating with the Nigerian government over the proposal, which would increase the number of jail spaces in the west African state. The investment of millions of pounds of British taxpayers' money is needed because conditions in existing Nigerian jails are so poor that prisoners would oppose their transfer on human rights grounds

One may add in parentheses that if human rights standards are 'met', prisoners will not be able to oppose their transfer, which will apparently become compulsory. And will arguments against such transfers not be undermined by the new provision for compulsory transfers of sentenced prisoners within the European Union?

These various examples illustrate just how deeply ambiguous the objectives of the projection of 'European' penal policy abroad may be. And then we have not yet begun to consider the role of 'security' in shaping these policies (Baker 2010). The relationship between penal policy, human rights and security is a large topic that cannot be discussed fully here. At the very least, however, it must be recognised that the standards that Europe sets in its criminal justice relationships with non-European countries are influenced by 'security concerns'. Decisions of the ECtHR, such as those in *Saadi,* and initiatives of various European bodies, to deal with 'extraordinary rendition',[23] for example, point to an awareness of the danger that the human rights values of European penology may be distorted by the external pressures that arise from dealing with a wider international community that does not recognise them, or that does not seek to apply them in the same way when it feels issues of security and international terrorism are raised. It is not yet clear, however, whether initiatives of this kind will be sufficient in the longer term to preserve these values in the face of ever more pressing claims that the security of the European population should trump other values.

[23] See amongst many examples, Marty (2006) and European Parliament (2006).

REFERENCES

Baker, E (2010) 'Governing Through Crime—The Case of the European Union' *European Journal of Criminology*, 7, 187–213.

Baker, E and Roberts, J (2005) 'Globalization and the New Punitiveness' in J Pratt, D Brown, M Brown, S Hallsworth and W Morrison (eds), *The New Punitiveness. Trends, Theories, Perspectives* (Cullompton, Willan Publishing).

Blair, A (2004) Speech by the Prime Minister, The Right Honourable Tony Blair, Lord Mayor's Banquet, Guildhall, 15 November 2004, available online at http://217.154.230.218/NR/rdonlyres/23B6E38C-DC30-48D8-BAC3-E256351AF119/0/MC_SP_lmbanquetblair_04.pdf.

Council of Europe (2001) *La peine de mort hors la loi! Le Conseil de l'Europe et la peine de mort* (Strasbourg: Conseil de l'Europe).

—— (2004) *Beyond Abolition* (Strasbourg, Council of Europe).

Daems, T (2008) *Making Sense of Penal Change* (Oxford, Oxford University Press).

De Hert, P, Gutwirth, S, Snacken, S and Dumortier, E (2007) 'La montée de l'Etat pénal: que peuvent les droits de l'homme?' in Y Cartuyvels, H Dumont, F Ost, M Van de Kerchove and S Van Drooghenbroeck (eds), *Les droits de l'homme, bouclier ou épée du droit pénal?* (Brussels, Facultés Universitaires Saint Louis).

Dumortier, E, Gutwirth, S, Snacken, S and De Hert, P (2012) 'The Rise of the Penal State: What can Human Rights do about it?' in S Snacken and E Dumortier (eds), *Resisting Punitiveness in Europe? Welfare, Human Rights and Democracy* (London, Routledge).

European Parliament (2006) 'Alleged Use of European Countries by the CIA for the Transportation and Illegal Detention of Prisoners'. Interim Report (Brussels, European Parliament) 2006/2027(INI) available online at www.europarl.europa.eu/sides/getDoc.do?type=TA&language=EN&reference=P6-TA-2006-0316.

Garland, D (1997) 'The Punitive Society: Penology, Criminology and the History of the Present' *Edinburgh Law Review*, 1, 180–99.

Garland, D and Young, P (1983) 'Towards a Social Analysis of Penality' in D Garland and P Young (eds), *The Power to Punish* (London, Heinemann).

Girling, E (2006) 'European Identity, Penal Sensibilities and Communities of Sentiment' in S Armstrong and L McAra (eds), *Perspectives on Punishment: The Contours of Control* (Oxford, Oxford University Press).

Hood, R and Hoyle, C (2008) *The Death Penalty: A Worldwide Perspective,* 4th edn (Oxford, Oxford University Press).

Hosein, G (2005) *Threatening the Open Society: Comparing Anti-Terror Policies in the US and Europe* (London, Privacy International).

Kelk, C (2000) *Nederlands detentierecht* (Deventer, Gouda Quint).

Kurki, L (2001) 'International Standards and Limits on Sentencing and Punishment' in M Tonry and R Frase (eds), *Sentencing and Sanctions in Western Countries* (New York, Oxford University Press).

Lewis, CS (1953) 'The Humanitarian Theory of Punishment' *Res Judicatae*, 6, 224–30.

Marty, D (2006) 'Alleged Secret Detentions and Unlawful Inter-State Transfers of Detainees Involving Council of Europe Member States' (Strasbourg, Council of Europe) Doc. 10957 available online at http://assembly.coe.int//Main.

asp?link=http://assembly.coe.int/Documents/WorkingDocs/doc06/edoc10957.htm?link=/Documents/WorkingDocs/Doc06/EDOC10957.htm.

Moerings, M (2003) 'Straffen met het oog op veiligheid: een onderneming vol risico's.' Inaugural lecture for the Chair in Penology, at Leiden University, 23 September 2003.

Morgan, R (2001) 'International Controls on Sentencing and Punishment' in M Tonry and R Frase (eds), *Sentencing and Sanctions in Western Countries* (New York, Oxford University Press).

Müller-Dietz, H (1978) *Strafvollzugsrecht* (Berlin, de Gruyter).

Myjer, E (2010) 'About the Human Rights Success Stories of the Council of Europe. Some Reflections on the Impact of the CPT upon the Case-law of the European Court of Human Rights' in M Groenhuijsen, T Kooijmans and T de Roos (eds), *Fervet Opus; Liber Amicorum Anton van Kalmthout* (Antwerp, Maklu).

Snacken, S (1999) 'Long-term prisoners and violent offenders' in *12th Conference of Directors of Prison Administration* (Strasbourg, Council of Europe).

—— (2006) 'A Reductionist Penal Policy and European Human Rights Standards' *European Journal on Criminal Policy and Research*, 12, 143–64.

—— (2011) *Prisons en Europe. Pour une pénologie critique et humaniste* (Brussels, Larcier).

Tonry, M (2001) 'Symbol, Substance, and Severity in Western Penal Policies' *Punishment & Society*, 3, 517–36.

Tulkens, F (2012) 'Human Rights as the Good and the bad Conscience of Criminal law' in S Snacken and E Dumortier (eds), *Resisting Punitiveness in Europe? Welfare, Human Rights and Democracy* (London, Routledge).

van Zyl Smit, D (2010a) 'Outlawing irreducible life sentences—Europe on the brink?' *Federal Sentencing Reporter*, 23, 39–48.

—— (2010b) 'Regulation of Prison Conditions' *Crime and Justice*, 39, 503–63.

van Zyl Smit, D and Snacken, S (2009) *Principles of European Prison Law and Policy. Penology and Human Rights* (Oxford, Oxford University Press).

Wacquant, L (2006a) *Parias urbains, Ghetto—Banlieus—Etat* (Paris, La Découverte).

—— (2006b) 'Penalization, Depoliticization, and Racialization: On the Over-incarceration of Immigrants in the European Union', in S Armstrong and L McAra (eds), *Perspectives on Punishment: The Contours of Control* (Oxford, Oxford University Press).

Walker, N (1987) *Crime and Criminology: A Critical Introduction* (Oxford, Oxford University Press).

## EUROPEAN COURT OF HUMAN RIGHTS

*Aerts v Belgium* 30 July 1998 (25357/94) (2000) 29 EHRR 50.

*Al-Saadoon and Mufdhi v United Kingdom* 2 March 2010 (61498/08) (2010) 51 EHRR 9.

*Barbar Ahmad and others v United Kingdom*, 10 April 2012 (24027/07, 11949/08, 36742/08, 66911/09 and 67354/09).

*Aliev v Ukraine* 29 April 2003 (41220/98).

*Alver v Estonia* 8 November 2005 (64812/01) (2006) 43 EHRR 40.

*Ashingdane v United Kingdom* 28 May 1985 (8225/78) (1985) 7 EHRR 528.
*Bouamar v Belgium* 27 June 1988 (9106/80) (1989) 11 EHRR 1.
*Bouchet v France* 20 March 2001(33591/96).
*Chahal v United Kingdom* 15 November 1996 (22414/93) (1997) 23 EHRR 413.
*Čiapas v Lithuania* 16 November 2006 (4902/02).
*Ciorap v Moldova* 19 June 2007 (12066/02).
*Cotlet v Romania* 3 June 2003 (38565/97).
*D v United Kingdom* 2 May 1997 (30240/96) (1997) 24 EHRR 423.
*D and others v Turkey* 22 June 2006 (24245/03).
*Dankevich v Ukraine* 29 April 2003 (40679/98) (2004) 38 EHRR 25.
*Dickson v UK* [GC] 4 December 2007 (44362/04) (2008) 46 EHRR 41.
*Dougoz v Greece* 6 March 2001 (40907/98) (2002) 34 EHRR 61.
*El Boujaïdi v France* 26 September 1997 (25613/94) (2000) 30 EHRR 223.
*Frerot v France* 12 June 2007 (70204/01).
*Golder v United Kingdom* 21 February 1975 (4451/70) (1979-80) 1 EHRR 524.
*Hamer v United Kingdom* 13 October 1979 (7114/75) (1982) 4 EHRR 139 (Commission).
*Harkins and Edwards v the United Kingdom* 17 January 2012 (9146/07 and 32650/07).
*Hatton and others v United Kingdom* 2 October 2001 (36022/97) (2002) 34 EHRR 1.
*Hatton and others v United Kingdom* [GC] 8 July 2003 (2003) 37 EHRR 28.
*Hirst v United Kingdom (no 2)* [GC] 6 October 2005 (74025/01) (2006) 42 EHRR 41.
*Ireland v UK* 18 January 1978 (5310/71) (1979-80) 2 EHRR 25.
*Jabari v Turkey* 11 July 2000 (40035/98).
*Kafkaris v Cyprus* 11 April 2006 (21906/04).
*Kafkaris v Cyprus* [GC] 12 February 2008 (21906/04) (2009) 49 EHRR 35.
*Mastromatteo v Italy* 24 October 2002 (37703/97).
*Mathew v the Netherlands* 29 September 2005 (24919/03) (2006) 43 EHRR 23.
*M C v Bulgaria* 4 December 2003 (39272/98) (2005) 40 EHRR 20.
*Messina v Italy (no 2)* 28 September 2000 (25498/94).
*Moustaquim v Belgium* 18 February 1991 (12313/86) (1991) 13 EHRR 802.
*N v United Kingdom* 27 May 2008 (26565/05) (2008) 47 EHRR 39.
*Öcalan v Turkey* 12 May 2005 (46221/99) (2005) 41 EHRR 985.
*Ostrovar v Moldova* 13 September 2005 (35207/03) (2007) 44 EHRR 19.
*Petra v Romania* 23 September 1998 (27273/95) (2001) 33 EHRR 5.
*Radovanovic v Austria* 22 April 2004 (42703/98) (2005) 41 EHRR 6.
*Ramirez Sanchez v France* [GC] 4 July 2006 (59450/00) (2007) 45 EHRR 49.
*Saadi v Italy* [GC] 28 February 2008 (37201/06) (2009) 49 EHRR 30.
*Sabou and Pircalab v Romania* 28 September 2004 (46572/99).
*Sawoniuk v UK* 29 May 2001 (63716/00).
*Selmouni v France* 28 July 1999 (25803/94) (2000) 29 EHRR 403.
*Soering v UK* 7 July 1989 (14038/88) (1989) 11 EHRR 439.
*Stafford v UK* [GC] 28 May 2002 (46295/99) (2002) 35 EHRR 32.
*Tyrer v UK* 25 April 1978 (5856/72) (1979-80) 2 EHRR 1.
*V v UK* 16 December 1999 (24888/94) (2000) 30 EHRR 121.
*Van der Ven v the Netherlands* 4 February 2003 (50901/99) (2004) 38 EHRR 46.
*Vinter and others v United Kingdom* 17 January 2012 (66069/09 and 130/10 and 3896/10).

*Weeks v United Kingdom* 2 March 1987 (9787/82) (1988) 10 EHRR 293.
*Winterwerp v the Netherlands* 24 October 1979 (1979-80) 2 EHRR 387.
*Yankov v Bulgaria* 11 December 2003 (39084/97) (2005) 40 EHRR 36.

## UK CASES

*R (on the application of Wellington) v Secretary of State for the Home Department* [2008] UKHL 72; [2009] 1 A.C. 335 (H.L.)
*Napier v Scottish Ministers* [2005] SC 229.

## US CASES

*Roper v Simmons* (543 US 551 2005)

## EU INSTRUMENTS

Council Framework Decision 2008/909/JHA of 27 November 2008 on the application of the principle of mutual recognition to judgments in criminal matters imposing custodial sentences or measures involving deprivation of liberty for the purpose of their enforcement in the European Union [2008] OJ L327/27.
Council Framework Decision 2008/947/JHA of 27 November 2008 on the application of the principle of mutual recognition to judgments and probation decisions with a view to the supervision of probation measures and alternative sanctions [2008] OJ L337/102.
Council Framework Decision 2009/829/JHA of 23 October 2009 on the application of the principle of mutual recognition to decisions on supervision measures as an alternative to provisional detention [2009] OJ L294/20.
Council Framework Decision 2004/757/JHA of 25 October 2004 laying down minimum provisions on the constituent elements of criminal acts and penalties in the field of illicit drug trafficking [2004] OJ L335/8.
Council Framework Decision 2002/475/JHA of 13 June 2002 on Combating Terrorism [2002] OJ L164/3.
European Council 'The Hague Programme: Strengthening Freedom, Security and Justice in the European Union' [2005] OJ C53/1.

# 2

# *Punishment and the Question of Europe*

TOM DAEMS

## I. INTRODUCTION: THE DEMISE OF ANCEL'S EUROPE

IN NOVEMBER 1973 Marc Ancel, one of Europe's most prominent penologists of the twentieth century, delivered a lecture on the 'Principal Aspects of Modern European Penology'. This happened at a symposium on Current Aspects of Penology, organised by the American Philosophical Society. Other invitees to the symposium included eminent American criminologists, such as Lloyd Ohlin and Franklin Zimring, as well as British *émigré* Leslie Wilkins. As a full-blooded European, Ancel was to some extent an outsider. In his speech looking back over the period since the Second World War, Ancel discussed the abolition of capital punishment, reforms in the reaction to youth delinquency, developments in sanctions entailing deprivation of liberty, and so on. However, at the moment when Ancel addressed his audience in Philadelphia, this first wave of reform had probably reached its peak and was in the process of slowing down. Moreover, all over the Continent there were prison riots, and crime rates were on the rise. Nonetheless, Ancel remained remarkably positive about the future of punishment in Europe. Demonstrating this optimism he mentioned that imprisonment as punishment was increasingly being questioned, and the idea of treatment (instead of mere punishment) was gaining further support. Ancel concluded with encouraging words about the prospects of European penology:

> European penology is again attracted to bold experiments despite the present challenge of crime. Personally I cannot reproach it for maintaining confidence in man and human nature, in spite of everything.
>
> (Ancel 1974: 259.)

Since the 1973 symposium a great deal has changed in the field of punishment. The US, in particular, embarked on a remarkable penal trajectory which can hardly have been predicted by contemporary observers. In his introduction to a 1969 special issue of *The Annals of the American Academy of Political and Social Science* devoted to 'The Future of Corrections', John P Conrad could still write that 'if the state of corrections is any indicator of the condition of civilization, Western man may be prospering better than he knows'. And he continued: 'Although there is much to be done, the present condition of corrections and its prospects for the future give rise to some optimism about the moral progress of man' (Conrad 1969: xii–xiii). Soon thereafter, however, the US reinstated the death penalty and witnessed the start of an unprecedented, more than six-fold, increase in its prison population. The American penal landscape today looks very different from the one Conrad and others had imagined in the late 1960s and early 1970s. Three decades later this state of affairs prompted the following observation from Richard Sparks:

> One special difficulty currently is the sometimes distracting sway of the American case as a pole of attraction. The sheer scale of incarceration in the United States, and its disparity from that in other countries, cries out for explanation. Yet the same disparity makes it difficult or impossible to calibrate US and European penal practices on the same scales. Can the penology of Europe and the penology of the United States make use of the same conceptual resources?
>
> (Sparks 2001: 165.)

Understandably, American penal developments have attracted a great deal of scholarly attention. As a result US punishment has, by now, been well documented, and the ways in which penal practice and discourse relate to American society have been extensively debated and analysed. But what happened in Europe in the meantime?

One of the purposes behind this book is to stimulate debate and foster research on European punishment—not so much in the sense of the role punishment has come to play in different European states separately, but rather in terms of the multiple ways in which 'Europe', in its various institutional incarnations (most notably, the Council of Europe and the European Union), has come to shape punishment in this part of the globe. Over the same period of time as the US experienced its much-debated penal experiment, Europe (and how it relates to the penal question) became entangled in its own intense process of transformation. Ancel's Europe no longer exists. Ancel delivered his speech at a time when the European continent was still divided between the East and the West, and when European institutions that intervened in (national) penal affairs were either non-existent or rather underdeveloped. This has changed dramatically over the past four decades. Since the fall of the Berlin Wall in 1989, in particular, the borders of Europe have shifted continuously following subsequent enlargements and a general move eastwards of the boundaries of the European Union and the Council of Europe. Classical divisions, such as the potato and pasta 'lines' that ran through Europe before the fall of communism, have become misleading as descriptions of the dynamics of contemporary Europe (Outhwaite 2008).

Indeed, Europe has increasingly become post-Western (Delanty 2003). At the same time, European institutions have come to play an increasingly important role in the area of the regulation of punishment. Within the framework of the Council of Europe in particular, much was done: the European Court of Human Rights turned into the ultimate arbiter of all sorts of disputes; with the establishment of the European Committee for the Prevention of Torture and Inhuman or Degrading Treatment or Punishment (CPT), the doors of prisons and other closed institutions opened for supervision and inspection; and the recommendations of the Council of Europe and the function of the Commissioner for Human Rights contributed in their way to the sensitisation and soft standardisation of numerous aspects of penal practice in the Member States. More recently, in particular since the late 1990s and even more so in the current post-Stockholm and post-Lisbon era, the (more powerful) European Union is (and will be) entering the penal terrain with increasing enthusiasm.

So if Europe has changed, and if Europe's involvement in penal matters has intensified and broadened, then perhaps the time has come for penologists to think more deeply *about Europe* in order to better understand punishment. In recent years the sociology of Europe, EU studies, European political philosophy and (European) cosmopolitanism have developed into thriving areas of research. However, thus far this literature has had no or only limited impact upon the study of punishment. This raises an obvious question: can it be fruitful for us to broaden our gaze and initiate a rendezvous with such adjacent fields of inquiry? Probably yes. This may be particularly appealing to those amongst us who prefer to think of European penology as an interdisciplinary field where legal scholarship, criminology, sociology and political science (should) meet in order to make sense of punishment in Europe. Moreover, such a rendezvous could also be attractive for the other part in this imaginary tête-à-tête: what can the study of punishment contribute to the understanding of Europe itself? Indeed, if it is true (and we believe it is) that 'the ways in which we punish, and the ways in which we represent that action to ourselves, makes a difference to the way we are' (Garland 1990: 276), then, what do the ways in which the Council of Europe and the European Union advise, instruct, persuade, and even force us to punish, reveal about us *as Europeans*?

This chapter is therefore set up as an invitation to explore, and establish connections between, two bodies of literature—that is, research on punishment and on Europe. It is built on the assumption that both parties in the dialogue may benefit from such interactions; that the whole is greater than the sum of its parts. We proceed by engaging with Ulrich Beck's recent writings on 'cosmopolitan Europe'. In particular, we suggest that penology may benefit from a second 'Beck-effect' (sections II and III): our aim is to demonstrate why we think this might be so (sections IV, V and VI). In line with our assumption that initiating a dialogue may be mutually beneficial, we will conclude with suggesting why the study of punishment should also interest Beck and other scholars who are active in the study of contemporary Europe (section VII).

## II. A SECOND 'BECK-EFFECT' IN PENOLOGY?

What do we mean when we speak about an 'effect'? The word 'effect' is often used with respect to the work of Michel Foucault. In the late 1970s *Discipline and Punish* sparked a first 'Foucault-effect', in particular in the study of punishment and control (Foucault 1977). Foucault's book fell on fertile soil, which to some extent had been prepared by a decade of critical research on the history of punishment, inter alia via studies of (rediscovered) Rusche and Kirchheimer (1968), Platt (1969), Rothman (1971), Scull (1977), Ignatieff (1978), and Melossi and Pavarini (1981). These so-called revisionist histories of punishment and control rejected the idea that history can be interpreted as a grand march forward, a linear process towards an increasingly humanised and civilised criminal justice system. Instead, the revisionists drew on a (neo-marxist) framework of (class) struggle, ideology and repression or, after the publication of *Discipline and Punish*, a Foucauldian framework of power, discipline and normalisation (Daems 2011).[1]

It is this meaning of 'effect' that we will use throughout this chapter, that is, the idea that a provocative book or thought-provoking series of articles is able to define research agendas for years to come. Speaking of an 'effect' in this way does not necessarily imply that scholars become close followers who are blindly devoted to the Master, nor that the foundations for a new school of thought are put into place. In fact, sometimes the opposite happens: 'effects' can also generate 'counter-effects'. In the case of Foucault, for example, *Discipline and Punish* not only gave rise to a distinctive stream of reflection and research, but also provoked critical theoretical responses and inspired empirical studies that were deliberately intended to prove him wrong and to highlight *other* dimensions of punishment. The introduction of Eliasian sociology by Pieter Spierenburg (1984) and Herman Franke (1990; 1995) in the sociology and history of punishment illustrates this nicely (Daems 2011). More recently, Philip Smith's (2008: 16) 'radically anti-Foucauldian position' formed part of a wider-ranging plea for a neo-Durkheimian framework, inspired by the so-called Yale strong program in cultural sociology. Seen from such a perspective, then, the 'Foucault effect' has sometimes been more about shock and provocation than about blind admiration and direct inspiration. Nonetheless, in both cases *Discipline and Punish*

[1] Interestingly, his later work on 'governmentality', mostly written between the late 1970s and his death in 1984, sparked a (second) 'Foucault-effect' in the 1990s and early 2000s (see eg Burchell et al 1991; Garland 1997).

made things move; or as Zygmunt Bauman (1990: 15) might have put it, the book has been conducive to 'defamiliarising' taken-for-granted views on punishment; that is, it assists in asking questions that 'make evident things into puzzles'.

The book *Risk Society* by German sociologist Ulrich Beck (1992) arguably has had a comparable 'effect' on research and debate about punishment. The original German-language edition of *Risk Society* was published in 1986, shortly after the world had been shocked by the nuclear disaster of Chernobyl. Risk moved to the forefront of public debate, and the book became a best-seller in Germany, with 60,000 copies sold in the first five years (Lash and Wynne 1992; Mythen 2004). Beck has been aptly described as a *Zeitgeist* sociologist (Skinner 2000: 160). His sociology is in particular concerned with 'the emerging new', rather than 'the old and the familiar'. For Beck, exploring and understanding the distinctive features of social transformations is one of the core tasks of the social sciences because 'it is precisely the turbulences which annoy people and drive them forward to face issues' (Beck and Beck-Gernsheim 1995: 10).

Unlike Foucault, whose work was explicitly concerned with the birth of the prison, Beck does not reflect in a direct way upon penal developments. Nonetheless, his writings on risk and reflexive modernisation have often been cited and have sensitised a generation of penologists to the pervasive presence of risk in contemporary penality. This has informed theory-building and empirical research on how we nowadays deal with crime, victimisation, prevention and punishment. Notions such as 'new penology', 'actuarial justice' or 'preventive justice' aim to capture some of the distinctive features of punishment in a risk society. The same is true for penological attention for aspects of risk calculation, new supervision practices, surveillance technologies, etc. At the same time, however, there has never been a Beckian school of thought. Moreover, at various occasions his work has been critically received, and has, in its wake, provoked 'counter-effects', for example from scholars who point at the enduring, and even increasing, influence and presence of the emotional and irrational dimensions of punishment; or from those who feel more attracted to the work of rivalling risk scholars, such as the writings of anthropologist Mary Douglas (1992) or of authors inspired by the later work of Michel Foucault (see, eg, O'Malley 2004).

## III. BECK'S COSMOPOLITAN TRILOGY AND THE QUESTION OF EUROPE TODAY

In this chapter we are not so much concerned with risk, but rather with Europe. Our focus therefore shifts to more recent work of Beck, even though there are clear links with Beck's earlier work on risk. Some even suggest that *Risk Society* already contains all the seeds of his subsequent writings (see, eg Vandenberghe 2001). Nevertheless, for our discussion in this chapter we are mostly interested in Beck's more recent writings devoted to the themes of globalisation, world risk society, cosmopolitanism and Europe—in particular, what Beck prefers to refer to as his cosmopolitan trilogy (Beck 2005a: xiii; Beck and Grande 2007a: xii). This trilogy is composed of the books *Power in the Global Age* (2005), *Cosmopolitan Vision* (2006) and *Cosmopolitan Europe* (2007) (co-authored with Edgar Grande). Central to this series of books is the radicalisation of the critique of methodological nationalism. This critique is not new. It goes back to the 1970s, 'when a number of sociologists argued that a major defect of existing social science was the treatment of nation-states *as though* they were closed, autonomous and self-contained units, and that this led to purely endogenous explanations of social change' (Fine 2006: 242–43). The notion, then, refers to the standpoint of social scientists who undertake research using concepts and categories associated with the nation state (Beck 2006: 24). For Beck, social scientists (and also politicians) continue to think in terms of the so-called 'zombie' category of the nation-state (Beck 2005a: xi). Whereas this may have been a defensible strategy for understanding society in its first modernity, this is no longer the case in the age of second modernity. A sociology that fails to acknowledge the pitfalls of methodological nationalism risks becoming a 'museum piece' (Beck 2005b). Such a sociology, so Beck explains, is beset by 'a failure to recognise—let alone research—the extent to which existing transnational modes of living, transmigrants, global elites, supranational organisations and dynamics determine the relations within and between nation-state repositories of power' (Beck 2005a: 23).

According to Beck, many of the problems that flow from methodological nationalism are being reproduced in comparative research: here too it is national societies that are being compared. Comparative research therefore presupposes nation-states as the basic units: 'Like a stamp collector, the social scientist starts from the assumption that social boundaries coincide with state boundaries and hence that the boundaries of research can and must also be fixed by the borders of the state' (Beck 2006: 28). Methodological nationalism also has deep consequences for how we deal with (global) inequalities. Within a nation-state, inequalities are usually legitimated in a 'reflexive' fashion, through reference to the 'merit system'. However, on a global scale such inequalities are legitimated in a non-reflexive manner, by the nation-state principle. What does this mean? The nation-state principle offers no defence of global inequalities based on reflection, but simply renders such inequalities invisible: 'the nation-state focus on national inequalities makes global inequalities disappear' (Beck 2005a: 26). As a result, people's attention is turned exclusively towards domestic issues.

So where does Europe fit in Beck's trilogy? In the two first instalments of the trilogy Beck devotes some attention to Europe (Beck 2005a: 230–31;

Beck 2006: 114–15, 163–77), and these cursory reflections are expanded in *Cosmopolitan Europe*, the closing episode of the trilogy. In this last book Europe is depicted as a special case of cosmopolitanisation. Beck and Grande highlight how Europe's unique history offers a fertile ground for developing cosmopolitanism. As they point out, the 'traditions of colonialism, nationalism, expulsion and genocide originated in Europe; but so too did the values and legal categories against which they are measured and condemned as crimes against humanity' (Beck and Grande 2007a: 9). For that reason they also speak of a self-critical Europe that has to confront its own history: Europe has created the ideologies and lived the experiences, but it also has erected the yardsticks against which we can judge them as 'evil'. As Beck explains: 'The awareness of global norms that founds political action arises post hoc, as it were, as a side effect of the violation of these same norms' (Beck 2006: 168).

As with the two other books of the trilogy, here also the main objective is to assist in transcending some misconceptions about Europe. At this moment, so Beck and Grande argue, Europe is either being understood as a collection of nation-states, or it is being approached as a large superstate in the making. In other words, conceptions of Europe too often use the nation-state model: 'Europe still suffers from misconstruing itself as a nation-state' (Beck and Grande 2007b: 69). But as Europe can become neither a state nor a nation, it cannot be thought of in terms of the nation-state (Beck 2008: 109). We need to approach Europe differently if we want to do justice to the *sui generis* character of European integration, that is, it being unique, not comparable to other historical models. Europe, then, should not be seen as the sum of a number of nation-states or a new emerging superstate, but rather as a dynamic and open political project. Beck and Grande therefore draw attention to the process of Europeanisation, that is, 'an institutionalized process of permanent change', which does not take place according to a master plan, but rather by means of the expansive logic of side effects:

> This innovation 'Europe' is a social construct, one which has until now obeyed a peculiar logic, namely, the *logic of side effects,* the logic of the unintended consequences of political decisions. Therein lies the peculiar modernity of Europe, and it is exactly for this reason that the project of European integration represents an exemplary field of study for the reflexive modernisation of modern societies.
>
> (Beck and Grande 2007a: 6.)

Europe, then, 'does not emerge on the open stage in a heroic political act but evolves behind the backs of actors through the power of side effects' (ibid: 36). This ongoing process of Europeanisation has deep and lasting consequences:

> The creation of interdependencies in every field of politics—the politics of mutual imbrication that makes Europeanization such a ubiquitous feature of our lives—is

> not a one-off form of cooperation that ultimately leaves the nation-states involved untouched. Rather, Europeanization seizes and transforms national sovereignty in the core of its being.
>
> (Beck 2003: 37.)

Because contemporary Europe tends to escape our available conceptual toolkit—being neither a super-state, nor an international organisation—we should abandon such outdated concepts and develop an alternative understanding of Europe. In order to give the political and institutional dimension of European governance its proper name, Beck and Grande introduce the concept of the 'European empire'. This European empire is 'post-imperial', so they argue, because it is no longer based on national demarcation and conquest, but rather on 'overcoming national borders, voluntarism, consensus, transnational interdependence and the political added value accruing from cooperation' (Beck and Grande 2007a: 53). Or as Beck has put it on another occasion:

> The cosmopolitan empire of Europe is notable for its open and cooperative character at home and abroad and therein clearly contrasts with the imperial predominance of the United States. Europe's undeniably real power is not decipherable in terms of nation-states. It lies instead in its character as a model of how Europe succeeded at transforming a belligerent past into a cooperative future, how the European miracle of enemies becoming neighbours could come about.
>
> (Beck 2008: 11.)

## IV. COMPARATIVE PENOLOGY AND METHODOLOGICAL NATIONALISM

The question of how to make sense of recent penal developments (for example, in terms of the uses or non-uses of imprisonment, of capital punishment, of alternative sanctions, of monetary fines) has attracted a great deal of scholarly attention. Indeed, western democracies seem to punish differently now compared with a few decades ago (Daems 2008). In recent years two major streams have developed in international penological research. On the one hand there is a group of scientists that points at the continuing strong influence of national political institutions, cultures and historical traditions. The emphasis usually is on differences and divergences in penal policy between different countries (eg Whitman 2003; Melossi 2004; Cavadino and Dignan 2006; Green 2008; Lacey 2008). On the other hand, there is a group of authors that focus on similarities and processes of convergence between different Western societies which are subject to similar structural and cultural changes (eg Christie 2000; Garland 2001; Pratt 2002, 2007; Wacquant 1999, 2006). Both have a lot to offer and we can learn a great deal from them. However, they both, for different reasons, tend to neglect the European dimension of the penal question.

Scholars belonging to the first group at times fall prey to methodological nationalism. Much comparative research is conducted from an exclusive national framework which suggests that one should only look at local practices and solely understand these against the background of the nation state. From this perspective, then, one is inclined to overstate the sovereignty and autonomy of nation states; such a comparative penology tends to feed the (wrong) impression that European states are in full control of the course of their penal trajectories. One recent plea for such a comparative penology can be found in the introduction to the book *Crime, Punishment, and Politics in Comparative Perspective*. Here editor (and eminent penologist) Michael Tonry states somewhat provocatively that only the local is relevant: 'Tip O'Neill, for many years speaker of the US House of Representatives, famously observed that "all politics are local." So are penal cultures and policies' (Tonry 2007: 1). Local cultures and policies are obviously of major importance, in particular in the field of punishment, but this 'either/or' style of reasoning[2] is not very helpful for alerting (European) penologists to the transnational dimensions of their subject matter. Such a privileging of national or local aspects is also present in the multiple uses of the term 'exceptionalism' in recent penological scholarship: 'American exceptionalism' (Poveda 2000; Steiker 2002), 'Dutch exceptionalism' (Downes and van Swaaningen 2007), 'English exceptionalism' (Tonry 2004: 51–70), 'French exceptionalism' (Tonry 2007: 37), 'Scandinavian exceptionalism' (Pratt 2008a,b). Each time, a state or group of states is being singled out and set apart: it is being suggested that one particular state or group of states is 'exceptional', and that it therefore escapes our 'normal' ways of understanding penal developments. 'Exceptional' developments call for 'exceptional' ways of making sense of penal developments which, therefore, can only apply, so the argument goes, to that particular state or set of states. The potential pitfalls stemming from methodological nationalism are not avoided by clustering states in different groups according to, for example, a typology of political economies (see eg Cavadino and Dignan 2006): also this type of comparative penology is first and foremost about studying separate, neatly circumscribed nation states which, in a second step, are to be grouped together because they share the same type of social and economic organisation.

But also scholars from the second group, who focus on the deeper transformations affecting contemporary societies, tend to neglect the fact that the European layer is quite distinctive and determinative for

[2] This 'either/or' style of reasoning is also present in Tonry's preface to the book *When Children Kill Children* by David Green, which offers a comparative study of the penal and political cultures in Norway and England and Wales: 'As Green makes clear, the differences in the emotions the two cases provoked, and in how they were handled, have nothing inherently to do with late-modernity and everything to do with differences in political and national cultures' (Tonry 2008: x).

socio-economic developments and, therefore, *also* for penal developments throughout Europe. If for decades aspects of (national) labour markets and social policy, culture, financial, fiscal and state budgetary matters have offered a pool of variables with which the sociologist of punishment could work, then it is quite plausible that, to the extent that European policy-making in those areas intensifies, these will *mutatis mutandis* also affect penal policy-making throughout Europe. Or to put it somewhat differently: if Europe becomes a source for social stability and transformation in itself (that is, if it starts to make sense to speak of a nascent 'European society' (Outhwaite 2008; Fligstein 2009)), then penology can no longer justify neglecting this European dimension of reality. We will need, therefore, to think more deeply about punishment and *European* society if we are to understand punishment in Europe now and what it may become in the future.

## V. TAKING EUROPE SERIOUSLY IN PENOLOGY

One of Beck's central messages is that we should take Europe seriously, and not approach it as a diverse collection of nation-states. Europe is a construction *sui generis*; it is a project that has its own characteristics (a 'European empire', as he prefers to call it), with a deep impact upon the daily lives of citizens within Europe's borders and a certain global *présence* (see above). Beck's suggestion that Europeanisation takes place according to the logic of 'side-effects', that is, by means of the unintended consequences of political decisions, is somewhat reminiscent of what Leon Lindberg once referred to as 'functional spill-over': 'the initial task and grant of power to the central institutions creates a situation or series of situations that can be dealt with only by further expanding the task and the grant of power' (Lindberg 1963: 10). Crime and punishment entered the EU agenda via this backdoor mechanism, in view of the potential 'security deficit' that was anticipated in the wake of the planned disappearance of Europe's internal borders; it was therefore an unintended side-effect of the freeing of the European internal market (Walker 2003; Baker and Harding 2009). The logic of 'side-effects' suggests, moreover, that a number of developments at a European level are closely connected; that is, penal policy becomes intertwined with other crime control policies, as well as policies that are unrelated to crime, because it tends to flow from previous 'grants of power'.

As a result we are nowadays confronted with a situation where Europe *as Europe* plays a much more important role on the crime scene than two decades ago. Frances Heidensohn (1991: 3) wrote in the early 1990s that: '"Europe" and all things European have become matters of increasing importance in the late twentieth century'. Nonetheless, and notwithstanding *some* activity in this respect, Heidensohn was not very impressed by what was going on at a European level:

> Crime policy at a European level is no one's business, although the Council of Europe does take an overall interest, it has no actual powers in these matters. Instead national governments and the supranational bodies make policies which affect crime rates and trends with little awareness of their crime-related consequences ... We face ... a future with some Eurocrime and Euroterrorism; whether we shall see Eurocops, Europrisons or Eurojustice is much less clear.
>
> (Heidensohn 1991: 12–13.)

From a contemporary perspective one can easily observe how key elements of the future predicted by Heidensohn—even those aspects that seemed to be unclear to her—have become reality. The term 'Eurocrime', for example, has by now become part of the standard vocabulary in Europe—even though it was used somewhat reluctantly in the beginning. In the mid-1990s it was argued that the term was only meaningful when used for crimes committed against the EU itself (such as agricultural fraud and budgetary fraud) (Anderson et al 1996: 15). Indeed, at that time the content of the term was still somewhat restricted because 'Eurocrime' suggests that there is 'a genuine criminal justice system' (ibid) which, at that time, was still far from reality. The gradually expanding role of the EU in the area of criminalisation would change this state of affairs quite dramatically (see eg Klip 2009). The Lisbon Treaty in particular, which offers an explicit legal basis for the adoption of criminal law directives, has opened the door for an EU policy on criminalisation. Consequently, the European Commission (2011b: 5) recently used the term Eurocrimes in a Communication where it reflected upon the further development of EU criminal policy under the Lisbon Treaty. Here, Eurocrimes are defined as those offences that are listed in Article 83, para 1 TFEU, referring to terrorism, trafficking in human beings, sexual exploitation of women and children, illicit drug trafficking, illicit arms trafficking, money laundering, corruption, counterfeiting of means of payment, computer crime and organised crime. These crimes, so the Commission argues, merit an EU approach 'due to their particularly serious nature and their cross-border dimension, according to the Treaty itself' (ibid).

Next to the material to work with—that is, crime—also the pan-European institutions that Heidensohn mentioned have to some extent materialised. We now have Eurocops and Eurojustice, although we label them somewhat differently—that is, Europol (the European Police Office), which became fully operational in July 1999, and Eurojust (the European Union's Judicial Cooperation Unit), which was established in 2002.[3] Moreover, even though

[3] www.europol.europa.eu/; http://eurojust.europa.eu/.

Europrisons will probably not become a reality in the foreseeable future, we have recently witnessed some highly interesting developments in this area which should attract the attention of penologists throughout Europe. On 12 March 2010 Viviane Reding, Vice-President of the European Commission responsible for Justice, Fundamental Rights and Citizenship, explained the EU's interest in Europe's prisons as follows:

> If people are detained in conditions bad enough to be considered degrading punishment, what judicial authority would authorise the transfer of a detainee to a place where he or she would face a substantial risk of being ill-treated? What does this mean for EU rules on prisoner transfers, due to be implemented by the end of 2011? These are supposed to allow Member States to repatriate foreign detainees even without their consent. For me it is therefore of crucial importance to improve prison conditions in Europe. Spreading alternatives to imprisonment and better prison management is one step that we can take in the near future. Of course prison conditions are first of all the responsibility of our 27 Member States, however, I will put pressure on all of them to live up to their responsibilities and I will publish a policy paper on prison conditions in Europe within the next 18 months.
>
> (Reding 2010: 4.)

Commissioner Reding kept her word: the announced Green Paper, *Strengthening mutual trust in the European judicial area—A Green Paper on the application of EU criminal justice legislation in the field of detention,* was published in June 2011. In this paper the Commission repeats that detention conditions and prison management are the prime responsibility of Member States, but that it is also interested in this issue 'because of the central importance of mutual recognition of judicial decisions for the area of freedom, security and justice' (European Commission 2011a: 2). Detention conditions are important in order to promote mutual trust and ensure the smooth functioning of mutual recognition instruments (such as the Council Framework Decisions on the European Arrest Warrant, the transfer of prisoners, mutual recognition of alternative sanctions and probation and the European Supervision Order). The EU, then, should become involved in prison matters in order to enhance mutual confidence and to avoid future cooperation in the judicial area being hampered by prison conditions that are below standard. Or as the Commission has put it:

> Without mutual confidence in the area of detention, European Union mutual recognition instruments that have a bearing on detention will not work properly, because a Member State might be reluctant to recognise and enforce the decision taken by another Member State's authorities. It could be difficult to develop closer judicial cooperation between Member States unless further efforts are made to improve detention conditions and to promote alternatives to custody.
>
> (European Commission 2011a: 4.)

It is too early to speculate about what will come out of this. Nonetheless, it is fascinating to observe how the European Commission's recent intervention in the area of detention further illustrates how the EU, by means of the mechanism of 'side-effects' or 'functional spill-over', has come to penetrate the *sancta sanctorum* of the European nation-state, that is, 'those very places where national sovereignty is given its overpowering yet most recondite expression' (Cassese 1996: 1). The tasks are, as Lindberg (1963: 10) suggested, 'inherently expansive': what started off as a project to integrate the coal and steel industries in Western Europe has come to penetrate areas that go straight to the heart of national sovereignty. Moreover, this also implies that the EU is entering territory that has been occupied and monopolised since decades by the Council of Europe. What will this bring for the future, and what does this mean for inter-institutional relations and dynamics within Europe? Mauro Palma, former President of the CPT, commented in March 2011 as follows on the (then upcoming) Green Paper of the European Commission:

> The Union has a clear interest in having satisfactory prison conditions in its member States, in order in particular to ensure the smooth functioning of mutual recognition instruments in the area of judicial cooperation. I believe this can be an opportunity, provided that the EU and the Council of Europe work in harmony. Together, the two organisations are capable of having a major impact on the treatment of prisoners throughout Europe.
>
> (Palma 2011: 3.)

The Council of Europe may, indeed, benefit from such cooperation in order to further its own agenda. Mauro Palma's CPT, for example, argued more than 15 years ago that the problem of prison overcrowding in Europe was 'sufficiently serious as to call for cooperation at European level, with a view to devising counter strategies' (CPT 1997: para 15). But will this potential be realised? Or can it be that we have entered a new era of competition between these two major institutional players? In the past, tensions have occasionally risen on topics as diverse as immigration, data protection and the rights of suspects of terrorism. Pan-European institutions do not always share the same agenda and there is no reason why this would be any different in the area of detention (Poncela and Roth 2006). In view of the predominantly instrumental rationale of the EU's interest in prison conditions—that is, to further judicial cooperation—the terrain of punishment may transform into a new site of potential conflict. A recent study of Framework Decision 2008/909/JHA of 27 November 2008 on the application of the principle of mutual recognition to judgments in criminal matters imposing custodial sentences or measures involving deprivation of liberty for the purpose of their enforcement in the European Union gives some food for thought in this respect: whereas the overt and declared objective of the Framework Decision is to promote the social rehabilitation of prisoners and to work in their interest, the more covert rationale seems to be to alleviate pressure on some of Europe's overcrowded prisons by making it easier (inter alia by means of abolishing double criminality and prisoners' consent) to return prisoners to their home countries (Vermeulen et al 2011; Vermeulen et al 2012).

Against such a background it is to be expected that the debate on the future of punishment *in* Europe will become more and more a debate on punishment *and* Europe: that is, the penal question then becomes an integral part of the larger and ongoing process of Europeanisation and, therefore, is uncoupled to some extent from the nation state focus. In order to promote and participate in such a European debate, different groups of penal practitioners have organised themselves, such as the European Organisation for Probation (CEP), which was already established in 1981, and which describes itself as 'the voice of probation in "Brussels"',[4] and, more recently, in October 2011, EuroPris (the European Organisation of Prison and Correctional Services), which was established with the specific intention of 'promoting ethical and rights-based imprisonment, exchanging information and providing expert assistance to support this agenda'.[5] Taking Europe seriously, as Beck suggests, then becomes indispensable for penology because a new era of policy-making and lobbying, opinion-formation and critique at a European level (and perhaps even a nascent European *penal* public sphere) seems to have dawned in the field of punishment. If European penology fails to engage more intimately with these and other developments it risks missing an important part of the ongoing process of the Europeanisation of the penal question.

## VI. EUROPE GOES GLOBAL

The debate about the borders of Europe usually focuses on how its external borders are being patrolled and securitised in order to tackle illegal immigration. Critics often capture these developments in the phrase 'Fortress Europe'. This is, indeed, an important and sinister part of the reality of contemporary Europe, as the images of human misery on the small Italian island of Lampedusa and the high death toll at the Union's borders testify.[6] However, Beck's notion of 'cosmopolitan Europe' also alerts us to another side of Europe, that is, its openness to the world. At first sight this term sounds somewhat paradoxical, since it encompasses 'the idea of

[4] www.cep-probation.org/.

[5] www.europris.org/.

[6] Since 1993 over 16,000 cases have been documented of people who died in their attempt of entering Europe or as a result of the EU's immigration policies; see www.unitedagainstracism.org/pdfs/listofdeaths.pdf.

"world citizenship", on the one hand, and the idea of a continent-wide, but nevertheless territorially limited political order, on the other' (Beck and Grande 2007b: 70). Nonetheless, the notion is particularly interesting because it invites reflection on the place of Europe in the world. Europe, so Beck argues, is a 'microcosm of global society': 'With growing transnational interconnections and obligations, Europe is becoming an open network with fluid boundaries in which the outside is already inside' (Beck 2006: 166).

Discussing Europe in these terms should happen cautiously because it makes one vulnerable for the critique of eurocentrism, that is, the fallacy of treating Europe as the world; as if Europe is the centre or the reference-point for understanding the globe and judging developments that take place outside of its borders. Nonetheless, one cannot deny that some ideas or visions are European in origin, or have found a hospitable environment within Europe, for example, in areas such as humanitarian aid (eg Red Cross or *Médecins sans Frontières*), environmental protection or, indeed, the abolition of capital punishment ('Europe is where there is no death penalty', according to a definition of Europe from French philosopher Jean-Pierre Faye (cited in Savater 2005: 43)). As Calhoun (2009: 646) recently suggested: 'a growing dimension of European self-awareness was that of being situated in a problematic world'. According to Calhoun, the idea of cosmopolitan Europe is rooted in an amalgam of three different sets of intellectual and popular images: (1) Europe as 'sophisticated', 'worldly wise'; (2) Europe as 'newly exciting' because of its unique experiment of political integration which has been pivotal to discussions about transcending the nation state (just as it previously was pivotal to imagining the nation state as the primary unit of politics); and (3) Europe as being 'at the center of imagining (and sometimes trying to act on) a cosmopolitan understanding of the world as a whole and itself as part. This is mostly an ethical perspective, rooted in Europe's old traditions of philosophical and religious universalism' (Calhoun 2009: 638).

This cosmopolitan dimension of Europe also becomes tangible if we look more closely at the history of monitoring places of detention by independent agencies in order to prevent torture and inhuman or degrading treatment or punishment. The idea of establishing a committee of experts that conducts unannounced preventive visits to places of detention all over the world originated in the mid-1970s when Jean-Jacques Gautier, a retired Swiss banker, decided to devote the rest of his life to the eradication of torture. To promote his proposal in 1977 Gautier founded the *Comité suisse contre la torture* (which became in 1992 the current Association for the Prevention of Torture). In 1978 Gautier's proposal was reworked to an optional protocol to the Convention Against Torture, which was then being prepared and negotiated within the UN. However, Gautier's proposal fell to a large extent on deaf ears. It was therefore decided to change strategy and to start lobbying at the regional level, that is, the Council of Europe. This proved to be a smart move because the idea of establishing such a visiting mechanism within Europe was received with much more enthusiasm within the Council of Europe.[7] As a result the European Convention for the Prevention of Torture and Inhuman or Degrading Treatment or Punishment was adopted in June 1987 and came into force on 1 February 1989. The first visit of the European anti-torture committee (CPT) that was established by this Convention (to Austria) took place in May 1990 (Evans and Morgan 1998). The CPT, in fact, became a self-declared 'cosmopolitan' expert body, accepting that its activities and the standards it develops *en cours de route* do not have any inherent borders. In its ninth general report it commented as follows on its place in the world: 'It is noteworthy that there is *no geographical restriction* upon the States which might be invited by the Committee of Ministers to accede to the Convention; *theoretically, at least, the world will be the limit*' (CPT 1999: para 14; emphasis supplied).

The successful adoption of the European Convention and the first experiences with the CPT in Europe provided a new impetus to attempts to realise a breakthrough on a global level. In 1990 the UN proposal was resubmitted by Costa Rica, and after a long and painstaking process the Optional Protocol to the Convention against Torture and other Cruel, Inhuman or Degrading Treatment or Punishment (OPCAT) was adopted in December 2002 (Evans and Haenni-Dale 2004; Boeglin 2005). Since the establishment of the Subcommittee on Prevention of Torture (SPT) following the entry into force of OPCAT (in June 2006), multiple contacts have taken place between the CPT and the SPT and a number of (former) members of the CPT have become members of the SPT.[8] The leading and facilitating role of the European body was symbolically confirmed at a conference organised in November 2009 in Strasbourg. Here, Victor Rodriguez Rescia, the then chairperson of the SPT, referred to the CPT as 'our elder brother and our partner and colleague in the prevention of torture' (CPT and APT 2010: 19). The fact that the CPT has been able to develop a much more intensive annual visiting programme than the SPT which, since its early inception, has suffered from a serious lack of sufficient resources, may imply that the CPT will remain the SPT's 'big brother' for many years to come (Daems 2012).

Europe, then, has undeniably functioned as a laboratory where 'cosmopolitan entrepreneurs' (to use one of Beck's other terms) could experiment

[7] Jean-Jacques Gautier had, in fact, a leading or facilitating role for Europe in mind already when he first started to think about developing and promoting this type of monitoring mechanism. In a letter of 25 September 1974 directed at Hélène Engel he launched the idea of persuading three or four European states to sign such a Convention amongst them and to take things further from there (Gautier 2003: 43). A few years later he would speak of a 'nucleus of committed states' in the fight against torture (Gautier 1980: 35).

[8] For example, Silvia Casale, a former member and chairperson of the CPT, was the first chairperson of the SPT.

with this preventive methodology which was, after all, still a revolutionary idea in the 1970s and 1980s, even in Europe (Cassese 1996). And yet, also here we can observe the power of the national outlook, as discussed by Beck. Earlier we discussed how Beck argues that the social sciences need to liberate themselves from the straitjacket of methodological nationalism in order to perceive existing world-wide inequalities more clearly. This observation also applies to prison conditions and the inequalities we can observe here, within Europe and across the globe; more particularly, it seems to be relevant for one of the core principles within the (European) normative *acquis* on governing the quality of prison conditions, a guiding principle for monitoring bodies such as the CPT and the SPT, that is, the principle of normalisation. This principle stipulates that living conditions behind bars and services provided for inmates should approximate as close as possible those in the community of free citizens, for example:

> A prison health care service should be able to provide medical treatment and nursing care, as well as appropriate diets, physiotherapy, rehabilitation or any other necessary special facility, in conditions comparable to those enjoyed by patients in the outside community. Provision in terms of medical, nursing and technical staff, as well as premises, installations and equipment, should be geared accordingly.
>
> (CPT 1993: para 38.)

> Life in prison shall approximate as closely as possible the positive aspects of life in the community.
>
> (European Prison Rules 2006, Rule 5.)

Putting this principle into practice is not that obvious. How can agencies such as the CPT establish standards that are being enjoyed in the outside world? What if law-abiding citizens in the free community enjoy little or no health care? (Morgan and Evans 1999). An additional problem, that moves centre-stage when we abandon the national focus, is that in practice the principle of normalisation is limited to a particular nation state: it does not guarantee the same standards for a Romanian, Moldovan or Finnish prisoner. Normalisation, as it is currently understood, is not a universal or absolute principle—it is a *relative* principle: the (outside) community mentioned in the quotes above is always a 'national' (outside) community.[9] The

[9] The same nation-state focus is implicitly present in its opposite, that is, the principle of 'less eligibility'. Sidney and Beatrice Webb defined this principle in 1910 as follows: 'The principle of "Less Eligibility"... that is, that the condition of the pauper should be "less eligible" than that of the lowest grade of independent labourer—is often regarded as a root principle of the reforms of 1834' (cited in Mannheim 1939: 56). The principle was introduced in the sociology of punishment by Georg Rusche (1978: 4) who formulated the reform implications of 'less eligibility' as follows: 'all efforts to reform the punishment of criminals are inevitably limited by the situation of the lowest socially significant proletarian class which society wants to deter from criminal acts. All reform efforts, however humanitarian and well-meaning, which attempt to go beyond this restriction are condemned to utopianism.' Jeremy Bentham

national outlook that Beck describes and criticises is therefore (implicitly) present in the principle of normalisation. This seems somewhat paradoxical: a European agency, such as the CPT, which operates explicitly on the basis of cross-border (or universal) principles that should guarantee the same levels of protection throughout Europe, needs to rely on the national perspective when prison conditions are being assessed.

This becomes even more pressing when we leave Europe, because on a global scale such inequalities become even more pronounced. But also here the principle of normalisation tends to be used within a national framework. In December 2007 the SPT paid a visit to the Maldives. This paradise for recently married couples celebrating their honeymoons in luxurious resorts also harbours some of the most horrific places of detention in the world: severe overcrowding, unhygienic living conditions, floggings, etc. Nonetheless, in terms of the provision of health care, the SPT remarked the following: 'it seems that the level of health care offered in prison is *equivalent to that of the population in general*, and it is free of charge' (SPT 2009: para 227, emphasis supplied). As long as inmates in the Maldives enjoy the same level of health care as other citizens in the outside community, all is fine. But is it? It is difficult to believe that the SPT really thinks it is. Such 'national' interpretations of normalisation raise an important and difficult issue for international organisations active in the field of monitoring closed institutions: it signals how questions of prison standards and their assessment are intricately bound up with much larger issues of global and redistributive justice which, obviously, are most often not within their reach.[10]

## VII. PUNISHMENT AND EUROPEAN SOCIETY

Let us now, by way of conclusion, address the dialogue from the other side of the table: What can the study of punishment contribute to our understanding of Europe? One of the central claims in penological research is

speaks of the principle of 'non-superiority': 'the ordinary condition of a convict doomed to punishment, which few or none but individuals of the poorest class are apt to incur, ought not to be made more eligible than that of the poorest class of subjects in a state of innocence and liberty' (cited in Mannheim 1939: 57).

[10] This is not only a problem outside of Europe. Art 9 of Council Framework Decision 2008/909/JHA of 27 November 2008 (transfer of prisoners) states the following: 'The competent authority of the executing State may refuse to recognise the judgment and enforce the sentence, if ... the sentence imposed includes a measure of psychiatric or health care or another measure involving deprivation of liberty, which ... cannot be executed by the executing State in accordance with its legal or health care system'. By including this ground for refusal in its Framework Decision, the EU seems to acknowledge that some EU Member States cannot provide adequate psychiatric or health care within their prison systems (see Vermeulen et al 2011: 48).

that, through the study of punishment, we can learn a great deal about our own societies and about ourselves (Garland 1990; Spierenburg 2004). What, then, do we reveal about ourselves as Europeans when we deal with penal questions in particular ways? What Dario Melossi once wrote about immigration in Europe, also applies to those being subjected to state punishment: 'in a sense on the very skin of the immigrants, Europeans are conversing about themselves, who they are, and where they want to go' (Melossi 1998: 57). Moreover, as Melossi suggests, this not only relates to who we *are* but also to what we can *become*. Indeed, as Loader and Sparks (2010: 123) recently argued: 'any discussion of the criminal question encodes in miniature a set of claims about the nature of the good society, and any attempt to answer it ... carries and projects a possible world, a desirable state of affairs'.

The ways in which we deal with outsiders reveals a great deal about our own identity; it signals where one group of people distinguishes itself from another group. Indeed, as Hildebrandt (2007: 58) explains, 'a people discriminates itself from other peoples in the way they criminalise behaviour, in the way they treat suspects and defendants and in the way they treat those that are judged and sentenced.' Throughout history punishment has at times become an important element in the identity politics of nation states: eg the remarkable decline of Finland's prison population has been associated with the fact that it felt itself to be 'out of line with the rest of the Nordic countries' (Christie 1993: 49); or Scotland's affinity for penal welfarism was linked to a sense of Scottishness 'defined as "other" to Thatcherism and Majorism in England and Wales' (McAra 2004: 49). In these cases punishment became an element in a much larger process of identity-construction. However, there is no reason why such questions about what punishment does and what it signifies should be restricted to the nation-state. Indeed, if Europe is increasingly working towards convergence in penal matters, then it becomes interesting to ask what kind of European penal identity (or identities, in view of potentially conflicting dynamics in contemporary Europe) is currently in the making.

Against this background, scholars who are intrigued by Europe should become interested in punishment because it may assist them in their attempts to understand European society better. Somewhat analogously to how Émile Durkheim turned to law as an indicator of the mode of integration of a society, one can wonder whether European (criminal) law, standard-setting and penal policy-making may offer us indicators of the mode of integration of European society. Unfortunately such questions are seldom asked in the field of European studies: with the exception of the intriguing question of the punishment of crimes against humanity, that is, those types of crimes that are by nature not bound to a nation-state framework (see Beck 2003: 34–36; Fine 2007: ch 6), punishment has hardly become a topic in the area of European studies. More generally, even though a great deal of scholarship on Europe is transdisciplinary in nature, the fields of criminology and penology are never mentioned as potential partners in such an enterprise:

> The intellectual undertaking of redefining cosmopolitanism is a trans-disciplinary one, which includes geography, anthropology, ethnology, international relations, international law, political philosophy and political theory, and now sociology and social theory.
>
> (Beck and Sznaider 2006: 2.)

This is, obviously, not new (see eg Cohen 1974), and probably criminology and penology are also to blame in part for not demonstrating with sufficient force why their topics of research deserve more attention from outsiders to the field.

There are, however, at least three additional reasons why scholarship on Europe could benefit from engaging more with penology. First of all, thinking about crime and punishment in Europe should make us cautious about some of the more sweeping statements about a nascent cosmopolitan Europe. Despite the influence of Europe which, as we have sought to demonstrate in this chapter, warrants special attention, we cannot simply do away with the enduring influence of the nation state in this area (Loader and Walker 2007). Moreover, thinking about punishment and crime control also reminds us of the fact that borders are often *not* blurring, but rather newly erected or fortified. Indeed, as Bauman (2004) once pointed out, the most important budgets of the new EU Member States were directed at the defences of the external borders of the EU. These developments sensitise us to the multiple, and at times conflicting, dynamics within contemporary Europe. Or to use once more a term that we introduced earlier in this chapter (section II): the work of Beck and much scholarship on Europe can probably benefit from a penological 'counter-effect' in order to amend or qualify some of the (rose-tinted) pictures of cosmopolitan Europe that tend to over-emphasise the emerging new transnational reality of Europe.

Secondly, there is what one might call an 'EU bias' at work in much debate and research on Europe. Although Beck repeatedly emphasises that Europe should not be equated with a specific institutional form and that therefore it cannot be restricted to the EU and its infrastructure (see eg Beck and Grande 2007a: 10), one can observe that in practice the focus is almost exclusively on the EU. This has the unfortunate consequence that the Council of Europe hardly receives any attention. In view of the financial and law-making power of the EU, as well as the wide-ranging impact of EU policy on European society, this is in part understandable. Nonetheless, this disproportionate attention to the EU still feels somewhat awkward, in particular at those moments when Beck discusses themes that have been at the heart of the Council of Europe's activities over the past six decades, such as the protection of human rights (eg Beck 2005a: 64ff; Beck 2006: 140ff).

Indeed, the Council of Europe describes itself as a 'house of human rights' and its primary goal has been formulated as 'to prevent barbarism from returning by protecting human rights and democracy throughout the continent' (Royer 2010: 3). Over the past decades it has established a track record of achievements in this area (see, eg, van Zyl Smit and Snacken 2009). A great deal of the activity that takes place at a European level disappears off the radar if the EU absorbs all of our attention.

Thirdly, and related to this EU bias, one can note a certain vagueness and even confusion in Beck's publications when he touches upon the normative dimension of his cosmopolitan Europe. Beck's cosmopolitanism is about an attitude of openness to other cultures, but it also includes an ethical orientation towards universal values and ideas. This distinguishes his cosmopolitanism from (postmodern) particularism (Beck 2006). Throughout his writings there are scattered remarks about the 'basic stock of common procedural and substantive norms' (Beck and Grande 2007a: 8) and the 'uniting and universally binding norms' (ibid: 14) of cosmopolitanism. However, what these are is either barely explained, or it becomes so self-evident that Beck's cosmopolitanism can hardly offer any normative guidance:

> Realistic cosmopolitanism presupposes a *universalistic minimum*. This includes substantive norms which must be upheld at all costs: that women and children should not be sold or enslaved, that people should be able to express their views about God or their government freely without being tortured or fearing for their lives—these norms are so self-evident that no violation of them could meet with cosmopolitan tolerance.
>
> (Beck 2006: 49.)

Beck suggests that cosmopolitan norms should be defined negatively rather than positively, that is, his cosmopolitanism seeks to avoid at all costs 'fascistic conformism ... systematic violation of human dignity, genocide and crimes against humanity' (Beck 2006: 59). Cosmopolitanism is about 'the common defence against evils' (ibid). At a certain point one draws a line, but where? According to one of Beck's critics this is one of the weaknesses of his cosmopolitanism: 'the normative content of Beck's cosmopolitanism remains frustratingly undertheorized' (Smith 2008: 259). Besides the fact that women and children should not be sold or enslaved, or that systematic violations of human dignity should be forbidden, he keeps silent. For example, if *systematic* violations of human dignity are not acceptable, does this then imply that *occasional* violations of human dignity are fine in Beck's cosmopolitan world?

Punishment may, in fact, be a good place to start to look for answers to questions about the normative content of European cosmopolitanism. Again, the Council of Europe in particular has been extremely active in the area of standard-setting, monitoring and sanctioning of 'uncivilised' penal practices throughout Europe. The topic of punishment, then, is not only interesting for analytic purposes in order to better understand Europe, but also to uncover the normative foundations of the kind of Europe in which we live and in which we would like to live.

## REFERENCES

Ancel, M (1974) 'Principal Aspects of Modern European Penology' *Proceedings of the American Philosophical Society*, 118, 254–59.
Anderson, M, Den Boer, M, Cullen, P, Gilmore, WC, Raab, CD and Walker, N (1996) *Policing the European Union* (Oxford, Clarendon Press).
Baker, E and Harding, C (2009) 'From Past Imperfect to Future Perfect? A Longitudinal Study of the Third Pillar' *European Law Review*, 34, 25–54.
Bauman, Z (1990) *Thinking Sociologically* (Oxford, Basil Blackwell).
—— (2004) *Europe. An Unfinished Adventure* (Cambridge, Polity Press).
Beck, U (1992) *Risk Society. Towards a New Modernity* (London, Sage).
—— (2003) 'Understanding the Real Europe' *Dissent*, Summer, 32–38.
—— (2005a) *Power in the Global Age. A New Global Political Economy* (Cambridge, Polity Press).
—— (2005b) 'How Not to Become a Museum Piece' *British Journal of Sociology*, 56, 335–43.
—— (2006) *The Cosmopolitan Vision* (Cambridge, Polity Press).
—— (2008) 'Re-Inventing Europe: A Cosmopolitan Vision' *Quaderns de la Mediterrània*, 109–16.
Beck, U and Beck-Gernsheim, E (1995) *The Normal Chaos of Love* (Cambridge, Polity Press).
Beck, U and Grande, E (2007a) *Cosmopolitan Europe* (Cambridge, Polity Press).
—— (2007b) 'Cosmopolitanism. Europe's Way Out of Crisis' *European Journal of Social Theory*, 10, 67–85.
Beck, U and Snzaider, N (2006) 'Unpacking Cosmopolitanism for the Social Sciences: A Research Agenda' *British Journal of Sociology*, 57, 1–23.
Boeglin, N (2005) 'History of the Optional Protocol to the UN Convention against Torture' in Inter-American Institute for Human Rights and Association for Prevention of Torture, *Optional Protocol to the United Nations Convention Against Torture and Other Cruel, Inhuman or Degrading Treatment or Punishment. A Manual for Prevention* (San José, Inter-American Institute for Human Rights).
Burchell, G, Gordon, C and Miller, P (eds) (1991) *The Foucault Effect. Studies in Governmentality* (London, Harvester Wheatsheaf).
Calhoun, C (2009) 'Cosmopolitan Europe and European Studies' in C Rumford (ed), *The Sage Handbook of European Studies* (London, Sage).
Cassese, A (1996) *Inhuman States. Imprisonment, Detention and Torture in Europe Today* (Cambridge, Polity Press).
Cavadino, M and Dignan, J (2006) *Penal Systems. A Comparative Approach* (London, Sage).
Christie, N (1993) *Crime Control as Industry. Towards GULAGS, Western Style?* (London, Routledge).

Cohen, S (1974) 'Criminology and the Sociology of Deviance in Britain. A Recent History and a Current Report' in P Rock and M McIntosh (eds), *Deviance and Social Control* (London, Tavistock Publications).
Conrad, JP (1969) 'Introduction (The Future of Corrections)' *Annals of the American Academy of Political and Social Science*, 381, xi–xiii.
CPT (1993) *3rd General Report on the CPT's Activities Covering the Period 1 January to 31 December 1992*, CPT/Inf (93) 12 (4 June 1993).
—— (1997) *7th General Report on the CPT's Activities Covering the Period 1 January to 31 December 1996*, CPT/Inf (97) 10 (22 August 1997).
—— (1999) *9th General Report on the CPT's Activities Covering the Period 1 January to 31 December 1998*, CPT/Inf (99) 12 (30 August 1999).
—— and APT (2010) *New Partnerships for Torture Prevention in Europe. Proceedings of the Conference. Strasbourg, 6 November 2009* (Strasbourg, Council of Europe).
Daems, T (2008) *Making Sense of Penal Change* (Oxford, Oxford University Press).
—— (2011) 'A Peculiar Sociology of Punishment' *Oxford Journal of Legal Studies*, 31, 805–23.
—— (2012) 'Koken met saffraan. Wereldwijd toezicht op vrijheidsberoving en het optioneel protocol bij het VN-Verdrag tegen foltering en andere wrede, onmenselijke of vernederende behandeling of bestraffing (OPCAT)' in L Pauwels and G Vermeulen (eds), *Update in de criminologie VI* (Antwerp, Maklu).
Delanty, G (2003) 'The Making of a Post-Western Europe: A Civilizational Analysis' *Thesis Eleven*, 72, 8–25.
Douglas, M (1992) *Risk and Blame: Essays in Cultural Theory* (London, Routledge).
Downes, D and Swaaningen, R van (2007) 'The Road to Dystopia? Changes in the Penal Climate of the Netherlands' in M Tonry and C Bijleveld (eds), *Crime and Justice in the Netherlands (Crime and Justice: A Review of Research (Volume 35))* (Chicago, University of Chicago Press).
European Commission (2011a) *Strengthening mutual trust in the European judicial area—A Green Paper on the application of EU criminal justice legislation in the field of detention.* COM(2011) 327, 14 June 2011.
—— (2011b) *Towards an EU Criminal Policy: Ensuring the effective implementation of EU policies through criminal law.* COM(2011) 573, 20 September 2011.
Evans, MD and Morgan, R (1998) *Preventing Torture. A Study of the European Convention for the Prevention of Torture and Inhuman or Degrading Treatment or Punishment* (Oxford, Clarendon Press).
Evans, MD and Haenni-Dale, C (2004) 'Preventing Torture? The Development of the Optional Protocol to the UN Convention Against Torture' *Human Rights Law Review*, 4, 19–55.
Fine, R (2006) 'Cosmopolitanism. A Social Science Research Agenda' in G Delanty (ed), *Handbook of Contemporary European Social Theory* (London, Routledge).
—— (2007) *Cosmopolitanism* (Abingdon, Routledge).
Fligstein, N (2009) *Euroclash. The EU, European Identity and the Future of Europe* (Oxford, Oxford University Press).
Foucault, M (1977) *Discipline and Punish. The Birth of the Prison* (New York, Pantheon Books).

Franke, H (1990) *Twee eeuwen gevangen. Misdaad en straf in Nederland* (Utrecht, Het Spectrum).
—— (1995) *The Emancipation of Prisoners. A Socio-Historical Analysis of the Dutch Prison Experience* (Edinburgh, Edinburgh University Press).
Garland, D (1990) *Punishment and Modern Society. A Study in Social Theory* (Oxford, Clarendon Press).
—— (1997) 'Governmentality and the Problem of Crime: Foucault, Criminology, Sociology' *Theoretical Criminology*, 1, 173–214.
—— (2001) *The Culture of Control. Crime and Social Order in Contemporary Society* (Oxford, Oxford University Press).
Green, DA (2008) *When Children Kill Children. Penal Populism and Political Culture* (Oxford, Oxford University Press).
Gautier, J-J (1980) 'The Case for an Effective and Realistic Procedure' in International Commission of Jurists and Swiss Committee Against Torture (eds), *Torture: How to Make the International Convention Effective. A Draft Optional Protocol* (Geneva, International Commission of Jurists).
—— (2003) 'Lettre de Jean-Jacques Gautier à Hélène Engel (25 septembre 1974)' in N Mischler (ed), *Jean-Jacques Gautier et la prévention de la torture: de l'idée à l'action. Recueil de textes* (Geneva, L'Association pour la prévention de la torture).
Heidensohn, F (1991) 'Introduction. Convergence, Diversity and Change' in F Heidensohn and M Farrell (eds), *Crime in Europe* (London, Routledge).
Hildebrandt, M (2007) 'European Criminal Law and European Identity' *Criminal Law and Philosophy*, 1, 57–78.
Ignatieff, M (1978) *A Just Measure of Pain. The Penitentiary in the Industrial Revolution, 1750–1850* (New York, Pantheon Books).
Klip, A (2009) *European Criminal Law: An Integrative Approach* (Antwerp, Intersentia).
Lacey, N (2008) *The Prisoners' Dilemma. Political Economy and Punishment in Contemporary Democracies* (Cambridge, Cambridge University Press).
Lash, S and Wynne, B (1992) 'Introduction' in U Beck, *Risk Society. Towards a New Modernity* (London, Sage).
Lindberg, LN (1963) *The Political Dynamics of European Economic Integration* (Stanford, Stanford University Press).
Loader, I and Walker, N (2007) *Civilizing Security* (Cambridge, Cambridge University Press).
Loader, I and Sparks, R (2010) *Public Criminology?* (Abingdon, Routledge).
Mannheim, H (1939) *The Dilemma of Penal Reform* (London, George Allen and Unwin).
McAra, L (2004) 'The Cultural and Institutional Dynamics of Transformation: Youth Justice in Scotland, England and Wales' *The Cambrian Law Review*, 35, 23–54.
Melossi, D (1998) 'Remarks on Social Control, State Sovereignty and Citizenship in the New Europe' in V Ruggiero, N South and I Taylor (eds), *The New European Criminology. Crime and Social Order in Europe* (London, Routledge).
—— (2004) 'The Cultural Embeddedness of Social Control: Reflections on a Comparison of Italian and North American Cultures Concerning Punishment'

in T Newburn and R Sparks (eds), *Criminal Justice and Political Cultures* (Cullompton, Willan Publishing).
Melossi, D and Pavarini, M (1981) *The Prison and the Factory. Origins of the Penitentiary System* (Basingstoke, MacMillan).
Morgan, R and Evans, MD (1999) 'CPT Standards: An Overview' in R Morgan and MD Evans (eds), *Protecting Prisoners. The Standards of the European Committee for the Prevention of Torture in Context* (Oxford, Oxford University Press).
Mythen, G (2004) *Ulrich Beck: A Critical Introduction to the Risk Society* (London, Pluto Press).
O'Malley, P (2004) *Risk, Uncertainty and Government* (London, Glasshouse).
Outhwaite, W (2008) *European Society* (Cambridge, Polity Press).
Palma, M (2011) Opening speech for the seminar 'Improving detention conditions through effective monitoring and standard-setting' organised within the framework of the Turkish Chairmanship of the Committee of Ministers of the Council of Europe, 17–18 March 2011, Antalya, Turkey.
Platt, A (1969) *The Child Savers. The Invention of Delinquency* (Chicago, University of Chicago Press).
Poncela, P and Roth, R (2006) *La fabrique du droit des sanctions pénales au Conseil de l'Europe* (Paris, La documentation Française).
Poveda, TG (2000) 'American Exceptionalism and the Death Penalty' *Social Justice*, 27, 252–67.
Pratt, J (2002) *Punishment and Civilization* (London, Sage).
—— (2007) *Penal Populism* (London, Routledge).
—— (2008a) 'Scandinavian Exceptionalism in an Era of Penal Excess. Part 1: The Nature and Roots of Scandinavian Exceptionalism' *British Journal of Criminology*, 48, 119–37.
—— (2008b) 'Scandinavian Exceptionalism in an Era of Penal Excess. Part 2: Does Scandinavian Exceptionalism have a Future?' *British Journal of Criminology*, 48, 275–92.
Reding, V (2010) 'The Future of European Criminal Justice under the Lisbon Treaty'. Speech delivered at the European Law Academy, Trier, 12 March 2010.
Rothman, DJ (1971) *The Discovery of the Asylum. Social Order and Disorder in the New Republic* (Boston, Little, Brown and Company).
Royer, A (2010) *The Council of Europe* (Strasbourg, Council of Europe Publishing).
Rusche, G (1978) 'Labor Market and Penal Sanction: Thoughts on the Sociology of Criminal Justice' *Crime and Social Justice*, 10 (Fall/Winter), 2–8.
Rusche, G and Kirchheimer, O (1968) *Punishment and Social Structure* (New York, Russell and Russell).
Savater, F (2005) 'Europe, both Needed and in Need' in D Lévy, M Pensky and JC Torpey (eds), *Old Europe, New Europe, Core Europe: Transatlantic Relations After The Iraq War* (London, Verso).
Scull, A (1977) *Decarceration. Community Treatment and the Deviant—A Radical View* (Englewood Cliffs, Prentice-Hall).
Skinner, J (2000) 'The Eruption of Chances Peak, Montserrat, and the Narrative Containment of Risk' in P Caplan (ed), *Risk Revisited* (London, Pluto Press).
Smith, P (2008) *Punishment and Culture* (Chicago, University of Chicago Press).

Smith, W (2008) 'A Cosmopolitan Sociology. Ulrich Beck's Trilogy on the Global Age' *Global Networks*, 8, 253–59.
Sparks, R (2001) 'Degrees of Estrangement: The Cultural Theory of Risk and Comparative Criminology' *Theoretical Criminology*, 5, 159–76.
Spierenburg, P (1984) *The Spectacle of Suffering. Executions and the evolution of repression: from a preindustrial metropolis to the European experience* (Cambridge, Cambridge University Press).
—— (2004) 'Punishment, Power, and History: Foucault and Elias' *Social Science History*, 28, 607–36.
Steiker, CS (2002) 'Capital Punishment and American Exceptionalism' *Oregon Law Review*, 81, 97–130.
Subcommittee on Prevention of Torture (2009) *Report on the Visit of the Subcommittee on Prevention of Torture and Other Cruel, Inhuman or Degrading Treatment or Punishment to the Maldives,* CAT/OP/MDV/1, 26 February 2009.
Tonry, M (2004) *Punishment and Politics. Evidence and Emulation in the Making of English Crime Control Policy* (Cullompton, Willan Publishing).
—— (2007) 'Determinants of Penal Policies' in M Tonry (ed), *Crime, Punishment, and Politics in Comparative Perspective (Crime and Justice, volume 36)* (Chicago, University of Chicago Press).
—— (2008) 'Preface' in DA Green, *When Children Kill Children: Penal Populism and Political Culture* (Oxford, Oxford University Press).
van Zyl Smit, D and Snacken, S (2009) *Principles of European Prison Law and Policy: Penology and Human Rights* (Oxford, Oxford University Press).
Vandenberghe, F (2001) 'Introduction à la sociologie (cosmo)politique du risque d'Ulrich Beck' *Revue du Mauss*, 17, 25–39.
Vermeulen, G, van Kalmthout, A, Paterson, N, Knapen, M, Verbeke, P and De Bondt, W (2011) *Cross-border Execution of Judgments Involving Deprivation of Liberty in the EU* (Antwerp, Maklu).
Vermeulen, G, Verbeke, P and De Bondt, W (2012) 'Materiële detentiecondities, strafuitvoering en overbrenging van gedetineerden in de EU. Een SWOTanalyse van het Kaderbesluit Overdracht Vrijheidsbenemende Straffen & Maatregelen' in L Pauwels and G Vermeulen (eds), *Update in de criminologie VI* (Antwerp, Maklu).
Wacquant, L (1999) *Les prisons de la misère* (Paris, Raisons d'agir).
—— (2006) *Parias urbains. Ghetto, banlieues, État* (Paris, Éditions La Découverte).
Walker, N (2003) 'The pattern of transnational policing' in T Newburn (ed), *Handbook of Policing* (Cullompton, Willan Publishing).
Whitman, JQ (2003) *Harsh Justice. Criminal Punishment and the Widening Divide between America and Europe* (New York, Oxford University Press).

# 3

# *Knowledge Politics and Penal Politics in Europe*

IAN LOADER AND RICHARD SPARKS*

> The work of an intellectual is not to mould the political will of others; it is, through the analyses that he does in his own field, to re-examine evidence and assumptions, to shake up habitual ways of working and thinking, to dissipate conventional familiarities, to re-evaluate rules and institutions and to participate in the formation of a political will (where he has his role as citizen to play).
>
> (Michel Foucault 1984.)

## I. INTRODUCTION: KNOWLEDGE-POLITICS, PENAL POLITICS, EUROPEAN POLITICS

IT IS WIDELY acknowledged that the texture and temperature of penal politics in any given time and place will have a bearing on the kinds of knowledge concerning punishment practices that are produced, taken up and used there. In what follows, we will rehearse a number of arguments—some familiar, and some perhaps more novel—about the significance, both practical and symbolic or ideological, of those relationships for the present and near futures of penal issues in Europe. Yet it can also be argued that, despite this general acceptance, the precise form, implications and effects of the relations between the contexts of knowledge production and those of policy formation and practical action, at least in the domains of crime and punishment, have hitherto rarely been made the topic of systematic

* We are most grateful to the organisers (subsequently editors) of the Oñati 'European Penology?' seminar, and to the other participants on that occasion. There have been at least three other audiences with whom we have had the chance to discuss some of these ideas in development. They are: the members of the GERN 'Interlabo' held in Edinburgh in May 2011; the participants in a memorial seminar celebrating the work of Richard Ericson at Green College, University of British Columbia in September 2011; and the audience at the WG Hart symposium at the Institute for Advanced Legal Studies in London in June 2012. We are grateful to the organisers of each of these events.

investigation, regardless of how many glancing references are made to the troubled relationship between them.

We have argued at some length in our book *Public Criminology?* (2010) that this lack of concerted inquiry is unfortunate, and that it stands in need of correction. For this reason we re-state and develop here the most relevant of those arguments. However *Public Criminology?* was self-admittedly a book whose main substantive examples and illustrations focused on British debates. It argued quite strongly that these examples raised issues that were in principle comparative and, increasingly, transnational in scope, but we did not explore those dimensions of the problem very much further in the book.[1] The discussion that is pursued throughout this volume about the current condition of European penology—whatever that is, and whatever it may become—seems an apt opportunity to begin to revisit those under-explored questions.

We will suggest that the state of these knowledge-policy figurations is in some quite strong and particular senses an *indicative* issue—one that provides insight into the terms on which policy is deliberated and made, and hence the mentalities and sensibilities that animate and undergird it. Exploring those dynamics is for this reason one of the more revealing challenges that comparative penological inquiry can set itself, even if that looks like a very oblique approach compared to more obvious and urgent questions such as prison populations, penal regimes and the uses of populist rhetoric in political campaigns. Yet the roles of knowledge in policy-making (its uses, abuses and non-uses; the predominance of some kinds of knowledge-claims over others, and so on) directly condition those other more plainly significant outcomes. There are a certain number of reports and observations (often arising for example from the invaluable country surveys published in the *European Journal of Criminology*) and a few intriguing observations of wider scope (notably Tonry 2004b) that lend support to this perception. At present however these seem to us to constitute at most the outlines of an agenda for research, rather than anything more definite. As we will also show, however, matters are quite otherwise in some other fields of policy and some other disciplines, and there is a good deal to be gained for scholars of criminology, criminal justice and penal politics from a sideways look across those disciplinary fences into the neighbouring fields.

[1] One reason for this omission is that we always conceived of *Public Criminology?* as the opening statement in a longer discussion, and planned to develop the position in various directions, both empirically and theoretically. Whilst this accounts to some extent for the somewhat schematic and manifesto-like quality of some of the arguments, we fully accept that the book stands or falls on its own merits and that we could not expect its critics and other readers to assume anything else. However, the present chapter and other papers that we are currently planning may be read as steps in the direction of a larger reconsideration of the place of crime and punishment in contemporary democratic politics.

Beyond the cross-national comparative issues with which we are at least somewhat familiar, however, there arises a still hazier set of outlines concerning the emergent penologies proper to European institutions themselves—the framings operated or mandated by various organs of the EU or the Council of Europe. Just as the prevailing penological wisdoms of individual countries at various points in their development have played their part in the formation of those political cultures and their particular regimes of social regulation and control, so, we might suggest, the generation of similar discourse on the European level tells us something about the self-understanding and aspirations of those polities too. As yet, in the field of penology broadly considered, we can find more corroboration for the general plausibility of some such claim (most significantly van Zyl Smit and Snacken 2009) than that we are able to document the roles of research and knowledge generation in influencing law, policy or practice. We can however point to a small number of research projects in other fields of scientific or social scientific knowledge that offer some guidance on what might be gained by exploring the knowledge–policy nexus more thoroughly, and where that might take us in terms of punishment policies and practices.

In short then there are two kinds of comparative question running through this discussion—the familiar cross-national sort, and the slightly less obvious cross-sectoral kind. There are also a number of issues concerning the salience of supranational, and especially European, agencies and institutions in shaping the future of knowledge production and use to some greater or lesser degree. The argument proceeds in the following steps. First, it briefly reminds us why raising the question of *penology* here at all is by definition to bring up certain problems about the social values and uses of scientific discourse. Second, it revisits certain themes raised by us in *Public Criminology?* concerning the positions of intellectual production vis-à-vis practical affairs, and hence about what is at stake in the choices that participants make about those matters. Third, it alludes to the somewhat scattered but important observations that are already available on these questions in suggesting that the institutional architecture that exists for research and research utilisation in different places is both an indicative and a practically consequential question in comparative criminological and penological research, and hence one that deserves to be explored much further. Fourth, it suggests, even more briefly and tentatively, that research on how knowledge and policy relate, or fail to relate, in respect of punishment and social control, will increasingly also have to focus on the level of European institutions as such. Finally, as well as sketching a few ideas on what a future research agenda on these issues may come to look like, we try to clarify why all this matters in terms of the relationships that exist, or the ones that we might hope to develop, between expert knowledges and democratic deliberation.

## II. 'PENOLOGY' IN THE SOCIOLOGY OF KNOWLEDGE—A BRIEF REMINDER

As Snacken and van Zyl Smit (this volume) note, 'penology' has been inflected somewhat differently in different European languages, and in particular in the distinct legal and administrative contexts and traditions in which it has developed. What the dictionary definitions generally have in common, however, is the primary and often taken-for-granted fact that making reference to penology at all involves asserting (or sometimes disputing) the grounding of current practices or reform proposals in the authority of scientific knowledge. The version of a dictionary definition for which one of us has to acknowledge authorial responsibility has it that penology is 'A term which ... covers the application of clinical, managerial or social scientific methods or expertise to the disciplined study and evaluation of penal institutions, especially prisons' (Sparks 2006: 290). From an historical and comparative point of view, Sparks continues, 'the particular histories of prison architecture and disciplinary regimes, as well as the minutiae of medico-psychiatric services, religious observance, diet and other aspects of the material infrastructure and social relations of penal institutions are largely unintelligible without reference to the intellectual inputs of the various penologies that have successively informed them' (ibid: 291).

A *locus classicus* for the latter longer and broader perspective is of course Foucault's discussion of the building-in of such practical *savoirs* into the very construction of penal institutions, their architecture, their fabric, their deployment of time and division of space (Foucault 1977: 27). On such an account the development of penal institutions and practices in modernity cannot but be seen as linked to various versions of expertise. There are of course moments, such as during the so-called decline of the rehabilitative ideal, when a prevailing orthodoxy of intervention is called into question and may fall into disrepute. Yet, that very case was precipitated in part by an expert intervention—Martinson's famous review article with its provocative conclusion that 'nothing works' (Martinson 1974; see also Cavender 2004)—even if the underlying motors of change may really have lain elsewhere.

This chapter certainly proceeds on the basis of a broader rather than more restrictive view of what 'penology' is—one that goes well beyond the technicist and instrumental assumptions sometimes associated with that term, and which are sometimes brought up in order to discredit it. On one side penology is a discursive arena that has open borders with the philosophy of punishment and aspects of legal theory. On the other its character has broadened markedly to incorporate a whole range of issues in the organisation, effects and ideological affiliations of penal institutions and their associated politics (see further Simon and Sparks 2012). On this view penology 'is the study of the social processes of punishment and penal control, which is to say, of the whole complex of laws, ideas and institutions which regulate criminal conduct' (Garland 1997: 181). Indeed, Garland goes on to argue that seen from this point of view, 'penology' is historically and intellectual the primary subject from which criminology is one line of evolutionary development:

> Understood in this more expansive sense, penological research *includes* the study of criminology, insofar as criminological ideas come to inform the practices of punishment and crime-control. This seems to me to be the right way to think about criminology: not as an academic subject—though it has certainly become one—but rather as a *practical* ingredient in the modern system of penal control. A penologist does not 'do' criminology. Instead, he or she *observes* it in operation, studying how criminological ideas have insinuated themselves into our penal institutions, shaping and legitimating our practices of punishment. For penologists, criminology is one of the discourses upon which penal practice is based, one of the knowledges that combines with penal power to create our modern system of penal control.
>
> (Garland 1997: 182.)

Whether or not we accept this slightly controversial way of framing the relationship between these nominated fields (a secondary consideration for our purposes), Garland is in our view quite correct in arguing that there is a continuing and rather fluid relationship between the ways in which certain modes of expert knowledge have envisioned responses to crime problems and the rise and fall of successive institutions and practices of crime control and their legitimating principles. Such reminders are, we suggest, quite necessary in an era when disaffection on the part of many criminologists and penal practitioners with the emotive tone of much political discourse on crime sometimes leads them to assert that their work has little or no influence on 'policy'—a position which we have elsewhere termed the doctrine or trope of 'successful failure', and one that we have been at some pains to interrogate quizzically (Loader and Sparks 2010: ch 1). Seen in this way it is more appropriate to argue that the effects of interventions on the level of expert knowledge, however defined and valued, are somewhat unpredictable and that they tend to escape the control of their originators. They may have delayed, unintended, counter-productive or perverse consequences. There may be battles for control or definition of a problem such that one set of expert knowers feel that it has been taken over by others, whom they often regard as charlatans or barbarians, or where they feel that something that properly sits within the domain of their expertise has become flooded by popular passions or demotic rhetoric. It is of the first importance for the project of this volume and for the argument of this chapter that these conditions may vary enormously between times and places and levels of decision-making.

Nevertheless it is almost never the case under conditions of modernity that expert knowledge-claims are irrelevant to the creation, implementation, evaluation, reform, legitimation or discrediting of institutions, policies and practices. We need not assume that those claims are either valid or benign in order to adopt this view. Simply, they are part of the process of the making and unmaking of those institutions and their position within political culture. Rather than focusing uniquely upon the supposed tendency of populist forms of penal politics to overwhelm expertise (a tendency which is in any case much more predominant in some countries than in others) it is in our view more instructive for analysts of problems of crime and punishment to interrogate the uses and abuses of those knowledges—the amplifications and appropriations, the erasures and distortions. Seen from this point of view the contention that surrounds criminal and penal questions nowadays presents a particular case of a paradox that sociologists of science see as pervasive. As Weingart has argued, one consequence of the 'scientisation' of society tends to be a politicisation of science (Weingart 1999). Or as Grundmann and Stehr have neatly framed the issue: 'If we speak about knowledge societies, we cannot remain silent about knowledge politics' (Grundmann and Stehr 2003: 183).

This leaves altogether open the question of what 'European penology' now is or may become. We know that Europe has been the point of origin of much of modern penology and that this has proceeded in a complex and varied set of relationships of exchange and mutual influence with the Americas and other parts of the world (eg Scharff-Smith 2004; Salvatore and Aguirre 1996; Melossi et al 2011). It is generally also suggested that after 1945 and into the twenty-first century, adherence to a developing set of human rights norms in penological matters has been part of the narrative of the maturation and growth of European institutions—first through the various organs of the Council of Europe, and latterly also through the expanding competencies of the EU with the consolidation of the 'Area of Freedom, Security and Justice' (AFSJ) following the Treaty of Lisbon (2009) and the adoption of the Stockholm Programme. Such developments are integral to the claim that Europe is in some sense a test-bed for a new form of cosmopolitanism (Calhoun 2010; Daems, this volume). It would be in this area, as much as others, that the notion of Europe as 'a civilisation', rather than an association of adjacent but discreet 'societies' (Roche 2010), would need to be realised. The distinct questions for a European penology would thus include not just the established activities of tracking convergent and divergent tendencies and their general and particular explanatory dynamics, but also which actors in what kinds of networks and institutional settings are now influencing developments at the European level, and with what effects? What kinds of knowledge do they claim in aid in determining policy, and who provides this? As well as the kinds of work that have already gained some insight into such matters—mainly to date from a legal/jurisprudential point of view and concerned with questions such as the protection of the rights of accused persons (Hodgson 2011) or those in confinement—the new circuits of power at a granular level. To which bodies of ideas, mobilising which sets of data, is reference made in those committee rooms? Which problems fill the inboxes and disturb the sleep of the key actors, and which claims to expert jurisdiction over those problems do they come to believe?

## III. REAPPRAISING THE PUBLIC ROLES OF CRIMINOLOGY

Unfortunately our book *Public Criminology?* does not provide answers to many of these question, if any at all. It is, however, in the first case a book about the production and circulation of knowledge—in particular, knowledge about crime and punishment (knowledge that we, like a lot of other people, usually call criminology or penology), and this is its relevance here. We took it that in thus attempting to locate these fields of social inquiry we were contributing to an understanding of the positioning of their practitioners vis-à-vis the worlds of practical intervention and policy formation. The book stands in a long tradition of studies in the sociology of knowledge in treating these as empirical questions, capable of hermeneutic recovery, with strong institutional affiliations and significant practical effects. What knowledge works here, now? Who is accredited an expert? How is this or that position/perspective used, filtered, appropriated, edited, rendered practicable, and so on. But as we come on to argue, these institutional questions also have major normative implications—the adjudication of arguments and claims between experts is also part and parcel of the struggle for a better politics of the criminal question and the penal question; and we therefore also need to be involved in debating what the conditions for that 'better politics' might be.

As we ultimately conceive it, that project relates less to the internal history of criminology as a discipline than to the much bigger, deeper and harder challenge of grasping the positions of criminal and penal questions in democratic politics, and of thinking through the terms in which (and the formats and institutions through which) those questions might be more fruitfully debated and decided. In our terms, investigating the kinds of 'publics' that are assembled in struggles around the crime question, and thinking about how the politics of order may be more closely aligned with a democratically-articulated 'public interest', remain key challenges. Examining the relation of knowledge to action, and in particular how science—however we conceive of and explore this arena—really engages in matters of contemporary controversy is a key preliminary stage in that discussion.

This relates to our argument in favour of criminology as a 'democratic under-labourer' (or DUL), our first attempt to get to grips with these problems. The DUL argument is that criminology inherently has three 'moments'—which we term the moments of discovery, of institutional-critical analysis, and that of normative deliberation—and that it is impoverished without giving proper weight to each. The DUL thus defends a pluralistic, intellectually capacious and fuzzy-bordered conception of criminology. It is not in the business of outlawing other people's best efforts on this subject, nor of setting up a 'new' paradigm or school of thought—yet another branded 'criminology' seeking to claim its own chapter in the textbooks and page in the publisher's catalogue. Democratic under-labouring is, rather, a disposition—a way of thinking and feeling about doing this, or indeed any, subject. It alludes to a practice whose 'formative intention' (Collins and Evans 2007) is the production of rigorous knowledge, but which also understands itself as engaging with a field in which applications of that knowledge never reduce to simple and transparent calculations. Seen from this point of view, criminology and penology inhabit and intervene in a world composed not simply of 'matters of fact' over which they can make legislative statements, but also always one of disputed 'matters of concern' (Latour 2004) which they can, alongside the various 'publics' who assemble around such matters, legitimately interpret and contest.

The criminologist as a democratic under-labourer has a commitment both to generating and disseminating knowledge *and* to a more deliberative politics of big public questions, such as the future of punishment and crime control. The DUL is, as such, necessarily implicated in developing public policy-making that is 'argumentative' (Hoppe 1999) or 'intelligent' (see for example Sanderson 2009), rather than simply 'evidence-based'. The under-labouring conception of these tasks is committed to participating within, and to facilitating and extending, institutional spaces that supplement representative politics with inclusive public deliberation about crime and justice matters, whether in local, state, or federal settings—or across emergent transnational arenas. In this regard, the public value of criminology or penology as democratic under-labouring lies not primarily in 'cooling down' controversies about crime and social responses to it, so much as in playing its part in figuring out ways to bring their 'heat' within the domain of democratic discussion and deliberative decision-making.

In developing this view we have made reference to the work of many scholars in and beyond the fields of criminology and penology. Among these there are perhaps two to which we have returned most frequently and which have assumed a faintly canonical status for us. The first of these involves some remarks by Tamar Pitch about the constitution of 'the criminal question':

> To study the criminal question is different from studying crime. It means that crime is not considered independently from the procedures by which is it defined, the instruments deployed in its administration and control and the politics and debates around criminal justice and public order. The criminal question can

> therefore be provisionally defined as an area constituted by actions, institutions, policies and discourses whose boundaries shift.
>
> (Pitch 1995: 52.)

Pitch then went on to advise those working on the field to 'be aware of the fact that the sociologist and the criminologist themselves contribute to the construction of the criminal question through their analyses, discourses, political interventions and debates' (ibid: 54). She also noted that 'what "the public" think of as crime and what, according to the "public" should be considered crime, or what cultural and symbolic significance is carried by law and criminal justice, is an integral aspect of the criminal question' (ibid). In our view, and the views of some of our collaborators (see further Melossi et al 2011) this position is helpful in drawing attention to the ways in which certain conceptions of the criminal question are embedded within—and so find their societal meaning and significance in—the distinctive concatenations of ways of thinking, doing and feeling that characterise certain political cultures at particular times and places. They are in this sense, for good or ill, literally institutionalised.

A second, closely related, thesis comes from Stanley Cohen's justly celebrated (if less read now than formerly) essay 'Footprints in the sand':

> The development of social scientific theory and knowledge takes place not simply within the heads of individuals, but within particular institutional domains. These domains are, in turn, shaped by their surroundings: how academic institutions are organized, how disciplines are divided and sub-divided, how disputes emerge, how research is funded and how findings are published and used. In criminology, an understanding of these institutional domains is especially important for knowledge is situated not just, or even primarily, in the 'pure' academic world, but in the applied domain of the state's crime control apparatus.
>
> (Cohen 1988: 67.)

'Footprints in the sand', as we explain at more length elsewhere (Loader and Sparks 2012) does something which we regard as very important and which we have to some extent tried to emulate. That is, it employs its own intellectual tools upon itself. It attempts to think *sociologically* about the production and consumption of knowledge, in this case criminological knowledge. To think about—and hence 'situate'—criminology in this manner is to ask where this activity is located, what its boundaries are, and what relations exist between criminology and the institutions which support it. It means attending, not only to the questions, approaches and knowledge claims that constitute the activity, but also to the conditions of possibility for different kinds of knowledge production, and to the circulation and effects of the knowledge produced, and hence to what Pierre Bourdieu called a 'field'. This orients enquiry towards where and how criminology is constituted, to its lines of vision and division, and to its relations to other fields—academic, legal, political, bureaucratic, journalistic, and so forth (Bourdieu 2004).

To turn these questions back upon the field of criminology—somewhat in the spirit of the late Richard Ericson, whose work returned time and again to the question of how criminological knowledge is produced and communicated within circuits of power (eg Ericson 2005)—is an attempt to promote grounded, comparative reflexive inquiry into the circumstances and uses of knowledge. In this spirit, *Public Criminology*'s principal object of enquiry is the relation between criminology and democratic politics; its focal concern lies in understanding how theory, research and reflection can best orient themselves towards the state of modern politics, and play their part in reaching towards a better politics of crime and its regulation. That better politics is something we want to explore further in forthcoming work. It is by nature both more evidence-informed and more deliberative, and reconciling those desiderata is no simple task.

Contrary to the allegations of some of our critics, who mistake our conciliation and tolerance for excessive detachment, there is a clear normative argument running through *Public Criminology?* We argue that the role of criminological or penological debate is best interpreted as one of seeking to contribute to a better politics of crime. But that conclusion deliberately comes at the end of a book that is first and foremost an attempt to develop something that has rarely been attempted—a sociology of scientific engagement in the relevant arenas. We mean by this an effort to construct a best-case interpretation of how social scientists understand their craft and position themselves in relation to the heated climate in which they commonly work nowadays—whether as experts, advisors, players, activists or prophets—and to clarify what is at stake in the debate between these personae. In trying to stake out these positions (or rather, this 'space of positions') we have found it helpful to look across not just into the neighbouring field of sociology (where the debate initiated by Michael Burawoy on 'public sociology' (Burawoy 2005) provides some but by no means all of the sort of material we need) but also further afield. We also point out, however, that what are for us metaphors (of heat and cold) have a more primary application in arenas like climate science where we can easily see that 'the science' and 'the politics' have become braided together in the most complex manner. What we take from social studies of (natural) science includes the recognition that even in the most technical fields questions about communication and engagement, applications and uses, ethics and accountability are of central significance.

In our view, commitments to and scepticism towards certain visions of science, and commitments to and scepticism towards certain conceptions of politics have been running tensions throughout the modern history of criminology. For these reasons the book revisits a certain number of indicative moments or cases, some of which will be at least partly familiar to many criminologists. These include the roles of expert advice in elite policy circles in Britain in the 1950s and 1960s; the nature of the challenge that these received from the radical criminologies of the 1970s (themselves responses to a political-cultural environment in which the criminal questions was already generating more heat) and a certain range of more recent examples of attempts to achieve a cooler, more dispassionate and more poised politics of crime control, whether by i) reaffirming legal guarantees, ii) buffering or insulating crime policy from the direct heat of political contention, or iii) reasserting the claims of scientificity and evidence-basedness (eg in the views of these matters advocated by experimental criminology and 'crime science'), or some combination of these.

It is not our aim to reject or endorse any of these moves in particular, although we are critical of some of their assumptions and some of their consequences. Neither, although some readers have mistakenly chosen to interpret our work in this way, are we arguing in support of a mushy consensualism or vague pluralism. We certainly are pluralists in our own way, but there is, we hope, nothing mushy or vague about our position. Instead we are pointing to the diverse answers that criminologists have produced to a set of questions about the public value of criminology or penology to democracy. Beyond the many substantive disagreements that animate these fields, what answers implicitly or explicitly arise to higher-order questions like these: What is the collective good that criminological enquiry seeks to promote? What modes of intervention—and what institutional arrangements—can best realise that good?

In the end, nothing could be further from our intentions than trying to pacify or conclude argument between proponents of different positions. Indeed our own stance—the thing we call thinking of criminology as an under-labourer for democracy—is at bottom an argument *in favour of argument*, meaning here more intense but mutually attentive and considerate debate between different positions and traditions of inquiry. For us, under-labouring equally includes the virtues of respect for evidence (indeed to the generation of evidence as a primary commitment—a 'formative intention') and of attentiveness to the 'circumstances of politics', as they have been called. Raising the quality of political discussion about the criminal question demands not just more evidence or more technical skills, or even dreaming up more policy innovations, but also a commitment to generating controversy, opening up and extending debate, challenging and provoking received public 'opinion' and political postures, not closing such discourse down. For us, the politics of crime control never reduces without remainder to calculation (hence our various references to the work of Latour (2004), among others). The criminologist as a democratic under-labourer has a commitment both to generating and disseminating knowledge and to a more deliberative politics of big public questions such as the future of punishment and crime control.

We are therefore not at all interested in criminology or penology for reasons of self-absorption or self-referentiality. Indeed we argue (in the spirit of Bourdieu's various discussions of the principle of reflexivity) that trying to objectify these matters is a key step in moving beyond and away from treating them as mere personal, idiosyncratic preferences or as being just matters of political *parti pris*, not available for discussion. Rather, as we have since gone on to detail further (Loader and Sparks 2012), these are inherently also *institutional* questions. Knowledge about crime and justice, we propose at the risk of stating the obvious (Loader and Sparks 2012: 7), doesn't just happen. The question of what comes to be known, from what theoretical perspectives, by what methods, about what crimes and ways of responding to crime, in what forms, and with what effects is conditioned by a whole range of institutions. These institutions employ researchers (permanently or temporarily); fund (or do not fund) research projects and programmes; permit (or refuse) access to data, research subjects and sites; offer outlets for publication; and use, abuse, champion or ignore the products of that research. Each of these institutions—universities, research councils, charities, think-tanks, consultancy firms, publishing houses, newspapers, broadcasters and new social media, campaign groups and lobbyists, political parties, prisons, police forces, government departments and so on—are themselves situated in economic, social and political contexts that shape how each of them think and can act. To study criminology as a 'field' is to explore how power relations and struggles between actors in these different institutional sites structure the knowledge that is (and is not) produced.

## IV. KNOWLEDGE-POLICY RELATIONS AND COMPARATIVE PENOLOGY

It is not our aim here to rehearse the recent history of debates about comparative criminal justice systems in Europe, nor the vexed question of their differential exposure to the currents of penal populism and the troubled political arithmetic of their prison populations (Tonry 2007; Snacken 2010; Lacey 2008). There is a basic contradiction between certain big theses—in particular, that nations most exposed to neo-liberal ideology and its consequent agitations and divisions are most prone to incarcerate more offenders—and those approaches that focus on more proximate cultural dynamics and which characteristically deny the viability of such general theorisations. Nelken has summarised such tensions with particular acuity and nuance (Nelken 2009; 2010). Certain contributions to these debates emphasise that the space for informed and dispassionate evidence-informed discussion to influence decision-makers may be a significant factor. Thus, Snacken's argument for the role of a 'democratic constitutional state' in resisting punitiveness (defending the erosion of the standing of offenders in the same sense that it defends the interests of other minorities) includes the premise that expert opinion will play a moderating and civilising role. Experts stand between political decision-makers and their exposure to direct pressure from or appeal to public opinion and thus defend the value of longer-term over immediate considerations, and the general interest of sectional and emotive appeal (Snacken 2010: 280, 282, passim). Similarly, Lappi-Seppälä describes the process of achieving sustained reduction in the prison population in Finland in the following terms:

> In Finland the criticism of the treatment ideology has since merged with that directed against an overly severe Criminal Code and the excessive use of custodial sentences. The resulting criminal political ideology was labelled as 'humane neo-classicism'. It stressed both legal safeguards against coercive care and the objective of less repressive measures in general. Between 1970 and 1990 all the main parts of Finnish criminal legislation have been reformed from these starting points. The reform ideology, which guided the law reforms from the early 1970s onwards, represented a pragmatic, non-moralistic approach to crime problems. In this framework, the role of criminal law as a means of crime policy occupies a much less prominent place than before.
>
> (Lappi-Seppälä 2006: 139.)

Here, the values associated with a cadre of expert opinion ('pragmatic, non-moralistic') seem to have depended for their realisation upon a confluence of perspective between key actors in positions of influence (politicians, civil servants, senior members of the judiciary) and expert opinion-formers outside the criminal justice system as such, including a certain degree of personal and social affinity amongst these groups.

On a less nationally specific level there is now, we might argue, a fairly readily available set of more or less standard terms to describe what it is that informed opinion is supposed to do in moderating the punitive temptation and defending the claims of rational discourse. Thus:

> To do this, criminal justice experts need to ensure that the key people are well-informed; provide information to and stimulate discussion among opinion formers, the media and the general public; challenge media misrepresentations; draw attention to how similar countries or jurisdictions cope differently; and bring the key people together to promote policy discussions, leading to decisions as to the direction in which policy ought to move.
>
> (Walmsley 2003: 77.)

These illustrations, which strike us as relatively representative, albeit that we cannot demonstrate this without adducing many more examples, all have many of the properties that we attribute to 'insulationist' postures, a point to which we return further below. To summarise briefly something that we have discussed at much greater length elsewhere (Loader and Sparks 2010), there is a widespread premise in many such discussions that the politics of crime and punishment have become so 'hot' that the only thing to be done is to remove them as far as possible from the crucible of impassioned public discourse, and hope they cool off. Only thus, so the argument runs, can rational deliberation and evidence-informed policy-making hold their own against the incitements of populist agitation. This appears to be something approaching the default position of many contributors, but it is a position we will wish to challenge.

On the whole, the matter is generally left to rest there. Expert (criminological) opinion carries more influence under some political conditions than others. Where it is attended to it is a force for good, which is to say for moderation, and for the channelling out of unseemly passions. This tends to mean that many contributors accept a relatively unquestioned view of the benefits of what has come to be termed 'evidence-based policy-making' (EBPM), even if their advocacy of that position ranges in tone from the moderate and cautious to the evangelical. As we have recently discussed at somewhat more length elsewhere (Loader and Sparks 2012), the most ebullient and optimistic versions of this support envisage what Hoppe (2005: 202) calls the 'scientization of the knowledge system', characterised by the 'instrumental use of research as data', in direct support of decision-making. Most knowledge utilisation, in crime policy or anywhere else, has not historically looked much like this, as any reasonably well-educated student of criminology, penology or social policy knows. Yet advocates of EBPM in criminal justice have in recent years come close to claiming that it should (see further Loader and Sparks 2012; Parsons 2002).

In the UK, a high watermark of the latter view came in a speech by then Labour Cabinet Minister David Blunkett in 2000: 'Tell us what works and why', the Minister enjoined. For Blunkett, it was 'self-evident that decisions on Government policy ought to be informed by sound evidence' (Blunkett 2000, cited by Parsons 2002: 43). What policy-makers require is 'to be able to measure the size of the effect of A on B. This is genuine social science and reliable answers can only be reached if the best social scientists are willing to engage in this endeavour' (ibid). This is plainly a direct governmental demand for explicit, instrumentally applicable knowledge—what one sceptical commentator called a view of evidence as things that can be 'added up, joined up and wired up' (Parsons 2002: 48). Blunkett's invitation certainly found a number of willing and conscientious takers. Nevertheless, many subsequent observations have been less sanguine than he might have hoped. There have been at least two very distinct lines of critical response to EBPM in criminal justice in Britain. The first suggests that it never really happened; 'they' were not serious, or at best they were intensely (and ideologically) selective. EBPM is, on this view, more rhetoric than practice, a scientific cloak for a series of thinly disguised political preferences (Hope and Walters 2008). The second says: 'it' did happen but its instrumentalism, and its association with the proliferation of governmental surveillance systems (audit trails, performance units, 'delivery' metrics etc) make EBPM inherently tied to a command-and-control logic of knowledge production and use (Parsons 2002).

This is a very potted version of an aspect of recent history in one country. It is a contentious and quite notable one both for the vigour with which the EBPM posture was propounded there and for the many critiques and allegations that the position was overwhelmed by political considerations even before it had been articulated (Tonry 2004a). Most other European countries have their own versions of such a story, though the outcomes may be very different. Occasionally, as in the Finnish case, these accounts describe a set of socio-cultural conditions that create sufficient proximity between the producers and users of penological knowledge to enable a certain programme of evidence-informed measures to be put into effect. Some others suggest that empirical criminological or penological knowledge generally finds itself in unequal competition with other dominant perspectives—the legal-constitutional framing of the criminal question usually trumps the social scientific one. Still others suggest that in circumstances of rapid socio-economic and political transformation the demands of politics, and the requirements of the security apparatus predominate. Not uncommonly, beleaguered criminological scholars forlornly note that their subject is simply too small and too institutionally weak to count for much in public discourse or policy-formation.

In our view this mosaic is a fascinating one, and is itself a fit subject for more systematic comparative study. In a suggestive and perhaps prescient, but relatively little cited, article Michael Tonry (2004b) argues that European societies (meaning here primarily those of Continental Europe, marking a contrast with those of the 'Anglo-Saxon' cultural space) are for a number of reasons well-placed to develop a concerted, cumulative criminological research infrastructure with the capacity to influence policy agendas. He includes as reasons for this their increasingly cosmopolitan and polyglot intellectual cultures, the development of pan-European research networks (notably but not exclusively under the auspices of the European Society of Criminology), the willingness of European governments to create long-term and politically independent research institutes and the insulation of key sites of intervention and opinion-leadership from direct politicisation. The latter, signified by such factors as the relative autonomy of civil servants, the judiciary and other professionals from intrusive political influence and controversy, creates conditions more favourable to 'rationalistic policy processes' (Tonry 2004b: 24) and more fruitful relations between experts and decision-makers.

It is no doubt possible to query aspects of this account of things, and Tonry himself is at pains to argue that someone else should take up the reins in a more thoroughgoing and systematic manner—a challenge that in our view remains largely unanswered. There is for example a grave danger of over-generalisation in respect of the (variously) English-speaking, Anglo-American or 'Anglo-Saxon' countries—a position which, for example, closer familiarity with the distinctions between the adjacent English and Scottish research and policy environments would do much to correct (McAra 2009; Henry 2009). Nevertheless the argument in favour of attentiveness to institutional arrangements both for conducting research and for constituting relations between the producers and users of expert knowledge is a powerful one. There are two unexamined aspects to Tonry's view that invite further interrogation. The first is that he tends to depict closer relations between experts and decision-makers as a self-evident and unqualified good. The second is that, ironically in retrospect, he has almost nothing to say about Europe as such. It is however perhaps on this level of engagement that many of the most intriguing and perplexing questions for 'European penology' now stand.

## V. RESEARCH, EXPERTISE AND THE QUESTION OF EUROPEAN PENOLOGY

Despite a growing number of manifestos for transnational perspectives (for example, Sheptycki and Wardak 2005; Bowling 2011), and of reflections upon the implications of globalisation for the analysis of crime and punishment (such as Aas 2007), most penological and other criminological research in Europe remains pitched at the comparative nation-state level. At the risk of casual empiricism, we might consider as a datum here the programme of the 2012 European Society of Criminology (ESC) Conference. Of more than 500 papers in the schedule, around 40 had the words 'Europe' or 'European' in the title. Of these, the great majority made reference directly to a geographical location ('... in a European trade Hub'), or used Europe as a comparative sampling frame. Some had a clear regional focus (such as 'Eastern European States' or 'the Balkans'). Others had regard either to convergences and divergences among a sub-set of European countries or to the relevance of certain over-arching concept (such as 'legitimacy' or 'trust') and to its bearing on the condition of criminal justice systems 'across Europe'. Some reported upon the development of a pan-European collaboration or research instrument, such as the European Social Survey. Certainly there is much evidence here of activity oriented towards mutual learning—much more, and in a much more developed state than would have been the case even when Tonry wrote. Some of this is expressly about seeking to develop common standards, best-practices and so on. The increasing level and intensity of such networking, often on emergent issues and practices (restorative justice, community sanctions and measures) reflects new ways of collaborating and exchanging, often only possible through novel institutional arrangements and partnerships, not least the working groups of the ESC itself. Nevertheless it does not seem unfair to suggest that in their predominant focus on comparison or convergences between national models many of these activities are recognisably the inheritors of earlier models. Only a relative handful made explicit reference to European institutions as such or to change at the constitutional level or to the future of Europe as a political or cultural entity.[2]

It is not our intention to deprecate any of this important work, or to argue that comparative research has ceased to be valuable—quite the contrary there remain many respects in which it is barely developed. The promotion of such work and the sheer hard work involved in overcoming the major logistic, linguistic and conceptual problems in multi-site research by multinational teams has occupied much effort and is a major achievement where it occurs.

At least until recently something similar might have been said of criminological and penological research that has benefited from funding under one or other of the EU's own research programmes. Consider here examples given in a recent Commission survey of research that it has supported (European Commission 2011). A number of these, although arising from new and vigorous international networks and collaborations, arguably fall within the category of comparative research rather than engaging the question of Europe as a distinct and level of rapidly increasing significance in the governance of crime and social order. However, the editorial commentary in the text, whilst not commenting on this contrast explicitly, certainly makes clear that there is a new policy context for such research to address. This is provided by the new responsibilities accorded to the EU following the Treaty of Lisbon. It summarises these, perhaps rather blandly, thus:

> [The AFSJ] aims at offering its citizens an area of freedom, security and justice without internal borders, with the ambition then of further increasing international cooperation in this area as well as increasing democratic accountability, judicial control and efficient decision-making processes.
>
> (2011: 6)

One consequence of this is an enhanced interest in 'serious and organised crime', notably human trafficking and drugs and large-scale financial offences, and on occasion a slightly airy and condescending tone in respect of 'other crime types', mundane problems of ordering, everyday insecurities and violences. Conclusions in respect of the latter can be underwhelming at best: 'the importance of a more equitable distribution of wealth and power on crime rates should not be underestimated' (ibid: 24).

[2] See here the more systematic, numericised analysis by Kim and Merlo (2011) in the ESC Newsletter, which also provides some sense of these trends since the inception of the conference in 2001.

These general trends will be familiar to anyone with a passing acquaintance with EU priorities in the crime control field. On the whole they suggest that much of the traditional stock in trade of criminological and penological scholarship (the troubles of youth, the adequacy of available interventions, their not infrequently perverse effects, and all the other mundane objects of police business and court schedules) falls beneath the horizon of attention of European policy elites. Indeed the concerns of the latter are characteristically expressed less by an interest in 'crime' or indeed in 'punishment' but rather ever more under the sign of *security*.

It is not our intention here to add to the extensive commentary that now exists on these developments. Studies of policing were perhaps the first (and arguably still best developed) to begin to track the wider effects of cooperation and the creation of new institutions at the European level (Anderson et al 1996; Walker 2008). Legal scholarship—so much more alert to the effects of treaty arrangements and constitutional questions than most social science—has demonstrated for some time now that in respect of relevant competencies the EU has increasingly shifted beyond the inter-governmental level (the level on which the greater part of penological inquiry remains firmly lodged) and in the direction of EU capacities (eg Mitsilegas 2009, 2011; Baker 2009, 2010). Alongside those bodies of work that document the many benefits that have historically flowed from European institutions on the level of the protection of individual human rights, including the rights of accused and convicted persons (van Zyl Smit and Snacken 2009), there now arises a parallel and contrasting critical literature that sees the encroaching securitisation of those institutions in much more threatening terms (for example, Bigo and Guild 2005; Guild 2009). Alongside the various protections reserved for those in possession of the full status of citizens, it is argued, there exist different tracks and different fate for Europe's 'denizens', especially perhaps the undocumented migrant (Aas 2011, 2012; Bosworth 2008) and other members of suspect populations. For observers in these emergent areas, the most pressing questions come to concern such matters as the uncertain location of sovereignty (Brown 2010), the contested prerogatives and powers of nation states versus other transnational actors and their refocusing of energy on the protection of their borders (both internal and external, material and symbolic) (Sassen 2005a, b), and the activation of powers to criminalise directed at novel targets and groups, including the allegation of a distinct 'criminal law of the enemy' (or sometimes 'enemy penality') (Fekete and Webber 2010) reserved for those groups defined as most menacing to the internal order of the European social space, whether they come in the shape of terrorists (Cancio Meliá 2011), traffickers, hackers or some other guise.

It is not for us to adjudicate the differing claims and commitments at issue in these debates here. If, however, it seems credible that they identify real and significant shifts in the location and uses of powers of detention, expulsion and relocation, then they become questions to which criminological and penological scholarship must attend. The immediate point at issue here is not one of trend-spotting, still less of futurological speculation. Rather it reverts directly to the questions about the civic roles of the social sciences, and specifically the public responsibilities of criminological and penological scholarship, with which we began.

Thus, for example, as the EU redefines its crime control efforts in terms of a security problematic, so its research agenda also shifts. Traditional criminological or penological concerns, such as those concerning legal guarantees, continue to play some part, perhaps especially those that go to questions of public anxieties and perceptions or to the direct corollaries of securitisation for civil liberties. However the dominant framing of relevance has arguably moved elsewhere. It reflects more immediately the concerns of the Stockholm Programme with the development of the new security architecture and its implications for such matters as police and intelligence cooperation, data exchange, surveillance, computer hacking and border control.[3] Unsurprisingly, therefore it is 'security' that now constitutes a distinct theme within the complex architecture of European research. As a recent call of the Seventh Framework (FP7) outlines it, this denominates a concern with 'governance', 'stability' and 'cohesion' in the face of fluid and uncertain cultural, economic and social space. Thus research is required on the 'governance of migration and mobility', 'security and democracy in the neighbourhood' (meaning here countries on the southern and eastern peripheries of the EU), but also more specifically within the 'Security' theme such matters as: intelligence against terrorism, explosives, forensic investigation techniques, 'the security of infrastructures and utilities', 'intelligent surveillance and border security', crisis management, interoperability of security systems and human trafficking.[4]

The questions that arise from these developments are both numerous and various. Suffice to note here that none of these framings are any longer uniquely social scientific or socio-legal in character, let alone 'criminological' or 'penological'. They are more accurately thought of

[3] 'The Stockholm Programme—An Open And Secure Europe Serving And Protecting Citizens', *Official Journal of the European Union*, (2010/C 115/01) http://eur-lex.europa.eu/LexUriServ/LexUriServ.do?uri=OJ:C:2010:115:0001:0038:EN:PDF.

[4] These objectives arise in several of the themes proposed for collaborative actions under the 2013 FP7 Cooperation Work Programme: Socio-economic Sciences and Humanities ((European Commission C (2012) 4536 of 9 July 2012). 'Security' however is also now a theme in its own right (Theme 10) ((FP7-SEC-2013-1) whose objective is 'to develop the technologies and knowledge for building capabilities needed to ensure the security of citizens from threats such as terrorism, natural disasters and crime, while respecting fundamental human rights' (ibid, p 6).

perhaps as socio-technical, and thus as comprehensively trans-disciplinary as well as trans-national. They have interests in territories and in borders but they are not driven by a conception of 'societies' as cultural or constitutional entities. They are unquestionably animated by a concern to harness various forms of expertise, but the *savoirs* they seek to harness are mainly technical, pragmatic, mobile and transferable. They are in this sense *governmental*, even if this refers to a level of governance distinct from the focusing of sovereign powers within the nation state with which we are more conceptually comfortable. There is also a relevant sense in which, as a product and producer of modern conceptions of penal social relations penology has traditionally taken the nation-state as its primary level of engagement. That has been the heart of sovereign power, the object, the problem and the solution; and national policy-makers have been the sometimes attentive, sometimes uninterested target audience. Our own previous work is in more ways than we might have wished or set out to achieve, part of this same tradition.

The shifts in the nature of knowledge-politics implied by these developments demand to be reckoned with, and that reckoning constitutes a daunting agenda for the near and medium-terms. Criminologists, penologists, even lawyers, cannot claim sole jurisdiction over this domain. It is arguable however that we have arrived at a point where there is a disconnection between our tradition penological concerns and aspirations and those same EU institutions. The growing capacity of European institutions in what we call penological matters is really part of the development of a common security framework. In the course of that development it is possible that not only are human rights priorities as traditionally conceived complicated and perhaps compromised, but so too are the sites of engagement or deliberation rendered less definite and less visible.

Several kinds of questions seem to arise. It is clearly high time for students of crime and punishment to start to take the lead from certain pioneers in policing (Anderson et al 1996), penology (van Zyl Smit and Snacken 2009) and criminal law (Baker 2009) and to begin to engage in earnest with the EU and Council of Europe not just a sponsors of research but as their objects.

## VI. IN LIEU OF CONCLUSIONS: PENALITY, SECURITY POLICY AND CIVIC SCHOLARSHIP

So what kind of research programmes, undertaken for what purposes, do these developments entail? Having argued fairly frequently against 'legislative utterance' on such matters (see especially Loader and Sparks 2010: ch 1), we feel compelled to proceed with some caution here. However, if there is indeed some sense of a growing disconnect between the priorities of European institutions and the concerns of most criminological and penological scholars, we can legitimately ask what is to be done about that? Is it simply about skilling up on developments in EU policy studies and EU law? Or is it a matter of opening channels to other perhaps more supple and alert disciplines? Or is it also and perhaps more particularly about re-framing our sense of the civic missions of our subjects and reappraising the forms of their engagement in a period when the political actors and communities that we associate with our nation-states are no longer the only, or perhaps even the most significant, ones that we need to address? The further these trends develop, the more pronounced would seem to be the danger of 'scalar' confusion (Valverde 2010) wherein we continue to focus on certain levels of governance long after some powers of decision-making have shifted elsewhere.

Scholars of penal questions have often aspired to act as members of, to use one widespread diction, 'epistemic communities' (Haas 1992; Zito 2001; Eriksen 2011). Such communities characteristically see themselves as parties to conversations in which their roles include creating space for knowledge in the interests of enlightened practice. This is one reason why debates on climate science are often taken to provide a paradigm for the development of the influence of an epistemic community. At the same time of course the less attractive features of the influence of such communities in modernity include their problematic relationship to democratic discussion involving wider publics. It has been argued quite extensively that the structure of European institutions can accentuate this propensity, conserving full participation in debate to insiders. Hence the well-known coinage 'commitology' (eg Pollack 2003) to describe the study of these processes as they are carried on in the committee rooms and conference suites. On the other face of this problem is the possibility that at least so far as the security problematic is concerned what is really called-for is knowledge-for-policy that directly supports already constituted political agendas in a technocratic fashion (Radaelli 1999), rather than focusing on bothersome normative questions or jurisprudential anxieties (Eriksen 2011). There is no doubt that European policy-making eagerly seeks expert input. Yet the nature of the forms of expertise in question shifts continually. The accreditation of experts is obscure and contestable and the conversation in which they are engaged frequently of low visibility and scant accountability. The values that many contributors to penological debate may cherish most dearly (those that we associate with the idea of the rule of law, for example, or with the enhancement of public deliberation on matters of common concern) may not turn out to be those that weigh most heavily in the committee rooms of the new comprehensive security strategists.

If we are to contribute to these debates in a democratising spirit, we need to understand this landscape and the possibilities and limits that it imposes better than most of us (the present authors very much included) yet do. In the face of the securitisation of traditional criminological and penological problems we need to ask tricky questions about the current dynamics of criminalisation; about uses of coercion beyond the traditional frameworks of national penal laws, about the protection of spaces of debate about these matters, and about which audiences if any are particularly disposed to attend to whatever we may have to say.

## REFERENCES


Aas, K (2007) *Globalization and Crime* (London, Sage).

—— (2011) 'Crimmigrant Bodies and Bona Fide Travellers: Surveillance, Citizenship and Global Governance' *Theoretical Criminology*, 15, 331–46.

—— (2012) "The Earth is One but the World is Not': Criminological Theory and its Geopolitical Divisions' *Theoretical Criminology*, 16, 5–20.

Anderson, M, den Boer, M, Cullen, P, Gilmore, W, Raab, C and Walker, N (1996) *Policing the European Union* (Oxford, Clarendon Press).

Baker, E (2009) 'The European Union's "Area of Freedom, Security and (Criminal) Justice" Ten Years On' *Criminal Law Review*, 833–50.

—— (2010) 'Governing through crime—the case of the European Union' *European Journal of Criminology*, 7, 187–213.

Bigo, D and Guild, E (eds) (2005) *Controlling Frontiers: Free Movement into and within Europe* (Aldershot, Ashgate).

Bosworth, M (2008) 'Border Control and the Limits of the Sovereign State' *Social & Legal Studies*, 17, 199–215.

Bourdieu, P (2004) *Science of Science and Reflexivity* (Cambridge, Polity Press).

Bowling, B (2011) 'Transnational Criminology and the Globalization of Harm Production' in M Bosworth and C Hoyle (eds), *What is Criminology?* (Oxford, Oxford University Press).

Brown, W (2010) *Walled States, Waning Sovereignty* (New York, Zone Books).

Burawoy, M (2005) 'For Public Sociology' *American Sociological Review*, 70, 4–28.

Calhoun, C (2010) *Cosmopolitanism and Belonging* (New York, Taylor and Francis).

Cancio Meliá, M (2011) 'Terrorism and Criminal Law: The Dream of Prevention, the Nightmare of the Rule of Law' *New Criminal Law Review*, 14, 108–22.

Cavender, G (2004) 'Media and Crime Policy: A Reconstruction of David Garland's *The Culture of Control*' *Punishment & Society*, 6, 335–48.

Collins, H and Evans, R (2007) *Rethinking Expertise* (Chicago, University of Chicago Press).

Cohen, S (1988) *Against Criminology* (New Brunswick, NJ, Transaction Publishers).

Ericson, R (2005) 'Publicizing Sociology' *British Journal of Sociology*, 56, 365–72.

Eriksen, EO (2011) 'Governance between expertise and democracy: the case of European Security' *Journal of European Public Policy*, 18, 1169–89.

Fekete, L and Webber, F (2010) 'Foreign nationals, enemy penology and the criminal justice system' *Race and Class*, 51, 1–25.

Foucault, M (1977) *Discipline and Punish* (Harmondsworth, Penguin).
—— (1984/1996) 'The Concern for Truth' in S Lotringer (ed), *Foucault Live: Collected Interviews, 1961–1984* (New York, Semiotext(e)).
Garland, D (1997) 'The Punitive Society: Penology, Criminology and the History of the Present' *Edinburgh Law Review*, 1, 180–99.
Grundmann, R and Stehr, N (2003) 'Social Control and Knowledge in Democratic Societies' *Science and Public Policy*, 30, 183–88.
Guild, E (2009) *Security and Migration in the 21st Century* (Cambridge, Polity Press).
Haas, P (1992) 'Introduction: Epistemic Communities and International Policy Coordination' *International Organization*, 46, 1–35.
Henry, A (2009) 'The Development of Community Safety in Scotland: A Different Path?', in A Crawford (ed), *Crime Prevention Policies in Comparative Perspective* (Cullompton, Willan Publishing).
Hodgson, J (2011) 'Safeguarding suspects' rights in Europe' *New Criminal Law Review*, 14, 611–65.
Hope, T and Walters, R (2008) *Critical Thinking about the Uses of Research* (London, Centre for Crime and Justice Studies).
Hoppe, R (1999) 'Policy Analysis, Science and Politics: From "Speaking Truth to Power" to "Making Sense Together"' *Science and Public Policy*, 26, 201–10.
—— (2005) 'Rethinking the Science–Policy Nexus: From Knowledge Utilization and Science Technology Studies to Types of Boundary Arrangements' *Poiesis and Praxis*, 3, 199–215.
Kim, B and Merlo, AV (2011) 'An examination of international or comparative studies under de aegis of the ESC' *Criminology in Europe*, 12, 6–7.
Lacey, N (2008) *The Prisoners' Dilemma: The Political Economy of Punishment in Comparative Perspective* (Cambridge, Cambridge University Press).
Lappi-Seppälä, T (2006) 'Reducing the prison population: long-term experiences from Finland' in, *Crime Policy in Europe* (Strasbourg, Council of Europe Publishing).
Latour, B (2004) *Politics of Nature: How to Bring the Sciences into Democracy* (Cambridge, Cambridge University Press).
Loader, I and Sparks, R (2010) *Public Criminology?* (London, Routledge).
—— (2012) 'Situating Criminology' in M Maguire, R Morgan and R Reiner (eds), *Oxford Handbook of Criminology*, 5th edn (Oxford, Oxford University Press).
McAra, L (2009) 'Scottish Youth Justice: Convergent Pressures and Cultural Singularities' *Déviance et Société*, 33, 383–98.
Martinson, R (1974) 'What Works?—Questions and Answers About Prison Reform' *The Public Interest*, 22–54.
Melossi, D, Sozzo, M and Sparks, R (eds) (2011) *Travels of the Criminal Question* (Oxford, Hart Publishing).
Mitsilegas, V (2009) 'The Third Wave of Third Pillar Law: Which Direction for EU Criminal Justice?' *European Law Review*, 34, 523–60.
—— (2011) 'The EU and the Implementation of International Norms in Criminal Matters' in M Cremona, J Monar and S Poli (eds), *The External Dimension of the Area of Freedom, Security and Justice* (Brussels, Peter Lang).
Nelken, D (2009) 'Comparative Criminal Justice: Beyond Ethnocentrism and Relativism' *European Journal of Criminology*, 6, 291–313.

—— (2010) *Comparative Criminal Justice: Making Sense of Difference* (London, Sage).

Parsons, W (2002) 'From Muddling Through to Muddling Up—Evidence Based Policy Making and the Modernisation of British Government' *Public Policy and Administration*, 17, 43–60.

Pitch, T (1995) *Limited Responsibilities* (London, Routledge).

Pollack, M (2003) 'Control Mechanism Or Deliberative Democracy?: Two Images of Comitology' *Comparative Political Studies*, 36, 125–55.

Radaelli, C (1999) *Technocracy and the European Policy Process* (London, Longman).

Roche, M (2010) *Exploring the Sociology of Europe* (London, Sage).

Sanderson, I (2009) 'Intelligent Policy Making for a Complex World: Pragmatism, Evidence and Learning' *Political Studies*, 57, 699–719.

Salvatore, R and Aguirre, C (eds) (1996) *The Birth of the Penitentiary in Latin America: Essays on Criminology, Prison Reform, and Social Control, 1830–1940* (Austin, University of Texas Press).

Scharff Smith, P (2004) 'A Religious Technology of the Self: Rationality and Religion in the Rise of the Modern Penitentiary' *Punishment & Society*, 6, 195–220.

Sheptycki, J and Wardak, A (eds) (2005) *Transnational and Comparative Criminology* (London, Glasshouse).

Sassen, S (2005) 'When National Territory is Home to the Global: Old Borders to Novel Borderings' *New Political Economy*, 10, 523–42.

Simon, J and Sparks, R (eds) (2012) *Handbook of Punishment and Society* (London, Sage).

Snacken, S (2010) 'Resisting Punitiveness in Europe' *Theoretical Criminology,* 14, 273–92.

Sparks, R (2006) 'Penology' in E McLaughlin and J Muncie (eds), *The Sage Dictionary of Criminology*, 2nd edn (London, Sage).

Tonry, M (2004a) *Punishment and Politics: Evidence and Emulation in the Making of English Crime Control Policy* (Cullompton, Willan Publishing).

—— (2004b) 'Criminology and Criminal Justice Research in Europe' in G Bruinsma, H Elffers and J de Keijser (eds), *Punishment, Places and Perpetrators: Developments in Criminology and Criminal Justice Research* (Cullompton, Willan Publishing).

—— (ed) (2007) *Crime, Punishment, and Politics in Comparative Perspective* (Chicago, University of Chicago Press).

Valverde, M (2010) 'Practices of Citizenship and Scales of Governance' *New Criminal Law Review*, 13, 216–40.

van Zyl Smit, D and Snacken, S (2009) *Principles of European Prison Law and Policy: Penology and Human Rights* (Oxford, Oxford University Press).

Walmsley, R (2003) 'Global incarceration and prison trends', *Forum on Crime and Society,* 3, 65–78, www.unodc.org/pdf/crime/forum/forum3_Art3.pdf.

Walker, N (2008) 'The pattern of transnational policing' in T Newburn (ed), *Handbook of Policing*, 2nd edn (Cullompton, Willan Publishing).

Weingart, P (1999) 'Scientific Expertise and Political Accountability: Paradoxes of Science in Politics' *Science and Public Policy*, 26, 151–61.

Zito, AR (2001) 'Epistemic Communities, Collective Entrepreneurship and European Integration' *Journal of European Public Policy*, 8, 585–603.

# 4

# *The Emerging Role of the EU as a Penal Actor*[*]

ESTELLA BAKER

## I. INTRODUCTION

CAPTURING 'THE EMERGING role of the European Union as a penal actor' is a challenging endeavour. A primary reason is that the EU does not perform just a single role, but has come to assume a variety of parts. The explanation for this state of affairs is substantially historical and relates to the original mission of (what we now know as) the Union to promote economic integration; the reluctance of Member States to pool national sovereignty in criminal law matters; and the relatively belated expansion in treaty competences to support political integration. The consequence is that the EU has increasing power as far as intervention in the penal sphere is concerned, yet its involvement can be hard to spot and can appear unstable and incoherent.

From a constitutional perspective, this fragmented persona reflects the broader tensions that have beset its evolutionary progress as a whole. Therefore, apart from contributing to the discussion in this volume, this chapter seeks to make an original addition to the developing literature on the Union's penal engagement. It does this by unravelling various penal roles that the Union has assumed to date and equating them with different elements in its evolving constitutional identity; that being the task of section III. Section IV then draws the strands together in order to discuss their penological and constitutional significance. Finally, the conclusion considers whether there are features of the Union's involvement in punishment that can be regarded as distinctively 'European'. Prior to executing these tasks, section II provides a basic guide to the legal framework of the Union in order to support the analyses that follow.

* A version of this chapter was presented to the European Society of Criminology's Working Party on Sentencing and Penal Decision-Making in Como, Italy, in April 2012. As well as those present at the original seminar in Oñati, I should like to thank those who attended the Como meeting for their comments, as well as Malcolm Ross for his encouraging observations on a draft.

## II. THE UNION'S LEGAL FRAMEWORK

To set the discussion in context, this section summarises the way in which the Union treaties have developed and distinguishes the relevant regulatory environments that have been created under them.

### A. The Treaties and the Rise and Demise of the Pillars

As the Union has evolved in scale and ambition, so its underpinning treaties have undergone increasingly prolific addition and amendment. This can cause confusion, especially when tracing the development of competence in a policy sphere, such as criminal law, that has been on a trajectory from a point on the periphery of Union affairs to a vicinity approaching their epicentre.

With one minor exception, the founding treaties of the 1950s did not confer any competence in criminal law matters upon the Union.[1] That remained so until November 1993, when the Maastricht Treaty entered into force. This consolidated the existing treaties into a new principal treaty, the European Community Treaty (ECT), and created a second principal treaty, the Treaty on European Union (TEU). The TEU contained a set of provisions that conferred some competence upon the Union in the field of 'justice and home affairs', including criminal law and sanctions. These provisions, and the law (or *acquis*) made under them, became known as the 'third pillar' of the Union. The consolidated provisions of the ECT and their accompanying *acquis* became known as the 'first pillar', and a further set of provisions in the TEU relating to 'common foreign and security policy' became known as the 'second pillar'.

Subsequently, in May 1999, the Amsterdam Treaty made substantial reforms to the third pillar, as a result of which it was renamed 'police and judicial cooperation in criminal matters'. However, the principal treaties remained the ECT and the TEU until December 2009, when the Lisbon Treaty made further extensive changes to the treaty architecture. In particular, the principal treaties were reconfigured and are now called the Treaty on the Functioning of the European Union (TFEU) and the TEU. Unlike their predecessors, they have 'the same legal value' (Article 1 TEU(L)) and, highly relevant here, they pave the way for the third pillar to 'dissolve' and for its *acquis* to become assimilated into that of the former first

[1] This was partly because these texts were focused on economic integration, but also because the Council of Europe had already been charged with responsibilities in the penal field (as well, of course, as the protection of human rights). Therefore, conferring some measure of penal authority on the embryo Union involved unnecessary duplication and risked confusion (Sir Igor Judge 2010).

pillar.[2] Also pertinent, the Union's Charter of Fundamental (that is, human) Rights (CFR, or the Charter) has been elevated in stature, so that it now has 'the same legal value as the treaties' (Article 6(1) TEU(L)), rendering it justiciable for the first time.

Despite the continuity in name, the pre- and post-Lisbon versions of the TEU are sufficiently distinct for the latter to be regarded as a newly constituted principal treaty. For that reason, and because the earlier Amsterdam reforms were so significant, care must be taken to distinguish between different versions of the TEU. Therefore, the chapter adopts the convention of identifying the relevant text through the use of a suffix that denotes the amending treaty that created it; thus: 'TEU(L)', 'TEU(A)' and 'TEU(M)'. In so far as necessary, it does likewise with respect to different versions of the ECT.

### B. Supranational versus Intergovernmental Regulatory Environments

Neither the founding treaties, nor the subsequent ECT, conferred any explicit competence in criminal law matters under the first pillar; that is, upon the European Community (Community) properly so called. That, though, did not mean that first pillar (Community) law was irrelevant to the penal context. On the contrary, the ECT provided some implicit competence to regulate by means of criminal law (Case C-176/03 *Commission v Council*; Case C-440/05 *Commission v Council*). And, because Community law was supreme over the internal laws of the Member States (Case 6/64 *Costa v ENEL*), it prevailed where conflicts with domestic criminal, including penal, laws occurred.

Supremacy is one of the two characteristics that conferred 'supranational' character upon Community law. The other is direct effect (Case 26/62 *van Gend en Loos*) provided certain qualifying criteria were met, individuals had the right to rely directly upon first pillar law before a national court. Together, these qualities conferred great potency upon Community law and demonstrated that the fields of competence that were covered by the ECT were those in which an intensive pooling of sovereignty had taken place between the Member States. This was in contrast to the third pillar.

Notwithstanding its foundation in the TEU, it was designed not to be invested with supranational character, but to remain intergovernmental in nature. That decision reflected a fundamental tension that can still be seen in the handling of criminal law matters at Union level. On the one hand, there is irrefutable evidence that *all* Member States recognise the practical

[2] Subject to a five-year transitional period: see Protocol No 36 to the TEU and the TFEU on Transitional Provisions, Title VII.

benefits that they stand to accrue from collaborating in criminal law matters. On the other hand, albeit to varying degrees (Besselink 2001), they recognise that such collaboration provokes special sensitivities because matters of criminal law and punishment are so intimately bound up with questions of citizenship, identity and statehood. That awareness has led them to be more reluctant to pool sovereignty in this field than most others. The interim solution was thus to create a dedicated collaborative environment within the framework of the treaties, but in a manner that remained consistent with the doctrine of state sovereignty under international law.[3] Accordingly, third pillar law was not supreme over the internal laws of the Member States, nor has it been established that it has capacity to have direct effect.[4]

In the light of this explanation, it should be clear why the decision to dismantle the pillar structure is so significant: it is effecting a paradigm shift whereby those areas of competence that were covered by the third pillar are transferring to the Union's supranational core. Hence, post-Lisbon penal law is supreme over Member States' internal laws and is directly effective if it satisfies the necessary criteria. Even though third pillar law had already assumed some supranational quality in the aftermath of the Amsterdam reforms (see Case C-105/03 *Pupino*),[5] this is a critical development in the history of the treaties (see further Baker and Harding 2009).

From the discussion so far, it can be surmised that the Union's plethora of penal roles is not a function of its evolutionary history per se, but one of shifting perspectives as to the most appropriate law and policy-making methodology for it to use. As the next section will show, a further confounding factor is that the constitutional goal of a particular penal role does not necessarily have to be reflected in the nature of the regulatory method that is employed in its pursuit.

## III. THE UNION'S ESTABLISHED ROLES AS A PENAL ACTOR

Altogether, eight distinct roles of the Union as a penal actor will now be discussed. The list is offered as a convenient framework for analysis and does not necessarily purport to be exhaustive. Structurally, it is organised according to the dominant type of governance arrangement that the roles

[3] The premise of the doctrine is that states enjoy autonomy over their own territories and are not subject to restrictions on their independence, other than those that they have accepted consensually. Nor, usually, may they exercise power in the territory of another state (Kittichaisaree 2001: 5).

[4] Arts 34(2)(b) and (c) TEU(A) state explicitly that Framework Decisions and decisions 'shall not entail direct effect', but the TEU says nothing about other third pillar instruments.

[5] Despite the tendency to paint supranationalism and intergovernmentalism as contrasting concepts, the reality is more nuanced (see Meyring 1997).

represent. Some types of Union activity display qualities that are consistent with more than one entry in the typology. Therefore, the categories overlap to some extent and should not be understood to be discrete.

### A. Roles that Express Supranationalism

The first two roles are treated as expressions of supranationalism because they are directed at promoting the core Union interest.

#### *i. Promoting the Use of Penal Law to Protect EU Assets*

As already noted, neither the founding treaties nor the ECT conferred any explicit penal competence upon the supranational component of the Union's structure. Superficially, that meant that the Community lacked the means to insist that penal measures were deployed to safeguard its assets and interests. However, the Court of Justice of the EU[6] (CJEU or the Court) was able to derive such a means from Member States' 'obligation of loyal cooperation'.

Now appearing in slightly amended language in Article 4(3) TEU(L), prior to the Lisbon reforms, this obligation was contained in Article 10 ECT and was composed of three interrelated duties. Two were couched in positive terms, and it is these that are relevant here. They mandated Member States to 'take all appropriate measures' to ensure that they fulfilled their obligations under the ECT and to 'facilitate the achievement of the Community's tasks'. The Court established that the discharge of these responsibilities required Member States to ensure the effective protection of Community assets, including through the deployment of their criminal justice systems (and thus their penal laws) if necessary (Case 68/88 *Commission v Greece*; Case C-265/95 *Commission v French Republic*). But when might it be 'necessary'?

In principle, the choice of means through which appropriate protection was secured was a matter for the Member State concerned (Case 68/88, para 24; Case C-265/95, para 33). However, that discretion was fettered by the overriding need to satisfy two principles. First, the steps that were adopted had to be akin to those that the Member State would deploy in an analogous, purely domestic situation: the principle of equivalence or assimilation. Second, the steps had in any event to be 'effective, proportionate and dissuasive': the principle of effectiveness itself (see further Harding 1997). Even though neither demanded the use of criminal law means,

[6] Formerly the European Court of Justice, but renamed as part of the Lisbon reforms. For simplicity, the new name will be used throughout the chapter.

logically, their application could crystallise into exactly that obligation (Case C-176/03 *Commission v Council* Opinion of Advocate General Colomer, para 43). Furthermore, because the principles applied both substantively and procedurally, they might have purchase at any (or all) stages of the criminal justice system, including that of dispensing punishment (see Case C-265/95 Opinion of Advocate General Lenz discussed in Baker 2002a).

Related to this generic treaty obligation, it became well-established practice for Community legislation to specify that Member States must punish violations with 'effective, proportionate and dissuasive' sanctions (see, eg, Council Directive 91/477/EEC, Article 16 as amended by Directive 2008/51/EC; Directive 2008/99/EC, Article 5). Just like the generic obligation, proper implementation of such provisions might dictate that penalties had to be penal in kind, rather than merely civil or administrative. Furthermore, the vocabulary of the effectiveness test implied that they should aim at retribution and deterrence, as opposed to other penological goals (see Baker 2002a; European Commission 2011b: 9).

That the Community legislature was competent to levy such requirements upon Member States was confirmed by the CJEU as recently as 2005, in the so-called '*Environmental Offences*' case (Case C-176/03 *Commission v Council*). However, the subsequent ruling, in 2007, in the so-called '*Ship Source*' case, revealed that the line between what the Community legislature did have the competence to do, and what it did not, was a fine one (Case C-440/05 *Commission v Council*, para 48). Specifically, it could not lay down more precise requirements, such as that Member States must impose sanctions of between X and Y terms of imprisonment, or X and Y levels of fine. Were it to be regarded as necessary to approximate penalties this exactly, it would be a matter for the Union to legislate in reliance upon its third pillar competence (Case C-440/05 *Commission v Council*, para 70).

As for that competence, with the advent of the third pillar, the Union acquired a dedicated legal basis upon which to adopt legislation that was aimed at protecting its assets and interests from abuse and misuse by means of the criminal law. The invigorated post-Amsterdam TEU provided expressly that it could legislate to establish 'minimum rules relating to the constituent elements of criminal acts and to penalties in the fields of organised crime, terrorism and illicit drug trafficking' (Articles 29 and 31(1)(e) TEU(A)). In principle, therefore, it was not problematic for relevant third pillar legislation to specify penalty requirements more precisely than was possible under the first pillar.

The sectoral measures that were adopted on the basis of this third pillar competence were protective of Union interests in two ways. Straightforwardly, certain of them targeted forms of criminality that threatened Union assets as their direct object; counterfeiting the euro, for instance (Council Framework Decision 2000/383/JHA; Council Framework Decision 2001/888/JHA). Others had that effect because they were aimed at combating illegitimate exploitations of the rights of free movement under the treaties (afforded to capital, goods, persons and services) and the associated dismantling of border controls (see, for example, Council Framework Decision 2002/629/JHA; Council Framework Decision 2002/946/JHA; Council Framework Decision 2004/68/JHA; Council Framework Decision 2004/757/JHA). Such behaviours harmed the Single Market, one of the core infrastructural assets of the Union. Thus, while the instruments had intergovernmental character, they pursued a supranational goal.

As far as the specific matter of punishment was concerned, the Council of Ministers (the Council) reached formal conclusions on the approximation of criminal sanctions in respect of third pillar instruments in 2002 (Justice, Home Affairs and Civil Protection Council 2002). In circumstances where it was judged inadequate to require Member States to introduce effective criminal penalties (in the technical sense explained above), they provided that punishment levels were to be set by reference to the following standard scale:

> Level 1: Penalties of a maximum of at least between one and three years' imprisonment.
> Level 2: Penalties of a maximum of at least between two and five years' imprisonment.
> Level 3: Penalties of a maximum of at least between five and 10 years' imprisonment.
> Level 4: Penalties of a maximum of at least 10 years' imprisonment (cases where very serious penalties are required).

As the words 'of at least' were included at each level, Member States were permitted to prescribe higher maxima if they wished (Justice, Home Affairs and Civil Protection Council 2002: 15). Notwithstanding that freedom, and that each level already consisted of bands of prescribed maxima, the existence of the scale attests to an underlying consensus at Union level that punishments should be proportionate, and thus retributive, in nature.

Now that the Lisbon Treaty is in force, Article 83 TFEU confers supranational competence upon the Union to legislate by means of directives to 'establish minimum rules' regarding the 'definition of criminal offences and sanctions' in either of two situations. Article 83(1) equates with the former third pillar competence and applies to a list of 'areas of particularly serious crime with a cross-border dimension'. They can be added to, but for the moment they are:

> terrorism, trafficking in human beings and sexual exploitation of women and children, illicit drug trafficking, illicit arms trafficking, money laundering, corruption, counterfeiting of means of payment, computer crime and organised crime.

Already, two directives have been adopted in reliance upon this provision (Directive 2011/36/EU; Directive 2011/92/EU). Both contain several

Articles that prescribe penalty levels and which appear to comply with the pre-Lisbon scale, implying that it continues to be adhered to.

Article 83(2), on the other hand, contains what is tantamount to an extended codification of the Court's rulings in the *Environmental Offences* and *Ship Source* cases. Designed to enable Union policies to be reinforced by the threat of criminal sanctions, it applies if approximation 'proves essential to ensure the effective implementation of a Union policy in an area which has been subject to harmonisation measures'. Now that the Union has this explicit competence, it is doubtful that it can still require Member States to adopt criminal penalties in reliance upon the obligation of loyal cooperation in Article 4(3) TEU(L). It does not follow, however, that the generic duty upon Member States to ensure that 'effective' measures are in place to secure the implementation of Union law has been disturbed. Thus, the principles established by the relevant pre-Lisbon case law survive intact.

### *ii. A Shield from National Penal Laws*

Paradoxically, in other circumstances, Community law provided a shield from the exercise of penal power. The scope for such an eventuality arose from the impossibility cleanly of severing economic from penal affairs, making it inevitable that factual situations would occur that engaged both Community and national penal laws. Where the respective norms clashed, the doctrines of direct effect and supremacy enabled legal and natural persons to seek relief from the application of penal provisions, thus giving primacy to the Union's supranational interest. Analytically, such a clash might occur in one, or more, of the following ways.

First, a penal provision might be incompatible with a primary rule of Community law, such as one of the rights of free movement, or another right under the ECT or Community legislation. If the national measure prevented the enjoyment of such a right, or had the potential or theoretical capacity to hinder its enjoyment, or to discourage its exercise, then the measure had to be disapplied. The same result would follow if, secondly, a penal measure, falling within the scope of the ECT, contravened one of the fundamental principles of Community law. The two of particular relevance in a penal context were proportionality and respect for fundamental rights.

Compliance with proportionality required that the least restrictive means should be used to attain a given goal. Its application as a shield from a penal measure is illustrated by the ruling in *Skanavi* (Case C-193/94). The case concerned a directive that required Union nationals who were resident in a host Member State to exchange their national driving licences for a Community licence. When its provisions were transposed into German law, the authorities added a penalty provision which stipulated that those who failed to comply were to be dealt with as though they were driving without a licence. Such conduct constituted a criminal offence that was punishable by a prison sentence of up to a year, or a fine. Asked whether the penalty clause was compatible with Community law, the CJEU found that it was not. The right to drive was distinct from the requirement to hold a valid licence, which was merely evidence of that right, and individuals' original national licences remained valid in other Member States. Therefore, the provision was disproportionate (Case C-193/94, paras 34–36).

The obligation to respect fundamental rights was more complicated. Akin to criminal competence, the founding treaties lacked any provisions that afforded safeguards for fundamental rights. Therefore, the CJEU took responsibility for insisting that such rights were respected as fundamental principles of Community law and for developing a suitable doctrine for their protection. In the quest for legitimacy, it grounded its doctrine in values and principles that the Member States had already accepted. Thus, it attached 'special significance' to the guarantees in the European Convention on Human Rights (ECHR), but it also regarded the 'constitutional traditions common to the Member States' and the 'international treaties for the protection of human rights on which [they had] collaborated or of which they are signatories' as sources of inspiration (Case C-260/89 *ERT*, para 41). Subsequently, its approach was codified in the TEU, albeit without reference to international instruments beyond the ECHR, and it is currently contained in Article 6(3) TEU(L).

A case in which it was argued, albeit unsuccessfully, that the execution of a punishment was contrary to Community law for being in breach of fundamental rights was that of *Kremzow* (Case C-299/95). Kremzow, an Austrian national, had been convicted in Austria of serious offences, for which he was serving a life sentence. In earlier litigation (*Kremzow v Austria*), the European Court of Human Rights had ruled that his sentence had been imposed in a manner that violated Article 6(3)(c) ECHR. As a 'citizen of the Union', Kremzow enjoyed a right of free movement under the ECT (then Article 8a ECT(M); subsequently Article 18 ECT(A); now Article 21 TFEU). Relying on the fact that the guarantees afforded by Article 6(3)(c) ECHR were recognised as fundamental rights in Community law (Case 17/74 *Transocean Marine Paint v Commission*; Case 155/79 *AM and S Europe Ltd v Commission*), he sought to establish that the execution of his prison sentence constituted an unlawful restriction upon his right of free movement under Community law.

The CJEU rejected the argument on the basis that Community law was not engaged. Kremzow's ability to move was 'purely hypothetical', meaning that his circumstances did not establish 'sufficient connection' with the ECT to fall within the Court's jurisdiction (Case C-299/95 para 16, criticised in Baker 1998). Were a case involving the same facts to occur now, it would be harder for the Court to escape the substantive issue. Not only has the law of Union citizenship developed very substantially (see, inter alia, Case C-184/99 *Grzelcyk*; Case C-314/99 *Baumbast*; Case C-135/08 *Rottmann*), but the protection afforded to fundamental rights has been shored up too. While these factors do not necessarily point to a different outcome, they might lead to a more convincing justification versed in terms of the punished citizen's lack of integrative ties with any other Member State. In cases involving other combinations of facts, claims based on a breach of fundamental rights might well be successful.

The final circumstance in which an individual could seek to challenge a penal measure for incompatibility with Community law occurred in situations where a Member State claimed to have a legitimate basis for acting contrary to the primary rules of the treaties. Such a claim could arise either where the Member State purported to rely upon a derogation that was written into the treaties or legislation, or where the pretext of its action was the pursuit of an interest that the CJEU recognised as consistent with the treaties (Case 33/74 *van Binsbergen*; Case 120/78 *Cassis de Dijon*; Case C-415/93 *Bosman*; Case C-55/94 *Gebhard*).

The Court policed both types of justification strictly, interpreting narrowly the grounds upon which they were available; requiring objective evidence that relevant action was necessary; and insisting that Member States must comply with the fundamental principles of Union law when it was taken. Thus, where a Member State applied a penal measure in reliance upon a justification, the legitimacy of its action could be challenged on the grounds that it infringed one or more of these requirements. Serving to sharpen the relevance to the current discussion, one of the commonly available grounds of derogation was 'public policy', a concept that captured actions by a Member State to safeguard the essential interests of its society (see, eg, Case C-36/02 *Omega Spielhallen*). Perhaps the clearest signal that a given interest genuinely had such a status was that conduct which threatened or harmed it was criminalised and punished by the Member State concerned (see Case C-348/09 *PI* Opinion of Advocate General Bot, para 36).

Among the provisions in respect of which Member States were permitted to rely upon this ground for derogation were those relating to the rights of free movement granted to economic actors under the ECT (Articles 39(3) and 46(1) ECT; now Articles 45(3) and 52(1) TFEU). Relatively early, the CJEU ruled that a Member State could justify steps to deny, or deprive, individuals of these rights where it could establish that they were necessary to combat 'a genuine and sufficiently serious threat to … one of the fundamental interests of society' (Case 30/77 *Bouchereau*, para 35). That an individual had been convicted of criminal offences could provide evidence that would sustain a judgement that she or he constituted such a threat, but only where it formed part of an assessment of that individual's personal conduct (Case 30/77 *Bouchereau*, para 28). Subsequently, these principles were codified in legislation (Council Directive 64/221/EEC, Article 3; now repealed and replaced by Directive 2004/38/EC, Article 27). Their application in a penal context is illustrated by the decision in *Calfa* (Case C-348/96).

The case concerned an Italian national who had been sentenced in Greece to three months' imprisonment and expulsion for life from the Greek territory for drug offences. Under the Greek Penal Code it was all but compulsory for the sentencing court to make the expulsion order. However, Calfa challenged its imposition as being an unlawful restriction on her right of free movement as a recipient of services (Article 49 ECT; now Article 56 TFEU). The CJEU agreed in principle that a Member State could justify taking such a step on the basis of the public policy derogation (Case C-348/96, para 22). However, it held that the Greek law was inconsistent with Community law because it applied automatically, without any enquiry into the personal conduct of the particular offender (Case C-348/96, paras 27–28). Analysed in penological terms, the decision is consistent with an inference that, where some form of incapacitation was called for, Community law tolerated measures of special incapacitation, but not those of general incapacitation (Zimring and Hawkins 1995).

The Lisbon reforms have not affected the principles that have just been explained, and they therefore remain good law.

## B. Roles that Express Intergovernmentalism

The next two roles are treated as expressions of intergovernmentalism because they concern cooperative ventures between the Member States (as Member States), and thus a realm of Union activity that has the primary purpose of furthering their domestic interests, rather than promoting those of the Union itself.

### *i. The Union as a Forum for Surmounting the Limitations of Member States' Sovereignty over Crime Problems and their Control*

Strikingly early, the Member States recognised, and began to exploit, the potential of the embryo Union to provide a collaborative forum for overcoming the limitations of their national sovereignties over crime and its control (see also Garland 1996). Initially this was done outside the treaty framework, the most significant initiative in terms of its enduring legacy being the creation of the Trevi network in 1975. The original mandate of the network was to combat terrorism and other forms of political extremism. During the next two decades, however, its remit was expanded to cover public order and training, drugs and organised crime, and the police and security issues linked to the creation of the Single Market (Lodge 1993). Ultimately, in 1993, its organisational infrastructure, together with its accumulated *acquis*, was absorbed into the Union to form the foundation of the third pillar (Lodge 1993; Baker and Harding 2009). Consistent with that developmental history, action taken under the third pillar had a strong strategic purpose in the generation of a coordinated response to terrorism and organised crime, especially that with a cross-border dimension.

Under the post-Lisbon treaties the strategic goal of combating cross-border crime has become more entrenched. Unlike the provisions that it replaced (Articles 29 and 31(1)(e) TEU(A)), Article 83(1) TFEU does not merely list the types of crime to which it applies, but defines the power of the Union to legislate as being to:

> establish minimum rules concerning the definition of criminal offences and sanctions in the areas of particularly serious crime *with a cross-border dimension resulting from the nature or impact of such offences or from a special need to combat them on a common basis*. [Emphasis added.]

In the course of discussing the first of the Union's penal roles above, it was seen that a series of sectoral measures was adopted on the basis of the old third pillar competence and that the Council developed a standard scale against which to calibrate penalty levels. It was also noted that the two post-Lisbon directives (Directive 2011/35/EU and Directive 2011/92/EU) appear to comply with it. Accordingly, there are no fresh points to note at this juncture.

### *ii. The Union as Facilitator of National Penal Systems: Creating an 'Area of Justice'*

When the Amsterdam Treaty entered into force in 1999, it became a formal objective of the Union 'to maintain and develop [itself] as an area of freedom, security and justice' (AFSJ) (Article 2 TEU(A)). Realisation of that ambition has emerged as a primary infrastructure project (European Council 1999; European Council 2004; European Council 2010), in the context of which measures that create capacity to enforce judicial decisions across the Union's internal borders are regarded as intrinsic to the notion of an 'area of justice' (European Council 1999, section B; European Council 2004, section 3; European Council 2010, section 3). As a result, the Union has adopted an increasingly dominant role in facilitating the 'free movement' of criminal justice, including criminal punishment, across its regulatory space.

Centre stage in constructing the area of justice is the growing family of instruments that are based upon the 'cornerstone' principle of mutual recognition (European Council 1998, para 39; European Council 1999, para I.10.33; Council of Ministers 2001). Simply stated, what mutual recognition demands is that judicial decisions that are produced in the course of criminal proceedings in one Member State are respected, and given effect, by the authorities of the other 26. Prima facie, it is immaterial that their subject matter would be dealt with in an entirely different way by the recognising state's criminal justice system, or that the decision does not correspond with the tenets of the latter's criminal procedure. Operating on the premise of mutual trust, effect should be given to the non-domestic decision on the basis that it is 'different but equal' (Chalmers et al 2010: 764). Thus, mutual recognition provides a different logistic from the one that was examined in the previous section for combating the deficiencies in Member States' abilities to exercise sovereignty over crime control.

The most famous member of the mutual recognition family is the European Arrest Warrant (EAW) that has replaced extradition between the Member States with a judicial system of surrender (Council Framework Decision 2002/584/JHA). However, it has four less prominent siblings that tackle the cross-border enforcement of punishments and/or post-trial disposal. All are founded in third pillar legislation. In order of adoption, they cover financial penalties (Council Framework Decision 2005/214/JHA); confiscation orders (Council Framework Decision 2006/783/JHA); custodial sentences (Council Framework Decision 2008/909/JHA); and probation orders and other types of alternative sanction (Council Framework Decision 2008/947/JHA). Although they have not actually complied, Member States were mandated to have completed the implementation of the last of these measures, and thus the entire package, by early December 2011.

While the details vary, each instrument creates a common framework whereby the responsibility for implementing a punishment that has been imposed in one Member State (the issuing state) can be assumed by the criminal justice authorities of another (the executing state). Therefore, their adoption entails the tacit endorsement by the Union of the full range of approaches that Member States take towards the imposition and implementation of punishment. Both the custodial sentence and the probation instruments add a supplementary Union element, however, as they share the professed aim of 'facilitating the social rehabilitation of the sentenced person' (Council Framework Decision 2008/909/JHA, Articles 3(1), 4(4) and 4(6); Council Framework Decision 2008/947/JHA, Article 1(1)). The former also mentions 'successful reintegration of the sentenced person into society' (Council Framework Decision 2008/909/JHA, Article 4(4)); and the latter, 'improving the protection of victims and of the general public' (Council Framework Decision 2008/947/JHA, Article 1(1)). Therefore, these latter measures provide some evidence that the goals of rehabilitation, reintegration and public protection are interlaced in the Union's thinking.

In order to secure the goal of delivering more effective and more efficient implementation, the instruments have certain core features. For example, the grounds upon which the executing state may decline to enforce a sentence are pre-defined, exhaustive and relatively narrow (Council Framework Decision 2005/214/JHA, Article 7; Council Framework Decision 2006/783/JHA, Article 8; Council Framework Decision 2008/909/JHA, Article 9; Council Framework Decision 2008/947/JHA, Article 11). Also, certain of the safeguards that are built into conventional (international law) mechanisms for conducting criminal justice across borders are at least partly jettisoned. Most notably, the instruments contain a common list of 32 forms of serious offending in relation to which there is no need to satisfy the requirement of double criminality before a transfer between national jurisdictions can take place (Council Framework Decision 2005/214/JHA, Article 5; Council Framework Decision 2006/783/JHA, Article 6; Council Framework Decision 2008/909/JHA, Article 7; Council Framework Decision 2008/947/JHA, Article 10).[7] Therefore, an executing state might have to enforce a punishment, notwithstanding that it was attracted by conduct falling outside the scope of its own criminal law.

These innovations have been made possible by operating a presumption that mutual trust exists between the criminal justice authorities of the Member States because all can be relied upon to respect fundamental rights and the other fundamental principles of Union law. Nevertheless, each instrument states explicitly that its provisions do not modify such obligations in any way (Council Framework Decision 2005/214/JHA, Article 3; Council Framework Decision 2006/783/JHA, Article 1(2); Council Framework Decision 2008/909/JHA, Article 3(4); Council Framework Decision 2008/947/JHA, Article 1(4)). That does not mean, of course, that theory and reality necessarily match up. In the cognate field of asylum law, the CJEU has ruled the equivalent presumption to have been rebutted by factual evidence that detention conditions did not satisfy fundamental rights' standards (Case C-411/10 *NS*). Therefore, it is not a foregone conclusion that, if tested through litigation, the presumption will stand in penal contexts.

Under the post-Lisbon treaty settlement, Article 82 TFEU has codified mutual recognition as the basis of judicial cooperation in criminal matters, including the enforcement of judicial decisions. Therefore, both the Union's role in facilitating the cross-border enforcement of punishment, and the approach that has just been sketched, are liable to endure if and when the current third pillar instruments come to be revised.

### C. Roles that Express Constitutionalism

Moving beyond supranationalism and intergovernmentalism, another strand in the Union's penal activities can be interpreted as consistent

[7] Usually the offences concerned must be punishable by a maximum sentence of at least three years' imprisonment according to the law of the issuing state. However, that requirement is waived in the case of financial penalties, and the list of offence types for which double criminality is not required is also extended to 39 in that Framework Decision. Member States may opt to preserve the requirement of double criminality in the case of custodial sentences and probation (Council Framework Decision 2008/909/JHA, Art 7(4); Council Framework Decision 2008/947/JHA, Art 10(4)).

with constitutionalism. This is because it relates to the Union's ability to construct a functional relationship with those who occupy its regulatory space, thereby earning legitimacy in their eyes as a governmental entity.

### *i. The Formal Institution of 'Citizenship of the Union'*

In 1993, the Maastricht Treaty inserted a new provision into the ECT by virtue of which 'citizenship of the Union' was conferred upon all those who hold the nationality of a Member State (Article 8 ECT(M), subsequently Article 17(1) ECT(A), now Article 20(1) TFEU). Further provisions invested citizens with a non-exhaustive list of identified rights (now contained in Articles 20–24 TFEU), the most significant of which is 'the right to move and reside freely within the territory of the Member States' (Articles 20(2)(a) and 21 TFEU). Like the economic rights of free movement, the CJEU has held this one to be directly effective (Case C-314/99 *Baumbast*). Consequently, it has provided a basis for challenging the compatibility of a considerable variety of national rules with Union law. In conjunction with action by the Community legislature, especially its adoption of the so-called 'Citizenship Directive' (Directive 2004/38/EC), this has created the conditions for a more comprehensive set of privileges of citizenship to become carved out and long since led the Court to forecast that 'Union citizenship is destined to be the fundamental status of nationals of the Member States' (Case C-184/99 *Grzelcyk*, para 31). What, though, of the relevance of these developments to the matter of punishment?

The case of *Kremzow*, discussed above, provides an early, albeit fruitless, illustration of an individual seeking to challenge the execution of a punishment as being contrary to his rights as a citizen of the Union. With the advent of a more sophisticated body of citizenship law further cases have started to materialise in which its interaction with punishment is in issue. Although few in number, they offer useful contributions to our emerging understanding of the Union as a penal actor.

One way in which they do so is by adding to what we know about the sorts of behaviours that are liable to elicit some form of punitive response. While still tentative, there is elementary evidence that those whose criminality results in an abusive claim to the rank of citizen, or constitutes an abuse of its privileges, will attract such a reaction (Case C-135/08 *Rottmann*; Case C-66/08 *Kozlowski*; Case C-145/09 *Tsakouridis*; Case C-348/09 *PI*).

Rather better fleshed out is a body of law that is starting to deal with the complications of the exercise of free movement for the question of where punishment should be implemented and enforced and/or what further consequences can ensue for a citizen once those processes are complete. One core determinate through which citizenship law is being shaped in general is the intensity of a migrant's ties with a host Member State. Consistent with that concern, the proposition that is emerging in the punishment field is that, during and after sentence, citizens should be dealt with in the Member State where they are most integrated in terms of their economic, family, and other social connections. Thinking back to the mutual recognition instruments on custodial sentences and probation, it has been seen that the idea surfaces there. It also arises in the setting of the EAW.

Among the purposes for which an EAW may be issued is to enable the enforcement of a custodial sentence or detention order (Council Framework Decision 2002/584/JHA, Articles 1(1) and 2(1)). However, the executing state may opt to execute the sentence in accordance with its domestic law, instead of surrendering the wanted individual if that person is 'staying in, or is a national or a resident of [that] Member State' (Council Framework Decision 2002/584/JHA, Article 4(6)). As a matter of everyday understanding, of these three trigger conditions, the one that seems to require the least degree of connection with the executing state is that of 'staying in'. Nevertheless, in *Kozlowski*, the CJEU ruled that it entailed a level of integration not dissimilar to residence, and must be assessed according to objective factors. They included 'in particular, the length, nature and conditions of [the person's] presence and the family and economic conditions which he has with the executing Member State' (Case C-66/08, para 48).

Given that the requirement to consider an individual's integrative ties is built into the mutual recognition instruments, the notion that it should colour decision-making must be supported in principle by the Member States.[8] When it comes to implementation, however, there are signs that it is causing legal and political difficulties. Understandably, public opinion is unsympathetic towards individuals who abuse the right of free movement by engaging in offending, especially when it is of a serious kind. Therefore, notwithstanding economic, humanitarian and social arguments in favour of allowing offenders to remain in a host Member State, governments experience heavy pressure to repatriate them to their Member State of nationality; a course of action they may favour anyway, as the case of *Calfa* has already illustrated.[9]

The context in which this tension falls to be reconciled is the Citizenship Directive (Directive 2004/38/EC). Although not concerned with punishment as such, Article 28 prescribes the circumstances in which a host Member State may deny individuals their rights of free movement and residence by expelling them from its territory. Bearing out the contemporary focus on integration, the scheme that it sets up provides tiered levels of protection from expulsion that are contingent upon status and length of residence. Those who are afforded the greatest protection are individuals who are

[8] Framework decisions required the unanimous vote of the Council in order to be adopted (Art 34(2)(b) TEU(A)).

[9] See also *Chindamo*, a case that attracted considerable controversy in the UK (*The Guardian* 2007).

citizens of the Union in their own right and who have been resident in their host Member State for at least 10 years. Such people can only be expelled on 'imperative grounds of public security'.

The need for *imperative* grounds indicates that the level of threat must be particularly high (Case C-145/09 *Tsakouridis*, para 41; Case C-348/09 *PI*, para 19) and 'public security' has an established meaning that spans internal and external security, but in a defence, as opposed to a criminal law, sense (Case C-145/09 *Tsakouridis*, para 44). Therefore, the elements combine to form a high bar for Member States to satisfy, limiting expulsion to exceptional cases (Directive 2004/38/EC, recital 24; Case C-145/09 *Tsakouridis*, para 40). Also, the legislative intention seems to have been that, for this elite category of migrants, integration should take priority over internal public security, so that criminality should not lead to expulsion. That understanding has been undermined, however, by two recent referrals to the CJEU.

In the first, that of *Tsakouridis* (Case C-145/09), the German authorities sought to expel a Greek national who had been born and raised in Germany after he was sentenced to six and a half years' imprisonment for drug dealing as part of a criminal gang. Rather than confirming that he enjoyed optimum protection under the directive, the Court described the type of criminality in which he had been involved as 'diffuse' and found that it 'could reach a level of intensity that might directly threaten the calm and physical security of the population as a whole or a large part of it.' (Case C-145/09 *Tsakouridis*, paras 45–47). Therefore, despite the intensity and depth of his integration into German society, the authorities were not necessarily precluded from determining that he was a threat to public security, and of a magnitude that might justify his expulsion. By virtue of this ruling it is arguable that the Court adjusted the normative balance that was written into the directive, broadening the concept of public security to give precedence to Member States' domestic efforts to incapacitate offenders over the Union's goal of promoting social integration.

The second case, that of *PI* (Case C-348/09), makes this even clearer. It too concerned a purported expulsion from Germany, this time of an Italian national who had been convicted of offences relating to the repeated sexual abuse of a minor who was a family member. Contrasting with *Tsakouridis*, the criminality here was of a type that meant that its effects were confined to the private sphere (Case C-348/09 *PI* Opinion of Advocate General Bot, paras 43–45). None the less, the Court found that it might be covered by the concept of 'imperative grounds of public security'. Of particular interest in the current context, it gauged its conclusion by reference to the Union's post-Lisbon competence under Article 83(1) TFEU to legislate with respect to the 'sexual exploitation … of children' and the punishment provisions of the so-called 'Child Pornography Directive' (Directive 2011/92/EU) that has been adopted in reliance upon it.

The directive is designed to combat the sexual abuse and sexual exploitation of children, as well as child pornography. To that end, it identifies a range of behaviours that Member States must criminalise. Those that relate to sexual abuse are set out in Article 3, and they include several that capture characteristics of Mr I's offending. In all cases the prescribed penalties are in the upper zone; that is, Levels 3 or 4 of the standard scale that was discussed above. Additionally, Article 9 of the directive sets out a list of aggravating factors, two of which were applicable to him. Drawing upon these pieces of evidence, the Court found that:

> it is open to the Member States to regard criminal offences such as those referred to in the second subparagraph of Article 83(1) TFEU [that is, the paragraph that was quoted in section Ai above] as constituting a particularly serious threat to one of the fundamental interests of society, which might pose a direct threat to the calm and physical security of the population and thus be covered by the concept of 'imperative grounds of public security' (para 28).

Therefore, such offences might justify expulsion in accordance with the Citizenship Directive 'as long as the manner in which [they] were committed disclose[d] particularly serious characteristics', a matter that it was for the national court to determine 'on the basis of an individual examination of the specific case before it' (ibid).

Having disposed of the 'public security' element of the test, the Court then addressed the matter of 'imperative grounds'. Reiterating a point made when discussing *Calfa*, the directive provides that expulsion is justified only when 'the personal conduct of the individual concerned … represent[s] a genuine, present threat affecting one of the fundamental interests of society or of the host Member State'. According to the Court, that requirement 'implies … the existence in the individual … of a propensity to act in the same way in the future' (para 30). To this settled law, it then added a contemporary gloss. Even when such recidivist or dangerous tendencies are present, the Member State must take account of those factors that are relevant to an individual's integration (length of residence, age, state of health, family and economic situation, social and cultural integration and the extent of any links with her or his home Member State) before taking an expulsion decision (para 32).

Several instructive points emerge from the ruling. First, it provides far more conclusive evidence that the Court is prepared to recalibrate the balance between Member States' ability to incapacitate offenders and the Union's mission to promote social integration than did the decision in *Tsakouridis*. Second, it corroborates the inference that was drawn from *Calfa* that there is nothing inherently objectionable about measures of special incapacitation from the perspective of Union law. Third, the Court's heavy reliance upon Article 83(1) TFEU and the Child Pornography Directive merits critical attention.

While it is true that Article 83 confers legislative competence with respect to the sexual exploitation of children, it will be recalled that it is in the context of 'particularly serious crime with a cross-border dimension'. Consequently, the business of the provision is with the most taxing forms of transnational organised crime, that are difficult for the authorities in a single jurisdiction to handle alone. It is thus aimed at offending of a different order of magnitude from that committed by Mr I, grave as his crimes were. Furthermore, in so far as his case involved a cross-border element, it derived from the fact of his migration and was nothing to do with his offending. As for the directive, not only did his convictions not stem from it, but the deadline for its implementation does not expire until December 2013 (Directive 2011/92/EU, Article 27). Therefore, the validity of pegging the decision upon these two sources is questionable. It also creates considerable uncertainty as to where the conceptual boundaries of 'public security' are now drawn. On the other hand, that the Court elected to reason in this way testifies to the steady emergence at Union level of a penal 'fabric' that is coming to comprise something more substantial than the sum of its constituent parts.

With the advent of the Lisbon reforms, the occasions when Union law is compelled to confront the interface between citizenship law and punishment will proliferate, causing the need to build upon the principles that have just been discussed.

### *ii. Duties of Citizenship and the Normative Construction of the Pan-Union Community*

One of the problematic aspects of Union citizenship is its parasitic nature: it is 'additional to and does not replace national citizenship' (Article 20(1) TFEU). The determination of nationality remains a matter of Member State competence, albeit that they must have due regard to Union law (Case C-135/08 *Rottmann*, para 41). That means both that many longer term occupants of the Union's territorial space are excluded from the institution entirely and that there is a distorted pattern of inclusion and exclusion as between the Member States. A second weakness is that, although citizens 'shall ... be subject to the duties provided for in the Treaties' (Article 20(2) TFEU), what these duties are is not explicit. Regarded in terms of the effort to anchor the Union on a robust constitutional footing and encourage its peoples to ally themselves to a coherent common identity, neither of these characteristics is helpful. On the contrary, they obstruct and obscure the Union's ability to construct relations with the full constituency of those to whom it stands in a position of governance. However, the Union is not resourceless when it comes to surmounting this constitutional gap and one of its most potent means of doing so is through its role as a penal actor.

The point here was beautifully put by Advocate General Mazák in his Opinion in the *Ship Source* case, when he said:

> In many respects, criminal law stands out from other areas of law. Availing itself of the most severe and most dissuasive tool of social control—punishments—it delineates the outer limits of acceptable behaviour and in that way protects the values held dearest by the community at large. As an expression essentially of the common will, criminal penalties reflect particular social disapproval and are in that respect of a qualitatively different nature as compared with other punishments such as administrative sanctions.
>
> Thus, more so than other fields of law, criminal law largely mirrors the particular cultural, moral, financial and other attitudes of a community and is especially sensitive to societal developments.
>
> (Case C-440/05 *Commission v Council*, paras 67–68 footnote omitted.)

He continued:

> the way in which this *ultimum remedium* of the law is used… indicates the social standards underpinning the community concerned and is therefore, in the last analysis, inherently related to the identity of that community.
>
> (Case C-440/05 *Commission v Council*, para 71.)

Although these observations imply that the existence of a criminal code should be understood as a marker of the fact that its creators regard themselves as inhabiting a recognisable community, there are suggestions elsewhere in the literature that it is possible for cause and effect to operate the other way round (see, eg, MacCormick 2007: ch 12).

Applied to the Union, what is interesting about this set of insights is that it suggests a mechanism through which its penal activities can operate to bypass at least some of the artificially created deficiencies in Union citizenship. In theory, through a basis in, and appeal to, the common values of its peoples, such activities can provide a facilitating force to bind them into a Union-wide community. They thus offer a framework through which to establish relations with a broader constituency than that of formal citizens and, by necessary implication, serve to define the more serious duties that are incumbent upon members of its community as a whole, whether they hold the rank of citizen or not (see further Baker 2002b). Having flagged this potentiality, it must however be noted that it is subject to an important caveat.

As a matter of empirical reality, the fact that the Union lacks its own criminal justice and punishment apparatus is liable to constitute a significant obstacle to the realisation of the theory. Its absence means that the Union must rely upon the resources of its Member States to implement and enforce the norms that it lays down. Therefore, authorship of the accompanying normative messages is likely to be ascribed to relevant national institutions; not to the Union. That creates an important disjuncture in the channel of communication between the Union and those whom it seeks to address that is liable to inhibit the development of a pan-Union community according to the process that has been sketched out.

As this strand of analysis does not derive from any specific initiative, it is untouched by the Lisbon reforms, except in so far as they are prompting greater penal activity on the part of the Union.

## D. The Union and Global Governance

Further roles of the Union relate to its participation in the mechanisms of global governance and its presence on the global stage. These can be dealt with quite briefly.

### *i. Promoting International Penal Norms within the EU*

A deceptive feature of the Union's *acquis* in the criminal field is that a sizeable proportion is made up of Council of Europe, OECD and UN instruments to which Member States are either obliged, or encouraged, to accede (Vermeulen and De Bondt 2009). Therefore, as well as generating penal measures of its own, the Union acts to promote the adoption within its Member States of norms that are a product of cooperation at international level.

Where punishment is concerned, the instruments fall into three broad categories. The first two relate to combating transnational organised crime and to the cross-border enforcement of sentences. As their inclusion is consistent with roles that have been analysed already, their detail will not be discussed now. By contrast, the third category raises a dimension to the Union's emerging penal profile that has not yet been subject to sufficient scrutiny. It concerns Member States' obligations to safeguard fundamental rights.

'Respect for human rights' is one of the founding values of the Union (Article 2 TEU(L)) and the treaties declare that any European state 'which respects the [Union's founding] values ... and is committed to promoting them may apply to become a member' (Article 49 TEU(L)). One of the means through which a state is required to demonstrate fulfilment of these criteria is via membership of the Council of Europe and accession to nominated instruments. They include the ECHR; Protocol 6 to the ECHR, which abolishes the death penalty in peacetime; and the European Convention Against Torture and other Cruel, Inhuman or Degrading Treatment or Punishment. Additionally, Member States are encouraged, but not obliged, to accede to Protocols 7 and 13 to the ECHR, which deal respectively with the right of review of sentence; the principle of *ne bis in idem*; and absolute abolition of the death penalty in all circumstances (see also Articles 2 and

50 CFR). All of these texts are principally or partially aimed at setting standards in the imposition, administration and enforcement of punishment and it can thus be seen that the Union has an important role in ensuring that they are transmitted into the internal legal orders of its Member States.

Under the post-Lisbon treaty settlement, the Union's commitment to ensuring that fundamental rights are protected has been strengthened significantly. The established pledge to respect fundamental rights, which 'shall constitute general principles of the Union's law' (Article 6(3) TEU(L)), is reiterated. However, it is now bolstered by a mandate for the Union to accede to the ECHR in its own right (Article 6(2) TEU(L))[10] and the decision to confer 'the same legal value as the Treaties' upon the CFR (Article 6(1) TEU(L). As the contents of the Charter substantially reproduce those of the ECHR and related instruments to which the Member States are signatory, this latter development offers the prospect of a separate, potentially potent, route through which relevant norms can become more deeply embedded within the Union. Furthermore, the Charter's provisions go further than simply to duplicate those of other instruments, giving it the capacity to offer more extensive fundamental rights' protection. Article 49(3), for example, provides a guarantee that the 'severity of penalties must not be disproportionate to the criminal offence', something that is not found in terms in the ECHR.

### *ii. The EU as a Penal Actor on the Global Stage*

Complementing its portfolio of internal roles, the Union engages as a penal actor outside its own borders. Predictably, the pattern of its external activities reflects that of its internal initiatives, including its commitment to ensuring that punishment is consistent with respect for fundamental rights. Thus, for example, it seeks to persuade third countries to abolish the death penalty and condemns publicly those who persist in conducting executions, even when they are principal allies such as the United States.[11]

Thanks to the mission to establish the Union as an AFSJ, increasing energy has been expended in recent years in developing an external dimension to the Union's penal profile. The focus for this effort has been provided by the series of five-year programmes to put the AFSJ in place: the so-called 'Tampere', 'Hague' and 'Stockholm' Programmes (European Council 1999;

[10] At the time of writing the accession negotiations are well advanced (Council of Europe 2011; Council of the European Union 2011). Nevertheless, the process is unlikely to reach a speedy conclusion because the accession treaty must first be individually ratified by each Member State in accordance with its domestic constitutional requirements: Art 218(8) TFEU.

[11] The precise terms in which it does so may be modified, however, depending on whether the offending party is perceived as an ally or a foe (Cardwell 2009: 76–77).

European Council 2004; European Council 2010). All have included a section on the external dimension, but the amount of space that has been devoted to the topic has increased markedly with each edition. As matters of penal policy fall under the AFSJ umbrella, by necessary implication it is now a conscious part of the Union's strategy to integrate them into its external affairs (European Council 2010, para 7.1).

The Lisbon reforms have already served to fuel this trend because the Stockholm Programme was adopted almost simultaneously with the Treaty's entry into force and its contents are premised on the new treaty settlement. Therefore, the section that deals with the external dimension capitalises upon a package of legal and institutional changes that aim to provide the Union with a clearer identity and enhanced effectiveness as an external actor. Apart from improving the framework for policy development, they should ensure greater coherence between the Union's internal and external instruments and facilitate cooperation with international organisations such as the Council of Europe and the United Nations (European Council 2010, para 7.1).

## IV. PENOLOGICAL AND CONSTITUTIONAL REFLECTIONS

In the light of the sketches in the previous section, what can be learnt about the emerging penological approach of the Union and the consequences of its activities for the shifting pattern of constitutional control over punishment?

### A. The Union's Penological Approach

From the material that has been discussed, the penological approaches that seem to have a place in the Union's armoury, or to have its endorsement, are retribution, involving principles of proportionality and parsimony in punishment (Case 68/88 *Commission v Greece*; Case C-193/94 *Skanavi*; Justice, Home Affairs and Civil Protection Council 2002); deterrence (Case 68/88 *Commission v Greece*); special, but not general, incapacitation (Case C-348/96 *Calfa*; Case C-348/09 *PI*); social rehabilitation and reintegration (Council Framework Decision 2008/909/JHA; Council Framework Decision 2008/947/JHA; Case C-66/08 *Kozlowski*; Case C-145/09 *Tsakouridis*); and protection of the public (Council Framework Decision 2008/947/JHA). Crudely appraised, this list suggests that the Union operates a penological 'cafeteria', with no eye for coherence or the development of an overarching strategy. However, a more nuanced picture emerges if the progressive incorporation of these various elements is analysed in terms of the timing of their introduction, origin (judicial or legislative), and the normative sphere to which they are applied. As timing is correlated with the other factors, it is a relatively straightforward task to conduct.

By definition, those of the Union's penal roles that pre-date the founding of the third pillar (those categorised as expressions of supranationalism and the normative construction of the pan-Union community), owe their initial development to judicial action because there was no dedicated penal basis in the treaties through which legislative initiative could be seized. For the same reason, their sphere of operation is heavily centred in the realm of economic and allied activity, reflecting the original scope of the treaties. Conversely, those roles that have developed in reliance upon the third pillar, or in the context of its existence (those categorised as expressions of intergovernmentalism and the construction of Union citizenship), are grounded in legislation that is founded in explicit treaty competence. Therefore, their motivational focus lies with crime and criminals, cut free from the need for an economic link. Put more simply, the older roles promote economic integration, whereas the more recent ones mirror the switch in attention and ambition to pursue political integration.

If the Union's penological portfolio is dissected by reference to this division then signs emerge of a corroborating bifurcatory pattern. The elements that fall on the former side of the line are retribution (proportionality and parsimony), deterrence, and special incapacitation; whereas those that fall on the latter are retribution (again), special incapacitation (again), social rehabilitation and reintegration, and protection of the public. Broadly speaking, the former group is consistent with a model of punishment that regards individuals as rational actors and is prevalent in economic discourse (see also von Hirsch et al 1999) and the latter with a perspective that subscribes to the more complex, multi-dimensional view of human agency that has currency in wider penological discussion. Therefore, a detectable shift in penological emphasis has occurred as the class of subjects of Union law has evolved from that of economic actors to that of (increasingly fully fledged) citizens. That does not mean though that the older parts of the penological architecture are in the process of becoming redundant; if anything, their prospective relevance has been bolstered by the new competence in Article 83(2) TFEU (see further European Commission 2011b).

Turning to the level of the Member States, a related, but not identical, bifurcatory effect has been shown to result from the Union's growing engagement with punishment. Economic interests and those that are quintessential to the successful development of Union citizenship (principally those that equate with the process of cross-border social and cultural integration) are afforded a privileged status by comparison with others that form part of the normative structure of national penal laws. Two processes are responsible. First, preference must sometimes be given to safeguarding Union assets and interests instead of those that would otherwise be a matter of national or sub-national priority (Article 4(3) TEU(L) and, especially,

Case C-265/95 *Commission v French Republic*); second, certain classes of individuals (natural and legal) can secure a full or partial exemption from punishments to which they would otherwise be subject in reliance upon Union law rights (Case C-348/96 *Calfa*; Case C-145/09 *Tsakouridis*). By these means the existing fabric of values that is enshrined in national penal laws threatens to become distorted, as do associated decisions about the allocation of penal resources.

The final points that emerge from the discussion relate to the impact of Union law upon the selection of punishments and what might be described as the ethos of the punishment process. Most conspicuously, if there is a penal feature that is equated with 'brand Europe', it is surely opposition to the death penalty. As has been seen, the Union can justly claim to act as one of its twin anchors, alongside, and fortifying, that which is constituted by the Council of Europe. Capital punishment is not the only punishment that the two bodies have joined forces to outlaw though. They have adopted a similar symbiotic stance in excluding torture, inhuman or degrading treatment or punishment from the legitimate penal repertoire (Article 3 ECHR; Case C-465/07 *Elgafaji*; Article 4 CFR). Added to that, through the development of fundamental rights' protection, the broader range of Convention guarantees that have a bearing on punishment have been absorbed into Union law. For example, the proposition that liability to criminal punishment must not be imposed or aggravated retrospectively has become deeply entrenched (Article 7(1) ECHR; Case 63/83 *Kirk*; Case C-168/95 *Arcaro*; Case C-105/03 *Pupino*; Article 49(1) CFR). Overall, therefore, the Union plays an important part in reinforcing an approach that aims to ensure that punishment is practised in a manner that respects not only the right to life, but the value of human dignity.

## B. Constitutional Significance

There is no doubt that the processes of European integration are having important consequences for the governance of punishment. However, it remains vital to preface a discussion of this subject with an unambiguous acknowledgement that the Member States of the Union (and yet more so, the broader constellation of European states) retain substantial autonomous sovereignty over penal affairs. Most situations in which punishment is in issue remain outside the scope of the treaties and, even when the Union has the prima facie competence to regulate, the principle of subsidiarity must be respected (Article 4(2)(j) TFEU). It restricts the sphere and extent of Union action to that in which 'the objectives of the proposed action cannot be sufficiently achieved by the Member States ... but can rather, by reason of the scale or effects of the proposed action, be better achieved at Union level' (Article 5(3) TEU(L)). If that criterion is not met, then the Union has no competence and the question of regulation falls to be determined at national level.

Even when the Union does have competence, the notion that its legislative interventions lead to outcomes in which 'one size fits all' is tantamount to a myth. On the contrary, Union instruments incorporate a substantial measure of deference to Member States' differing penal cultures and practices (see further Lappi-Seppälä 2008). Take, for example, the design of the Union's standard scale (Justice, Home Affairs and Civil Protection Council 2002). Its aim of establishing proportionate punishments is compromised by a visible effort to accommodate divergent degrees of punitiveness among the Member States; hence, the scale is comprised of bands of maxima, and wide ones at that.

Deference to national policies and practices is also integral to the mutual recognition instruments. Although, as a matter of Union law, each establishes a common framework for cross-border cooperation, they also each demarcate responsibility for different aspects of the punishment process in such a way that, in principle:

— the internal law of the issuing State determines the decision to impose punishment (Council Framework Decision 2005/214/JHA, Article 5; Council Framework Decision 2006/783/JHA, Article 6; Council Framework Decision 2008/909/JHA, Article 7; Council Framework Decision 2008/947/JHA, Article 10); and
— the internal law of the executing State, governs its implementation once cross-border transfer has occurred (Council Framework Decision 2005/214/JHA, Article 9; Council Framework Decision 2006/783/JHA, Article 12; Council Framework Decision 2008/909/JHA, Article 17; Council Framework Decision 2008/947/JHA, Article 13).[12]

Thus, while they establish processes that fall within the scope of Union law because they are governed by the parent instrument, much of their detailed operation is conducted according to the domestic laws of the respective Member States.

Notwithstanding these points of counterbalance, it should none the less be apparent that the constitutional control of punishment is undergoing significant modification and reorganisation as the Union gains stature and legitimacy as a penal actor. There are various ways in which this can be illustrated, one of the more straightforward being from the perspective of the doctrine of separation of powers.

[12] The executing state is, however, charged with some responsibilities towards the issuing state. For example, it must inform the issuing State of certain matters relating to the execution of the sentence. In some instances, such information may cause the issuing State to revise its decision to seek enforcement in the executing State or result in the task of enforcement reverting back to it.

It will be assumed for the purposes of discussion that, within national systems, the legislature is responsible for determining sentencing powers and policies; the judiciary for applying them to individual offenders; and the executive for then executing sentences (Ashworth 2010, ch 2, esp 51–52). Until relatively recently, the effects of the Union's ascendancy had only been visited upon national legislatures through the loss of autonomy that is integral to the discharge of Union law obligations (Article 4(3) TEU(L)). For some, that loss is objectionable on sovereignty grounds, but that is not the issue here. What is, is the interconnected issue of whether and how the separation of powers plays out at Union level. Hypothetically, perhaps, the evolving constitutional framework might merit a clean bill of health if that element of the legislative function that has been pooled by the Member States has been conferred upon the legislature at Union level, and its legislature is of an equivalent democratic character to those at national level. However, the reality is that neither of these conditions is met.

In circumstances where a relevant Union norm derives from legislation the problem lies with the composition of the Union legislature. Under the third pillar it was the Council (Article 34(2) TEU(A)), the institution that is composed of members of the executives of the Member States (Article 16(2) TEU(L), formerly Article 203 ECT). Under the first pillar and the post-Lisbon treaties the normal arrangement has become that the legislature is composed of the Council acting in conjunction with the European Parliament (Article 251 ECT; now Article 294 TFEU). Although the latter arrangement represents an improvement on the former one, both conflate the executive and legislative roles. Exacerbating matters, national legislation may be inspired by a ruling of the CJEU or obligation to incorporate an externally sourced penal norm that has been endorsed by the Union. In those instances, there is no correspondence at all in terms of compliance with the separation of powers as between the national and Union levels of government.

Until relatively recently, there would have been nothing to add with respect to the judicial and executive arms of government. However, Union law has started to affect these too. A natural consequence of the growth in Union penal law and of the post-Lisbon treaty settlement is to fuel an increase in the number of cases that relate to punishment that are being referred to the CJEU. That in turn expands the potential for questions of the interpretation of Union law to determine whether or not individuals who are subject to penal proceedings are rightly held in custody; all the more so now that the Charter is justiciable (see further Reding 2010). Explicitly to cater for these latter cases, an expedited procedure has been introduced for securing rulings from the Court (Article 267 TFEU). Its existence underlines the fact that the CJEU may now have a direct hand in deciding how sentences are applied to individual offenders. Rather than a challenge to the doctrine of separation of powers, this is a vertical extension of the judicial role to a constitutional level above that of the nation-state.

Thanks to the introduction of the mutual recognition instruments, the sphere of operation of national executives is also being extended in so far as they place the responsibility for implementing a sentence that has been imposed by the courts of one Member State upon the authorities of another. Contrasting with the vertical extension to the sphere of operation of the judicial branch, the extension here is horizontal, across national borders.

A different perspective from which to appraise the constitutional consequences of the Union's increasing engagement with punishment is through the substance of its effects. Attention was drawn above to the ways in which it is prompting a partial revision to the normative hierarchies that are associated with Member States' penal laws, so that promoting economic prosperity and cross-border integration are elevated as objectives by comparison with those interests and values that form the conventional targets of penal protection. From a penal perspective, this seems somewhat unorthodox and is a state of affairs that is difficult to square with the declarations in the treaties that the Union shall respect:

— Member States' 'national identities';
— their 'essential State functions, including ... maintaining law and order and safeguarding national security'; and, explicitly,
— their 'different legal systems and traditions' with respect to development of the AFSJ (Articles 4 TEU(L) and 67 TFEU respectively).

The underlying cause of this constitutional tension is the Union's reliance upon Member States' penal apparatus, which denies it the independent means of establishing that certain interests and values are fundamental to *Union* society (*cf* Case C-440/05 *Commission v Council* Opinion of Advocate General Mázak above). Its presence is symptomatic of a further point that also comes through from other directions.

Slowly, signs are emerging that Member States are becoming less free to arrange their penal affairs without regard for their impact upon the Union 'space'. In *Tsakouridis*, for example, the Advocate General suggested that a Member State that wished to expel an individual once a punishment had been enforced had to 'state precisely in what way that decision does not prejudice the offender's rehabilitation' (Case C-145/09 *Tsakouridis* Opinion of Advocate General Bot, para 95). This was not simply to protect that individual's rights, but 'in the interests of the Union in general' because, once expelled, she or he would be able to exercise the right to move freely to other Member States. Thus it was 'in the general interests that the conditions of his release should be such as to dissuade him from committing crimes and, in any event not risk pushing him back into offending' (ibid). His view was subsequently endorsed by the CJEU (para 50).

Considerably earlier, the Court had sent a similar message when it portrayed the failure of the French authorities to combat vandalism against imported goods as having the potential to cultivate a 'climate of insecurity' that might affect the Single Market as a whole (Case C-265/95 *Commission v France,* especially para 17). Now that it inspects penal matters through the lens of the AFSJ, the proposition that Member States' choices as penal actors must be informed by their implications for the Union at large is only likely to be encouraged (see also Case C-137/09 *Josemans* Opinion of Advocate General Bot). Should it become pervasive, the statement at the outset of this discussion that Member States retain substantial autonomous sovereignty over their *general* penal affairs will be subject to important qualification. That observation exposes a final point with which to close this part of the discussion.

An intricate model of constitutional accountability is evolving in Europe that rests upon a matrix of vertical (nation–state–EU; nation–state–ECHR/ Council of Europe) and horizontal (inter–nation–state; EU–ECHR/Council of Europe) elements. As a case study, the penal field demonstrates this particularly well and it may be that, from it, an alternative (or complementary) paradigm of constitutional checks and balances is emerging to remedy the current fracture in the separation of powers. What is certain is that the juxtaposition of the Union's increasingly active involvement in punishment and the increasingly intense inter-relationship between its legal order and that of the Convention has already prompted some focused reflection by the European Commission as to the prospective consequences (Reding 2010; European Commission 2011a). Presumably, the Court's ruling in *NS* (Case C-411/10) will be having a similar sobering effect. Should that decision be replicated in a penal setting, so that the presumption of mutual trust threatened to become inoperable, it can be anticipated that a Member State whose fundamental rights' standards were found wanting would come under considerable pressure from others to take tangible steps to rectify matters.

## V. CONCLUSION

This chapter has sought to demonstrate that the European Union has developed a portfolio of penal roles, and to enhance understanding of its contribution as a penal actor by examining their penological and constitutional significance. It is appropriate to conclude with some comments on the extent to which its engagement with punishment supports the proposition that there is such a thing as a distinctively 'European penology'. If there is, then, owing to its size and influence, the activities of the Union ought to play an increasingly significant part in defining and sustaining it. Not only are 27 of the 47 members of the Council of Europe full members of the Union at the time of writing, but some of the remainder are drawn into its sphere of penal regulation through their preparations for membership or because they have association agreements with the Schengen zone.[13] Thus the Union has a claim to represent the most intense embodiment of 'Europeanness' that is presently available.

The first part of the previous section analysed the Union's penological approach and identified a number of features that could be said to characterise it: a degree of birfurcation in the treatment of economic and integration interests by comparison with others, both at Union and Member State levels; abolition of the death penalty and of torture, inhuman or degrading treatment or punishment; and a general ethos that punishment should be conducted in a manner that respects human dignity. Of these, the one that stands out is the first. Its inclusion seems unusual from a standard penological perspective; but, by the same token, it is the only feature that is definitively an expression of the Union's own. Seen through its eyes, the pursuit of these interests is of the essence in terms of its mission and culture. Therefore, it would be very odd if its penal profile was not evolving in such a way as to further and protect them, and, understood in that light, the fact that it is doing so is not so unorthodox in terms of accepted doctrine on the function of penal law.

As for the remainder of the list, there is a high degree of coincidence and entanglement between the Union's normative message and that which is broadcast by the Council of Europe and through the Convention's legal order. There is thus an analytical basis for distinguishing the approach of the Union, on the one hand, from that of 'Europe', on the other. If a distinctively European penology exists, part of the case must rest on the basis that it is these latter characteristics that describe it. By itself, however, this rationale is not convincing because it can be argued that what the characteristics actually typify is a *Western* approach to punishment, rather than one that is specifically European. To take the case the necessary stage further, something extra is needed and it is here that the second strand in the ongoing discussion falls into place.

In a globalising world, it would be ridiculous to suggest that Europe is unique as a setting in which ideas about punishment and its management are being transmitted across national borders (Baker and Roberts 2005; Jones and Newburn 2007; Newburn and Sparks 2004). There is, though, something special about its cultural, legal and political dynamics that has led to the creation of an infrastructure that encourages such transmission and has stretched the parameters of the penalising state, vertically and horizontally, while simultaneously inventing a novel mode of multi-level accountability through which to contain it. In ensuring that this is at all feasible, one factor above all others is vital: that the complex series of legal and political relationships upon which the whole scheme rests is characterised

[13] Prospective Member States must implement the whole of the Union's existing *acquis* prior to their accession. The states that have signed association agreements with the Schengen zone are Iceland, Liechtenstein, Norway and Switzerland.

by a high degree of respect for the rule of law, within and transcending the participatory states. Thus, it is arguable that what is distinctively 'European' about European penology is not just the intrinsic character of its punishments, but the way in which the pursuit of integration, on the one hand, and the premium that is placed on the rule of law, on the other, is reconfiguring their governance. In both respects, the role of the Union is pivotal.

## REFERENCES

Ashworth, AJ (2010) *Sentencing and Criminal Justice*, 5th edn (Cambridge, Cambridge University Press).

Baker, E (1998) 'Taking European Criminal Law Seriously' *Criminal Law Review*, June, 361–80.

—— (2002a) 'The Duty of National Criminal Justice Authorities to Enforce Community Law' in PJ Cullen and S Jund (eds), *Criminal Justice Cooperation in the European Union after Tampere*, Series of Publications by the Academy of European Law in Trier Volume 33 (Cologne, Bundesanzeiger).

—— (2002b) 'Criminal Jurisdiction, the Public Dimension to Effective Protection and the Construction of Community-Citizen Relations' in AA Dashwood, C Hillion, JR Spencer and A Ward (eds), *Cambridge Yearbook of European Legal Studies 2001*, Volume 4 (Oxford, Hart Publishing).

—— and Harding, CS (2009) 'From Past Imperfect to Future Perfect? A Longitudinal Study of the Third Pillar' *European Law Review*, 34, 25–54.

—— and Roberts, JV (2005) 'Globalisation and the New Punitiveness' in J Pratt, D Brown, M Brown, S Hallsworth and W Morrison (eds), *The New Punitiveness: Trends, Theories, Perspectives* (Cullompton, Willan Publishing).

Besselink, LFM (2001) 'Sovereignty, Criminal Law and the New European Context' in P Alldridge and C Brants (eds), *Personal Autonomy, the Private Sphere and the Criminal Law* (Oxford, Hart Publishing).

Cardwell, PJ (2009) *EU External Relations and Systems of Governance* (London, Routledge).

Chalmers, D, Davies, G and Monti, G (2010) *European Union Law*, 2nd edn (Cambridge, Cambridge University Press).

Council of Europe (2011) *Draft Legal Instruments on the Accession of the European Union to the European Convention on Human Rights*, CDDH-UE (2011)16 Final version, Strasbourg.

Council of Ministers (2001) *Programme of Measures to Implement the Principle of Mutual Recognition in Criminal Matters* [2001] OJ C12/10.

Council of the European Union (2011) *Accession of the Union to the European Convention for the Protection of Human Rights and Fundamental Freedoms—State of Play*, 18117/11, Brussels.

European Commission (2011a) *Strengthening Mutual Trust in the European Judicial Area—A Green Paper on the Application of EU Criminal Justice Legislation in the Field of Detention*, COM(2011) 327 final, Brussels.

—— (2011b) Communication from the Commission to the European Parliament, the Council, the European Economic and Social Committee and the Committee of the

Regions, *Towards an EU Criminal Policy: Ensuring the Effective Implementation of EU Policies through Criminal Law*, COM(2011) 573 final, Brussels.
European Council (1998) Presidency Conclusions of the Cardiff European Council, 15 and 16 June.
—— (1999) Presidency Conclusions of the Tampere European Council on the Creation of the Area of Freedom, Security and Justice, 15 and 16 October, *Bulletin EU 10-1999*.
—— (2004) *The Hague Programme: Strengthening Freedom, Security and Justice in the European Union* [2005] OJ C53/01.
—— (2010) *The Stockhom Programme—An Open and Secure Europe Serving and Protecting Citizens* [2010] OJ C115/01.
Garland, D (1996) 'The Limits of the Sovereign State: Strategies of Crime Control in Contemporary Society' *British Journal of Criminology*, 36, 445–71.
Harding, CS (1997) 'Member State Enforcement of European Community Measures: The Chimera of 'Effective' Enforcement' *Maastricht Journal of European and Comparative Law*, 4, 5–24.
Jones, T and Newburn, T (eds) (2007) *Policy Transfer and Criminal Justice: Exploring US Influence over British Crime Control Policy* (Maidenhead, Open University Press).
Judge, Sir Igor (2010) '30 Years on: Reflections on the Future', 14th Annual Lecture of the Judicial Studies Board, London, March 17.
Justice, Home Affairs and Civil Protection Council (2002) 2423rd Council Meeting, 7991/02 Press Release (Presse 104), Luxembourg, 25/26 April.
Kittichaisaree, K (2001) *International Criminal Law* (Oxford, Oxford University Press).
Lappi-Seppälä, T (2008) 'Trust, Welfare and Political Culture: Explaining Differences in National Penal Policies' *Crime and Justice: A Review of Research*, 37, 313–87.
Lodge, J (1993) 'Internal Security and Judicial Cooperation' in J Lodge (ed), *The European Community and the Challenge of the Future*, 2nd edn (Houndmills, Palgrave Macmillan).
MacCormick, N (2007) *Institutions of Law: An Essay in Legal Theory* (Oxford, Oxford University Press).
Meyring, B (1997) 'Intergovernmentalism and Supranationality: Two Stereotypes for a Complex Reality' *European Law Review*, 22, 221–47.
Newburn, T and Sparks, R (eds) (2004) *Criminal Justice and Political Cultures: National and International Dimensions of Crime Control* (Cullompton, Willan Publishing).
Reding, V (2010) 'The Future of European Criminal Justice under the Lisbon Treaty', Speech/10/89 delivered at the European Law Academy, Trier, 12 March.
The Guardian (2007) 'Court Rejects Challenge over Chindamo Deportation Ruling', 31 October, www.guardian.co.uk/uk/2007/oct/31/humanrights.immigrationpolicy.
Vermeulen, G and De Bondt, W (2009) *EULOCS The EU Level Offence Classification System: A Bench-mark for Enhanced Internal Coherence of the EU's Criminal Policy*, IRCP-series volume 35 (Antwerp, Maklu).
Von Hirsch, A, Bottoms, AE, Burney, E and Wikström, P-O (1999) *Criminal Deterrence and Sentence Severity: An Analysis of Recent Research* (Oxford, Hart Publishing).
Zimring, FE and Hawkins, G (1995) *Incapacitation: Penal Confinement and the Restraint of Crime* (Oxford, Oxford University Press).

## EU TREATIES

European Community Treaty (Amsterdam version).
European Community Treaty (Maastricht version).
Treaty on European Union (Amsterdam version).
Treaty on European Union (Lisbon version).
Treaty on the Functioning of the European Union.

## EU INSTRUMENTS AND LEGISLATION

Charter of Fundamental Rights of the European Union [2010] OJ C83/389.

Council Directive 64/221/EEC of 25 February 1964 on the co-ordination of special measures concerning the movement and residence of foreign nationals which are justified on the grounds of public policy, public security or public health [1963-64] OJ English Special Edition 117.

Council Directive 91/477/EEC of 18 June 1991 on control of the acquisition and possession of weapons [1991] OJ L256/51.

Council Framework Decision 2000/383/JHA of 29 May 2000 on increasing protection by criminal penalties and other sanctions against counterfeiting in connection with the introduction of the euro [2000] OJ L140/1.

Council Framework Decision 2001/888/JHA of 6 December 2001 amending Framework Decision 2000/383/JHA on increasing protection by criminal penalties and other sanctions against counterfeiting in connection with the introduction of the euro [2001] OJ L329/3.

Council Framework Decision 2002/584/JHA of 13 June 2002 on the European arrest warrant and the surrender procedures between Member States [2002] OJ L190/1.

Council Framework Decision 2002/629/JHA of 19 July 2002 on combating trafficking in human beings [2002] OJ L203/1.

Council Framework Decision 2002/946/JHA of 28 November 2002 on the strengthening of the penal framework to prevent the facilitation of unauthorised entry, transit and residence [2002] OJ L328/1.

Council Framework Decision 2004/68/JHA of 22 December 2003 on combating the sexual exploitation of children and child pornography [2004] OJ L13/44.

Council Framework Decision 2004/757/JHA of 25 October 2004 laying down minimum provisions on the constituent elements of criminal acts and penalties in the field of illicit drug trafficking [2004] OJ L335/8.

Council Framework Decision 2005/214/JHA of 24 February 2005 on the application of the principle of mutual recognition to financial penalties [2005] OJ L76/16.

Council Framework Decision 2006/783/JHA of 6 October 2006 on the application of mutual recognition to confiscation orders [2006] OJ L328/59.

Council Framework Decision 2008/909/JHA of 27 November 2008 on the application of the principle of mutual recognition to judgments in criminal matters imposing custodial sentences or measures involving deprivation of liberty for the purpose of their enforcement in the European Union [2008] OJ L327/27.

Council Framework Decision 2008/947/JHA of 27 November 2008 on the application of the principle of mutual recognition to judgments and probation decisions with a view to the supervision of probation measures and alternative sanctions [2008] OJ L337/102.

Directive 2004/38/EC of the European Parliament and of the Council of 29 April 2004 on the right of citizens of the Union and their family members to move and reside freely within the territory of the Member States [2004] OJ L158/77.
Directive 2008/51/EC of the European Parliament and of the Council of 21 May 2008 amending Council Directive 91/477/EEC of 18 June 1991 on control of the acquisition and possession of weapons [2008] OJ L179/5.
Directive 2008/99/EC of the European Parliament and of the Council of 19 November 2008 on the protection of the environment through criminal law [2008] OJ L328/28.
Directive 2011/36/EU of the European Parliament and of the Council of 5 April 2011 on preventing and combating trafficking in human beings and protecting its victims, and replacing Council Framework Decision 2002/629/JHA [2011] OJ L101/1.
Directive 2011/92/EU of the European Parliament and of the Council of 13 December 2011 on combating the sexual abuse and sexual exploitation of children and child pornography, and replacing Council Framework Decision 2004/68/JHA [2011] OJ L335/1.

## CJEU CASE LAW

Case 26/62 *NV Algemene Transport- en Expeditie Onderneming van Gend en Loos v Netherlands Inland Revenue Administration* [1963] ECR 3.
Case 6/64 *Flaminio Costa v ENEL* [1964] ECR 1141.
Case 17/74 *Transocean Marine Paint v Commission* [1974] ECR 1063.
Case 33/74 *Johannes Henricus Maria van Binsbergen v Bestuur van de Bedrijfsvereniging voor de Metaalnijverheid* [1974] ECR 1299.
Case 30/77 *R v Bouchereau* [1977] ECR 1999.
Case 120/78 *Rewe-Zentral AG v Bundesmonopolverwaltung für Branntwein ('Cassis de Dijon')* [1979] ECR 649.
Case 155/79 *AM and S Europe Ltd v Commission* [1982] ECR 1575.
Case 63/83 *R v Kent Kirk* [1984] ECR 2689.
Case 68/88 *Commission v Greece 'Greek Maize'* [1989] ECR 2965.
Case C-260/89 *ERT v Dimotiki* [1991] ECR I-2925.
Case C-415/93 *Union Royale Belge des Sociétés de Football Association ASBL and Others v Jean-Marc Bosman and Others* [1995] ECR I-4921.
Case C-55/94 *Reinhard Gebhard v Consiglio dell'Ordine degli Avvocati e Procuratori di Milano* [1995] ECR I-4165.
Case C-193/94 *Criminal proceedings against Sofia Skanavi and Konstantin Chryssanthakopoulos* [1996] ECR I-929.
Case C-168/95 *Criminal proceedings against Luciano Arcaro* [1996] ECR I-4704.
Case C-265/95 *Commission v French Republic 'French Farmers'* [1997] ECR I-6959.
Case C-299/95 *Friedrich Kremzow v Republik Österreich* [1997] ECR I-2629.
Case C-348/96 *Criminal proceedings against Donatella Calfa* [1999] ECR I-11.
Case C-184/99 *Grzelcyk v Centre public d'aide sociale d'Ottignies-Louvain-la-Neuve* [2001] ECR I-6193.

Case C-314/99 *Baumbast and R v Secretary of State for the Home Department* [2002] ECR I-7091.
Case C-36/02 *Omega Spielhallen und Automatenaufstellungs GmbH v Oberbürgermeisterin der Bundesstadt Bonn* [2004] ECR I-9609.
Case C-105/03 *Criminal proceedings against Maria Pupino* [2005] ECR I-5285.
Case C-176/03 *Commission of the European Communities v Council of the European Union 'Environmental Offences'* [2005] ECR I-7879.
Case C-440/05 *Commission of the European Communities v Council of the European Union 'Ship Source'* [2007] ECR I-9097.
Case C-465/07 *Meki Elgafaji and Noor Elgafaji v Staatssecretaris van Justitie* [2009] ECR I-921.
Case C-66/08 *Proceedings concerning the execution of a European arrest warrant issued against Szymon Kozlowski* [2008] ECR I-6041.
Case C-135/08 *Janko Rottmann v Freistaat Bayern* [2010] ECR I-1449.
Case C-137/09 *Marc Michel Josemans v Burgemeester van Maastricht* [2010] ECR I-13019.
Case C-145/09 *Land Baden-Württemberg v Panagiotis Tsakouridis* [2010] ECR I-11979.
Case C-348/09 *PI v Oberbürgermeisterin der Stadt Remscheid*, judgment of 22 May 2012, not yet reported.
Cases C-411/10 *NS v Secretary of State for the Home Department* and C-493/10 *ME and Others v Refugee Applications Commissioner, Minister for Justice, Equality and Law Reform*, judgment of 21 December 2011, not yet reported.

## COUNCIL OF EUROPE INSTRUMENTS

European Convention for the Protection of Human Rights and Fundamental Freedoms CETS 005.
European Convention Against Torture and other Cruel, Inhuman or Degrading Treatment or Punishment CETS 126.

## EUROPEAN COURT OF HUMAN RIGHTS CASE LAW

*Kremzow v Austria* 21 September 1993 (12350/86) (1994) 17 E.H.R.R. 322.

# 5

# *Approximation of Sanctions within the European Union*[*]

ROLAND MIKLAU

## I. SOME GENERAL ASPECTS OF SENTENCING CRIMINAL OFFENCES

THE SENTENCING PROCESS in criminal matters aims at the individualisation of criminal justice reactions to undesirable and criminalised behaviour of individuals found guilty by a court. The proper and adequate application of sanctions therefore requires high degrees of flexibility and judicial discretion, as well as proportionality between the seriousness of the criminal act, the personal situation and history of the offender, and the sentence applied (see further van Zyl Smit and Ashworth 2004).

The definition of criminal offences often covers a wide range of diverse actions or omissions of varying degrees of seriousness. Most definitions, even of the more serious offences, include cases where the individual fault (the degree of culpability or *mens rea*) of certain individuals participating in the offence may be minor. Many criminal justice systems take that into account by providing broad frames of punishment (eg prison terms) or a number of penalty levels with generally low minima or no minima at all. Additionally, suspended sentences and alternatives, such as fines, community service and measures of diversion, may be applicable according to the respective provisions of the Penal Code or general sentencing guidelines.

The maximum sentences provided for different forms of criminal behaviour on the other hand generally reflect the (hierarchy of) legally protected values *(Rechtsgüter)*. These are oriented towards the aim of general prevention, and bear highly symbolic significance. They are part of the visible arsenal of social reactions to misdeeds that serve to provide psychological reconciliation through citation in the media reporting crime, amongst other things.

In order to achieve such reconciliation and reassurance within society, while at the same time providing for an adequate individualisation of

[*] Editing of this chapter, in particular as to references, was assisted by Lee Coulthard.

the sanction for a criminal act, the relative autonomy of the different components and stages of the criminal process is an indispensable prerequisite. Lawmakers approach offences in a highly abstract way, within which the objectives of general prevention of undesirable acts and harm prevail. When a serious offence arouses public emotions and fear, media reports often refer to the frame of punishment in the law, emphasising the available maximum. The trial judge, usually dealing with the case much later, takes a more rational view, based on his or her professional experience as well as on the 'collective wisdom' inherent in the theoretical and practical orientation acquired by the judiciary and reflected in the jurisprudence over time. Generally speaking, the sentence applied should fit the objective of individualisation, where considerations of individual prevention and treating the offender are more concrete than other aspects. In the phase of implementing the sentence, in particular after part of a prison sentence has been served, primary attention is devoted to offenders' prospects for reintegration into society and to their rehabilitation.

Each of those stages of the criminal process has its own relevance to identifying and handling crime. Although the stages mentioned are interrelated and influence each other, they are also autonomous and partially independent of each other. The criminal justice system, viewed as a whole, possesses a stigmatising weapon and a helping hand at the same time.

Taking into account the different functions of penalty frames and punishment levels, national legal systems have developed multi-tier structures and scales for penalty frames—some systems preferring more general and broad frames, others rather sophisticated multiple tiers (Frase 2001). The approach that is adopted also depends on the relationship between the legislature and the judiciary.

In most systems the majority of actual sentences are normally meted out in the lower third of the available penalty frame: at least, this tends to be a reference or starting point. Sentencing practice often deviates from the prescribed scales for a variety of reasons (such as regional sentencing styles and traditions, social or individual severity assessments and individual culpability assessments). Sentencing practices may change considerably over time, irrespective of actions taken by the legislator.

## II. TRANSNATIONAL COMPARISON OF SENTENCING FRAMES AND PENALTIES

The significance and validity of cross-border comparisons of statutory sentencing scales and structures are much lower than often believed, and frequently do not reflect actual sentencing practice. There are no internationally agreed and harmonised principles for the transformation of sentencing frameworks into penalties and, more particularly, into prison terms handed down in concrete cases. There are no binding international sentencing guidelines; it would hardly be feasible to seek harmonisation in that area. Making decisions on sentences is considered to be a core task of an independent judiciary, subject only to appeal procedures. In particular, the duration of prison sentences and the actual period of time served in prison are determined by national traditions, local practices, judicial perceptions and pragmatic considerations such as prison capacity and the (un)availability of alternative sentencing options and (early) conditional release, as well as pardon and amnesty practices. The time spent in prison varies accordingly.

The actual period of time spent in prison might, in practice, be a relatively better transnational comparator than the statutory sentencing tiers and possibly even than the prison terms formally imposed by courts. This is because the level of a maximum penalty for certain (forms of) offences under national law is frequently closely related to the specific national offence structure and sentencing frames, and does not necessarily reflect the seriousness of the offence or the actual sentencing practice. Let us mention just one example: the lowest maximum sentence for the offence of (simple) theft is six months' imprisonment in Austria (para 127 of the Penal Code) and five years' imprisonment in Germany (para 242 of the Penal Code). Here we have two countries with very similar criminal codes; yet, irrespective of the maximum in Germany being 10 times higher than in Austria, the actual sentencing practices in the two jurisdictions are absolutely comparable: Germany on average is actually a bit more lenient than Austria.

The relevance of sentencing levels to the achievement of the main objectives of criminal justice (general and individual prevention of offending) is generally considered to be very limited, at least concerning 'classical' crime. Much criminological research, in particular as to recidivism rates, has demonstrated a very high degree of interchangeability of different penalties as to their dissuasive effects (see eg von Hirsch et al 1999; Ashworth 2010: 79). Providing and applying harsher sentences normally has very limited effects, and if so, they are mostly temporary. Replacing severe sanctions by milder ones does not seem to change crime and recidivism patterns significantly. This scientifically well-established phenomenon is in stark contrast to the impact that heavier sanctions are frequently assumed to have when the issue of appropriate punishments is debated—and not only in the course of populist discussions.

## III. APPROXIMATION OF SANCTIONS IN THE EUROPEAN UNION

### A. Developments up to the Lisbon Treaty

Before the Treaty of Lisbon came into force, the EU Council, acting on the basis of the EU Treaty and in particular the 'third pillar' that dealt with justice and home affairs, adopted several legal instruments (Framework

Decisions) that involved an approximation of the elements of certain criminal offences. The main objective was the establishment of a minimum level of criminalisation for more serious offences and offences against the financial interests of the Community. The standard formulation of the provision on sentencing in such instruments requires that the offences concerned are punishable by 'effective, proportionate and dissuasive' sanctions.

The European Council of Tampere (October 1999, the only meeting of the EU Heads of State and Government which was exclusively devoted to justice and home affairs) advocated 'efforts to agree on common definitions, incriminations and *sanctions*'[1] (emphasis added) in respect of a limited number of criminal offences. This conclusion was related to the stated commitment that mutual recognition of judicial decisions (both criminal and civil) should in the future be a cornerstone of the proclaimed 'Area of Freedom, Security and Justice', a concept modelled to some extent on the 'Internal Market'.[2]

After the entry into force of the Treaty of Amsterdam (1999) the Council, on the basis of Articles 31 and 34 TEU, adopted Framework Decisions which laid down minimum levels for the upper limit (maximum) of (prison) penalties (minima-maxima, requiring a number of years' imprisonment) to be provided by national law in respect of specified offences—mainly, but not exclusively, serious ones. Examples include a minimum-maximum penalty of eight years' imprisonment for the fraudulent making or altering of currency,[3] and a minimum-maximum penalty of four years' imprisonment in respect of certain money laundering offences. In addition, penalties which may give rise to extradition are often stipulated in such instruments (which amounts to imprisonment of at least one year, thereby bringing the penalties within the scope of the European extradition regimes).[4]

In adopting these Framework Decisions the Council, as a rule, followed proposals by the European Commission. Several Member States supported the main objectives of these drafts, including the proposals for minimum-maximum sanctions as described above. A number of Member States, however, had difficulties with aligning the envisaged minima-

[1] European Council, 'Tampere European Council 15 and 16 October 1999 Presidency Conclusions' available online at www.europarl.europa.eu/summits/tam_en.htm, para 48.

[2] See in this regard the Commission communication of 26 July 2000 on mutual recognition of final decisions in criminal matters COM (2000) 495 final. On the validity of this approach, see (Peers 2004).

[3] Council Framework Decision 2000/383/JHA of 29 May 2000 on increasing protection by criminal penalties and other sanctions against counterfeiting in connection with the introduction of the euro [2000] OJ L140.

[4] Initially the Council of Europe's 1957 European Convention on Extradition and latterly under Council Framework Decision 2002/584/JHA of 13 June 2002 on the European arrest warrant and the surrender procedures between Member States [2002] OJ L190.

maxima with the structure and internal coherence of their national penalty tiers and frameworks (eg the proposed maxima of four, six or eight years' imprisonment do not fit into structures providing for three, five and 10 years maxima only as standard upper limits). Therefore, a need for establishing a general approach to approximation of sentences emerged.

In April 2002, on the occasion of negotiating a Framework Decision on combating the sexual exploitation of children and child pornography, the Council adopted 'Conclusions on the approach to apply regarding approximation of penalties'.[5] In these 'Conclusions' the Council stated that 'in order to allow Member States to preserve the coherence of their national penalty systems, a certain flexibility is needed when approximating criminal sanctions'. The Council agreed on the following standardised scale of four levels of criminal penalties:

> Level 1: maximum of at least between one and three years of imprisonment.
> Level 2: maximum of at least between two and five years of imprisonment.
> Level 3: maximum of at least between five and 10 years of imprisonment.
> Level 4: maximum of at least 10 years of imprisonment (cases where very serious penalties are required).

No successful attempt was undertaken to agree on upper limits for penalties (maxima-maxima) that ought not to be exceeded by national law. Not even a clause stating that a Member State, when adopting one of these four levels in internal law, should only provide for higher penalties where this is necessary in order to maintain the coherence in its national penalty system, was accepted by all Member States. The Commission did not present any proposal to that effect. The endeavours by the EU decision-making bodies in the field of harmonisation and approximation of sentences therefore give a rather one-sided picture. They show a clear tendency towards more severe sentences without any upward cap: this is not a balanced endeavour. It is one of the reasons why we cannot really speak about harmonisation. The overwhelming motivation was rather a punitive one, focused more on being 'effective' and 'dissuasive' than on being 'proportionate'. This has been the dominant attitude of the Commission, supported by some big countries, in the field of criminal law in general.

It is noteworthy in this context that this EU policy on sentencing does not follow the long-standing and balanced crime policy line developed by the Member States of the Council of Europe, notwithstanding the fact that all EU nations are also Member States of that organisation. Recommendation R (92) 17 of the Council of Europe Committee of Ministers 'concerning

[5] Council document of 25 April 2002 on the approach to apply regarding approximation of penalties 9141/2002.

consistency in sentencing' stipulates that aiming at such consistency 'should not lead to more severe sentences' and that 'sentencing practice should be subjected to critical appraisal so as to avoid undue severity'. Obviously, the EU Commission and a majority of Member States did not apply such critical appraisal in their deliberations on approximating sentences.

## B. Recent Developments

The Treaty of Lisbon, which entered into force on 1 December 2009, changed the previous legislative procedures. It integrated the former 'third pillar' (justice and home affairs) into community law and consequently extended co-decision-making of the European Parliament and the Council as well as the 'Qualified Majority Principle' within the Council to the field of criminal law.

The articles of the Treaty that deal with criminal law follow the lines developed earlier in the EU as regards the approximation of the definitions of offences and penalties as well as the principle of mutual recognition of judgments and other judicial decisions. Article 83 of the TFEU serves as the new basis for establishing 'minimum rules concerning the definition of criminal offences and sanctions in the areas of particular serious crime with a cross-border dimension'. Article 83 lists the following as such areas of crime: terrorism, trafficking in human beings and sexual exploitation of women and children, illicit drug trafficking, illicit arms trafficking, money laundering, corruption, counterfeiting of means of payment, computer crime and organised crime. The designated 'minimum rules' can be extended to other areas 'if this proves essential to ensure the effective implementation of a Union policy in an area which has been subject to harmonisation measures'—a kind of additional criminal law competence in other fields of harmonisation created by EU law.

In terms of substance these provisions do not change very much in relation to criminalisation and the approximation of sanctions. Most of the criminal offences that they cover had already been the subject of Framework Decisions before Lisbon. They may now be the subject of Directives that have a similar legal character (except that the supervisory role of the Court of the European Union in controlling implementation by the Member States has been significantly enhanced). The Stockholm Programme adopted by the European Council in 2010 is not much more concrete as to 'common definitions of criminal offences and common minimum levels of maximum sanctions'.

In 2009 (before Lisbon) the European Commission presented two proposals for new Framework Decisions on trafficking in human beings[6] and

[6] Commission Communication of 25 March 2009 on a proposal for a Council Framework Decision on combating the sexual abuse, sexual exploitation of children and child pornography, repealing Framework Decision 2004/68/JHA COM (2009) 135 final.

on the sexual exploitation of children and child pornography,[7] designed to replace the existing instruments that date from 2002[8] and 2004[9] respectively. These drafts contained new obligations to criminalise and again included minimum-maximum penalties. But the proposed minimum levels of six, 10 and 12 years' imprisonment were not in conformity with the general Council conclusions adopted in 2002, referred to above under section IIIA, which provided for four penalty levels and a certain degree of flexibility for national legislators.

The proposals for the two new Framework Decisions were transformed into draft directives and negotiated after the TFEU acquired legal force. In the meantime the Directive on human trafficking had been adopted.[10] Its Article 4 now provides for minima-maxima of five and 10 years. The 'considering' paragraph 12 even states that this was 'based on' levels 3 and 4 of the approach to the application of the approximation of penalties by the Council conclusions of 24/25 April 2002. However, it is in fact not in full conformity with those 'conclusions', since it does not allow the legislator a margin of flexibility as to those maxima (except the possibility of providing penalties even higher than the stated maxima).

The Directive on sexual exploitation and child pornography has been adopted as well.[11] The minima-maxima envisaged by the Commission have been modified, but still contain one minimum-maximum level of eight years' imprisonment (Art 4 p.3); this is not in line with the Council conclusions of 2002, although according to considering paragraph 11, those conclusions 'should be kept in mind in the light of the Lisbon Treaty'.

### C. Sanctions against Legal Entities

The EU legal instruments referred to above, as a rule, also contain an article on sanctions for legal persons (commercial companies and other entities). This article stipulates that such sanctions *shall* include 'criminal or non-criminal fines' and *may* include other sanctions. Due to the diversity of regulations on criminal or non-criminal responsibility of legal persons in

[7] Commission Communication of 25 March 2009 on a proposal for a Council Framework Decision on preventing and combating trafficking in human beings, and protecting victims, repealing framework decision 2002/629/JHA COM (2009) 136 final.

[8] Council Framework Decision 2002/629/JHA of 19 July 2002 on combating trafficking in human beings [2002] OJ L203.

[9] Council Framework Decision 2004/68/JHA of 22 December 2003 on combating the sexual exploitation of children and child pornography [2004] OJ L13.

[10] Council Directive 2011/36/EU of 5 April 2011 on preventing and combating trafficking in human beings and protecting its victims, and replacing Council Framework Decision 2002/629/JHA [2011] OJ L101.

[11] Council Directive 2011/92/EU of 13 December 2011 on combating the sexual abuse and sexual exploitation of children and child pornography, and replacing Council Framework Decision 2004/68/JHA (OJ L335).

the Member States the harmonising effect of such provisions (which in similar form can nowadays also be found in many UN and Council of Europe conventions) is extremely limited.

Nevertheless, more efforts to approximate sanctions against legal entities would seem desirable in view of the much more extended trans-border activities of commercial companies and the emphasis of the EU on the internal market. This is all the more so since the dissuasive effects of such sanctions and, even more importantly, the preventative effect of such sanctions on legal persons with established structures of responsibility and legal advisers certainly outweigh the deterrent and preventive effects of criminal sanctions on most individuals.

## IV. CONCLUSIONS

The frequently wider scope of offences within EU Framework Decisions and Directives leads to greater obligations to criminalise certain behaviour or to extend existing definitions of criminal offences. This can create specific problems in countries with a tradition of strict (restrictive) definitions of the elements of crime and which adhere to the principle of mandatory prosecution in criminal procedure and/or to a double-track structure of penal law (with a separate system of administrative penal law, or *Ordnungswidrigkeiten*). During deliberations in Council working groups, some Member States (Denmark, Sweden, Finland, the Netherlands, Germany, and Austria) often tried to limit or restrict the definition of offences, or to reduce higher minima-maxima suggested by the Commission.

The overall criminalising tendencies of EU legal instruments seem to have two root causes. First, there is an assumed necessity to make the burden of proof for law enforcement and judicial authorities less onerous and to facilitate indictments and judgments against offenders in instances where it is difficult for the prosecution to present evidence of all the elements of a crime defined in a traditionally restrictive manner. Secondly, there is a general trend to more punitiveness derived from the endeavour to step up the 'fight against crime', in particular in view of new forms of trans-border and organised crime in a region with open internal borders. This tendency is shared by politicians and policy-makers in most Member States.[12]

The punitive tendency also seems to be the main motivating factor behind the objective to approximate sanctions by providing minimum levels for maximum sanctions. It has to be admitted that, in view of the different structures of national penalty systems, hardly any kind of legislative 'sentencing approximation' other than the enactment of minima-maxima is

[12] On 'populist punitiveness' generally, see Bottoms (1995); on the pressures of trans-border crime, see Fletcher et al (2008: 11); see also Baker (2010) and in this volume.

conceivable. It is significant, however, that no real attempt has been made to provide for maximum-maximum penalties as well. So the approximation endeavours represent an 'upward' penalising and a clearly one-sided model: that of more punitiveness. In practice, the minimum-maximum approach is of extremely limited value for achieving the proclaimed objective of more 'harmony' in sentencing among Member States because, as noted in sections I and II, maximum sentencing levels are only weakly correlated with actual sentencing patterns. At the same time the minimum-maximum approach is prone to interfere with the structure and coherence of national sentencing scales. The unwanted side-effects of such rather symbolic harmonisation may outweigh the 'harmonising' value.

On the other hand, in the field of penalties against legal entities no substantial efforts to introduce an 'approximation policy' have been undertaken so far. This seems inconsistent with the overall EU emphasis on the internal market and with the increasing international attention for the responsibility of legal entities under penal law.

The European Commission obviously largely disregards the Council Conclusions of 2002 on the four levels (margins) of penalties, in particular the involved flexibility which the Council considered necessary. The Commission and policy-makers in some Member States seem to adhere to a somewhat naïve belief as to the dissuasive effect of criminal law in general and of (maximum) criminal sentences in particular. Criminological research clearly does not support this simple approach; it has demonstrated, in particular, that the clearance and prosecution rates of most offences are by far more important if one aims at deterrence of crime (see Ashworth 2010: 79; von Hirsch et al 1999).

It could be questioned whether the unbalanced belief in punitiveness and the tendency to wider criminalisation is in line with the generally accepted principle of criminal law being a measure of last resort (*ultima ratio* principle), endorsed in para 3.3.1 of the recent 'Stockholm Programme' of the European Council of Heads of State and Government.

A final thought for the reader: is the 'sentencing policy' of the EU in full conformity with Article 49.3 of the Charter of Fundamental Rights of the European Union, which stipulates that 'the severity of penalties must not be disproportionate to the criminal offence'? This proportionality principle ought to be a central guideline not only for sentencers but also for the legislators of all levels.

## REFERENCES

Ashworth A (2010) *Sentencing and Criminal Justice*, 5th edn (Cambridge, Cambridge University Press).

Baker, E (2010) 'Governing Through Crime—The Case of the European Union' *European Journal of Criminology*, 7, 187–213.

Bottoms, A (1995) 'Philosophy and Politics of Punishment and Sentencing', in C Clarkson and R Morgan (eds), *The Politics of Sentencing Reform* (Oxford, Oxford University Press).

Fletcher, M, Lööf, R and Gilmore, B (2008) *EU Criminal Law and Justice* (Cheltenham, Edward Elgar Publishing).

Frase, R (2001) 'Comparative Perspectives on Sentencing Policy and Research' in M Tonry and R Frase (eds), *Sentencing and Sanctions in Western Countries* (Oxford, Oxford University Press).

Peers, S (2004) 'Mutual Recognition and Criminal Law in the European Union: Has the Council got it Wrong?' *Common Market Law Review*, 41, 5–36.

van Zyl Smit, D and Ashworth, A (2004) 'Disproportionate Sentences as Human Rights Violations' *Modern Law Review*, 67, 541–60.

Von Hirsch, A, Bottoms, AE, Burney, E and Wikström, P-O (1999) *Criminal Deterrence and Sentence Severity: An Analysis of Recent Research* (Oxford, Hart Publishing).

## EU INSTRUMENTS AND LEGISLATION

Commission communication of 26 July 2000 on mutual recognition of final decisions in criminal matters COM(2000) 495 Final.

Commission communication of 25 March 2009 on a proposal for a council framework decision on combating the sexual abuse, sexual exploitation of children and child pornography, repealing framework decision 2004/68/JHA COM (2009) 135 final.

Commission communication of 25 March 2009 on a proposal for a council framework decision on preventing and combating trafficking in human beings, and protecting victims, repealing framework decision 2002/629/JHA COM (2009) 136 final.

Council directive 2011/36/EU of 5 April 2011 on preventing and combating trafficking in human beings and protecting its victims, and replacing Council Framework Decision 2002/629/JHA [2011] OJ L 101.

Council directive 2011/92/EU of 13 December 2011 on combating the sexual abuse and sexual exploitation of children and child pornography, and replacing Council Framework Decision 2004/68/JHA (OJ L 335).

Council document of 25 April 2002 on the approach to apply regarding approximation of penalties 9141/2002.

Council Framework Decision 2000/383/JHA of 29 May 2000 on increasing protection by criminal penalties and other sanctions against counterfeiting in connection with the introduction of the euro [2000] OJ L 140.

Council Framework Decision 2002/584/JHA of 13 June 2002 on the European arrest warrant and the surrender procedures between Member States [2002] OJ L 190.

Council Framework Decision 2002/629/JHA of 19 July 2002 on combating trafficking in human beings [2002] OJ L 203.

Council Framework Decision 2004/68/JHA of 22 December 2003 on combating the sexual exploitation of children and child pornography [2004] OJ L 13.

European Council, 'Tampere European Council 15 and 16 October 1999 Presidency Conclusions' available online at http://www.europarl.europa.eu/summits/tam_en.htm, accessed on 15 August 2012.

Part Two

# Cross-Cutting Issues

# 6

# *The Processes of Criminalisation of Migrants and the Question of the European Union as a 'Land of Immigration'**

DARIO MELOSSI

THE OVERREPRESENTATION OF migrants in the criminal justice systems of the countries that make up the EU is a well-established fact. Processes of criminalisation seem inherently to be tied to immigration policies oriented toward exclusion, given also the close connection between the lack of regular legal status and such processes. I claim, and in this chapter I shall try to show, that the question of the status of the EU as a 'land of immigration' is of paramount importance in order to understand and fight the processes of criminalisation of immigrants. Moreover, I would especially like to ask, how could the intense and complex public debate necessary in order to make the EU a 'land of immigration' take place, if there is no common, democratic European 'public sphere', no access to a genuine intra-European political debate? The absence of such a debate is closely connected to the lack of a European common sphere of social and public interaction, an issue which is in part attributable to, and in part revealed by, the lack of a common language (a lack that the wishful thinking of a small cosmopolitan European leadership will be unable to remedy).

* Elements of this chapter were presented at a Conference at the Monash University Prato Center in 2009, and at a Workshop on 'European Penology?' (22–23 July 2010) of the International Institute for the Sociology of Law, Oñati, Spain. They have also found their way into other publications such as Melossi (2012, 2013). I would like to thank the editors of this collection for their comments on a first draft of this chapter (even if they are obviously not responsible for the final outcome), and the Center for the Study of Law and Society, University of California, Berkeley, where I was a guest in the fall of 2010 and summer of 2011.

## I. THE OVERREPRESENTATION OF NON-EU CITIZENS IN PRISON

Let us proceed from what is a matter of fact: in certain parts of the EU the representation of non-EU citizens in prison is many times their share of the general population.

**Table 6.1: Overrepresentation of foreigners in EU prison systems**

| | Percent of foreigners in prison pop.[1] | Percent of foreigners/ foreigners extra-EU in general pop.[2] | Estimate of the rate of overrepresentation[3] |
|---|---|---|---|
| Austria | 45.8 | 10.5/6.57 | **4.36–6.97** |
| Belgium | 41.1 | 9.7/3.12 | **4.23–13.17** |
| Bulgaria | 1.9 | Missing | |
| Cyprus | 59.6 | 15.9/5.47 | **3.74–10.89** |
| Czech Republic | 7.3 | 4/2.71 | **1.82–2.69** |
| Denmark | 21.9 | 6/3.9 | **3.65–5.61** |
| Estonia | 39.4 | 15.9/15.08 | **2.47–2.61** |
| Finland | 10.3 | 2.9/1.85 | **3.55–5.56** |
| France | 19.2 | 5.8/3.77 | **3.31–5.09** |
| Germany | 26.3 | 8.7/5.6 | **3.02–4.69** |
| Greece | 43.9 | 8.4/6.97 | **5.22–6.29** |
| Hungary | 3.8 | 2/0.82 | **1.9–4.63** |
| Ireland | 10.8 | 8.6/1.68 | **1.25–6.42** |
| Italy | 36.9 | 7/4.95 | **5.27–7.45** |
| Latvia | 1 | 17.4/16.97 | 0.05 |
| Lithuania | 1.2 | 1.1/1.03 | **1.09–1.16** |
| Luxemburg | 69.5 | 43/5.9 | **1.61–11.77** |

*(Continued)*

[1] At 10 June 2010 (source: International Centre for Prison Studies, King's College, University of London).

[2] Percentage of foreigners/foreigners from countries outside the EU27 in the general population (on 1 January 2010; source: EUROSTAT).

[3] I divided the number in the first column by both numbers in the second column: the result is the estimate in the third column, somewhere in between the two numbers. Why is that? Because we do not have a distinction of the percentages of inmates according to whether they are simply foreigners, or foreigners from outside of the EU, information that we have instead about the general population of foreigners. Now, most inmates are from countries outside the EU so the second term of the estimate is probably more precise. There are, however, two important exceptions to such a rule of thumb: 1) the situation has changed with the admission of Romania to the EU, because the number of Romanians incarcerated in several countries is substantial, and 2) in many smaller countries, such as Belgium or Luxembourg, a substantial number of inmates come from neighbouring EU countries.

| | Percent of foreigners in prison pop. | Percent of foreigners/ foreigners extra-EU in general pop. | Estimate of the rate of overrepresentation |
|---|---|---|---|
| Malta | 40.1 | 4/2.39 | 10.02–16.77 |
| The Netherlands | 27.7 | 3.9/2.04 | 7.10–13.57 |
| Poland | 0.7 | 0.1/0.07 | 7–10 |
| Portugal | 20.2 | 4.3/3.42 | 4.69–5.90 |
| Romania | 0.7 | Missing | |
| Slovakia | 1.8 | 1.2/0.47 | 1.5–3.82 |
| Slovenia | 10.8 | 4/3.78 | 2.7–2.85 |
| Spain | 35.5 | 12.3/7.25 | 2.88–4.89 |
| Sweden | 28.7 | 6.3/3.47 | 4.55–8.27 |
| United Kingdom | 12.9[4] | 7/3.92[5] | 1.84–3.29 |
| European Union (27 countries) | 21.7 | 6.5/4.03 | 3.33–5.38 |

Analysis of this table could certainly be a research task in itself. For now, it will be enough to notice that there are *grosso modo* three groups of countries among the 27. A first group is what we could call the large, traditional immigration countries. Especially in former colonial countries, such as France or the United Kingdom, there may be naturalised citizens, often from former colonies, who are in prison because of social mechanisms not unlike those that lead to foreigners' imprisonment, but obviously they do not show up in foreigners' statistics. In Southern European countries, in contrast, what is characteristic is their high level of undocumented migrants (Calavita 2005), caused by the almost impossible task of immigrating legally, especially for reasons of work. Particularly in these countries, the criminal justice system provides the only type of institutional 'care' and 'welfare' available to 'criminal' migrants, who are almost always undocumented and therefore devoid of political or social citizenship (paradoxically, criminal migrants in prisons enjoy standards which may be higher than those endured by undocumented migrants held in ad hoc detention centres). Finally, there are Eastern European countries, where, generally speaking, there are almost no migrants and therefore no migrants in prison. As a matter of fact, these countries often have higher imprisonment rates. Many are emigrant countries, such as Poland and Romania, much as Italy might have been, for instance, until about half a century ago.[6]

[4] Data for England & Wales.
[5] Data for the UK.
[6] Compulsory transfers of sentenced prisoners to their countries of origin if they are within the EU will pose particular problems for Eastern European countries when they come into

A comparison with the United States is particularly instructive (Melossi 2013). On the one hand, the total number of people imprisoned in the United States is staggering. In contrast, the number of prisoners in Europe, especially Western Europe, is relatively limited. The US imprisonment rate is above 700 per 100,000 whereas the European average, at least in Western Europe, wavers around 100 per 100,000, and even those countries where there has been recently quite an increase, such as the UK, Spain and the Netherlands, are still below or close to 150 per 100,000 (Snacken 2010: 274). On the other hand, if one considers the *percentages* of foreigners that are part of those larger numbers, the situation reverses itself. The percentage of non-citizens in prison in the US—at least the ones counted—is probably less than the number of non-citizens in the general population. On 30 June 2010, for instance, a reported 95,977 non-citizens were held in the custody of state or federal correctional authorities. Overall, about 6 per cent of state and federal inmates at midyear 2010 were not US citizens, whereas the percentage of the population which is foreign-born in the US is about 12 per cent (an unknown percentage of whom have in the meanwhile become citizens). As we have seen, it is instead extremely high in Europe, so high in fact (as shown in Table 6.1) as to surpass even the 'disproportionality' in imprisonment in the United States in terms of ethnicity (between five and six times, for African Americans (Mauer and King 2007)).

The social mechanisms that may produce such data are the most various, from the high visibility of migrants' crime vis-à-vis the extremely low visibility of other kinds of crime ('crime in the streets' vs 'crime in the suites'!), to the specific crimes that only migrants can commit; from the public and legislative prejudice against migrants, to the discriminatory behaviour of many public institutions; from the migrants' deprivation of the fundamental right to have an efficient defence, to the impossibility of applying to migrants a host of pre- and post-trial benefits that keep natives out of prison but that railroad foreigners into detention. And of course this without even mentioning the basic issue of the social, economic, cultural and legal condition of disadvantage from which many migrants start! In any case, the immigrant group that is by far the most criminalised in Europe, and especially in Southern Europe, is the undocumented migrant; in the case of minors, the so-called 'unaccompanied minor'.[7]

force in December 2012: Poland has negotiated a five-year exception, but this rule will eventually hit it too, and will have a big impact in others, such as Lithuania, immediately.

[7] A number of studies have shown that between 70 and 80 per cent of the migrants who are arrested, reported, convicted or detained in Italy are 'undocumented'.

## II. MIGRATION AND PROCESSES OF CRIMINALISATION

This is however no earth-shattering news to the expert! Sociologists and criminologists have been interested in the relationship between immigration and various so-called 'social pathologies' (Lemert 1951), at least since the conjunction of mass migration with the emergence of their disciplines in North America at the beginning of the twentieth century. Perhaps also today in Italy, and in Europe more generally, an intellectual and political development might unfold that would be familiar to other countries and historical periods characterised by mass migrations. In the United States, after the initial nativist moral panic about immigration, the Chicago School of Sociology eventually produced a more balanced and 'normalised' view of the relationship between migration processes and deviance (Park 1928; Park et al 1925; Shaw and McKay 1942), according to which migrants' criminal behaviour was connected to societal disorganisation. This was not specific to immigrant groups but had to do with the very processes of migration, assimilation and integration into American society. The Chicago School authors were also quick to point out that generally 'first generation' migrants tended to reproduce the criminal habits of their society of origin, whereas second generations slowly assumed the levels and types of criminality typical of the environment where they found themselves. In fact, public concern began to shift toward the generations successive to the original immigrants: their integration, and their possible contribution to phenomena of deviance and crime.

More recently, using data on US imprisonment organised by place of birth, Rumbaut et al (2006: 71) showed that the rates of incarcerated foreign-born males of *all* American ethnic groups are systematically lower than the incarcerated US-born (second-generation or later) males in each group. Likewise, Robert Sampson (2006), following in the footsteps of the Chicagoan tradition, noted that first generations are in a sense 'protected', by their relationships with their original families, within tried and true 'ethnic niches', which separate the migrant youth from the more obviously criminogenic currents of the context in which they find themselves. Their cultures of origin are often crime-averse, and this is especially the case within so-called 'ethnic enclaves' (Stowell et al 2009; Martinez and Valenzuela 2006; Stowell 2007). However, when their offspring integrate within American society, one of the unfortunate consequences of the integration process is their participation in cultures that are characterised by a higher level of crime and violence. In fact, as the Chicago classic tradition teaches us, once they exit their ethnic enclaves, social controls decrease because of the new anonymity and heterogeneity.

It is not that surprising if immigrants try their best to avoid what may be socially perceived as deviant or criminal behaviour. After all, migrants have much more to lose than so-called natives. Generally serious criminal convictions carry with them the danger of the additional sanction of deportation and, beyond that, there is always around the migrant, as Sayad suggested (2004), a 'double suspicion'. 'Punishment' is to the foreigner more serious than to the native and it is reasonable for migrants to be—contrary to stereotype—hyperconformists. This is even more the case once they have established themselves in their new social settings. Americans of ethnic origins felt, after a few generations, more 'American' than the average member of the population. They also reached integration goals, which in terms of wealth and social prestige (Jenks 1983), are higher.

European criminological discourse about migration took off in the middle of the twentieth century, between the 1950s and 1960s. Public discussion about migration flows from Southern and Eastern Europe toward the West and the North of Europe followed a roughly similar pattern (Ferracuti 1968). The question of 'migration and crime' was however not at the centre of attention, especially in Southern Europe, until the 1990s (Tonry 1997; Haen Marshall 1997). Also Southern Europe, after the economic crisis of the early 1970s linked to so-called 'oil crisis' and the transition from a 'Fordist' to a 'post-Fordist' type of economy, became a place of attraction for migratory in-flows from other continents (Calavita 2005; De Giorgi 2006).

One of the most specific characteristics of the immigration situation in Italy today—and that could be extended to most parts of Western Europe—appears to me to be the peculiar irrationality of immigration laws, that seem to have had a distinct 'criminogenic' effect. Here too, the familiar complaint was raised that 'our data undoubtedly show that foreigners in our country commit a disproportionate amount of crimes relative to their number' (Barbagli 2008: 104). The Caritas (2009) organisation has demonstrated, however, that in Italy, foreigners' contribution to crime rates—measured by reports to the police—is very close to the rate of Italians, especially if one takes into consideration the demographic profile of the two groups. If, by immigrants, one therefore means *documented* immigrants, in Italy the preoccupation with their contribution to crime is certainly exaggerated. And as to the *undocumented* ones, one should remember that the connection to be established is between deviant behaviour and the *condition* of lack of documents, not some kind of 'personal quality' of undocumented foreigners. Generally speaking, undocumented foreigners are people who entered legally (for instance on a tourist visa) or who acquired the proper documents for work, but subsequently lost the right to stay—a particularly harsh problem in the current situation of economic crisis, given that work is one of the premises for being able to maintain the permit to stay legally in the country (that is, also in the EU).

The problem is of course that the condition of being without documents places the foreign citizen within a set of restrictions that increase all the risk factors for criminal behaviour enormously (besides making them more visible to official agencies of control). In other words, the problem of the relationship between the documented status and the risk of deviant behaviour is first of all a legislative and more generally normative one which concerns Italy, as well as many other countries members of the EU, because of the cumbersome nature of entry procedures. Unskilled labour is the kind of labour de facto in demand and, especially in such cases, until the beginning of the economic crisis, those who aspired to come and work in Europe tried to enter by any means possible with the idea that subsequently they would get a regular permit to stay. The hunger for labour of European societies was such that, sooner or later, some kind of individual or collective amnesty provision would be enacted—thereby recognising the rational, albeit unlawful, strategy of the migrants—not to mention the importance of their contribution to the welfare of the country.[8] However, this situation creates a sort of 'gap' in the migrant's biography, when he or she has no chance to work legally. It therefore makes it more likely that they will become involved in a variety of illegal or downright criminal 'occupations'.

The nature of the problems has been heavily affected by the recent economic crisis, which has much increased migrants' unemployment. A report by the European Commission (2009) to the European Parliament showed that the rate of unemployment for third-country (documented) nationals had gone from 13.6% in 2008 to 18.9% in 2009 (8.4% for nationals) in the EU 27. The consequence has been that:

> overall immigration to developed countries has slowed sharply as a result of the economic crisis, bringing to a virtual halt the rapid growth in foreign-born populations over the past three decades. In the two years since the onset of the global economic crisis, temporary workers flows, business migration, and 'unregulated' flows such as illegal immigration and free movement within certain parts of the EU have experienced the largest decreases.
>
> (Papademetriou et al 2010: 1.)

In the case of Italy, this is probably connected also to the attitude of hostility which has been created deliberately by previous governments in both its more and less official aspects. For instance, according to the Italian Research Institute ISMU (2010), there has been a definite slowdown of new immigrant entries into Italy in 2010: about 100,000 fewer than in 2007, the last pre-crisis year (a fall of 40 per cent). It is interesting to note that the percentage of foreigners in prison has also declined slightly in Italy, by 2.6 per cent between 2010 and 2012.[9]

[8] Routinely, Italian studies have shown that at least half of the regular, documented male immigrants bore witness to the fact that they found themselves without documentation for a period, whereas most women came to Italy for family reunifications at the request of those very immigrants (Melossi 1999; Ambrosini 2009).

[9] ISMU, newsletter of 8 March 2012.

Exactly as happened in the US in the 1920s, first with the introduction of admission quotas and then especially with the great depression of 1929, the changed scenario may be conducive to a shift of attention from first generations of migrants coming into the country to the integration of so-called 'second generations', the children of immigrants. To the traditional North American distinction between 'first' and 'second' immigrant generations is added, in Europe and especially in Southern Europe, a tripartite distinction between 'undocumented' migrants, first-generation migrants and second-generation migrants. Whereas in Europe undocumented migrants (and their corresponding category among minors, 'unaccompanied minors') seem to suffer the bulk of the criminalisation process, the relationship between first and second generations is similar to that in the US, as far as criminalisation processes are concerned.

## III. THE IMPORTANCE OF LEGAL STATUS

As already noted, starting in the 1980s, Italy and Spain also became receiving countries, at least until 2008. In those years, Italian and Spanish immigration laws seemed to 'welcome' immigrants exclusively as workers (Calavita 2005). However, their legal status is usually contingent on temporary work permits that are difficult to get because of very complex procedures. Permanent residence is quite hard to obtain, and the result is that immigrants are 'useful' as 'labour power', as they are willing, or compelled, to work, under conditions and for wages that are part of a substantially 'post-Fordist' setting of social and economic circumstances. Racialisation and criminalisation are central elements of this process of immigrants' marginalisation.

A very important aspect of all this is how legal status is proven (Melossi 2013). Even when we consider how many foreigners are in US prisons, it is really uncertain what the sources of data are. The information about foreigners in American prisons seems in fact to be in part derived from self-reporting (Hickman and Suttorp 2008), in part from counting only foreigners in ICE (US Immigration and Customs Enforcement) institutions, and in part—in the most accurate cases—foreign-born inmates (Guerino et al 2011).

However, the issue of how legal status is proven is paramount to processes of criminalisation. Comparing the European and the American situations, one element, which is not often considered in American literature on migration and crime, is the issue of the possession by recent immigrants of legal documentation that enables them to work. Work is an essential element of integration, and in many European countries, the possession of legal documents is a prerequisite for work. For example, in Italy today, as we have seen, the process of criminalisation is usually related not so much to the status of immigrant as to the status of 'undocumented' immigrant. In contrast, it may be easier for a foreign citizen to integrate him- or herself in the US because of the lack of a national identity document, which may facilitate hiring based on a false assumption of citizenship, and therefore increase the likelihood of employment and 'making an honest living'. Such a false assumption may extend even to those who find themselves in detention. I would like to point out, in other words, what would seem like a paradox: the greater ease with which undocumented migrants may deceive potential employers in the US might protect them—and American society!—from the risk of crime, whereas the European obsession with discovering migrant crime may increase the likelihood of its occurrence. This possibility is intensified by the fact that, in many European countries, it is the business of ordinary police forces to control and check on strangers. As yet, this is something that is not as pervasive in the US, although this is precisely what the recently passed Arizona law would encourage (something, however, that is not uncontested if it is true that, in May 2010, the City Council of Los Angeles decided to boycott the state of Arizona because of its immigration bill—given that in this city the police behaviour called for in the new Arizona law[10] would indeed be highly problematic!).

In continental Europe, especially in the nineteenth century, strangers, together with prostitutes and vagrants, were the original subjects of police prevention powers and it is ingrained in much legislation, which reflects a certain part of public opinion, that the stranger is dangerous by definition. The tradition of the continental European police state is quite important here. The persistence of this tradition in many of the constituent countries of the EU is a real challenge to the construction of the EU—not only to its immigration policy but to the Union itself. That kind of statist tradition has to be overcome and set aside if we need to have an actually working EU and, even more so, sensible immigration policies. Laws of immigration are nowadays quite restrictive in Europe, and in Italy more specifically, because they are aimed at suppressing 'unlawful' immigration, rather than at *regulating* immigration: the resources destined to combating illegal entries are very much greater than those targeted at immigration services. Therefore, in a situation in which great parts of Europe, and specifically Italy, at least before the current economic crisis, did not have sufficient labour to match demand, migrants came to Europe undocumented and notwithstanding the restrictions on them. They have been waiting for the (at least in the pre-crisis era) unavoidable amnesty provision in order to be 'regularised'

[10] Which would allow among other things the possibility of ordinary local police enquiring about the citizenship status of people stopped, an aspect of the Arizona law the constitutionality of which was affirmed by the US Supreme Court on 25 June 2012 (other aspects of the law were struck down).

(Calavita 2005). In between, a dangerous period of lack of documentation has ensued, fraught with the necessity for all sorts of illegalities, a true situation—as has been noted by Valeria Ferraris (2009)—of 'institutionalised irregularity'.

In other words, the easier the processes of legal integration in the host society (residency and naturalisation), the lower the criminalisation: conversely, the harder the process of legal inclusion, the higher the numbers of criminalised foreigners. In a comparative study, James Lynch and Rita Simon (1999) pointed out that 'immigrant nations', such as the US, Canada and Australia, have relatively open immigration policies and high proportions of foreign-born resident populations. Germany[11] and Japan ('non-traditional immigrant nations') have restrictive immigration policies, strict policies for the control of resident aliens, and restrictive naturalisation policies. France and the United Kingdom have restrictive admission policies based on nationality and origin, but naturalisation policies are relatively open. Comparing the incarceration rates, the pattern that emerges across the seven nations is that overall, immigrants in traditional immigrant receiving countries have lower criminalisation rates than those in non-traditional immigrant nations. The apparent relationship between the inclusiveness of immigration policies and the criminal involvement of aliens suggests that the more restrictive the policy, the greater the criminalisation of foreigners.

## IV. EUROPE, A 'LAND OF IMMIGRATION'

Immigration is an eminently European, and specifically EU, issue. As already pointed out, there is a paradox at work here, because policies of restriction, which are invoked on the ground also of defending natives from migrants' crime, end up creating the preconditions for increased criminalisation of migrants (both harsher social reaction but also at the same time a higher level of criminal behaviour by the migrants). The difficulties with treating the whole issue of migration seriously is but one (not secondary) aspect, I believe, of the more general difficulty that the EU has with policies about matters of common import, that go deeply into the cultural spheres of the various European countries and that are at this point impossible to treat as mere 'international' issues. However, the lack of a genuine European public sphere makes this kind of public conversation very unlikely.

[11] At least until 1998, when the new red-green government proclaimed aloud that *Deutschland ist ein Einwanderungsland!* 'Germany is an immigration land!' (Monte 2002).

At the same time, it also seems to me that, beyond this overall difficulty, we are facing a more specific 'socio-criminological difficulty'. This has to do with a style of criminological thinking that has gone back to a purely ancillary vision of the discipline and that completely ignores the wisdom of the 1960s sociology of deviance, which showed that one of the (unintended?) results of greater repression is, at least in part, more intense and committed criminal behaviour. Such 'criminological difficulty' would not have such a devastating effect, however, were it not for an utter lack of ideas, conceptions and imagination on the issue of immigration. Whereas recent developments in the law of the EU have supposedly 'communitarised' the matter of immigration, from the Treaty of Amsterdam (1999) all the way to the most recent 'Stockholm Programme', such developments—within the rather depressing status of the whole European enterprise lately—have by and large remained on paper, with the various national governments bickering bitterly among themselves about the fundamentals of the immigration phenomenon. The need for immigrants, to counter Europe's very low level of demographic reproduction, has been consistently underestimated, compelling would-be migrants to try and come undocumented or often under the guise of asylum-seekers, and thus exposing themselves and their families to the risk of being criminalised in one way or another.

It is quite well-known that the political framework that has caused such incredibly restrictive and myopic policies in more or less all European countries, jealously guards its own competence on the subject of immigration and is quite forgetful of the communitarisation of the matter! Immigration as a scapegoat, a kind of ball thrown back and forth between fast-rising extreme right groups, which have made xenophobia and racism their *raisons d'être*, and the moderate majorities of centre-right and centre-left, which exploit such dangerous issues for opportunistic electoral gain, has become one of the mainstays of European politics. This has of course been of assistance to all kinds of marginal or downright criminal economic enterprises, which have found in the provision of cheap undocumented immigrant labour their hope of surviving in a market where they would otherwise have had no hope whatsoever.

The alternative to all of this would be to move towards the basic and frank recognition of Europe as a 'land of immigration'. The historical acceptance by the new German government in 1998 of Germany as an *Einwanderungsland* should be applied to the rest of Europe: *Europa ist ein Einwanderungsland*! Such a decision would however imply the need for some clear concept of what 'Europe', and more specifically the EU, is, and what it stands for. It would also imply a debate about the issue, and of the procedural channels necessary to make such a debate happen. The question of migration in Europe, with all those other questions to which it is usually, rightly or wrongly, connected, such as those of security and crime, is prima facie the kind of issue that cannot be discussed (only) in the very many languages that characterise Europe today as a political entity—because the problem is transnational, and similarly transnational are the decisions and the policies to be made and implemented. To be shy about such matters simply means to give in to what is going on in many European countries today, where issues such as that of migration are not longer discussed in rational terms and are often the object of a localistic and para-Fascist jargon.

## V. DEMOCRACY AND SOCIAL CONTROL IN THE EU

I believe that the very possibility of such a debate is one and the same thing as the very possibility of the existence of an EU! The making of the EU began exactly at the time when communicative action had installed itself at the centre of the construction of social order and cohesion, in the first half of the 'American century', when social sciences discovered that the very foundations of social order lay in linguistic and symbolic interaction. Questions of 'social control' had to have precedence, therefore, for the very sake of social order, over questions of 'State' (Melossi 1990; 2005). In the US, however, the fundamental presupposition for this communicative action was the existence of a common language. It is certainly true that multilingual political communities have existed and do exist! But these are either very small (Switzerland), or characterised by what is clearly a majority language and always on the brink of secession (Canada) or, in the past, empires rather than democracies (the classic example being the Hapsburg Empire). The crucial issue seems to be, in this respect, the very question of communication and language, a question that is strictly linked with the political weakness of the whole construction.

In the German Federal Constitutional Court's 1993 decision about the constitutionality of the Maastricht Treaty (Wegen and Kuner 1994), the Court declared 'admissible' but not 'well-founded' the complaint about the 'diminution of democracy' that the transformation envisioned in the Maastricht treaty would have brought about for the citizens of the German Federal Republic. The argument centred around the concept of 'living democracy', the idea, that is, that democracy cannot be conceived only as a formal requirement but that it has to be lived and legitimated by ongoing citizen participation. According to the argument of the Court as developed by the German legal theorist, Dieter Grimm—who was a member of the Court—the very substance of democracy, if not its form, is based in the existence of certain minimal conditions of 'pluralism, internal representativity, freedom and capacity for compromise of the intermediate area of parties, associations, citizens' movements and communication media'

(Grimm 1995: 293; see also Melossi 2005).[12] Now, it is quite apparent that in Europe, today as in 1993, there is no European system of political parties, there are no European social movements (or perhaps we could say, they are only now starting to emerge; we shall come back to this crucial point) and there are of course no European mass media. There is therefore no European public sphere, and no 'European democracy' would then appear to be possible. Grimm then goes on to trace the root cause of such a situation to the absence of a common European language, because even the only language that could aspire to play such a role, English, in most European countries is functionally spoken by very small groups of citizens, especially in Southern Europe.

The problem pointed out by Grimm here is the lack of a collective identity constituted through a 'capacity for transnational discourse' (Grimm 1995: 297). This is a *structural* weakness of the EU. That does not mean—as it has been unfortunately misunderstood (Habermas 1995, 1998)—that such a weakness would be caused by the absence of some kind of traditional foundation, a *Volksgemeinschaft* to be found in the past. On the contrary, I believe a 'capacity for transnational discourse' would imply a vision of Europe grounded in the future, in a project, in a 'new Europe' created in the same way in which European colonists created a 'New World' in America. Such a vision could only ground itself in the existence of a vibrant and effective European public sphere. In particular, it seems to me important to realise that the process of construction of a democratic political will has to unfold at the very level of the public which is interested in that will formation. The 'democratic deficit' is therefore not simply an institutional phenomenon, which concerns the limited powers of the European Parliament, but is a deficit of the public sphere and of the formation of political will—an argument that cannot simply be counteracted by the usual and cynical assertion that we simply need a European democratic process that takes place in the same way and to the same extent as the process within nation states, where, 'of course', elites are those who conduct the conversation! Such a position—leaving aside the question of its desirability—is a kind of argument that might have been put forward in the second half of the nineteenth century. On the contrary, the need for the kind of conversation that is deeply grounded among the larger masses, especially for what concerns the fundamental decisions of a European political community, of a European *polity*, is absolutely essential to a theory of democracy. In fact, the construction of unified and central standpoints, able to overcome the tendency to fragmentation and drift, was the way in which the problem of social control had been framed in North America at the beginning of the twentieth

[12] The German Constitutional Court eventually 'saved' the constitutionality of the Maastricht Treaty because the want of democratic participation at the European level was seen as somehow compensated by the residual democratic life in the Member States.

century—when the very concept of 'social control' emerged (Melossi 1990). A few years before, however, Durkheim had written memorably on the democratic state as a 'strong' state, better able than any other political form to warrant an effective communication channel between political elites and the masses (Durkheim 1958: 86–96). The role of the elites is to help establish those channels, those communication processes, that are able to organise and coordinate 'the public'. In other words, what happens today within the sundry national publics—i.e. constituted within *one* (or one *dominant*) language—shall happen tomorrow within a transnational conversation. The need of a modern democratic society to involve and mobilise its masses will be satisfied only through such a process. If we can ascertain the need for a European public that speaks the same language, from a perspective of social control by the elites, the need to articulate the standpoint of masses that wish to question their role as passive objects of elites' manipulation will be even stronger. It is quite clear in my view that such masses will be absolutely powerless and ineffective if they are not able to locate themselves at the same level of discourse as the elites.[13]

Certainly, the question of 'elites' is a vexed one, for the actual lived democratic life as well as for social scientists. And elites are not all the same. It seems to me therefore that, within a process of constituting this new political entity, the EU, there is a plurality of political, cultural, legal 'elites', vying for their particular visions and their particular sets of interests and values. So that these elites—no matter their stance—may be effective, though, it is necessary for them to be able to concur on creating a common European discourse. Otherwise, they cannot play their specific role, which consists of developing those vocabularies that become common motives for action among the great masses of people. Their function would then remain at the level of good intentions, and we know where good intentions are usually said to lead. Cosmopolitanism (Beck and Sznaider 2006; Hudson 2008) is very fine but, if it does not have legs on which to walk, it is empty ideology, and may even be counterproductive by eliciting a dangerous backlash. The question is therefore not whether elitism is good or bad, the problem is that, insofar as it is elitism, it is quite ineffective!

There have been elites which have fulfilled a very important role by developing, promoting and defending a human rights agenda for Europe (van Zyl Smit and Snacken 2009). The usual justifications of elite processes, that they are sometimes necessary in view of the complexity of a policy issue (such as punishment or migration), the linguistic and other barriers, or even

[13] Trying to shift the whole question toward a problem of 'simple' 'translation' will not help. Habermas, for instance, tries, surprisingly, to underplay this issue (Habermas 2001: 19). Neil Walker (2003) discusses it in the context of the 'translation' from national to supranational constitutional frameworks. On the 'cultural embeddedness' of language and particularly of social control language see Melossi (2001).

a lack of interest from the general public, are however exactly the problem! The general public is in fact interested, instead, by the jingoistic and localistic vernacular jargon of right-wing political groupings, whether particularistic, pseudo-secessionist political enterprises, or neo-Fascist formations. The problem is that the position of enlightened elites hitherto seems to have been almost one of hoping that the general public does not notice them, when they proclaim the importance of a European Constitution or when they defend the rights of immigrants or detainees. They prefer to talk to politicians who are at the top. This may perhaps have worked when Europe was a distant concept, that did not reach into the daily lives of individuals and families of 27 countries. No longer is this so. This argument is after all very similar to the argument—advanced by many sociologists of punishment—that one of the reasons why imprisonment rates are so high in the US and quite low in (most) European countries is because generally in Europe the matter of punishment is managed by bureaucratic governmental institutions—even when of a judicial nature. It is claimed that such bureaucratic bodies are (more) immune to the nefarious populism that infests all levels of political and judicial decision-making in the United States, where public prosecutors and even judges can be elected or at least electorally removed from their posts. Europe would enjoy an enlightened elitism, in other words.

At the same time, there would not be anything mechanical in the idea that a transnational conversation, a modern democratic society based in the involvement and mobilisation of its masses, would lead to the EU becoming a 'land of immigration'. This would have to be the hoped-for result of political struggle. It would be within that struggle that the goal might be achieved—exactly as happened with the creation of many nation states in the nineteenth century, starting with Italy and Germany, when the development of a national consciousness (and later on of a *class* national consciousness) was the result of the emergence of social movements within which a new oppositional and transformative language was being created. The fundamental issue, therefore, in order to tackle head-on the conundrum of the creation of a European 'public sphere', seems to turn into the question of a *constituent process*, a process that goes together with the formation of a common language and of a common sphere of public interaction. We could even state, in Durkheimian fashion, that the coming into being of such a common language may be taken to be an 'indicator' of the real, social, 'thick' existence of a European Constitution.

## VI. BORDER 'SECURITY' IN FORTRESS EUROPE

Many years ago, the sociologist Kai Erikson (1966), in reconstructing the waywardness of seventeenth-century Massachusetts Puritans, put forward an interesting idea, according to which, through the extended public discussion of crucial instances of deviance, communities converse within themselves, about their identity and where they want to go. Likewise, I would submit that, through this crucial issue of immigration, we Europeans have been conversing for some time now about ourselves, who we are, and where we want to go. The talk about immigrants' criminal and cultural deviance, with which European mass-media are replete, might therefore be considered as an arena in which we Europeans debate the existence, nature and essential characteristics of a European identity that appears to be very problematic indeed.

Unfortunately, if we consider the reality of today's *European* policies of migration and border control, we seem to be quite far away from the ideal of Europe, and the EU, as a 'land of immigration'. Katja Franko Aas (2011) has recently explored the nature of surveillance and crime control in connection with the new reality of global governance. In the EU the coupling of surveillance and crime control has increasingly played a role in constructing a particular type of globally divided polity. This has connected with a deep transformation in our notions of citizenship. As in a new version of the old Greek democracy, the category of citizenship is fragmented into an array of figures which go from the 'bona fide global citizen'—as Aas calls her—to the regular immigrant, to the undocumented 'other', a fragmentation that the traditional liberal language of citizenship has a hard time accounting for.

As I mentioned, most of our efforts in organising the area of 'freedom, liberty and justice' seem to have gone into a ceaseless effort to patrol the external borders, that duplicates, at the European level, what national governments have already been doing—something which has also brought about forms of competition between the newborn European policing efforts and the more entrenched national policies, squabbles which would have been almost ludicrous, were it not for their impact on the lives of thousands and thousands of would-be immigrants. This for instance happened in the sort of competition between Frontex (see below) and the separate bilateral Italian-Libyan efforts in patrolling the Mediterranean Sea, which may have been one of the reasons for some of the misunderstandings between Italy and the rest of Europe in the 'crisis' of 2011, when the flow of migrants landing on Italian shores in Lampedusa increased sharply and suddenly in the first few months of 2011 (see Giuseppe Campesi's analysis (2011) of the way in which the Euro-Mediterranean 'border-control regime' has been reacting to the so-called 'Arab Spring').

Indeed, reading the official definition of 'the roles and responsibilities' of Frontex from the official site,[14] one would think that it does indeed make sense to talk of a 'Fortress Europe':

> Schengen countries are obliged to deploy sufficient staff and resources to ensure a 'high and uniform level of control' at the external borders of the Schengen area. They must also ensure that border guards are properly trained. EU and Schengen

[14] http://frontex.europa.eu/operations/roles-and-responsibilities.

> Associated Countries also assist each other with the effective application of border controls via operational cooperation, which is coordinated by the EU agency Frontex. Its main task is to augment and to add value to, border control activities of the Member States. Thus the agency is also mandated to assist EU countries in raising and harmonizing border management standards with the aim of combating cross-border crime while making legitimate passage across the external border of the EU faster and easier.

A further glance at the site will show that 'irregular migration' is seen as a very large part indeed of that 'cross-border crime'. These policies seem today to have a broad political support in Europe—even if there are increasing signs, especially in Southern Europe, that the rising preoccupations with economic difficulties are pushing the question of immigration (and the related issue of crime) into second place (for instance, according to the European Report on Security coordinated by Italian sociologist Ilvo Diamanti (2012)). At the same time, it should also be made clear that the right-wing groups, which are militantly against immigrants and more inclusive immigration policies, are as vehemently opposed to the EU. And in all public opinion polls the overlapping of right-wing political alignment and enmity against both immigration and the process of 'Europeanisation' (so to speak), is quite consistent.

The fact of the matter is that there are a number of concepts of Europe. The idea and the type of policies, which are often expressed with the moniker 'Fortress Europe', belong within nationalist groupings, in each European country. Such groupings, by referring to a restrictive policy that discriminates against the immigrants and by invoking some kind of 'European' tradition, often based on religion and race, in support of it, try to balance their hatred for migration and the political difficulty (which is however diminishing very fast) of asking for downright withdrawal from the EU. In other words, what I am suggesting is a true divorce from a traditionalist concept of 'Europe'—a concept that for many centuries has belonged together with economic exploitation, racism and colonialism—and the idea instead of a specific political entity, the EU, as something to be built together, by the European peoples and immigrants, based on premises which are indeed the opposite of those of the 'European tradition'. Europe is one thing, the EU another. I believe that the moniker 'Fortress Europe' is justified only if the former takes over the process of building the latter. But this is a matter for political and cultural struggle; it is in no way something that should be taken for granted. Europeans cannot really converse among themselves about the question of immigration without building a common house of language and culture, able to sustain the public debate that would be needed. The question of a more rational and humane approach to the issue of immigration in Europe is therefore strictly intertwined with the process of making the EU itself. Immigrants are indeed those who have not only the highest stake but also the greatest ability to be part of the process and, at the same time, of the debate necessary to make it unfold.

## REFERENCES

Aas, KF (2011) '"Crimmigrant" bodies and bona fide travelers: Surveillance, citizenship and global governance' *Theoretical Criminology*, 15, 331–46.

Ambrosini, M (2009) 'L'ennesima ultima sanatoria', in www.lavoce.info, 1 September 2009, www.lavoce.info/articoli/pagina1001254.html.

Barbagli, M (2008) *Immigrazione e sicurezza in Italia* (Bologna, il Mulino).

Beck, U and Sznaider, N (2006) 'Unpacking Cosmopolitanism for the Social Sciences: A Research Agenda' *British Journal of Sociology*, 57, 1–23.

Calavita, K (2005) *Immigrants at the Margins: Law, Race, and Exclusion in Southern Europe* (New York, Cambridge University Press).

Campesi, G (2011) 'The Arab Spring and the Crisis of the European Border Regime: Manufacturing Emergency in the Lampedusa Crisis' EUI Working Paper, RSCAS 2011/59. Available online at http://cadmus.eui.eu/handle/1814/19375.

CARITAS/Migrantes, Redattore Sociale (2009) 'La criminalità degli immigrati: dati, interpretazioni, pregiudizi', in Agenzia Redattore Sociale, *Guida per l'informazione sociale. Edizione 2010* (Capodarco di Fermo, Redattore Sociale).

De Giorgi, A (2006) *Re-Thinking the Political Economy of Punishment: Perspectives on Post-Fordism and Penal Politics* (Aldershot, Ashgate).

Diamanti, I (ed) (2012) *L'insicurezza sociale ed economica in Italia e in Europa: Significati, immagine e realtà* (Pavia, Fondazione Unipolis, Bologna and Osservatorio di Pavia).

Durkheim, E (1958) *Professional Ethics and Civic Morals* (Glencoe, Free Press).

Erikson, K (1966) *Wayward Puritans* (New York, John Wiley).

European Commission (2009) *Report from the Commission to the European Parliament and the Council: First Annual Report on Immigration and Asylum* (SEC (2010) 535).

Ferracuti, F (1968) 'European Migration and Crime' in ME Wolfgang (ed), *Crime and Culture: Essays in Honor of Thorsten Sellin* (New York, Wiley).

Ferraris, V (2009) 'Migrants' Offside Trap: A Strategy for Dealing with Misleading Rules and a Hostile Playing Field' in J Shapland and P Ponsaers (eds), *The Informal Economy and Connections with Organized Crime: The Impact of National Social and Economic Policies* (The Hague, Boom Legal Publishers).

Grimm, D (1995) 'Does Europe Need A Constitution?' *European Law Journal*, 1, 282–302.

Guerino, P, Harrison, PM and Sabol, WJ (2011) *Prisoners in 2010. Bulletin of December 2011*, Bureau of Justice Statistics, Office of Justice Programs (Washington DC, US Department of Justice).

Habermas, J (1995) 'Comment on the Paper by Dieter Grimm: "Does Europe Need a Constitution?"' *European Law Journal*, 1, 303–07.

—— (1998) 'On the Relation between the Nation, Rule of Law, and Democracy' in J Habermas, *The Inclusion of the Other* (Cambridge, MA, MIT Press).

—— (2001) 'Why Europe Needs a Constitution' *New Left Review*, 11, 5–26.

Haen Marshall, I (ed) (1997) *Minorities, Migrants, and Crime* (London, Sage).

Hickman, LJ and Suttorp, MJ (2008) 'Are Deportable Aliens a Unique Threat to Public Safety? Comparing the Recidivism of Deportable and Nondeportable Aliens' *Criminology & Public Policy*, 7, 59–82.

Hudson, B (2008) 'Difference, Diversity and Criminology: The Cosmopolitan Vision' Theoretical Criminology, 12, 275–92.
ISMU (2010) *16th Report on Migrations* (from *La Repubblica*, 13 December 2010).
Jencks, C (1983) 'Discrimination and Thomas Sowell' *The New York Review of Books*, 3 March.
Lemert, EM (1951) *Social Pathology: A Systematic Approach to the Theory of Sociopathic Behavior* (New York, McGraw-Hill).
Lynch, JP and Simon, RJ (1999) 'A Comparative Assessment of Criminal Involvement Among Immigrants and Natives Across Seven Nations' *International Criminal Justice Review*, 9, 1–17.
Martinez, R Jr and Valenzuela, A Jr (eds) (2006) *Immigration and Crime: Race, Ethnicity and Violence* (New York, New York University Press).
Mauer, M and King, RS (2007) *Uneven Justice: State Rates of Incarceration By Race* (Washington DC, The Sentencing Project).
Melossi, D (1990) *The State of Social Control: A Sociological Study of Concepts of State and Social Control in the Making of Democracy* (Cambridge, Polity Press).
—— (ed) (1999) *Multiculturalismo e sicurezza in Emilia-Romagna: prima parte* (Emilia-Romagna, Progetto Città Sicure).
—— (2001) 'The Cultural Embeddedness of Social Control: Reflections on the Comparison of Italian and North-American Cultures Concerning Punishment' *Theoretical Criminology*, 5, 403–24.
—— (2005) 'Security, Social Control, Democracy and Migration within the "Constitution" of the EU' *European Law Journal*, 11, 5–21.
—— (2013) 'Punishment and Migration between Europe and the United States: A Transnational "Less Eligibility"?' in J Simon and R Sparks (eds), *Handbook of Punishment and Society* (London, Sage).
—— (2012) 'The Processes of Criminalization of Migrants and the Borders of "Fortress Europe"', in J McCullock and S Pickering (eds), *Borders and Crime: Pre-Crime, Mobility and Serious Harm in an Age of Globalization* (Basingstoke, Palgrave Macmillan).
Monte, M (2002) 'Le politiche di immigrazione in Germania: la criminalità degli immigrati di II e III generazione.' Thesis in Criminology, Faculty of Law, University of Bologna, Academic Year 2001–2002.
Papademetriou, DG, Sumption, M and Terrazas, A with Burkert, C, Loyal, S and Ferreo-Turrion, R (2010) *Migration and Immigrants, Two Years after the Financial Collapse: Where Do We Stand?* (Washington, DC, Migration Policy Institute).
Park, RE (1928) 'Human Migration and the Marginal Man' in RE Park, *On Social Control and Collective Behaviour* (Chicago, University of Chicago Press).
—— Burgess, EW and McKenzie, RD (1925) *The City* (Chicago, University of Chicago Press).
Rumbaut, RG, Gonzales, RG, Komaie, G, Morgan, CV and Tafoya-Estrada, R (2006) 'Immigration and Incarceration. Patterns and Predictors of Imprisonment among First- and Second-Generation Young Adults', in R Martinez Jr and A Valenzuela Jr (eds), *Immigration and Crime: Race, Ethnicity and Violence* (New York, New York University Press).
Sampson, R (2006) 'Open Doors Don't Invite Criminals' *New York Times*, March 11.

Sayad, A (2004) *The Suffering of the Immigrant* (Cambridge, Polity Press).
Shaw, C and McKay, HD (1942) *Juvenile Delinquency and Urban Areas* (Chicago, University of Chicago Press).
Snacken, S (2010) 'Resisting Punitiveness in Europe?' *Theoretical Criminology*, 14, 273–92.
Stowell, JI (2007) *Immigration and Crime: Considering the Direct and Indirect Effects of Immigration on Violent Criminal Behavior* (New York, LFB Scholarly Press).
Stowell, JI, Messner, SF, McGeever, KF and Raffalovich, LE (2009) 'Immigration and the Recent Violent Crime Drop in the United States: A pooled, cross-sectional time-series analysis of metropolitan areas' *Criminology*, 47, 889–928.
Tonry, M (ed) (1997) *Ethnicity, Crime, and Immigration: Comparative and Cross-National Perspectives* (Chicago, University of Chicago Press).
van Zyl Smit, D and Snacken, S (2009) *Principles of European Prison Law and Policy: Penology and Human Rights* (Oxford, Oxford University Press).
Walker, N (2003) 'Postnational Constitutionalism and the Problem of Translation' in JHH Weiler and M Wind (eds), *European Constitutionalism Beyond the State* (Cambridge, Cambridge University Press).
Wegen, G and Kuner, C (1994) 'Germany: Federal Constitutional Court Decision Concerning the Maastricht Treaty' *International Legal Materials*, 33, 388–444.

# 7

# *Youth Justice Policy in Europe—Between Minimum Intervention, Welfare and New Punitiveness*[1]

FRIEDER DÜNKEL

## I. INTRODUCTION

IN THE LAST 20 years, youth justice[2] systems in Europe have undergone considerable changes, particularly in the former socialist countries of Central and Eastern Europe. However, differing and sometimes contradictory youth justice policies have also emerged in Western Europe. So-called neo-liberal[3] tendencies can be seen particularly in England and Wales, and also in France and the Netherlands (Cavadino and Dignan 2006: 215 ff; Cavadino and Dignan 2007: 284 ff; Goldson 2002: 392 ff; Tonry 2004; Muncie and Goldson 2006; Bailleau and Cartuyvels 2007; Muncie 2008; Cimamonti et al 2010). In other countries, such as Germany and Switzerland, a moderate system of minimum intervention with priority given to diversion and of educational measures has been retained (Dünkel,

[1] I am deeply grateful to my friend Dirk van Zyl Smit of the University of Nottingham, who revised the present chapter not only linguistically, but also gave very important support for a more stringent outline of the chapter.

[2] A note on terminology: where possible, we have used the terms 'youth' and 'youth justice' in this chapter. The term 'juvenile' is also still in use in a number of international, European and national instruments, where it usually refers to persons under the age of 18 years. We have used it in this way too. However, the Convention on the Rights of the Child uses the term 'child' to refer to anyone under the age of 18 years. We have not followed this usage of 'child', as it is not always appropriate in this context. Finally, we use the term 'young adults' to refer to persons between the ages of 18 and 21 who are treated as youths or juveniles.

[3] The meaning of the term 'neo-liberal', which sometimes is used synonymously with the concept of Garland's 'culture of control', contains different concepts and aspects that cannot be simply characterised by more repressive sanctions or sentencing (see Crawford and Lewis 2007: 30 ff). These include the criminalisation of anti-social behaviour (ASBOs), increased use of youth custody, managerialism and the reduction of risk by social exclusion, rather than by integrating vulnerable offender groups through specific programmes.

Grzywa, Horsfield and Pruin 2011). In many countries, elements of restorative justice have been implemented.

This chapter evaluates youth justice policies and practice in Europe from a comparative perspective.[4] The focus is on tendencies in youth justice legislation and on the sentencing practice of prosecutors and judges in youth courts. Attention is also paid to the traditional 'welfare' and 'justice' models of youth justice and how they have become intertwined in modern European practice. The claim that a 'new punitiveness' is the prevailing strategy is questioned and attention is drawn to the practice of many youth justice systems, which seem to be fairly resistant to neo-liberal policies. Snacken has recently sought to explain why continental European countries in general have succeeded in resisting 'penal populism' (Snacken 2012: 247 ff). In the conclusion this reasoning is applied to youth justice systems in particular.

## II. CONTEMPORARY TRENDS IN YOUTH JUSTICE POLICY

Across Europe, policies based on the notions of the subsidiarity and proportionality of state intervention against youth offenders are in force or emerging afresh in most, if not all, countries. Recently however, in several European countries, we have also witnessed developments that adopt a contrary approach. These developments intensify youth justice interventions by raising the maximum sentences for youth detention and by introducing additional forms of secure accommodation. The youth justice reforms in the Netherlands in 1995 and in some respects in France in 1996, 2002 and 2007 should be mentioned in this context, as should the reforms in England and Wales in 1994 and 1998 (Kilchling 2002; Cavadino and Dignan 2006: 215 ff; Cavadino and Dignan 2007: 284 ff; Junger-Tas and Decker 2006; Bailleau and Cartuyvels 2007; Junger-Tas and Dünkel 2009). The causes of the more repressive or neo-liberal approach in some countries are manifold. It is likely that the new punitive trend in the US, with its emphasis on retribution and deterrence, was not without its impact in some European countries, particularly England and Wales.

These developments at the national level, which is the primary focus of this chapter, have to be understood against the background of international and regional instruments that set standards for youth justice. Most important in this regard is the 1989 UN Convention on the Rights of the Child, a binding international treaty that all European states have ratified. It makes clear that

[4] The comparison is based largely on a survey of 34 countries conducted by the Criminology Department at the University of Greifswald (Dünkel, Grzywa, Horsfield and Pruin 2011). The project was funded by the European Union (AGIS programme) and by the Ministry of Education of the Federal State of Mecklenburg-Western Pomerania in Germany.

the common and principal aim of youth justice should be to act in the 'best interests of the child'—'child' defined for the purpose of this Convention as a person under the age of 18 years—and to provide education, support and integration into society for such children. These ideas are developed further in the 1985 UN Standard Minimum Rules for the Administration of Juvenile Justice and at the European level in the recommendations of the Council of Europe, in particular Recommendation No Rec(2003)20 of the Committee of Ministers to Member States concerning new ways of dealing with juvenile delinquency and the role of juvenile justice and Recommendation No Rec(2008)11 of the Committee of Ministers to Member States concerning juvenile offenders subject to sanctions or measures (Dünkel 2009; Dünkel, Grzywa, Horsfield and Pruin 2011: 1861 ff).

### A. Responsibilisation and Neo-liberalism

In England and Wales, and to some extent elsewhere, the concept of responsibilisation has become a pivotal category of youth justice.[5] Responsibilisation is not limited to young offenders, but increasingly parents are held criminally responsible for the conduct of their children.[6] Making parents more responsible may have a positive impact. There is empirical evidence that parental training, combined with child support at an early stage, has positive preventive effects (Lösel et al 2007; Lösel 2012). However, it is not necessary to criminalise parents. Ideally, parental training should be offered by welfare agencies (as is the case in Germany and the Scandinavian countries) and not be enforced by penal sanctions (Junger-Tas and Dünkel 2009: 225 ff).

A positive aspect of making young offenders take responsibility for their actions is that it has contributed to the expansion of victim-offender reconciliation (*Täter-Opfer-Ausgleich*), mediation and reparation. In the English context, however, it is more problematic, as it has been accompanied by the abolition of the previously rebuttable presumption that 10- to 14-year-olds may lack criminal capacity. Although in practice the presumption had been relatively easy to rebut, its formal abolition in 1998 was an indication of determination to hold even very young offenders responsible for their actions. The tendencies in English youth justice may be regarded as symptomatic of a neo-liberal orientation, which can be characterised by the key terms of responsibility, restitution (reparation), restorative justice

[5] See critically, Crawford and Lewis (2007: 27), and Cavadino and Dignan (2006: 68 ff) with regards to the 'managerial' and the 'getting tough' approach.

[6] See, for example, the so-called parenting order in England and Wales or similar measures in Belgium, Bulgaria, France, Greece, Ireland or Scotland; and see Pruin (2011: 1559 ff).

and (occasionally openly publicised) retribution. These so-called '4 Rs' have replaced the '4 Ds' (diversion, decriminalisation, deinstitutionalisation and due process) that shaped the debates of the 1960s and 1970s (Dünkel 2008). The retributive character of the new discourse is exemplified by the requirement that community interventions should be 'tough' and 'credible'. For example, the 'community treatment' of the 1960s was replaced by 'community punishment' in the 1980s and 1990s. Cavadino and Dignan attribute these changes to the so-called 'neo-correctionalist model' that has come to dominate official English penology (Cavadino and Dignan 2006: 210 ff; Bailleau and Cartuyvels 2007; Muncie 2008).

There are many reasons for the increase in neo-liberal tendencies, as defined by Garland and other authors (Garland 2001a; Garland 2001b; Roberts and Hough 2002; Tonry 2004; Pratt et al 2005; Muncie 2008). Some are to be found in the renewed emphasis on penal philosophies such as retribution and incapacitation, and in related sentencing policies that demonise youth violence, often by means of indeterminate sentences. There are also underlying socio-economic reasons. More repressive policies have gained importance in countries that face particular problems with young migrants or members of ethnic minorities and that have problems integrating young persons into the labour market, particularly where a growing number of them live in segregated and declining city areas. They often have no real possibility of escaping life as members of the 'underclass', a phenomenon that undermines 'society's stability and social cohesion and create mechanisms of social exclusion' (Junger-Tas 2006: 522 ff). They are at risk of being marginalised and eventually criminalised. In this context, recidivist offending is a major concern. Therefore in England and Wales, France, and Slovakia for example, many of the more punitive changes to the law are restricted to recidivist offenders.

It should be emphasised, however, that, in the case of most continental European countries, there is no evidence of a regression to the classical penal objectives and perceptions of the eighteenth and nineteenth centuries. Overall, there is continued adherence to the prior principle of education or special prevention, even though 'justice' elements have also been reinforced. The tension between education and punishment remains evident. The reform laws that were adopted in Germany in 1990, in the Netherlands in 1995, in Spain in 2000 and 2006, in Portugal in 2001, in France and Northern Ireland in 2002, as well as in Lithuania in 2001, the Czech Republic in 2003 or in Serbia in 2006 are examples of this dual approach. The reforms in Northern Ireland and in Belgium in 2007 are of particular interest, as they strengthened restorative elements in youth justice, including so-called family group conferencing or youth conferencing (Northern Ireland), and thus arguably contribute to responsiblisation in this way without necessarily being neo-liberal in fundamental orientation (Christiaens et al 2011; O'Mahony and Campbell 2006; Doak and O'Mahony 2011).

It must be recognised, however, that, even in countries with a moderate and stable youth justice practice, the rhetoric in political debates is sometimes dominated by penal populism with distinctly neo-liberal undertones. Nevertheless, this does not necessarily result in a change, as can be demonstrated by a German example. At the end of 2007 several violent crimes in subways (which were filmed by automatic cameras) led to a heated public debate about the necessity to increase the sanctions provided by the Juvenile Justice Act. The leader of the Christian Democratic Party (CDU) of the federal state of Hesse, Roland Koch, made this a core element of his electoral campaign by proposing the use of boot camps and other more severe punishments for juvenile violent offenders. He also referred to the fact that the offenders had immigrant backgrounds in xenophobic statements. Within a few days almost 1000 criminal justice practitioners and academics had signed a resolution against such penal populism and in January 2008 the CDU lost the elections. Since then, penal populism has not been made a prominent feature of electoral campaigns again; the CDU had gone too far. Muncie (2008: 109) refers to this debate in Germany and interprets it as an indicator for increased punitiveness. Yet, youth justice practice in Germany has remained stable and sentencing levels relatively moderate (Heinz 2009; 2011a; 2011b; 2012).

## B. Diversion, Minimum Intervention and Community Sanctions

If one regards the developments in the sanctions and measures that are applicable to young offenders, there has been a clear expansion of the available means of diversion. However, these are often linked to educational measures, or merely function to validate norms by means of a warning (Dünkel, Pruin and Grzywa 2011). Sometimes, however, the concern for minimum intervention still means that diversion from prosecution leads to no further steps being taken at all.

Everywhere it is proclaimed that deprivation of liberty should be a measure of last resort. In practice the level of what is meant by 'last resort' varies across time and in cross-national comparison. England and Wales, for example, experienced sharp increases of the juvenile prison population in the 1990s, but the reduction of immediate custody by 35 per cent from 1999 to 2009 contradicts the assumption that the adoption of a more punitive rhetoric necessarily leads to a continued growth in these numbers. Spain and a few other countries have also shown increases in the use of youth custody in recent years, but in general recent developments go in the other direction. This is particularly true for Central and Eastern European countries. In some of these countries, such as Croatia, the Czech Republic, Hungary, Latvia, Romania and Slovenia, the high level of diversion and community sanctions and the low level of custodial sanctions characteristic of continental Western European and Scandinavian countries have been achieved, whereas others, such as Lithuania, Russia and Slovakia, still use deprivation of liberty more often, albeit not as frequently as in Soviet times.

With the exception of some serious offences, the vast majority of youth offending in Europe is dealt with out of court by means of informal diversionary measures: for example, in Belgium about 80 per cent, Germany about 70 per cent (Dünkel, Pruin and Grzywa 2011: 1684 ff). In some countries, such as Croatia, France, the Netherlands, Serbia and Slovenia, this is a direct consequence of the long-recognised principle of allowing the prosecution and even the police a wide degree of discretion—the so-called expediency principle. Exceptions, where such discretion is not allowed, can be found in some Central and Eastern European countries, but in these cases one should note that, for example, property offences that cause only minor damage are not always treated as statutory criminal offences. Italy, to take a further example, provides for a judicial pardon which is similar to diversionary exemptions from punishment, but awarded by the youth court judge. So, there is a large variety of forms of non-intervention or of imposing only minor (informal or formal) sanctions.

Constructive measures, such as social training courses (Germany) and so-called labour and learning sanctions or projects (the Netherlands), have also been successfully implemented as part of a strategy of diversion. Many countries explicitly follow the ideal of education (Portugal), while at the same time emphasising prevention of re-offending, that is, special prevention (as in Recommendation No. Rec(2003)20 of the Committee of Ministers to Member States concerning new ways of dealing with juvenile delinquency and the role of juvenile justice).

## C. Restorative Justice

One development that appears to be common to Central, Eastern and Western European countries is the application of elements of restorative justice policies to young offenders. Victim-offender reconciliation, mediation, or sanctions that require reparation or apology to the victim have played a particular role in all legislative reforms of the last 15 years. Pilot mediation projects were established in the 1990s in Central and Eastern European countries such as Slovenia (since 1997) and the Czech Republic. They are predominantly linked to informal disposals (diversion).

In some countries, legislation provides for elements of restorative justice to be used as independent sanctions by youth courts. In England and Wales, for example, this is done by means of reparation or restitution orders, and in Germany by means of so-called *Wiedergutmachungsauflage*, victim-offender reconciliation as an educational directive (see §§ 10 and 15 of the

Juvenile Justice Act). Family group conferences—originally introduced and applied in New Zealand—form part of the law reform of 2007 in Belgium. These conferences are forms of mediation that take into account and seek to activate the social family networks of both the offender and the victim. Even before the Belgian reform project, the youth justice reform in Northern Ireland had introduced youth conferences, which have been running as pilot projects since 2003. In addition the Northern Irish reform made provision for reparation orders: an idea that had been introduced in England and Wales in 1998 (O'Mahony and Campbell 2006; Doak and O'Mahony 2011).

Whether these restorative elements actually influence sentencing practice or are merely a 'fig leaf" seeking to disguise a more repressive youth justice system can only be determined by taking into account the different backgrounds and traditions in each country. Victim-offender reconciliation has attained great quantitative significance in the sanctioning practices of both the Austrian and the German youth courts.[7] If one also takes community service into account as a restorative sanction in the broader sense, the proportion of all juvenile and young adult offenders who are dealt with by such—ideally educational—constructive alternatives increases to more than one-third (Heinz 2012).

In Italy the procedural rules for youth justice introduced in 1988 have led to a move away from a purely rehabilitative and punitive perspective, to a new conception of penal procedure. Restorative justice measures have gained much more attention, and victim-offender mediation can be applied at different stages of the procedure: during the preliminary investigations and the preliminary hearing when considering 'the extinction of a sentence because of the irrelevance of the offence', or in combination with the suspension of the procedure with supervision by the probation service (*Sospensione del processo e messa alla prova*).

## D. Youth Justice Models

If one compares youth justice systems from a perspective of classifying them according to typologies, the 'classical' orientations of both the justice and the welfare models can still be differentiated (Doob and Tonry 2004: 1 ff; Pruin 2011). However, one rarely, if ever, encounters the ideal types of welfare or justice models in their pure form. Rather, there are several examples of mixed systems, for instance within German and other continental European youth justice legislation.

[7] Roughly 8% of all sanctions imposed on juveniles, see Dünkel (2011a: 587); for *Austria* see Bruckmüller (2006).

There is a clear tendency in youth justice policy in recent decades to strengthen the justice model by establishing or extending procedural safeguards, also to what may be regarded as welfare measures. This tendency includes a stricter emphasis on the principle of proportionality in the sense of avoiding both sentences and educational measures that are disproportionately harsh.

Other orientations that are not necessarily based squarely on 'justice' or 'welfare' are significant too. Restorative justice has already been mentioned. Minimum intervention, too, plays a part but so also do the neo-liberal tendencies towards harsher sentences and 'getting tough' on youth crime (Albrecht and Kilchling 2002; Tonry and Doob 2004; Jensen and Jepsen 2006; Junger-Tas and Decker 2006; Bailleau and Cartuyvels 2007; Ciappi 2007; Patanè 2007; Cimamonti et al 2010; Pruin 2011). Tendencies towards minimum intervention, that is the prioritisation of informal procedures (diversion), including offender-victim-reconciliation and other reparative strategies, can also be viewed as independent models of youth justice: a 'minimum intervention model' (Cavadino and Dignan 2006: 199 ff, 205 ff). Cavadino and Dignan identify not only a 'minimum intervention model' (priority of diversion and community sanctions) and a 'restorative justice model' (priority of restorative/reparative reactions), but also a 'neo-correctionalist model', which, as mentioned previously, is particularly characteristic of contemporary trends and developments in England and Wales (Cavadino and Dignan 2006: 210 ff).

Here, too, there are no clear boundaries, for the majority of continental European youth justice systems incorporate not only elements of welfare and justice philosophies, but also minimum intervention (as is especially the case in Germany, see Dünkel 2006; 2011), restorative justice and elements of neo-correctionalism (for example, increased 'responsibilisation' of the offenders and their parents, tougher penalties for recidivists and secure accommodation for children). Rather, differences are more evident in the degree of orientation towards restorative or punitive elements. In general, one can conclude that European juvenile justice is moving towards mixed systems that combine welfare and justice elements, which are further shaped by the trends mentioned above.

## III. REFORM STRATEGIES

Against this background of a range of old and newly prominent ideas combined with somewhat fractured models, one can identify a number of reform strategies.

In many Western European countries such strategies seem to have been relatively well planned. In Austria, Germany and the Netherlands, the community sanctions and restorative justice elements that were introduced by the reforms in 1988, 1990 and 1995 respectively were systematically and extensively piloted. Nationwide implementation of the reform programmes was dependent on prior empirical verification of the projects' practicability and acceptance. The process of testing and generating acceptance—especially among judges and the prosecution service—takes time. Continuous supplementary and further training is required, which is difficult to guarantee in times of social change, as has been the case in Central and Eastern Europe. Yet, reform of youth justice through practice (as developed in Germany in the 1980s) appears preferable to a reform 'from above', which often fails to provide the appropriate infrastructure.

As a result of major political changes at the end of the 1980s, more drastic reform was required in the countries of Central and Eastern Europe. The situation as it existed at the time was not uniform across the region but differed amongst groups of countries. One group was comprised of the Soviet republics, Bulgaria, Romania and to some degree the German Democratic Republic (East Germany) and Czechoslovakia. These countries had developed a more punitively oriented youth justice policy and practice. On the other hand, there were Hungary, Poland and Yugoslavia, which had rather moderate youth justice policies with many educational elements.

Across Central and Eastern Europe, developments since the early 1990s have been characterised by a clear increase in the levels of officially recorded youth crime. The need for youth justice reform, a widely accepted notion in all of these countries, stemmed from the need to replace old (often Soviet or Soviet-influenced) law with (Western) European standards as contained in the principles of the Council of Europe and the United Nations. This process has, however, produced somewhat different trends in criminal policy.

Since the early 1990s, there has been a dynamic reform movement both in law and in practice. It is exemplified not only in numerous projects but also in the appointment of law reform commissions for and, in many cases, in the adoption of reform legislation in, for example, Estonia, Lithuania, Serbia, Slovenia and the Czech Republic.

On the one hand, the development of an independent youth justice system is a prominent feature of these reforms: see, for example, developments in the Baltic states, Croatia, the Czech Republic, Romania, Russia, Serbia and Slovakia, as well as in Turkey. In this connection the importance of procedural safeguards and entitlements that also take the special educational needs of young offenders into account has been recognised. However, in the Baltic states there are as yet no independent youth courts. In Russia the first model youth courts are up and running in Rostov-on-Don and in a few other cities (Shchedrin 2011).[8] Such a project has also been

[8] Recently (2011) the Russian parliament (*Duma*) rejected a proposal to introduce a separate youth court system on a nationwide base. Opponents, including the Orthodox Church, had warned against a state instrument of arbitrary prosecution and unwarranted interference

established in Romania in Brasov (Păroşanu 2011). However, in general, the required infrastructure for the introduction of modern, social-pedagogical approaches to youth justice and welfare is widely lacking.

In order to deter recidivists and violent young offenders in particular, some of this new legislation not only involves new community sanctions and possibilities of diversion, but also retains tough custodial sentences. The absence of appropriate infrastructure and of widespread acceptance of community sanctions still results in frequent prison sentences. However, developments in Russia, for example, show that there has been no return to past sanctioning patterns, where roughly 50 per cent of all young offenders were sentenced to imprisonment. Instead, forms of probation are now quantitatively more common, and more frequently used than sentences of imprisonment.

What is becoming clear in all Central and Eastern European countries is that the principle of imprisonment as a last resort (*ultima ratio*) is being taken more seriously and the number of custodial sanctions reduced. However, it has to be noted that youth imprisonment or similar sanctions in the former Yugoslavian republics, and to a lesser extent also in Hungary and Poland, had already been the exception during the period before the political changes at the beginning of the 1990s.

Regarding community sanctions, the difficulties of establishing the necessary infrastructure are clear. Initially, the greatest problem in this respect was the lack of qualified social workers and teachers. This has remained a problem, as to a great extent the appropriate training courses have not yet been fully introduced and developed (Dünkel, Pruin and Grzywa 2011). Again one has to differentiate, as there are exceptions: Poland has a long tradition in social work. Also in the former Yugoslavia social workers were trained, following the introduction of 'strict supervision' as a special sanction in 1960.

The concept of 'conditional' criminal responsibility (related to the ability of discernment) as long expressed in German and Italian law—has recently been adopted in Estonia (2002), the Czech Republic (2003) or Slovakia (for 14-year-olds, see Pruin 2011: 1566 ff). This is another interesting development, for it reflects a tendency for reforms in the countries of Central and Eastern Europe to have been influenced by Austrian and German youth justice law as well as by international standards. Despite obvious and undeniable national particularities, there is a recognisable degree of convergence among the systems in Western, Central and Eastern Europe.

in the realm of the family. Supporters hoped to see a child-friendly institution that reduces juvenile delinquency and child homelessness and makes parents more responsible for their offspring. The influence of the Orthodox Church was of major importance in denying juvenile justice reforms.

## IV. UNRESOLVED ISSUES

Although on the basis of comparative research one may speak, albeit cautiously, of an emerging European philosophy of juvenile justice, which includes elements of education and rehabilitation (apparent in, for example, the recommendations of the Council of Europe), the consideration of victims through mediation and restoration, and the observance of legal procedural safeguards, there are some issues on which such a development is not as clear. In this regard we consider the age of criminal responsibility and its corollary, the age at which offenders cease to be regarded as juveniles and are treated as adults. The latter issue also raises the question of whether there should be some mechanism for the converse, namely allowing juveniles to be tried in adult courts.

### A. Age of Criminal Responsibility

There is no indication of a harmonisation of the age of criminal responsibility in Europe. Indeed, the 2008 European rules for juvenile offenders subject to sanctions or measures (Rec (2008)11, see Council of Europe 2009) recommend no particular age, specifying only that some age should be specified by law and that it 'shall not be too low' (rule 4).

The minimum age of criminal responsibility in Europe varies between 10 (England and Wales, and Switzerland), 12 (Netherlands, Scotland and Turkey), 13 (France), 14 (Austria, Germany, Italy, Spain and numerous Central and Eastern European countries), 15 (Greece and the Scandinavian countries)[9] and even 16 (for specific offences in Russia and other Eastern European countries) or 18 (Belgium). After the recent reforms in Central and Eastern Europe, the most common age of criminal responsibility is 14 (see Table 7.1).

The ages of criminal responsibility have to be defined further: whereas we can talk of a really low age of criminal responsibility, for example in England and Wales, in many countries only educational sanctions imposed by the family and youth courts are applicable at an earlier age (for example, France and Greece). Also in Switzerland the youth court judge can only impose educational measures on 10- to 14-year-olds (who are, however, seen as criminally responsible), whereas juvenile prison sentences are restricted to those aged at least 15. The same is the case in the former Yugoslavian republics of Croatia, Kosovo, Serbia and Slovenia for 14- and 15-year-old offenders. Further still, some countries, such as Lithuania and

[9] The age was lowered to 14 in Denmark in January 2010. Subsequently however, a new government was elected and Denmark has reverted to the Scandinavian consensus and raised the age of criminal responsibility to 15 again.

**Table 7.1: Comparison of the age of criminal responsibility and age ranges for youth imprisonment**

| Country | Minimum age for *educational* measures of the family/ youth court (juvenile welfare law) | Age of criminal responsibility (juvenile criminal law) | Full criminal responsibility (adult criminal law can/must be applied; juvenile law or sanctions of the juvenile law can be applied) | Age range for youth imprisonment/ custody or similar forms of deprivation of liberty |
|---|---|---|---|---|
| Austria | | 14 | 18/21 | 14–27 |
| Belgium | | 18 | 16[b]/18 | 14–21 |
| Belarus | | 14[c]/16 | 14/16 | 14–21 |
| Bulgaria | | 14 | 18 | 14–21 |
| Croatia | | 14/16[a] | 18/21 | 14–21 |
| Cyprus | | 14 | 16/18/21 | 14–21 |
| Czech Republic | | 15 | 18/18 + (mitigated sentences) | 15–19 |
| Denmark[d] | | 15 | 15/18/21 | 15–23 |
| England/ Wales | | 10/12/15[a] | 18 | 10/15–21 |
| Estonia | | 14 | 18 | 14–21 |
| Finland[d] | | 15 | 15/18 | 15–21 |
| France | 10 | 13 | 18 | 13–18 + 6 m./23 |
| Germany | | 14 | 18/21 | 14–24 |
| Greece | 8 | 15 | 18/21 | 15–21/25 |
| Hungary | | 14 | 18 | 14–24 |
| Ireland | | 10/12/16[a] | 18 | 10/12/16–18/21 |
| Italy | | 14 | 18/21 | 14–21 |
| Kosovo | | 14 | 18/21 | 16–23 |
| Latvia | | 14 | 18 | 14–21 |
| Lithuania | | 14[c]/16 | 18/21 | 14–21 |
| Macedonia | | 14[c]/16 | 14/16 | 14–21 |
| Moldova | | 14[c]/16 | 14/16 | 14–21 |
| Montenegro | | 14/16[a] | 18/21 | 16–23 |

*(Continued)*

| Country | Minimum age for *educational* measures of the family/ youth court (juvenile welfare law) | Age of criminal responsibility (juvenile criminal law) | Full criminal responsibility (adult criminal law can/must be applied; juvenile law or sanctions of the juvenile law can be applied) | Age range for youth imprisonment/ custody or similar forms of deprivation of liberty |
|---|---|---|---|---|
| Netherlands | | 12 | 16/18/21 | 12–21 |
| Northern Ireland | | 10 | 17/18/21 | 10–16/17–21 |
| Norway[d] | | 15 | 18 | 15–21 |
| Poland | 13 | | 15/17/18 | 13–18/15–21 |
| Portugal | 12 | | 16/21 | 12/16–21 |
| Romania | | 14/16 | 18/(20) | 14–21 |
| Russia | | 14[c]/16 | 18/21 | 14–21 |
| Scotland | 8[e] | 12[e]/16 | 16/21 | 16–21 |
| Serbia | | 14/16[a] | 18/21 | 14–23 |
| Slovakia | | 14/15 | 18/21 | 14–18 |
| Slovenia | | 14/16[a] | 18/21 | 14–23 |
| Spain | | 14 | 18 | 14–21 |
| Sweden[d] | | 15 | 15/18/21 | 15–21[g] |
| Switzerland | | 10/15[a] | 18[f] | 10/15–22 |
| Turkey | | 12 | 15/18 | 12–18/21 |
| Ukraine | | 14[c]/16 | 18 | 14–22 |

[a] Criminal responsibility resulting in juvenile detention (youth imprisonment or similar custodial sanctions under the regime of the Ministry of Justice).
[b] Only for traffic offences and exceptionally for very serious offences.
[c] Only for serious offences.
[d] Only mitigation of sentencing without separate youth justice legislation.
[e] The age of criminal prosecution is 12, but for children from eight up to the age of 16 the children's hearings system applies, thus preventing more formal criminal procedures.
[f] Art 61 of the Swiss Criminal Code for adults provides for a special form of detention, a prison sentence for 18–25-year-old young adult offenders who are placed in separate institutions for young adults, where they can stay until they reach the age of 30.
[g] Youth custody. There are also special departments for young offenders in the general prison system (for young adults up to about 25 years of age).

Russia, employ a graduated scale of criminal responsibility, according to which only more serious and grave offences can be prosecuted from the age of 14, while the general minimum age of criminal responsibility lies at 16 (for a summary, see also Pruin 2011). Such a graduation of the age of criminal responsibility must be criticised, as it is contrary to the basic philosophy of juvenile justice that sanctions should refer to the individual development of maturity or other personality concepts, rather than to the seriousness of the offence (see also the criticism under section IV.C).

Whether these notable differences can in fact be correlated to variations in sentencing, is not entirely apparent. For within a system based solely on education, under certain circumstances the possibility of being accommodated as a last resort in a home or in residential care (particularly in the form of closed or secure centres, as in England and Wales and France) can be just as intensive and of an equal or even longer duration than a sentence of juvenile imprisonment. Furthermore, the legal levels of criminal responsibility do not necessarily give any indication of whether a youth justice or welfare approach is more or less punitive in practice. What happens in reality often differs considerably from the language used in the reform debates (Doob and Tonry 2004: 16 ff). Legal changes that formally make the regime more intensive are sometimes the result of changes in practice, and sometimes they contribute to changes in practice. The effect of these changes varies too. Despite the dramatisation of events by the mass media that sometimes lead to changes in the law, there is often, in Germany for instance, a remarkable continuity and a degree of stability in youth justice practice (Dünkel 2006; 2011).

### B. Young Adults

There are also interesting developments in the upper age limits of criminal responsibility (the maximum age to which juvenile criminal law or juvenile sanctions can be applied). The central issue in this regard is the extension of the applicability of juvenile criminal law—or at least of its specifically educational measures—to 18- to 20-year-old young adults, as occurred in Germany as early as in 1953 (see also the recent reforms in Austria, Croatia, Lithuania and the Netherlands; Pruin 2007; Dünkel and Pruin 2011; 2012).

This tendency is rooted in a criminological understanding of the transitional phases of personal and social development from adolescence to adulthood and a recognition that such transitions are taking longer. Over the last 50 years, the phases of education and of integration into working and family life (the establishment of one's 'own family') have become prolonged well beyond the age of 20. Many young people experience developmental-psychological crises and difficulties in the transition to adult life, and increasingly such difficulties continue to occur into their mid-twenties (Pruin 2007; Dünkel and Pruin 2011; 2012). Furthermore, new neuro-scientific evidence indicates that maturity and psycho-social abilities are fully developed only in the third decade of life (Weijers and Grisso 2009: 63 ff; Loeber et al 2012: 336 ff; Bonnie, Chemers and Schuck 2012, chapters 4 and 5).

An increasing number of states have statutory provisions for imposing educational and other sanctions of the youth justice law on young adults. Historically however, such laws have not always had the same impact in practice. While in Germany the laws applicable to juveniles are applied in more than 90 per cent of the cases concerning young adults who commit serious crimes (overall average: more than 60 per cent; see Dünkel 2011a), in most other countries this has remained the exception. One reason is that in Germany the jurisdiction of the juvenile court has been extended to young adults, whereas in other countries the criminal court for adults is responsible for this age group but can impose some of the measures otherwise reserved for juveniles (for example, in the former Yugoslavia, which introduced this possibility in 1960, see Gensing 2011). The Yugoslavian experience is a good example of how substantive and procedural laws have to be harmonised in order to prevent counterproductive effects of such provisions. There was therefore good reason in 1998 for Croatia, a former Yugoslavian state, to transfer the jurisdiction on young adults to the juvenile courts. Austria took the same step in 2001.

In other instances, keeping young adults fully in the adult framework does not mean that they cannot in practice be treated very much like juveniles. In the Netherlands, for example, the general criminal law provides for a plethora of alternative sanctions, which can be seen as educational or rehabilitative (for example, community service) and which are not provided in German criminal law for adults.

## C. Transfer to Adult Criminal Courts or Jurisdiction (Waiver Procedures)

While raising the upper limit of the definition of juvenile may be seen as a way of imposing more appropriate sentences on immature young adults and extending the scope of youth justice, there is also an opposite trend, most prominent in the USA (Stump 2003) but also found in many European countries (Pruin 2011), of referring children for trial in adult courts. Such referrals have a distinctively punitive purpose.

In some European countries, such as Scotland and Portugal, juvenile offenders from the age of 16 onwards can be dealt with in the adult criminal justice system. Beyond that, in other countries, juvenile offenders can be transferred from the youth court to the adult court, where so-called waiver or transfer laws provide for the application of adult criminal law to certain offences (Stump 2003; Bishop 2009; Weijers et al 2009; Beaulieu 1994: 329 ff; Goldson and Muncie 2006: 91 ff; Keiser 2008). This is in fact a qualified limitation of the scope of juvenile justice (Hazel 2008: 35) and a lowering of the minimum age for the full application of adult criminal law.

Some countries provide for the application of adult criminal law for serious offences, for example, in Belgium for rape, aggravated assault, aggravated sexual assault, aggravated theft, (attempted) murder and (attempted) homicide by juveniles aged 16 or older. Since the law reform of 2006, prior to which juveniles had been tried by adult courts, so-called Extended Juvenile Courts have had the competence to conduct such trials.[10] In the Netherlands, the youth court remains competent as well, but the general criminal law can be applied to 16- and 17-year-old juveniles. In 1995 the requirements were relaxed. The seriousness of the criminal offence, the personality of the young offender, or the circumstances under which the offence is committed can lead to the application of adult criminal law. The law provides the judge with a great deal of discretion. In most cases, in practice it is the seriousness of the offence that leads to the application of adult criminal law. In England and Wales juveniles, even at the age of 10, can be transferred to the adult criminal court (Crown Court) if charged with an exceptionally serious offence (including murder and crimes that would in the case of adult offenders carry a maximum term of imprisonment of more than 14 years). The Crown Court has to apply slightly different rules for the protection of juveniles in this case. The number of juvenile offenders who are sent to the Crown Court has fluctuated over the last 25 years, with no indication of a clear-cut trend in either direction.

In Serbia and in Northern Ireland, transfers are limited to juveniles who have been charged with homicide, or who are co-accused with adult offenders. In the latter case, there is an interesting alternative as well: the juvenile has to be referred back to the youth court for sentencing following a finding of guilt (O'Mahony 2011). In Ireland, in exceptional cases like treason or crimes against the peace of nations, but also for murder or manslaughter, juveniles are tried by the Central Criminal Court before a judge and jury.

In France, in contrast, less serious offences, rather classed as misdemeanours, are brought before an adult court: since 1945 in cases of misdemeanours (*contraventions des quatre premières classes*) juvenile offenders are judged by a Police Court which can issue reprimands or fines. Since 2002, the competences of the Police Court have been conferred on a specific 'proximity judge', who is neither a lawyer nor a youth justice specialist, but has the competence to 'punish' juveniles up to a certain level (Castaignède and Pignoux 2011).

[10] Only the most serious crimes should be dealt by the (adult) Crown Court, but this regulation was outlawed by the Constutional Court, see Christiaens et al (2011: 115 ff). Besides this possibility for waivers, traffic offences are always judged by (adult) police courts.

In Scotland there are no waivers or transfer laws, but the same effect can be achieved in another way. In most severe cases the juvenile offender will not be transferred to the children's hearings system. Formally, this is not a transfer to the adult criminal court, because the criminal court has original competence to try all cases, even if in practice the vast majority are transferred to the children's hearings system. However, Scotland shares the idea that in very serious cases the offenders should not be dealt with by the juvenile criminal system but in the adult criminal system.

Countries, like those in Scandinavia that do not have specialised juvenile jurisdictions, thus (naturally) do not have provision for transfers either. It should be emphasised though, that, in general, in the Scandinavian countries the same regulations apply in cases of 'aggravated' as well as 'normal' offences.

The application of adult law to juveniles through waivers or transfer laws can be regarded as a systemic weakness in those jurisdictions that allow it (Stump 2003). Whereas normally the application of (juvenile) law depends on the age of the offender, transfer laws or waivers rely on the type or seriousness of the committed offence. The justification for special treatment of juvenile offenders (as an inherent principle of youth justice) is challenged by such provisions (Keiser 2008: 38). The fundamental idea is to react differently to offences that are committed by offenders up to a certain age, based on their level of maturity or on their ability of discernment. Waivers or transfer laws question this idea for serious offences. On the one hand, the maximum age of criminal responsibility should signify—independently from the type of offence—from what age onwards a young person is deemed 'mature enough' to receive (adult) criminal punishment. On the other hand, however, the introduction of 'transfer laws' holds to responsibility those very offenders who often lack the (social) maturity to abstain from crime, or even fully to differentiate right from wrong. Furthermore, it is hard to imagine that the same juvenile would be regarded as not fully mature when charged with a 'normal' offence, but fully criminal responsible for a serious offence. As Weijers and Grisso have put it: 'An adolescent has the same degree of capacity to form criminal intent, no matter what crime he commits' (Weijers and Grisso 2009: 67). A systematic approach would treat all offences equally.

States with transfer laws or waivers often argue that these laws are justified by the alleged deterrent effect of more severe sanctions on juvenile offenders.[11] Additionally, they claim that waivers are needed as a 'safety

[11] In Belgium, the possibility of waivers is officially based on the need to compensate the high age of criminal responsibility, which is set at 18 years (Christiaens et al 2011). In Germany the same arguments are used to fight for the application of adult criminal law to young adults, that is those of from 18 to 20 years of age (Dünkel 2011a: 587 ff; Dünkel and Pruin 2011; 2012).

valve' (Weijers et al 2009) for the juvenile courts because juvenile law does not provide adequate or suitable options for severe cases.[12] However, so far criminological research has not found evidence for positive effects of transfers or waivers. In fact, research has suggested that transferring juveniles to adult courts has negative effects on preventing offending, including increased recidivism.[13]

The second argument misses the point as well: does adult criminal law provide adequate or suitable options for reacting to severe criminality? How do we measure effectiveness? If we look at recidivism rates, then long prison sentences—the typical reaction by adult criminal law to serious offending—are relatively ineffective in preventing further crimes (Killias and Villettaz 2007: 213). Research results furthermore show that a lenient, minimum-interventionist juvenile justice system does not produce more juvenile offenders than an active and punitive one (Smith 2005: 192 ff).

In practice, transfers may be of declining significance in Europe. In the Netherlands the number of transfers to the adult court has been reduced considerably: whereas in 1995 16 per cent of all cases were dealt with by the adult criminal court, this figure was only 1.2 per cent in 2004 (Weijers et al 2009: 110).[14] In Belgium the use of transfers is very limited as well: transfer decisions amount to 3 per cent of all judgments (Weijers et al 2009: 118 with references to regional differences). In Ireland, adult criminal courts are competent in less than 5 per cent of all cases against juveniles. In Poland, from 1999 to 2004 the number of cases transferred to public prosecutors swung between 242 and 309, or 0.2–0.3 per cent of all cases tried by the courts (Stańdo-Kawecka 2011).

Even if waivers and transfer laws are of little significance in practice in most countries, they are nonetheless systemic flaws that ultimately undermine the special regulations for juvenile offenders. Additional safeguards in adult courts are unable to compensate for them (Keiser 2008: 38).[15] Therefore the UN Committee on the Rights of the Child recommends abolishing all provisions that allow offenders under the age of 18 to be treated

[12] These arguments do ultimately show fear of, and intolerance towards, juveniles' misconduct (Hartjen 2008: 9).

[13] Bishop (2009: 97 ff) emphasises that the negative effects of transfer laws are found among those who receive community sanctions as well.

[14] This has to do with the range of youth custody sentences: until 1995 youth courts in the Netherlands had the competence to impose youth prison sentences of up to six months only. The reform law extended it to two years in the case of 16- and 17-year-old juveniles. Therefore juvenile judges only rarely have to transfer a case in order to arrive at a 'proportionate' sentence: see Pruin (2011: 1571).

[15] The European Court for Human Rights has not found that such trials in adult courts necessarily violate the European Convention of Human Rights, but in *T and V v The United Kingdom* (2000) 30 EHRR 121 the case concerning the 10-year-old murderers of James Bulger, a significant minority of the judges took the view that trying such young offenders in an adult court would inevitably violate their rights.

as adults, in order to achieve full and non-discriminatory implementation of the special rules of youth justice to all juveniles under the age of 18 years (Committee on the Rights of the Child 2007: paras 34, 36, 37 and 38; Doak 2009: 23).

## V. SUMMARY AND CONCLUSION

Juvenile justice systems in Europe have developed in various forms and with different orientations. Looking at sanctions and measures, the general trend reveals the expansion of diversion, combined in some countries with educational or other measures that aim to improve the compliance with the norm violated by the juvenile offender (*Normverdeutlichung*). Mediation, victim-offender reconciliation or family group conferences are good examples of such diversionary strategies.[16] On the other hand, from an international comparative perspective, systems based solely on child and youth welfare are on the retreat. In Europe more or less 'pure' welfare-orientated approaches exist only in Belgium[17] and Poland, whereas, for instance, in Latin American countries, which traditionally were oriented to the classic welfare approach, the changes towards the justice model are more visible (Tiffer-Sotomayor 2000; Tiffer et al 2002; Gutbrodt 2011).

Across Europe, elements of restorative justice have been implemented, both in countries which to some extent adopt neo-liberal or neo-correctional approaches and in those with a relatively strong welfare orientation. In addition, educational and other measures, which try to improve the social competences of young offenders, such as social training courses and cognitive-behavioural training and therapy, have been developed more widely. These developments are in line with international juvenile justice standards. The 2003 recommendation of the Council of Europe on new ways of dealing with juvenile delinquency clearly emphasises the development of new, more constructive community sanctions also for recidivist and other problematic offender groups. This maintains the traditional idea of juvenile justice as a purely, special 'educational' system of intervention designed to prevent the individual from reoffending.

Although the ideal of using deprivation of liberty only as a measure of last resort for juveniles has been hailed as desirable across Europe, it cannot

[16] However, diversion in the sense of non-intervention has been restricted, particularly for recidivist offenders, in some countries such as England and Wales, France and the Netherlands.

[17] The Scottish practice of sending juvenile offenders up to the age of 16 to the children's hearings system could also be characterised as a welfare approach. The Belgian case is difficult to classify: since the reform law of 2006 it has contained a mixture of educational, restorative and punitive measures (eg imprisonment for up to 30 years for juveniles appearing before the Extended Juvenile Court).

be denied that in some countries neo-liberal orientations have influenced juvenile justice policy and, to a varying extent, also practice (see Muncie 2008 with further references). The widening of the scope for youth detention in England and Wales, France and the Netherlands may be interpreted as a 'punitive turn'. And indeed the youth prison population in these countries did increase considerably in the 1990s. Muncie refers to public debates and academics in other countries (including Scandinavian ones) and comes to the conclusion that:

> such commentaries clearly suggest that not only in the USA and England and Wales but throughout much of Western Europe, punitive values associated with retribution, incapacitation, individual responsibility and offender accountability have achieved a political legitimacy to the detriment of traditional principles of juvenile protection and support.
>
> (Muncie 2008: 110.)

This conclusion reflects only a facet of the full reality. A different reality emerges, however, when one considers the practice of juvenile prosecutors, courts, social workers and youth welfare agencies and projects such as mediation schemes. These continue to operate in a reasonably moderate way and thus to resist penal populism. Deprivation of liberty remains the truly last resort in Scandinavia and indeed in most other regions and countries (von Hofer 2004; Storgaard 2004; Haverkamp 2007).[18] This differentiated picture of a 'new complexity' (Habermas 1985) is the main message of the research presented by the major comparative study on juvenile justice legislation and sentencing practice in Europe (Dünkel, Grzywa, Horsfield and Pruin 2011) on which this chapter is largely based (see in detail Dünkel, Pruin and Grzywa 2011; Dünkel, Grzywa, Pruin and Šelih 2011).

Sonja Snacken has sought to explain why many European countries could resist penal populism and punitiveness (Snacken 2010; 2012). She has emphasised that European states are constitutional democracies strongly oriented towards the welfare state, democracy and human rights. These fundamental orientations, which can be found most clearly in many continental Western European states, and particularly in Scandinavian states (Lappi-Seppälä 2007; 2010), serve as 'protective factors' against penal populism.

It is undoubtedly true that penal populism does not halt at the gates of youth justice (Pratt et al 2005; Ciappi 2007; see also Garland 2001a; 2001b; Roberts and Hough 2002; Tonry 2004; Muncie 2008). Generally speaking however, the same factors that have allowed such punitiveness to be resisted in many European countries apply even more strongly to youth

[18] See, for the fairly stable sentencing practice in Juvenile and Adult Criminal Law in Germany, Heinz (2009; 2011a; 2011b); Dünkel (2011a). There is no evidence of a 'punitive turn' in Germany.

justice. Moreover, juvenile offending is different from that of adults. Its episodic nature allows for more tolerance and moderate reactions.

The relative invulnerability of youth justice to punitive tendencies is reinforced by the strong framework of international and European human rights standards that apply to it, courtesy of the 1989 UN Convention on the Rights of the Child and the other instruments mentioned above. More specifically, these instruments also emphasise the expansion of procedural safeguards, on the one hand, and the limitation or reduction of the intensity of sentencing interventions, on the other hand.

Clearly more needs to be done, and this chapter has highlighted three areas in which policies are still unresolved, also at the international and European level. One step forward would be to raise the age of criminal responsibility to at least the European average of 14 or 15.[19] A second step would be to build on the interesting initiatives to increase the maximum age at which young offenders can be treated as if they were juveniles. This could do much to protect a potentially vulnerable group and to divert them from a career of adult crime.

Thirdly, the contrary tendency towards trying juveniles as adults should be resisted. It is not only doctrinally dubious, as explained above, but carries the risk of increasing directly the impact of the worst features of the adult criminal justice system on young offenders.

In sum, youth justice policy as reflected in legislation and practice in the majority of European countries has successfully resisted a punitive turn. While there is more work to be done in areas where policy is not yet clear, it is realistic to hope that neo-liberal approaches will be moderated, even in England and Wales, France or the Netherlands where they are rhetorically most prominent, and that the ideal of social inclusion and reintegration will be the *Leitmotiv* for juvenile justice reforms of the twenty-first century.

## REFERENCES


Albrecht, H-J and Kilchling, M (eds) (2002) *Jugendstrafrecht in Europa* (Freiburg, Max-Planck-Institut für ausländisches und internationales Strafrecht).

Bailleau, F and Cartuyvels, Y (eds) (2007) *La justice pénale des mineurs en Europe—Entre modèle Welfare et infléxions néo-libérales* (Paris, L'Harmattan).

Bishop, DM (2009) 'Juvenile Transfer in the United States' in J Junger-Tas and F Dünkel (eds), *Reforming Juvenile Justice* (Dordrecht, Springer).

Bonnie, R J, Chemers, B M and Schuck, J, (2012) (eds), *Reforming Juvenile Justice: A Developmental Approach* (Washington/D.C, National Research Council of the National Academies).


[19] See Hammarberg (2008).

Bruckmüller, K (2006) 'Austria: A Protection Model' in J Junger-Tas and SH Decker (eds), *International Handbook of Juvenile Justice* (Dordrecht, Springer).

Castaignède, J and Pignoux, N (2011) 'France' in F Dünkel, J Grzywa, P Horsfield and I Pruin (eds), *Juvenile Justice Systems in Europe—Current Situation and Reform Developments*, 2nd edn (Mönchengladbach, Forum Verlag Godesberg).

Cavadino, M and Dignan, J (2006) *Penal Systems. A Comparative Approach* (London, Sage).

—— (2007) *The Penal System: An Introduction*, 4th edn (London, Sage).

Christiaens, J, Dumortier, E and Nuytiens, A (2011) 'Belgium' in F Dünkel, J Grzywa, P Horsfield and I Pruin (eds), *Juvenile Justice Systems in Europe—Current Situation and Reform Developments*, 2nd edn (Mönchengladbach, Forum Verlag Godesberg).

Ciappi, S (2007) *La nuova punitività—Gestione dei conflitti e governo dell'insicurezza* (Soverina Mannelli, Università Rubbettino).

Cimamonti, S, di Marino, G and Zappalà, E (eds) (2010) *Où va la justice des mineurs? (Allemagne, Espagne, France, Italie, Russie)* (Torino, G. Ciappichelli Editore).

Council of Europe (ed) (2009), *European Rules for juvenile offenders subject to sanctions or measures*, (Strasbourg, Council of Europe Publishing).

Crawford, A and Lewis, S (1987) 'Évolutions mondiales, orientations nationales et justice locale: les effets du néo-liberalisme sur la justice des mineurs en Angleterre et au Pays de Galles' in F Bailleau and Y Cartuyvels (eds), *La justice pénale des mineurs en Europe—Entre modèle Welfare et infléxions néo-libérales* (Paris, L'Harmattan).

Doak, J and O'Mahony, D (2011) 'Developing Mediation and Restorative Justice for Young Offenders across Europe' in F Dünkel, J Grzywa, P Horsfield and I Pruin (eds), *Juvenile Justice Systems in Europe—Current Situation and Reform Developments*, 2nd edn (Mönchengladbach, Forum Verlag Godesberg).

Doob, AN and Tonry, M (2004) 'Varieties of Youth Justice' in M Tonry and AN Doob (eds), *Youth Crime and Justice (Crime and Justice,* Volume 31) (Chicago, University of Chicago Press).

Dünkel, F (1997) 'Jugendstrafrecht in Europa—Entwicklungstendenzen und Perspektiven', in F Dünkel, A van Kalmthout and H Schüler-Springorum (eds), *Entwicklungstendenzen und Reformstrategien des Jugendstrafrechts im europäischen Vergleich* (Bonn, Forum Verlag Godesberg).

—— (2006) 'Juvenile Justice in Germany—Between Welfare and Justice' in J Junger-Tas and SH Decker (eds), *International Handbook of Juvenile Justice* (Dordrecht, Springer).

—— (2008) 'Jugendstrafrecht im europäischen Vergleich im Licht aktueller Empfehlungen des Europarats' *Neue Kriminalpolitik*, 20, 102–14.

—— (2011a) 'Germany', in F Dünkel, J Grzywa, P Horsfield and I Pruin (eds) *Juvenile Justice Systems in Europe—Current Situation and Reform Developments*, 2nd edn (Mönchengladbach, Forum Verlag Godesberg).

—— (2011b)'Werden Strafen immer härter? Anmerkungen zur strafrechtlichen Sanktionspraxis und zur Punitivität', in B Bannenberg and J-M Jehle (eds), *Gewaltdelinquenz. Lange Freiheitsentziehung. Delinquenzverläufe* (Mönchengladbach, Forum Verlag Godesberg).

Dünkel, F and Pruin, I (2011) 'Young Adult Offenders in the Criminal Justice Systems of European Countries' in F Dünkel, J Grzywa, P Horsfield and I Pruin (eds), *Juvenile Justice Systems in Europe—Current Situation and Reform Developments*, 2nd edn (Mönchengladbach, Forum Verlag Godesberg).

Dünkel, F and Pruin, I (2012) 'Young adult offenders in the criminal justice systems of European countries' in F Lösel, A Bottoms and D Farrington (eds), *Lost in Transition? Young adult offenders in the criminal justice system* (Abingdon, Routledge).

Dünkel, F and Stańdo-Kawecka, B (2011) 'Juvenile Imprisonment and Placement in Institutions for Deprivation of Liberty—Comparative Aspects' in F Dünkel, J Grzywa, P Horsfield, and I Pruin (eds), *Juvenile Justice Systems in Europe—Current Situation and Reform Developments*, 2nd edn (Mönchengladbach, Forum-Verlag Godesberg).

Dünkel, F, Pruin, I and Grzywa, J (2011) 'Sanctions Systems and Trends in the Development of Sentencing Practices', in F Dünkel, J Grzywa, P Horsfield and I Pruin (eds), *Juvenile Justice Systems in Europe—Current Situation and Reform Developments*, 2nd edn (Mönchengladbach, Forum Verlag Godesberg).

Dünkel, F, Grzywa, J, Horsfield, P and Pruin, I (eds) (2011) *Juvenile Justice Systems in Europe—Current Situation and Reform Developments*, 2nd edn (Mönchengladbach, Forum Verlag Godesberg).

Dünkel, F, Grzywa, J, Pruin, I and Šelih, A (2011) 'Juvenile justice in Europe—Legal aspects, policy trends and perspectives in the light of human rights standards', in F Dünkel, J Grzywa, P Horsfield and I Pruin (eds), *Juvenile Justice Systems in Europe—Current Situation and Reform developments*, 2nd edn (Mönchengladbach, Forum Verlag Godesberg).

Garland, D (2001a) *The Culture of Control: Crime and Social Order in Contemporary Society* (Chicago, University of Chicago Press).

—— (ed) (2001b) *Mass Imprisonment: Social Causes and Consequences* (London, Sage).

Gensing, A (2011) 'Jurisdiction and characteristics of juvenile criminal procedure in Europe', in F Dünkel, J Grzywa, P Horsfield and I Pruin (eds), *Juvenile Justice Systems in Europe—Current Situation and Reform Developments*, 2nd edn (Mönchengladbach, Forum Verlag Godesberg).

Goldson, B (2002) 'New punitiveness. The politics of child incarceration' in J Muncie, G Hughes and E McLaughlin (eds), *Youth Justice: Critical Readings* (London, Sage).

—— (2011) '"Time for a Fresh Start", but is this it? A Critical Assessment of The Report of the Independent Commission on Youth Crime and Antisocial Behaviour' *Youth Justice*, 11, 3–27.

—— and Muncie, J (2006) *Youth, crime and justice* (London, Sage).

Gutbrodt, T (2011) *Jugendstrafrecht in Kolumbien* (Mönchengladbach, Forum Verlag Godesberg).

Habermas, J (1985) *Die neue Unübersichtlichkeit* (Frankfurt/Main, Suhrkamp).

Hammarberg, T (2008) *Memorandum following visits to the United Kingdom* (5–8 February and 31 March–2 April 2008) CommDH(2008)27Strasbourg, 17 October.

Hartjen, CA (2008) *Youth, Crime and Justice. A Global Inquiry* (New Brunswick/NJ, Rutgers University Press).

Haverkamp, R (2007) 'Neuere Entwicklungen im Jugendstrafrecht in Schweden und Finnland' *Recht der Jugend und des Bildungswesens*, 55, 167–90.
Heinz, W (2009) 'Zunehmende Punitivität in der Praxis des Jugendkriminalrechts? Analysen aufgrund von Daten der Strafrechtspflegestatistiken', in Bundesministerium der Justiz (ed), *Das Jugendkriminalrecht vor neuen Herausforderungen? Jenaer Symposium* (Mönchengladbach, Forum Verlag Godesberg).
—— (2011a) 'Neue Straflust der Strafjustiz—Realität oder Mythos?' *Neue Kriminalpolitik*, 22, 14–27.
—— (2011b) 'Neue Lust am Strafen. Gibt es eine Trendwende auch in der deutschen Sanktionierungspraxis?' in K Kühl and S Seher (eds), *Rom, Recht, Religion: Symposion für Udo Ebert zum 70. Geburtstag* (Stuttgart, Mohr Siebeck).
—— (2012) 'Das strafrechtliche Sanktionensystem und die Sanktionierungspraxis in Deutschland 1882–2010 (Stand: Berichtsjahr 2010) Version: 1/2012', Internet-Publication www.uni-konstanz.de/rtf/kis/sanks12.pdf.
Jensen, EL and Jepsen, J (eds) (2006) *Juvenile Law Violators, Human Rights, and the Development of New Juvenile Justice Systems* (Oxford, Hart Publishing).
Junger-Tas, J (2006) 'Trends in International Juvenile Justice—What Conclusions Can be Drawn?' in J Junger-Tas, and SH Decker (eds), *International Handbook of Juvenile Justice* (Dordrecht, Springer).
Junger-Tas, J and Decker, SH (eds) (2006) *International Handbook of Juvenile Justice* (Dordrecht, Springer).
Junger-Tas, J and Dünkel, F (eds) (2009) *Reforming Juvenile Justice* (Dordrecht, Springer).
Kaiser, G (1985) 'International vergleichende Perspektiven zum Jugendstrafrecht' in H-D Schwind, U Berz, G Geilen, RD Herzberg and G Warda (eds), *Festschrift für G. Blau* (Berlin, Walter de Gruyter).
Keiser, C (2008) 'Jugendliche Täter als strafrechtlich Erwachsene? Das Phänomen der "Adulteration" im Lichte internationaler Menschenrechte' *Zeitschrift für die gesamte Strafrechtswissenschaft*, 120, 25–67.
Killias, M and Villettaz, P (2007) 'Rückfall nach Freiheits- und Alternativstrafen: Lehren aus einer systematischen Literaturübersicht' in F Lösel, D Bender and JM Jehle (eds), *Kriminologie und wissensbasierte Kriminalpolitik. Entwicklungs- und Evaluationsforschung* (Mönchengladbach, Forum Verlag Godesberg).
Lappi-Seppälä, T (2007) 'Penal Policy in Scandinavia' in M Tonry (ed), *Crime, Punishment, and Politics in Comparative Perspective (Crime and Justice,* Volume 36) (Chicago, University of Chicago Press).
—— (2010) 'Vertrauen, Wohlfahrt und politikwissenschaftliche Aspekte—International vergleichende Perspektiven zur Punitivität', in F Dünkel, T. Lappi-Seppälä, C Morgenstern and D van Zyl Smit (eds), *Kriminalität, Kriminalpolitik, strafrechtliche Sanktionspraxis und Gefangenenraten im europäischen Vergleich* (Mönchengladbach, Forum Verlag Godesberg).
Loeber, R, Hoeve, M, Farrington, D P, Howell, J C, Slot, W, and van der Laan, P H (2012), 'Overview, Conclusions, and Policy and Research Recommendations', in Loeber, R, Hoeve, M, Slot, W, and van der Laan, P H (eds), *Persisters and Desisters in Crime from Adolescence into Adulthood. Explanation, Prevention and Punishment*, (Farnham, Ashgate).

Lösel, F (2012) 'Offender treatment and rehabilitation: What works?' in M Maguire, R Morgan and R Reiner (eds), *The Oxford Handbook of Criminology*, 5th edn (Oxford, Oxford University Press).
Lösel, F, Stemmler, M, Beelmann, A and Jaursch, S (2007) 'Universelle Prävention dissozialen Verhaltens im Vorschulalter mit dem Elterntraining von EFFEKT: Eine Wirkungsevaluation' in F Lösel, D Bender and J-M Jehle (eds), *Kriminologie und wissensbasierte Kriminalpolitik. Entwicklungs- und Evaluationsforschung* (Mönchengladbach, Forum Verlag Godesberg).
Muncie, J (2008) 'The "Punitive Turn" in Juvenile Justice: Cultures of Control and Rights Compliance in Western Europe and in the USA' *Youth Justice*, 8, 107–21.
Muncie, J and Goldson, B (eds) (2006) *Comparative Youth Justice* (London, Sage).
Nelken, D (2009) 'Comparative criminal justice: Beyond ethnocentrism and relativism' *European Journal of Criminology*, 6, 291–311.
O'Mahony, D and Campbell, C (2006) 'Mainstreaming Restorative Justice for Young Offenders through Youth Conferencing: The Experience in Northern Ireland' in J Junger-Tas and SH Decker (eds), *International Handbook of Juvenile Justice* (Dordrecht, Springer).
O'Mahony, D and Doak, J (2009) 'Restorative Justice and Youth Justice: Bringing Theory and Practice Closer Together in Europe' in J Junger-Tas and F Dünkel (eds), *Reforming Criminal Justice* (Berlin, Springer).
Păroşanu, A (2011) 'Romania' in F Dünkel, J Grzywa, P Horsfield and I Pruin (eds) *Juvenile Justice Systems in Europe—Current Situation and Reform Developments*, 2nd edn (Mönchengladbach, Forum Verlag Godesberg).
Patanè, V (ed) (2007) *European Juvenile Justice Systems* (volume 1) (Milan, Giuffrè Editore).
Pratt, J, Brown, D, Brown, M, Hallsworth, S and Morrison, W (eds) (2005) *The New Punitiveness. Trends, theories, perspectives* (Cullompton, Willan Publishing).
Pruin, I (2007) *Die Heranwachsendenregelung im deutschen Jugendstrafrecht. Jugendkriminologische, entwicklungspsychologische, jugendsoziologische und rechtsvergleichende Aspekte* (Mönchengladbach, Forum Verlag Godesberg).
—— (2011) 'The Scope of Juvenile Justice Systems in Europe' in F Dünkel, J Grzywa, P Horsfield and I Pruin (eds), *Juvenile Justice Systems in Europe—Current Situation and Reform Developments*, 2nd edn (Mönchengladbach, Forum Verlag Godesberg).
Roberts, J and Hough, M (eds) (2002) *Changing Attitudes to Punishment: Public opinion, crime and justice* (Cullompton, Willan Publishing).
Shchedrin, N (2011) 'Russia' in F Dünkel, J Grzywa, P Horsfield and I Pruin (eds) *Juvenile Justice Systems in Europe—Current Situation and Reform Developments*, 2nd edn (Mönchengladbach, Forum Verlag Godesberg).
Smith, DJ (ed) (2010) *A New Response to Youth Crime* (Cullompton, Willan Publishing).
Snacken, S (2010) 'Resisting punitiveness in Europe?' *Theoretical Criminology*, 14, 273–92.
—— (2012) 'Conclusion: Why and How to Resist Punitiveness in Europe?', in S Snacken and E Dumortier (eds), *Resisting Punitiveness in Europe? Welfare, Human Rights and Democracy* (London, Routledge).

Snacken, S and Dumortier, E (eds) (2012) *Resisting Punitiveness in Europe? Welfare, Human Rights and Democracy* (London, Routledge).
Stańdo-Kawecka, B (2011) 'Poland' in F Dünkel, J Grzywa, P Horsfield and I Pruin (eds) *Juvenile Justice Systems in Europe—Current Situation and Reform Developments*, 2nd edn (Mönchengladbach, Forum Verlag Godesberg).
Storgaard, A (2004) 'Juvenile Justice in Scandinavia' *Journal of Scandinavian Studies in Criminology and Crime Prevention*, 5, 188–204.
Stump, B (2003) *'Adult time for adult crime'—Jugendliche zwischen Jugend- und Erwachsenenstrafrecht* (Mönchengladbach, Forum Verlag Godesberg).
Tiffer-Sotomayor, C (2000) *Jugendstrafrecht in Lateinamerika unter besonderer Berücksichtigung des Jugendstrafrechts in Costa Rica* (Mönchengladbach, Forum Verlag Godesberg).
Tiffer-Sotomayor, C, Llobet Rodríguez, J and Dünkel, F (2002) *Derecho Penal Juvenil* (San José/Costa Rica, DAAD).
Tonry, M (2004) *Punishment and Politics* (Cullompton, Willan Publishing).
Tonry, M and Doob, AN (eds) (2004) *Youth Crime and Justice (Crime and Justice,* Volume 31) (Chicago, University of Chicago Press).
Von Hofer, H (2004) 'Crime and Reactions to Crime in Scandinavia' *Journal of Scandinavian Studies in Criminology and Crime Prevention*, 5, 148–66.
Weijers, I and Grisso, T (2009) 'Criminal Responsibility of Adolescents: Youth as Junior Citizenship', in J Junger-Tas and F Dünkel (eds), *Reforming Juvenile Justice* (Dordrecht, Springer).
Weijers, I, Nuytiens, A and Christiaens, J (2009) 'Transfer of Minors to the Criminal Court in Europe: Belgium and the Netherlands', in J Junger-Tas and F Dünkel (eds), *Reforming Juvenile Justice* (Dordrecht, Springer).

## EUROPEAN COURT OF HUMAN RIGHTS CASE LAW

*T and V v United Kingdom* 16 December 1999 (24724/94) (2000) 30 EHRR 121.

## COUNCIL OF EUROPE INSTRUMENTS

Recommendation No. Rec (2003) 20 of the Committee of Ministers to Member States concerning new ways of dealing with juvenile delinquency and the role of juvenile justice adopted by the Committee of Ministers on 24 September 2003 at the 853rd meeting of the Ministers' Deputies.
Recommendation No. Rec (2008) 11 of the Committee of Ministers to Member States concerning juvenile offenders subject to sanctions or measures adopted by the Committee of Ministers on 5 November 2008 at the 1040th meeting of the Ministers' Deputies.

# 8

# *Community Sanctions and European Penology*

FERGUS MCNEILL

## I. INTRODUCTION

THE NUMBERS OF offenders under supervision in the community have grown rapidly in recent decades. In most jurisdictions in and beyond Europe, offenders under supervision (whether as an alternative to prosecution or sentence, as a community sentence in its own right, or as part of a post-custody licence) heavily outnumber those detained in custody. To give two examples, in Germany in 2008 the prison population was around 73,000 (Federal Statistics Office/*Statistisches Bundesamt* 2008), whereas an estimated 225,000 persons were under some form of supervision (Federal Statistics Office/*Statistisches Bundesamt* 2011; Morgenstern and Hecht 2011); in June 2010 in England and Wales the prison population was 83,500 whilst the population of offenders under statutory supervision in the community was 241,500 (Ministry of Justice 2010). Systems and practices of offender supervision have also developed swiftly in Central and Eastern Europe, where nascent probation systems have been a part of post-Soviet era criminal justice reforms.

Pan-European figures are hard to establish, given the wide range of definitions and forms of community sanctions and differences in official recording of their use but Van Kalmthout and Durnescu's (2008) extensive recent survey suggests considerable expansion of the use of such sanctions in almost all European jurisdictions. Durnescu (2008) estimated that about 2 million people were incarcerated in Europe at the time of his survey, and about 3.5 million were subject to some form of community sanction. The fact that almost all prisoners are (eventually) released, often under some form of supervision, means of course that many 'custodial' sentences also involve community-based supervision, whereas the converse is not the case. As Robinson, McNeill and Maruna argue, therefore, '[t]he vast majority of the "ordinary" (but barely visible) business of supervised punishment therefore plays out daily in probation or parole offices, and in supervisees' homes, rather than in custodial institutions' (Robinson et al 2012).

But besides their increasing scale and reach, the intensity of supervisory sanctions has also developed considerably in recent decades, moving beyond traditionally rehabilitative measures to include unpaid work, medical, psychological or substance misuse treatment, mandatory drug or alcohol testing, exclusion orders and residence conditions, curfews, house arrest and electronic monitoring as well as other innovations. Under criminal law, the use of supervisory sanctions before trial or sentence is increasing, but supervision has also emerged under civil law (eg in the UK's Anti-Social Behaviour Orders) and in administrative forms (eg again in the UK's use of Multi-Agency Public Protection Arrangements). New forms of supervision directed at foreign nationals, migrants and refugees have also emerged.

One driver of this expansion and adaptation, at least in some jurisdictions, is increasing political and public concern about the costs of imprisonment and of reoffending (ie offending during or after criminal sanctions). A recent policy paper in the UK estimated that the 'vicious cycle' of reoffending by ex-prisoners costs the UK economy £7–10 billion per year (Ministry of Justice 2010).

The potential role of community supervision in reducing these costs has become a key interest of contemporary penal policy; particularly in relation to using such sanctions and measures to displace shorter custodial sentences which have higher costs per day and are typically associated with high reconviction rates. To give one example of the possible savings: in the Netherlands, the notional cost of a two-month prison sentence is between 10,800 and 24,000 EUR, while the total costs of community sanctions that can substitute for such a sentence range between 600 and 2,000 EUR. Some argue (somewhat more controversially) that, as well as being much less expensive than imprisonment, community supervision can produce lower reoffending rates.

This remarkable expansion and adaptation, along with the recurring claims of greater 'efficiency' or 'effectiveness' that have been made for supervisory sanctions, should have ensured that such sanctions became a key focus of contemporary penology in Europe and elsewhere. Instead, despite the influence and standing of Stan Cohen's (1985) *Visions of Social Control*, it is the growth of 'mass incarceration' that has preoccupied scholars, unwittingly allowing the neglect of the parallel development of 'mass supervision'. This neglect has analytical and practical consequences. It skews academic, political, professional and public representations and understandings of the penal field, and in consequence it produces a failure to deliver the kinds of analyses that are now urgently required to engage with political, policy and practice communities grappling with the challenges of delivering justice efficiently and effectively in fiscally straitened times—and with the challenges of communicating the meaning, nature, legitimacy and utility of supervisory sanctions to an insecure public (see McNeill 2011).

This chapter aims principally to issue a challenge to European penologists to take community sanctions more seriously, and to begin to sketch out how we might do so.[1]

## II. DEFINING AND VIEWING THE (SUB-)FIELD

Observant readers will already have noticed a certain slippage in terminology: I have referred sometimes to 'offender supervision', sometimes to 'supervision in the community', sometimes to 'community supervision' and sometimes to 'community sanctions'. Whatever we call it, this is clearly a penal subfield around which it is difficult to draw precise boundaries, which is described and labelled differently in different places, and which has been characterised by the regular renamings that come with innovation, differentiation and a perennial quest for credibility and legitimacy (see Robinson et al 2012). Raynor's preferred term, 'community penalties', reflects his jurisdictional home (England and Wales) and suffers (as he acknowledges) from its failure to include the large populations subject to some form of supervision following release from custody (Raynor 2007). In other Anglophone jurisdictions (principally in North America and Australasia), terms like 'community corrections' are used. Though these are broader in scope, they have the disadvantage of implying a particular form of practice (correctionalist), which is far from universal in its application, even in the jurisdictions in which the term is used.

Given the avowedly European focus in this collection, it makes sense to settle on the commendably neutral, if somewhat technical, European label 'community sanctions and measures' (CSM), defined by the Council of Europe as:

> [those sanctions and measures] which maintain the offender in the community and involve some restriction of his liberty through the imposition of conditions and/or obligations, and which are implemented by bodies designated in law for that purpose. The term designates any sanction imposed by a court or a judge, and any measure taken before or instead of a decision on a sanction as well as ways of enforcing a sentence of imprisonment outside a prison establishment.
>
> (Council of Europe 1992: Appendix para 1.)

[1] This chapter draws heavily on the ultimately successful application for a COST Action on Offender Supervision in Europe (COST Action IS1106: www.cost.eu/domains_actions/isch/Actions/IS1106). That application was co-authored by Kristel Beyens, Miranda Boone, Ioan Durnescu, Martine Herzog-Evans, Christine Morgenstern, Gwen Robinson and myself. This chapter gives me a welcome opportunity to acknowledge my intellectual debt to these co-authors, and more generally, to the many colleagues who have participated since 2007 in the European Society of Criminology Working Group on Community Sanctions. Both the COST application and therefore this chapter are really the products of our conversations over the last five or six years.

What this definition lacks in depth, it makes up for in breadth: it succeeds in capturing not just the wide array of penalties handed down by courts (sometimes called 'front door' measures) which fall between non-supervisory penalties (eg fines) and custodial sentences, but also statutory post-custodial ('back-door') measures associated with early release schemes (such as parole). The use of the term 'measures' (as well as 'sanctions') allows for attention to be paid to measures imposed pre-court and/or in lieu of prosecution, rather than restricting our attention to those that are imposed by judicial or quasi-judicial bodies.

Clear though it is, this definition is all form and no function. As Robinson, McNeill and Maruna note:

> In the most general terms, what community sanctions and measures have in common is some form of oversight or supervision of individuals' activities whilst maintaining them in the community. What 'supervision' entails, the ends or purposes to which it is oriented and who assumes responsibility for it, are all dimensions of variation internationally and historically.
>
> (Robinson et al 2012.)

Putting this a different way, we have here a kind of formal or legal scaffold, but it tells us very little about the kind of building whose construction it facilitates. It tells us little about the substance or the essence of community sanctions and measures. Of course, as Barbara Hudson's (2003) excellent introductory text on punishment both argues and demonstrates, there are many ways to construct and examine the objects of the penological gaze. Just as criminology is a 'rendezvous discipline', so penology is a quintessentially interdisciplinary subject that compels and requires criminological, legal, philosophical and sociological scrutiny, as well as raising fundamental political and practical questions. Community sanctions need to be scrutinised from all of these different vantage points.

In similar vein, Tonry's (2006) commanding and authoritative overview of the purposes and functions of sentencing also provides a neat framework for analysing penal sanctions. Tonry distinguishes between sentencing's purposes or normative functions (that is, its justifications), its primary functions (these being the proper distribution of punishment; the prevention of crime; and the communication of threat, censure and of social norms), its ancillary functions (in contributing to the management of an efficient and effective justice system, and in securing legitimacy and public confidence) and its latent functions (the ways in which it reflects self-interest, ideology and partisanship, and how and what it communicates informally).[2]

[2] In the Mertonian sense, the normative, primary and ancillary functions of punishment are all 'manifest' functions, in that they are all explicitly stated and understood, though perhaps to varying degrees and in different ways by different parties to the process. Of course, depending

Though he does not explain his framework in these terms, we might suggest that, albeit with notable exceptions, philosophers and jurists tend to study and discuss the normative functions and primary purposes of sentencing, criminologists tend to examine its ancillary functions and sociologists tend to study its latent functions. The same taxonomy of perspectives can be applied to community sanctions; we can explore their purposes or normative functions, their primary functions, their ancillary functions and their latent functions, provoking respectively legal and philosophical enquiry, criminological research and analysis, and sociological interpretation.

## III. REVIEWING THE (SUB-)FIELD

Although there is some 'normative' literature (especially in Germany) addressing the legal and constitutional requirements of forms of supervision, it remains relatively under-theorised as well as under-researched in comparative perspective. In recent years the most prominent strand of research in the field has addressed the effectiveness of specific forms of community sanction or supervision. It is worth noting that there are at least two separate sets of questions here. One concerns the effectiveness of one type of sanction vis-à-vis another (usually prisons versus community); the other concerns the effectiveness of particular styles of or approaches to supervision or intervention within the legal framework that the sanction requires.

The latter question—about the effectiveness of particular methods and approaches—has been a particular preoccupation in anglophone jurisdictions (for an excellent overview, see Raynor and Robinson 2009), although it has also been the focus of much attention and development in Scandinavia and the Low Countries. Under the general banner of 'What Works?', much of this research has been sponsored by national governments (eg the Home Office in England and Wales) and limited to the evaluation of programmes which, despite the amount of energy and investment directed at them, are only accessed by a small minority of offenders subject to supervision, even in those jurisdictions that are most committed to such programmes. At a recent CEP (the European Probation Organisation) event, concerned with sharing European experience around the accreditation of such programmes and co-sponsored by the Scottish Centre for Crime and Justice Research, discussions revealed that Northern Ireland may put the highest proportion of persons subject to supervision through such programmes. But even there, only about one in three people under supervision is involved in such work. In most other jurisdictions the ratio is less than one in 10.

on one's point of view, at least some of the manifest and the latent functions of punishment might also be seen as Mertonian *dysfunctions*, in terms of their adverse social consequences.

It is perhaps not surprising therefore that, even within this primarily evaluative body of scholarship, it is increasingly recognised that research and development needs to move beyond a focus on special programmes and toward an examination of routine practices of supervision if significant improvements in reoffending outcomes are to be delivered (McNeill et al 2010). More critically minded and culturally sensitive scholars have also highlighted the need to attend to the risks associated with 'policy transfer' around 'What Works?': specifically the transfer of programmes which may be effective in one context to others with different penal cultures and offender populations (Canton 2009).

Of course, even within a principally evaluative paradigm preoccupied with effectiveness questions, major methodological and conceptual challenges are generated by the broader question of the effectiveness of different types of sanctions themselves (see McNeill and Whyte 2007: ch 2). While it may (perhaps) be possible to specify the components of a structured, manualised programme, so as to somehow isolate independent, extraneous and dependent variables, the kinds of scaffold referred to in the last section are in and of themselves much too insubstantial to permit any meaningful evaluation of their aggregate 'effects'.

These more prosaic questions of technical efficiency and effectiveness therefore drive us back towards other prior projects of enquiry which are at least threefold. We need to examine: (1) the lived experience of supervision for those subject to and affected by it; (2) the construction of cultures and practices of supervision by those that deliver it; and (3) the multiple contexts of supervision (material, social, political, cultural, organisational, professional and legal) that shape and structure it. In other words, we need to move beyond the narrowly evaluative, criminological enquiry that has dominated the subfield, to produce a more inter-disciplinary and more critical mode of analysis that draws on and extends beyond legal, philosophical and sociological traditions. We need to analyse the nature of community sanctions as socially constituted institutions of punishment, as culturally constructed and contingent practices and as lived experiences.

## A. Constituting Sanctions: The Identities and Purposes of Supervision[3]

Perhaps one of the reasons for the failure to displace or marginalise the prison in the popular, penal-political or in the penological imagination, rests in the historical origins of community sanctions in many jurisdictions, particularly where they emerged not as punishments but rather as measures

[3] This section, and the two that follow it, draw extensively upon and update Sparks and McNeill (2009).

imposed (primarily in anglophone countries) *instead* of punishment, or (primarily in countries with Roman law traditions) as a form of suspended punishment. This peculiar non-status as a mode of punishment may have suited liberal and progressive reformers who were so often trying to divert first-time and/or minor offenders from the demoralising dangers of imprisonment and into nascent forms of social welfare services (for the Scottish example, see McNeill 2005). However, its legacy in the context of late-modern penal populism and of contemporary public sensibilities has been a legitimation crisis for sanctions cast around remedial, rehabilitative and reintegrative intentions that are seen, rightly or wrongly, as being principally concerned with the interests and needs of 'offenders'.

In those jurisdictions where both social trust and welfare provision are in short or declining supply, where inequality is rising and where penal politics is febrile, it is not difficult to see how and why such intentions and concerns cease to connect with public sensibilities. In general terms therefore, the social, economic, cultural and political dynamics elucidated in, for example, the works of Garland (2001), Melossi (2008), Simon (2007) and Wacquant (2009) arguably conspire to produce a shrinking conceptual space for community sanctions. These late-modern dynamics (and indirectly the more 'dystopian' or 'catastrophic' readings of them, on which see Daems (2008)) deprive community sanctions of the sorts of moral, cultural and political resources upon which they have historically drawn. Instead, they tend to be cast as the kind of undue indulgence discussed above. As Garland (2001) puts it, where the offender ceases to be seen as a 'poorly socialised misfit' and becomes instead either an opportunistic, illicit consumer (to be controlled through target-hardening or increased surveillance) or alternatively a dangerous, threatening outsider (to be despatched, incapacitated or deported), support for more inclusive penal-welfarist strategies wanes. As I have already suggested, this is not to say that supervision in the community declines in volume, rather it serves to reveal how supervision's uses, forms, meanings and character are compelled to change and to find new routes to legitimacy.

But before discussing these changes, it is necessary to note a second problem perhaps posed by the origins of community sanctions as measures of *diversion from* punishment; a problem that may partly explain the slower progress of human rights discourses in the field of community sanctions than in relation to imprisonment. This problem rests in the sense in which the origins of community sanctions in many jurisdictions lie in acts of sovereign or executive clemency or mercy. Thus recipients of such sanctions were seen not as being diverted from punishment because they *deserved* to be so diverted; rather they were granted such sanctions (whether probation or parole) because the state elected not to proceed with the measures of punishment to which it *was* nonetheless entitled. As philosophers of punishment have pointed out, part of the point of mercy is that it is undeserved (Smart 1969; Murphy 1988; Walker 1991). For that reason it is not something to which someone can easily extend a rights claim.

Though in many jurisdictions community sanctions now find themselves located in an explicit or implicit tariff of penalties (whether enshrined in sentencing laws and guidelines, penal codes or merely in professional practices), there remains in several other jurisdictions a stubborn public (and sometimes professional) perception that the ordering of such a sanction is an act of judicial or executive largesse. When this perception is combined with any public suspicion that the largesse is tied to some non-legal or non-judicial consideration (for example, making cost savings or gaining some political or diplomatic advantage), public cynicism may be the result. This has two main implications for human rights: first, in the social and political climate discussed above it generally militates against parsimonious approaches to sentencing and release decisions; secondly, it constructs those subject to supervision as recipients of mercy and thereby de facto deprives them of the moral basis for legitimate claims to any entitlements to community sanctions (rather than custodial ones) and to fair treatment in the execution of community sanctions.

The durability of the perception that the subjects of supervision are recipients of mercy (ie they are seen as having been 'let off') has vexed probation policy-makers and practitioners for decades (eg the Morison Report 1964; Casey Report 2008). To some extent, it perhaps reflects the failure of community sanctions to make significant inroads into public consciousness. Public opinion research tends to show very little public understanding of the nature and requirements of contemporary community sanctions, though some support for their aims and methods does exist (Allen and Hough 2008; Maruna and King 2008). To address the credibility and legitimacy issues that arise from the 'marketing' problems of CSM, there have been attempts in some jurisdictions to create identities for CSM that are more focused on managing risk and public protection, on delivering punishment in the community, or on recasting them as principally reparative in nature (see Robinson et al 2012). At the same time, the traditional view of probation as means of re-educating or correcting the corrigible so as to enable their social integration and inclusion has been downplayed (though not necessarily abandoned). In very broad terms, and in some jurisdictions more than others, we might summarise these developments as suggesting a drift away from what Gearty (2006) would perhaps describe as a concern with the claim rights of offenders (linked to a concern with *their* flourishing and well-being) and towards protecting the liberties of potential victims and of communities (see Canton 2008). Paraphrasing Melossi, we might say that in some guises at least, community sanctions have become less a site where offenders are made fit for enjoying the rights and responsibilities of the social contract (with the intention *rétablir dans ses droits*), and more a mechanism for managing the ways in which they are deemed to threaten the liberties of others, and thus the social contract itself.

### B. Constructing Sanctions: Practising Supervision

If this sounds somewhat dystopian, and perhaps over-emphasises developments in anglophone jurisdictions, it might be more accurate to describe community sanctions in general as facing a perennial tension regarding the extent to which they are defined and constructed around the purposes of public protection, penal reductionism and/or rehabilitation/ social inclusion. Despite the pressures noted above, in most jurisdictions all three purposes endure in some form or other, and in some places a more explicit commitment to the pursuit of reparation or mediation has been added where CSM services have sought to engage much more directly with victims.[4] In some jurisdictions, policy-makers and practitioners have gone so far as to argue that the three purposes are interdependent, for example casting both the inclusion (or integration) of offenders and the reduction of the use of imprisonment as means by which public protection can and should be enhanced (Robinson and McNeill 2004; McNeill and Whyte 2007).

However, the elevation of public protection as the dominant purpose or meta-narrative in some jurisdictions (Robinson and McNeill 2004)—even where such discourses are used as a means of re-legitimating welfarist practices (see McNeill et al 2009)—is far from unproblematic. To promise public protection seems to make sense during times when people are insecure about the pace and scale of change in western societies, and in this respect the contemporary preoccupation with risks might suggest that the position of community sanctions can be secured by promising to manage and reduce risks and thus to protect. However, there is a paradox at the heart of protection and there are risks with risk: to promise to protect is to confirm the existence of a threat, and thus to legitimise and reinforce fear (Douglas 1992). Whenever and wherever supervision agencies commit themselves to the assessment and management of risks, or even worse define themselves in those terms, they expose themselves not to the likelihood of failure, but to its inevitability. Not all risks are predictable and not all harms are preventable. Even being excellent at assessing and managing risks most of the time (assuming that this could be achieved) would not protect probation from occasional, spectacular failures and the political costs that they carry (McCulloch and McNeill 2007; McNeill 2011).

[4] Here we mean 'real' victims of extant crimes, as opposed to 'potential' victims of future crimes.

A further related problem with public protection is that it tends to dichotomise the interests and rights of offenders and the interests and rights of victims and communities in a zero-sum game (McCulloch and McNeill 2007). It becomes not just a case of protecting 'us' from 'them', but a case of setting 'our' safeties and liberties against 'theirs' (see also Canton 2008). For supervision agencies in some jurisdictions at least this has led to public and political pressure for more secure or incapacitating forms of control; forms of control that serve, at least in the short term, to reassure. But the traditional mechanisms of protection associated with community sanctions are to be found in the support of longer-term processes and projects of change and reintegration which provide relatively little security and reassurance in the short-term. Thus although changed ex-offenders ('desisters', in contemporary parlance) who have internalised and committed to the responsibilities of citizenship may offer a better prospect for a safer society in the long term, change programmes and services look somewhat feeble when set against the increasingly threatening offender that communities are taught to fear. In this context, where supervision is cast as just one in a range of means of securing public protection, and where it lacks a distinctive moral purpose or penal-cultural identity, they remain in the shadow of the always more incapacitating, always more punishing prison. Even within the community, they have to compete against or seek re-legitimation through the promise of new technologies like remote electronic monitoring which, on some accounts, aspire to create the 'virtual prison' in the community (Roberts 2004).[5] In this sense, community sanctions are vulnerable to what we might cast not as the penal temptation (*pace* Wacquant) but as a less and less satiable appetite for incapacitation.

And yet, evidence is emerging in various jurisdictions that penal practitioners—even in those jurisdictions where risk-based discourses and technologies have made the greatest advances—can resist and subvert, as well as sometimes being co-opted to, these pressures. Thus Deering's (2011) recent analysis of the accounts of probation practitioners in England and Wales uncovers a familiar combination of pragmatic adherence to government aims and continued commitment to ideals about the possibility and value of individual change and development, as well as a stubbornly social (or sociologically positivistic) analysis of the causes of crime (see also McNeill et al 2009). Deering doesn't really acknowledge or discuss the implicit tensions in this position; that is, the tension between a belief that crime is a product of social and structural factors and a practice rooted in supporting individual change and empowerment. The durable practice ideology that he uncovers remains one in which the practice

[5] Of course as Mike Nellis (2009) has pointed out, electronic monitoring in and of itself does not incapacitate—it merely provides a new means of monitoring and perhaps securing compliance with curfew conditions or home detention.

focus is on individual rather than social change; on crime rather than criminalisation; on better coping with the stresses of disadvantaged lives rather than moderating the forces that generate these pressures; in essence on the processing of private troubles rather than the confrontation of social issues. That said, he is surely right to note that the continuation of an essentially humanitarian ethos in probation practice is probably (from the probationer's point of view) an important moderator of more punitive and exclusionary policy discourses.

## C. Experiencing Sanctions: The Lived Realities of Supervision

With respect to offenders' and ex-offenders' human rights, the implications of the ascendancy of public protection are perhaps obvious: first, their access to community sanctions (whether instead of custody or as mechanisms for early release) can become conditional on assessments of the risks[6] involved in their liberation, irrespective of the sometimes dubious basis of such assessments; secondly, they may not be required to consent to the forms of supervision to which they find themselves subject, since these measures are not aimed at their interests; thirdly, sanctions may come to be loaded with more onerous and intrusive conditions, in the putative public interest; fourthly, combinations of the involuntary nature of supervision and its more onerous conditions may increase the likelihood of technical violations[7] of community sanctions; and fifthly, violations may lead to greater penalties than would have been imposed at first instance. Under these conditions, community sanctions can all too easily become a driver of incarceration rates, rather than a brake upon them (see Simon 1993). For those caught up in such systems and practices, questions of legitimacy and procedural justice in the administration of community sanctions become no less pressing than they are for those in custody.

Even leaving aside the pressures and problems generated by the dominance of public protection, the punitive effects of community sanctions have rarely been recognised or discussed, perhaps particularly because they have until comparatively recently been cast as essentially benign, inclusive, welfarist measures with reintegrative intent. But of course, as the history of penal welfarism itself so clearly illustrates, the pursuit of welfare can often result in consequences that are experienced as being highly punishing by those on the receiving end (Garland 1985; see also Daems 2008). It is

[6] This is not the place for a discussion of the accuracy of risk assessment, but it should be noted that professional assessments of risk are not immune to the wider social and political pressures discussed above.

[7] By technical violations, we mean breaches of the conditions of supervision as opposed to the commission of further offences.

worth noting, for example, that the limited empirical evidence available about probationers' recollections of their experience—even at the peak of penal welfarism and in an avowedly welfarist jurisdiction (Scotland in the 1960s)—suggests that probation has always been simultaneously about helping, holding (both in the sense of support and in the sense of constraint) and hurting (McNeill 2009).

With respect to the hurts that punishment generates, there is, of course, an extensive body of scholarship, in the tradition of Gresham Sykes' (1958) seminal work, on the pains of imprisonment. More recent iterations of this literature point not just to the peculiar pains of life in 'supermax' conditions (King 2005), but also to the pains and harms of mass incarceration itself (Haney 2005), and to the pains and harms suffered by prisoners' partners and families, through 'secondary prisonization' (Comfort 2007). Perhaps more directly pertinent here are the pains of penal rehabilitation in its current risk-focused guise. Thus, for example, we find evidence of burgeoning resentment amongst English prisoners towards what apparently seems to them to be the capricious and illegitimate exercise of 'soft power' by prison psychologists involved in key decisions about prisoner progression or release (Crewe 2009; and more generally Maruna 2011). In similar vein, Lacombe's (2008) ethnographic study of prisoners in an English prison-based sex offender programme reveals the ways in which risk-based rehabilitation invites and requires them to contort their perceptions and presentations of self in line with the requirements of the particular programme or process to which they are subject. Cox's (2012) compelling ethnographic analysis of the pains of youth imprisonment (albeit in a US state) reveals a similar picture.

These pains of risk-based rehabilitation extend beyond the prison too. The traditional absence of punitive intent in probation or criminal justice social work (alluded to above) does not necessarily entail an absence of 'penal bite'; at least if studies of those subject to community supervision are to be taken seriously. For example, researchers at the RAND Corporation in the USA found that there are intermediate sanctions which surveyed prisoners equate with prison in terms of punitiveness. For some individuals, intensive forms of probation 'may actually be the more dreaded penalty' (Petersilia and Deschenes 1994: 306; see also Petersilia 1990; Payne and Gainey 1998; May and Wood 2010). More recently, Durnescu (2011) has specifically explored the 'pains of probation' as experienced in Romania. Alongside deprivations of time and the other practical and financial costs of compliance, and limitations on their autonomy and privacy, probationers also reported the pain of the 'forced return to the offence' and the pain of a life lived 'under a constant threat'. The threat in question in Durnescu's (2011) study was that of breach or revocation, and with it further punishment, but the works referred to in the last paragraph also point to the threat of failing to persuade a probation officer, a psychologist, or some other professional that one's 'riskiness' can be and is being properly addressed and managed.

In one sense, there may be little that is truly novel in this. For a prisoner of the Eastern State Penitentiary in the nineteenth century, placed in silent and solitary confinement in the hope that he would repent and make his peace with his Maker, the pains of penitentiary reform were doubtless profound. His project of 'coercive soul transformation' may have been designed and delivered somewhat differently than that directed at the late-modern risk-bearing prisoner or probationer—but both are subjected to disciplinary regimes (Foucault 1977). But what may be peculiarly demanding for late-modern penal subjects (inside or outside of prison) is that, rather than being left to deal, before God, with their own sinfulness and redemption, they are compelled to *display* the malleability of their riskiness, to *perform* its reduction and manageability. At least in some risk-based systems, it is the credibility of this performance which will determine progression in and release from punishment. In these circumstances, rehabilitation is both disciplinary and punishing in a particularly potent way (see Crewe 2012).

Perhaps presaging these developments, Edgardo Rotman drew an important distinction between anthropocentric and authoritarian rehabilitation:

> The authoritarian model of rehabilitation is really only a subtler version of the old repressive model, seeking compliance by means of intimidation and coercion. Rehabilitation in this sense is essentially a technical device to mould the offender and ensure conformity to a predesigned pattern of thought and behaviour ... The anthropocentric or humanistic model of rehabilitation, on the other hand, grants primacy to the actual human being rather than metaphysical fixations or ideologies, which long served to justify the oppressive intervention of the state. Client centred and basically voluntary, such rehabilitation is conceived more as a right of the citizen than as a privilege of the state. A humanistic public policy regarding crime implies the idea of human perfectibility, which at the level of rehabilitation includes not only the offenders themselves, but also the society that bred them and the institutions and persons involved in their treatment.
>
> (Rotman 1994: 292.)

This distinction, and more specifically its implication that the person engaged in rehabilitation must be treated as a moral subject and not as a material object to be manipulated or adjusted in the interests of others, seems central to many of the claims that can be made for and against rehabilitation—and to broader questions about the legitimacy of rehabilitation (in its various guises; see Robinson 2008, McNeill forthcoming) and of its relationships with institutions of punishment, whether custodial or community-based.

## IV. CONCLUSIONS: DEVELOPING COMPARATIVE AND EUROPEAN PENOLOGY

Despite my earlier call for more thoroughly interdisciplinary analyses of community sanctions, it is obvious, on reviewing this chapter, that it is the product of a principally sociological engagement with the topic. In a sense, therefore, this brief and selective exploration of the existing literature on supervisory sanctions does little more than to underline the need to more comprehensively review and synthesise existing analyses, as well as to generate new knowledge about such sanctions as a set of situated social practices which can and must be analysed in comparative context, taking into account how they are differently experienced, practiced and constituted in different places—and to what effect.

Although interested scholars have begun to take important first steps towards comparative work (eg Dünkel and Spieß 1983; Hamai et al 1995; van Kalmthout and Durnescu 2008), existing publications (in the form of edited collections) have tended to rely principally on single nation descriptive accounts of probation systems, services and practices, and to emphasise policy rather than practice or theoretical issues, with limited comparative analyses provided. That gap—in comparative analyses of community sanctions as constituted, as practised, as experienced—constitutes an important lacuna in the existing literature on comparative penology itself (eg Rusche and Kirchheimer 1939; van Kalmthout and Tak 1988; Downes 1988; Cavadino and Dignan 2006; Dünkel et al 2010; Lappi-Seppälä 2012). This body of work has tended to privilege the analysis of imprisonment rates/regimes and macro-level explanations for jurisdictional variations. Valuable though this is, it is increasingly recognised that deeper and richer understandings of penal cultures and practices are required to make sense of differences in approaches to punishment (Nelken 2009), and that systems, practices and experiences of supervision (and not just prison rates and regimes) must be a part of such analyses.

Returning to the arguments with which we started, the development of such analyses seem to matter now more than ever, for both analytical and practical purposes. At an international or transnational level, supervision began to emerge as an important topic in the early 1990s when the United Nations and the Council of Europe tried to strengthen community sanctions to reduce the use of imprisonment but also tried to establish minimum standards for such sanctions so as to ensure that human rights were respected. Both organisations involved national stakeholders as well as NGOs and scientific experts in the preparations of suitable documents to support these goals. Nevertheless, the United Nations Standard Minimum Rules for Non-Custodial Sanctions and Measures (the Tokyo Rules) from 1990 and the Council Europe's *Recommendation No. R (92) 16 on the*

*European rules on community sanctions and measures* from 1992—neither of which is binding on Member States—gained little attention in the Member States.

In the years since, in particular after 2001, other topics, such as the 'fight' against organised crime, terrorism or corruption, became priorities on the international agenda. In the EU, where criminal policy remains largely within the competence of the Member States, 'mutual trust based on mutual understanding' is of key importance for efficient cooperation in that field—this was recently affirmed in the 'Stockholm programme' that sets policy priorities in the area of justice, freedom and security ([2010] OJ C115). More specifically, a European Council Framework Decision from 2008 on 'supervision of probation measures and alternative sanctions' now requires Member States to supervise offenders sentenced in another state and thus to implement 'foreign' supervision orders. Mutual understanding based on mutual knowledge of such orders and practices has therefore become crucial in managing such transfers. Yet recent seminars that have brought together practitioners, scholars and policy makers reveal that this understanding is still lacking, partly because of the limitations in academic study of this field alluded to above.

But the Framework Decision is important for another reason: it raises the profile and import of the EU itself as a significant actor in the penal field (see Baker, this volume), specifically with reference to community sanctions. Thus, for example, and without going into the detail of the Framework Decision itself, the 'scientific experts' supporting the then Belgian Presidency of the EU in working towards the implementation of the Framework Decision, noted the following:

> Member States ... differ in their reliance on explicit purposes of sentencing. Some refer explicitly to the aims of rehabilitation and prevention of recidivism for community sanctions and measures ... others leave it up to the court to assess whether a CSM can fulfil 'the aims of the punishment'.
>
> This should not raise a particular problem for transfers under the [Framework Decision], so long as all parties understand that the [Framework Decision] itself states in article 1 its objectives as: 'facilitating the social rehabilitation of sentenced persons, improving the protection of victims and the general public, and facilitating the application of suitable probation measures and alternative sanctions in cases of offenders who do not live in the state of conviction'.
>
> (Snacken and McNeill 2012: 1)

Though this statement concerns the purposes of *transferring* supervision, in some senses it can be interpreted as establishing common pan-European meta-purposes (or in Tonry's terms, normative and primary functions) for community sanctions themselves. Other European instruments have less force than the Framework Decision but they nonetheless suggest convergence in what we referred to above as the constitution of sanctions; in the elaboration of their identities and purposes (see Morgenstern 2002; 2009). Thus similar statements of purpose can be found in the Council of Europe Probation Rules R 1:

> Probation agencies shall aim to reduce re-offending by establishing positive relationships with offenders in order to supervise (including control where necessary), guide and assist them and to promote their successful social inclusion. Probation thus contributes to community safety and the fair administration of justice.

The CEP (the European organisation of probation services) Statement on Probation Values and Principles equally emphasises that 'Social inclusion is a requirement of social justice and a key guiding principle in probation practice' (para 3). Thus, it seems that, as Snacken and McNeill (2012: 1) argue:

> there is an emerging consensus at the pan-European level that, whereas all penal sanctions, including deprivation of liberty, aim at reducing re-offending and protecting victims and the general public, *a particular characteristic of probation measures is their emphasis on working with offenders in the community and fostering their social rehabilitation and inclusion.* [Emphasis added.]

Some suggest that such developments represent a useful and important bulwark against the broader social, political and cultural forces discussed above; against an Anglo-American-style 'new punitiveness' or a 'culture of control' (Snacken 2010). These developments can be seen as providing a potential brake on dystopian or catastrophic developments in penality generally and as an alternative means of the re-legitimation of community sanctions in particular. In another sense, these kinds of developments may function at the analytical level as a resource for imagining different and more constructive penologies (Daems 2008).

It may be obvious by now that I have a great deal of sympathy with this position; I have already alluded briefly above to the risks associated with policy transfer. Of course, the tendency when such arguments are made is to think about the importation of the 'harsh justice' (Whitman 2003) represented in some Anglo-American influences, models and practices. But whether we regard the transnational influence of *European* institutions and organisations as benign or malign depends largely on the extent of our political and normative sympathies with their values and effects. Moreover, beyond the question of the 'leniency vectors' (Zimring and Johnson 2006) that such institutions and organisations may or may not represent, profound questions about the political legitimacy of their influence on state-level criminal justice also arise.

In principle therefore, critiques of and concerns about policy transfer need to be considered and applied both *within Europe* and at the *European* level. It follows that securing the benefits and protections of a richer and more developed comparative penology necessarily entails a more developed

European penology. The recent development of networks of researchers and practitioners in Europe—at all career stages—engaged in such work opens up the possibility of sharing existing academic and practice-based knowledge; of building comparative analytical frameworks and other inter-disciplinary methodological innovations; of supporting collaborative research activity (across jurisdictions and disciplines), building research capacity; of developing the skills of young researchers; and thus of creating new insights, theories and perspectives about penality within and across Europe *and* about European penology. The argument of this chapter has been that, within these broader projects, the inter-disciplinary study of community sanctions and offender supervision in Europe must be seen as an increasingly important part.

Perhaps through such endeavours, we may at least aspire to develop both comparative penology and European penology so that both can contribute more effectively to the development of justice and security in Europe. That contribution matters not least where we seek not a Europe in which experts, policy networks and elites preserve liberal values from populist assault, but where we aspire instead to developing scholarship which, through its engagement with public policy, practice and debate, supports a 'better politics of crime and regulation' itself—both within and across European states (Loader and Sparks 2010: 117, and this volume).

## REFERENCES


Allen, R and Hough, M (2007) 'Community Penalties, Sentencers, the Media and Public Opinion', in L Gelsthorpe and R Morgan (eds) *The Handbook of Probation* (Cullompton, Willan Publishing).

Canton, R (2008) 'Nonsense upon Stilts? Human Rights, The Ethics Of Punishment and the Values of Probation', Professorial Inaugural Lecture, De Montfort University, 7 May 2008.

—— (2009) 'Taking Probation Abroad' *European Journal of Probation*, 1, 66–78.

Casey, L (2008) *Engaging Communities in Fighting Crime: A Review (Casey Report)* (London, Cabinet Office).

Cavadino, M and Dignan, J (2006) *Penal Systems. A Comparative Approach* (London, Sage).

Cohen, S (1985) *Visions of Social Control* (Cambridge, Polity Press).

Comfort, M (2007) *Doing Time Together. Love and Family in the Shadow of the Prison* (Chicago, University of Chicago Press).

Cox, A (2012) 'Doing the Programme or Doing me? The Pains of Youth Imprisonment' *Punishment & Society*, 13, 592–610.

Crewe, B (2009) *The Prisoner Society. Power, Adaptation and Social Life in an English Prison* (Oxford, Oxford University Press).

—— (2012) 'Depth, Weight, Tightness: Revisiting the Pains of Imprisonment' *Punishment & Society,* 13, 509–29.

Daems, T (2008) *Making Sense of Penal Change* (Oxford, Oxford University Press).
Deering, J (2011) *Probation Practice and the New Penology* (Farnham, Ashgate).
Douglas, M (1992) *Risk and Blame. Essays in Cultural Theory* (London, Routledge).
Downes, D (1988) *Contrasts in Tolerance* (Oxford, Clarendon Press).
Dünkel, F and Spieß, G (eds) (1983) *Alternativen zur Freiheitsstrafe. Strafaussetzung zur Bewährung und Bewährungshilfe im internationalen Vergleich* (Freiburg, MPI).
Dünkel, F, Lappi-Seppälä, T, Morgenstern, C and van Zyl Smit, D (eds) (2010) *Kriminalität, Kriminalpolitik, strafrechtliche Sanktionspraxis und Gefangenenraten im europäischen Vergleich* (Mönchengladbach, Forum).
Durnescu, I (2008) 'An Exploration of the Purposes and Outcomes of Probation in European Jurisdictions' *Probation Journal*, 55, 273–81.
—— (2011) 'Pains of Probation: Effective Practice and Human Rights' *International Journal of Offender Therapy and Comparative Criminology*, 55, 530–45.
Federal Statistics Office/*Statistisches Bundesamt* (2008). *Strafvollzugsstatistik—Fachserie 10 Reihe 4.1.* Wiesbaden.
—— (2011) *Bewährungshilfe—Fachserie 10 Reihe 3.* Wiesbaden.
Foucault, M (1977) *Discipline and Punish* (London, Allen Lane).
Garland, D (1985) *Punishment and Welfare* (Aldershot, Gower).
—— (2001) *The Culture of Control* (Oxford, Oxford University Press).
Gearty, C (2006) *Can Human Rights Survive? The Hamlyn Lectures 2005* (Cambridge, Cambridge University Press).
Hamai, K, Ville, R, Harris, R, Hough, M and Zvekic, U (eds) (1995) *Probation Round the World. A Comparative Study* (London, Routledge).
Haney, C (2005) *Reforming Punishment. The Psychological Limits to the Pains of Punishment* (Washington, American Psychological Association).
Hudson, B (2003) *Understanding Justice*, 2nd edn (Buckingham, Open Unversity Press).
King, R (2005) 'The Effects of Supermax Custody', in A Liebling and S Maruna (eds) *The Effects of Imprisonment* (Cullompton, Willan Publishing).
Lappi-Seppälä, T (2012) 'Criminology, Crime and Criminal Justice in Finland' *European Journal of Criminology*, 9, 206–22.
Loader, I and Sparks, R (2010) *Public Criminology?* (London, Routledge).
McCulloch, P and McNeill, F (2007) 'Consumer Society, Commodification and Offender Management' *Criminology and Criminal Justice*, 7, 223–42.
McNeill, F (2005) 'Remembering probation in Scotland' *Probation Journal*, 52, 25–40.
—— (2009) 'Helping, Holding, Hurting: Recalling and reforming punishment', 6th annual Apex Lecture, at the Signet Library, Parliament Square, Edinburgh, 8 September 2009. Available online at: https://pure.strath.ac.uk/portal/files/521675/strathprints026701.pdf.
—— (2011) 'Probation, Credibility and Justice' *Probation Journal*, 58, 9–22.
—— (forthcoming) 'When Punishment is Rehabilitation' in G Bruinsma and D Weisburd (eds) *The Springer Encyclopedia of Criminology and Criminal Justice* (New York, Springer).

McNeill, F and Whyte, B (2007) *Reducing Reoffending. Social Work and Community Justice in Scotland* (Cullompton, Willan Publishing).
McNeill, F, Raynor, P and Trotter, C (eds) (2010) *Offender Supervision. New Directions in Theory, Research and Practice* (Cullompton, Willan Publishing).
McNeill, F, Burns, N, Halliday, S, Hutton, N and Tata, C (2009) 'Risk, Responsibility and Reconfiguration: Penal Adaptation and Misadaptation' *Punishment & Society*, 11, 419–42.
Maruna, S (2011) 'Why Do They Hate Us? Making Peace Between Prisoners and Psychology' *International Journal of Offender Therapy and Comparative Criminology*, 55, 671–75.
Maruna, Sand King, A (2008) 'Selling the Public on Probation: Beyond the Bib' *Probation Journal*, 55, 337–51.
May, DC and Wood, PB (2010) *Ranking Correctional Punishments. Views From Offenders, Practitioners and the Public* (Durham NC, Carolina Academic Press).
Melossi, D (2008) *Controlling Crime, Controlling Society. Thinking about Crime in Europe and America* (Cambridge, Polity Press).
Ministry of Justice (2010) *Breaking the Cycle. Effective Punishment, Rehabilitation and Sentencing of Offenders* (London, Ministry of Justice).
Morgenstern, C (2002) *Internationale Mindeststandards für ambulante Strafen und Maßnahmen* (Mönchengladbach, Forum)
—— (2009) 'European initiatives for harmonisation and minimum standards in the field of community sanctions and measures' *European Journal of Probation*, 1, 128–41.
Morgenstern, C and Hecht, A (2011) 'Rechtstatsachen zur Führungsaufsicht im kriminalpolitischen Kontext' *Bewährungshilfe*, 58, 177–95.
Morison Report (1964) *Report of the Departmental Committee on the Probation Service*. Cmnd 1650 (London, HMSO).
Murphy, J (1988) 'Mercy and Legal Justice' in JG Murphy and J Hampton (eds) *Forgiveness and Mercy* (Cambridge, Cambridge University Press).
Nelken, D (2009) 'Comparative Criminal Justice. Beyond Ethnocentrism and Relativism' *European Journal of Criminology*, 6, 291–311.
Nellis, M (2009) 'Surveillance and Confinement: Explaining and Understanding the Experience of Electronically Monitored Curfews' *European Journal of Probation*, 1, 41–65.
Payne, BK and Gainey, RR (1998) 'A Qualitative Assessment of the Pains Experienced on Electronic Monitoring' *International Journal of Offender Therapy and Comparative Criminology*, 42, 149–63.
Petersilia, J (1990) 'When Probation Becomes more Dreaded than Prison' *Federal Probation*, 54, 23–27.
Petersilia, J and Deschenes, EP (1994) 'Perceptions of punishment: Inmates and staff rank the severity of prison versus intermediate sanctions' *The Prison Journal*, 74, 306–28.
Raynor, P (2007) 'Community Penalties: Probation, 'What Works', and Offender Management', in M Maguire, R Morgan and R Reiner (eds) *Oxford Handbook of Criminology*, 4th edn (Oxford, Oxford University Press).
Raynor, P and Robinson, G (2009) *Rehabilitation, Crime and Justice* (Basingstoke, Palgrave Macmillan).

Roberts, J (2004) *The Virtual Prison. Community Custody and the Evolution of Imprisonment* (Cambridge, Cambridge University Press).
Robinson, G (2008) 'Late-modern Rehabilitation: The Evolution of a Penal Strategy' *Punishment & Society,* 10, 429–45.
Robinson, G and McNeill, F (2004) 'Purposes Matter: Examining The 'Ends' of Probation Practice', in G Mair (ed) *What Matters in Probation* (Cullompton, Willan Publishing).
Robinson, G, McNeill, F and Maruna, S (2012) 'Punishment *in* Society: The Improbable Persistence of Community Sanctions', in J Simon and R Sparks (eds) *The Sage Handbook of Punishment and Society* (London, Sage).
Rotman, E (1994) 'Beyond Punishment', in A Duff and D Garland (eds) *A Reader on Punishment* (Oxford, Oxford University Press).
Rusche, G and Kirchheimer, O (1939) *Punishment and Social Structure* (New York, Columbia University Press).
Simon, J (1993) *Poor Discipline. Parole and the Social Control of the Underclass 1890–1990* (Chicago, University of Chicago Press).
—— (2007) *Governing Through Crime. How The War on Crime Transformed American Democracy and Created a Culture of Fear* (New York, Oxford University Press).
Smart, A (1969) 'Mercy', in HB Acton (ed) *The Philosophy of Punishment* (London, Macmillan/St Martin's Press).
Snacken, S (2010) 'Resisting Punitiveness in Europe' *Theoretical Criminology*, 14, 273–92.
Snacken, S and McNeill, F (2012) 'Scientific Recommendations' in D Flore, S Bosly, A Honhon and J Maggio (eds) *Probation Measures and Alternative Sanctions in the European Union* (Cambridge, Intersentia).
Sparks, R and McNeill, F (2009) 'Incarceration, Social Control and Human Rights', research paper prepared as part of the International Council on Human Rights Policy's (ICHRP) Project on Social Control and Human Rights. Available online at www.ichrp.org/files/papers/175/punishment_and_incarceration_sparks_and_mcneill.pdf.
Statistisches Bundesamt (2009) *Strafvollzug—Demographische und kriminologische Merkmale der Strafgefangenen am 31.03.2008*—Fachserie10 Reihe 4.1.
Sykes, G (1958) *The Society of Captives. A Study of a Maximum-Security Prison* (Princeton, Princeton University Press).
Tonry, M (2006) 'Purposes and Functions of Sentencing' in M Tonry (ed) *Crime and Justice: a Review of Research (Volume 34)* (Chicago, University of Chicago Press).
Van Kalmthout, A and Durnescu, I (eds) (2008) *Probation in Europe* (Nijmegen,Wolf Legal Publishers).
Van Kalmthout, A and Tak, PJP (1988) *Sanctions Systems in Member States of the Council of Europe, Part 1: Deprivation of Liberty, Community Service and Other Substitutes* (Deventer, Kluwer Academic Publishers).
Wacquant, L (2009) *Punishing the Poor* (Durham NC, Duke University Press).
Walker, N (1991) *Why Punish?* (Oxford, Oxford University Press).
Zimring, F and Johnson, D (2006) 'Public Opinion and the Governance of Punishment in Democratic Political Systems' *The ANNALS of the American Academy of Political and Social Science*, 605, 265–80.

## COUNCIL OF EUROPE INSTRUMENTS

Council of Europe (1992) *Recommendation No. R (92) 16 of the Committee of Ministers to member states on the European rules on community sanctions and measures* adopted by the Committee of Ministers on 19 October 1992 at the 482nd meeting of the Ministers' Deputies.

## EU INSTRUMENTS AND LEGISLATION

Council Notice of 4 May 2010 on the Stockholm programme—an open and secure Europe serving and protecting citizens [2010] OJ C115/01.

Council Framework Decision 2008/947/JHA of 27 November 2008 on the application of the principle of mutual recognition to judgments and probation decisions with a view to the supervision of probation measures and alternative sanctions [2008] OJ L337/102.

# 9

# *Remand Detention in Europe: Comparative and Pan-European Aspects as Elements of a Wider European Penology*

CHRISTINE MORGENSTERN

## I. INTRODUCTION: REMAND DETENTION AS A MATTER FOR PENOLOGY

WHY A CONTRIBUTION on remand detention in a book on penology? The easy answer to that question is: because it is about imprisonment. However, from a legal point of view this is not self-evident: the German term *Pönologie* describes a rather narrow field of research which is concentrated on the sentence of imprisonment. Even if 'penology' in the English (and European) usage is interpreted more widely, the key element is *poena*—punishment, sanction, penalty. But this is precisely what pre-trial detention must not be, since during its imposition the offender as a suspect or as an accused person is still presumed to be innocent. Article 6(2) of the European Convention of Human Rights (ECHR) stipulates that: 'Everyone charged with a criminal offence shall be presumed innocent until proved guilty according to law.' This norm serves as the European expression of the presumption of innocence, which is a common heritage of different European legal traditions (Stuckenberg 1998: 573; Pradel 1992: 14).[1] The ECHR is binding law, partly with constitutional status, in all 47 Member States of the Council of Europe. In most Member States the presumption of innocence is also codified in national law, ie, in the constitution or in the code of criminal procedure. Obviously,

[1] Great importance is attributed to the presumption of innocence in Anglo-American criminal law (common law). Sometimes the superiority of the common law over the continental systems (civil law) has been deduced from the mistaken belief that this presumption does not exist in the continental systems, or that it is a lot weaker (see Stuckenberg 1998: 251 ff with many references).

remand detention is in tension with this principle (see eg Duff 1986: 139). It may therefore only be used as a provisional procedural measure of last resort to secure the criminal process (Trechsel 2006: 503) against the risk that the accused may abscond or interfere with evidence, or to protect actual or potential victims against further offending (although the latter ground is disputed).

From the human rights point of view, therefore, detention on remand is first and foremost a form of deprivation of liberty and as such only allowed under strict conditions. In addition to Article 6(2) of the ECHR, Article 5(1) of the ECHR safeguards the right to liberty by prescribing that: 'No one shall be deprived of his liberty save in the following cases and in accordance with a procedure prescribed by law.' The normative justification of remand detention follows from Article 5(1)(b) ECHR, which allows 'the lawful arrest or detention of a person effected for the purpose of bringing him before the competent legal authority on reasonable suspicion of having committed an offence or when it is reasonably considered necessary to prevent his committing an offence or fleeing after having done so'.

From the point of view of a criminologist, however, there are indications that pre-trial detention is often not (only) used for a designated legally justified purpose, but also misused for other objectives, such as obtaining a confession or as 'shock therapy' for juvenile offenders. Empirical research from various countries suggests 'that remand custody is used more as an immediate punishment and as a security measure to protect society against "dangerous" elements ... than as an instrument to secure the presence of the suspect at the trial' (Raes and Snacken 2004: 514 for Belgium). Similar practices are reported for ethnic minorities in England and Wales (Ashworth and Redmayne 2010: 240) or for juveniles in Germany (Kowalzyck 2008: 275). The hybrid character is highlighted by the fact that remand detention is retrospectively treated as part of the sentence by law: the time served in pre-trial detention is deducted from the sentence of imprisonment in all Member States of the European Union (van Kalmthout et al 2009b: 84). This is an indispensable act of fairness, but it also raises concerns for penology because it may impact on the sentencing decision. In Germany, only a little more than half of all pre-trial detainees are sentenced to an unconditional prison sentence. The rest receive a suspended prison sentence (about 40 per cent) or a fine (about 10 per cent), whereas only very few are acquitted (Heinz 2010: 84, data for 2008). Data for England and Wales show that about 50 per cent of all those remanded in custody (32 per cent in magistrates' court cases) are sentenced to a term of imprisonment, roughly 30 per cent to a non-custodial sanction and around 15 per cent are acquitted (Player et al 2010: 242, data for 2007). These results hint at a disproportionate use of remand detention. However, it also can be argued that the contrary is the case: perhaps judges tend to consider the time spent in remand detention as adequate to meet the retributive aim of punishment, and adjust the sentence accordingly. Both interpretations are empirically hard to validate: probably both are true in individual cases, although the English data seem to point in the former direction. The fact remains that a considerable number of inmates experience imprisonment only in the form that can just be regarded as incompatible with the 'rehabilitative ideal', ie in remand custody (Heinz 2010: 94).

This is important from the perspective of a prison researcher interested in the internal dynamics of imprisonment. In reality, the suspect probably experiences remand detention very much as punishment—particularly if he only spends time in a remand facility and is then released. It has been observed that living conditions in pre-trial detention facilities throughout Europe are often worse than those in prisons for sentenced prisoners. For example, in France so-called short-stay prisons are affected by massive overcrowding (with an occupancy rate of more than 140 per cent), which was manifestly criticised by the Council of Europe Commissioner for Human Rights after his visit to French prisons in 2008 (Hammarberg 2008). Similarly, several of the cases in which the European Court of Human Rights (ECtHR) found a violation of Article 3 of the ECHR in the form of degrading treatment were related to the conditions in a remand institution.[2] In *Savenkovas v Lithuania* the Court noted: 'In addition, as a remand prisoner, the applicant had been obliged to stay in such cramped conditions some 23 hours a day, with no access to work, or educational or recreational facilities'.[3] Accordingly, it concluded that the severely overcrowded and insanitary conditions of the applicant's detention at the Lukišk s Remand Prison amounted to degrading treatment, in breach of Article 3 of the Convention. Additionally, the European Committee for the Prevention of Torture and Inhuman or Degrading Treatment or Punishment (CPT) has observed that activities in many remand prisons are extremely limited. In its standards the CPT comments that:

> The organisation of regime activities in such establishments—which have a fairly rapid turnover of inmates—is not a straightforward matter. Clearly, there can be no question of individualised treatment programmes of the sort which might be aspired to in an establishment for sentenced prisoners. However, prisoners cannot simply be left to languish for weeks, possibly months, locked up in their cells, and this regardless of how good material conditions might be within the cells.
>
> (European Committee for the Prevention of Torture and Inhuman or Degrading Treatment or Punishment (CPT) 2010: 21.)

[2] *Savenkovas v Lithuania* App no 871/02 (ECtHR, 11 November 2009). *Peers v Greece* (2001) 33 EHRR 51 is another example.
[3] *Savenkovas v Lithuania*, para 81.

More recently the European Union has become involved in this field and has formulated a Framework Decision on remand detention and possible alternatives.[4] From the point of view of European comparative criminology and criminal law it is therefore interesting to see how the activities of the different European institutions may have influenced legislation and the practice of remand detention in Europe, and thus possibly led to a specifically 'European' perspective on it.

## II. REMAND DETENTION: QUANTITATIVE SIGNIFICANCE AND SCOPE IN EUROPE

### A. (How) Can we Compare within Europe?

Apart from identifying common problems with regard to remand detention within Europe, it is important to assess the quantitative significance and scope from a comparative perspective. This will be indispensable in order to explore what 'Europe stands for' (see Snacken and van Zyl Smit, this volume) and it will be of practical importance for the envisaged closer cooperation within the EU. Comparative research needs to develop a common understanding for the subject under consideration. In the previous section it is argued that remand detention serves procedural purposes, ie, to prevent a suspect from absconding or from tampering with evidence or witnesses. The justice system needs him or her to be present and at its disposal—in fact, the etymology of the word 'remand' (coming from the Latin *re-* and *mandare*, literally 'order back') points to this original meaning. For this period of custody the term 'pre-trial' detention is also often used, but it is obvious that remand detention may last longer, as it may extend beyond the beginning of the trial.[5] Even if the procedural needs of the justice system with regard to the investigation may diminish once the trial has begun, those with regard to the risk of absconding may remain. The problem for comparative research in Europe is rather situated at the end of the trial: does a conviction end the remand detention period? What about systems that separate the conviction from the sentence, and detain offenders who

[4] Council Framework Decision 2009/829/JHA of 23 October 2009 on the application, between Member States of the European Union, of the principle of mutual recognition to decisions on supervision measures as an alternative to provisional detention OJ L294/20, see below IIIE for details.

[5] The term 'remand detention' is a more neutral one. Inconsistencies in the legal terms are widespread throughout Europe: in German, *Untersuchungshaft*—literally 'investigation detention'—is the term used in the legislation, although it is absolutely clear that it lasts until the final conviction, thus not only during trial but through appeal and cassation procedures. In other languages, 'provisional' detention (*prisión provisional* in Spanish; *détention provisional* in French) can be found. Often also the preventive/precautionary aspect is expressed, as in the Italian *custodia cautelare*.

have been convicted but not yet sentenced? What about the time spent in prison during appeal (or cassation) procedures?

In his introduction to *Criminal Procedure in Europe,* Vogler notes: 'There are stark differences between levels of pre-trial remand around Europe, apparently demonstrating very different levels of procedural commitment to the presumption of innocence and pre-trial release' (Vogler 2008: 26). The basis of this statement has to be scrutinised closely. The data referred to are the remand imprisonment rates taken from statistics compiled on behalf of the Council of Europe (SPACE I)[6] and the International Centre for Prison Studies (ICPS).[7] Prisoner rates have often been used in recent years to assess and compare different levels of punitiveness in Europe or the world. It has become clear that much additional information and profound knowledge of legal, social and political factors that influence these rates in different countries are needed to interpret these numbers in a sensible way (see eg Dünkel and Morgenstern 2010: 5). However, despite their shortcomings, such rates provide at least a useful starting point to explore these questions.

## B. European Data

Here we use the most recent data from SPACE I. Figure 9.1 ranks the remand prisoner rates (remand prisoners per 100,000 of the total population); additionally the lighter column shows the prisoner rate (all prisoners per 100,000 of the population) for the respective country.[8]

Some of 'the usual suspects' can be found at the top in both rankings: Latvia, Estonia and to a lesser extent also Lithuania show both high remand and overall prisoner rates. At the other end we find Finland, Sweden and Norway for both categories. But we can observe some significant differences

[6] Council of Europe Annual Penal Statistics (SPACE I) (see Aebi and Delgrande 2011). The statistics are available online from 1999 onwards: www3.unil.ch/wpmu/space/space-i/annual-reports/.

[7] International Centre for Prison Studies, World Prison Population List and World Pre-trial/Remand Imprisonment List, www.prisonstudies.org.

[8] Only 30 countries are shown—the smaller European countries and Russia are missing. The arithmetical mean that is included in the graph relates to the countries shown. Russia had an estimated remand prisoner rate of 96 in 2007, while the overall prisoner rate was 617, according to the data of the ICPS. Since then the imprisonment rate has dropped to 559 (2011) but no information is available with regard to the rate of remand imprisonment. The US with an overall imprisonment rate of 743 has a remand imprisonment rate of 149 (September 2009, Source: ICPS).

Sometimes the *percentage* of remand prisoners is used also for comparative approaches (see eg Player et al 2010: 237). This does not make much sense: having a low share of remand prisoners obviously only means that relatively more prisoners are already serving their sentence and does not necessarily have anything to do with a strong commitment to procedural human rights. It may show that the prison sentences in a given country are very long, for example, as Player et al (2010) recognise in the case of England. *Rates* are therefore mostly preferable.

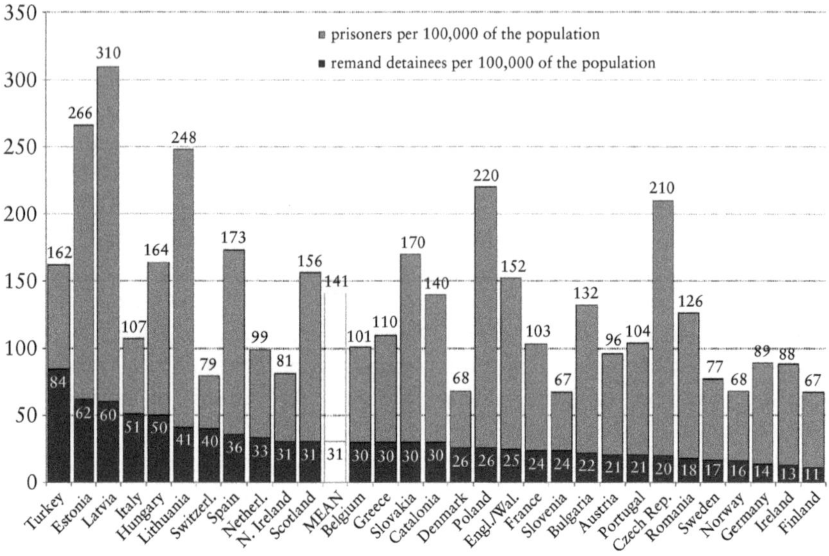


**Figure 9.1: Remand prisoners and prisoners in selected European states, 2009**
Source: SPACE I 2011 and own calculations.

in both rankings as well: Turkey has the highest remand prisoner rate in the sample, but ranks only ninth with regard to all prisoners. Italy and, perhaps more surprisingly, Switzerland have very high remand rates but clearly below-average overall prisoner rates; to a lesser degree this is also true for the Netherlands. Divergent tendencies can also be seen in the other direction: compared to other Western European states England and Wales is notorious for its high rate of imprisonment but is well below average with regard to remand detainees. The same is true for Poland. In general, the numbers in Figure 9.1 indicate that remand detention has a significant impact on the overall prison population in Europe, but that this impact varies considerably between countries. We can also note that in countries suffering from high prisoner rates, remand imprisonment does not always contribute greatly to their overall prisoner rate. On the other hand, it seems as if some countries are able to contain their overall prison population but still have a large problem in terms of remand detention. Indeed, in countries such as Italy, Switzerland and, to a lesser degree the Netherlands, the remand prison population forms between 40 and almost 50 per cent of the overall prison population (see also Figure 9.2). If we assume that no or only very limited efforts are made to offer work, activities or treatment to remand prisoners, this poses a serious problem, not only for the prisoners but also for the prison authorities.

When we compare such numbers, however, we need to take into account that the remand prisoner population might be composed differently, depending on the country. In fact, SPACE I mentions five different categories of prisoners that (potentially) make up the total prison population: three categories relate to prisoners who are dealt with in the criminal process but who are not finally convicted; the fourth category is 'sentenced prisoners' and the fifth is 'others'. The latter is a very heterogeneous category that may include foreigners detained pending deportation, mentally ill prisoners in specialised institutions, prisoners in transit etc. The three categories that are of interest for our purposes are currently labelled 'untried (investigation and trial phase) prisoners', 'prisoners convicted but not yet sentenced' and 'prisoners convicted and sentenced who have appealed or who are in the statutory limit of doing so'. Figure 9.2 shows data for the remand prison population as percentage of the overall prison population—subdivided, where possible, into its subgroups. Not all countries provide consistent data, so only 15 countries were selected to illustrate the impact of the different categories.

In some cases, namely Italy or Turkey, a significant part of the population held in remand institutions have already been convicted (and sentenced) in the first instance but have appealed. For comparative research it is very important to take into account that these prisoners are counted

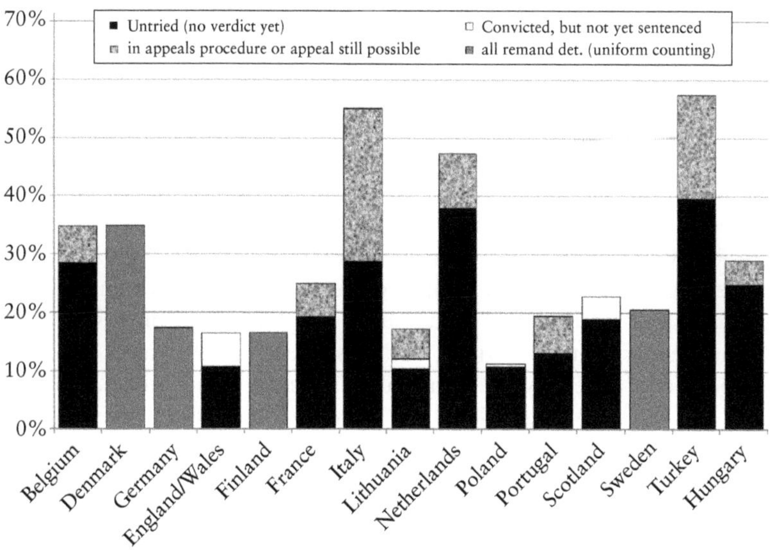


**Figure 9.2: Percentage of remand prisoners, subdivided in different categories, 2009**

Source: SPACE I 2011 and own calculations.

as *sentenced prisoners* in other countries—this is particularly the case in common law systems. England and Wales, for example, has a relatively small percentage of remand prisoners (16 per cent). This includes the group of 'convicted but not yet sentenced' prisoners that does not exist in the continental systems (as in the latter, conviction and sentencing are occur at the same sitting). Next to differences that can be explained by the type of legal system, there are also technical explanations that one needs to take into account when interpreting the above-mentioned numbers. For example, Poland and Lithuania provide data for all three sub-groups of remand prisoners, although conviction and sentencing are always pronounced in the same decision as in the other continental systems. This probably results from a misunderstanding about what was meant by these categories.

### C. Different Scope

The statistics discussed in the previous subsection highlight the different scopes of remand detention and notions behind them. This prompts questions about why there are such different notions, and whether the underlying legal principles differ. We have seen that the legal status of remand prisoners depends on two factors: the first factor has to do with criminal procedure (ie, the need for certain restrictive measures); while the second relates to the presumption of innocence which implies that a remand prisoner should be treated differently from a sentenced prisoner. This latter principle plays a central role in the theoretical underpinning of remand detention as well as of the criminal justice system as a whole. The role and scope of the presumption are not entirely clear, not within certain jurisdictions and even less in a comparative perspective. They vary from a mere rule about the burden of proof, to an overarching principle to guarantee procedural rights of the suspect or accused (see Darbyshire 2008: 39; Ashworth and Redmayne 2010: 29 and, generally, Stuckenberg 1998 with many references). One difference relates to the period during which the presumption has an effect on those detained during a criminal process: while in most European countries persons are presumed innocent until the sentence has been confirmed by the court of final instance, in others, namely in England and Wales (Morgan 1994: 183 and 195) this is not (necessarily) the case. The same is true for Northern Ireland according to the Criminal Justice (Northern Ireland) Order 2003, for Ireland (Article 71 Irish Prison Rules 2007) and for Scotland (Jones 1994: 529 and 536), even if its legal system is not a common-law but a mixed one. From a European perspective both concepts seem acceptable as the ECtHR explicitly acknowledged that the English practice meets the criteria of Article 6(2) and Article 5(1) of the

ECHR.[9] The Court has, however, been criticised by several (continental) scholars for lowering the standard to the lowest common denominator (see eg Esser 2002: 287; Trechsel 2006: 519).

Nevertheless, Figure 9.2 shows that even where the scope of remand detention is the same, the extent to which remand detention affects persons in appeals procedures may differ significantly. In Italy, there are more remand prisoners involved in appeal procedures than untried or unconvicted. A relatively high proportion can also be seen in Turkey and the Netherlands. In contrast, older data from Germany indicate that only relatively few remand detainees are in appeals procedures.[10] Differences may be caused by different legal cultures and structures, and by resource allocation for the judiciary. In particular, in some countries the propensity to appeal is stronger than in others, or appeal procedures are extremely protracted. Since 2006 the European Commission for the Efficiency of Justice (CEPEJ) has compiled reports for the Council of Europe that also discuss the length of criminal proceedings and the proportion of verdicts appealed against. The fragmentary and inconsistent data obtained, however, do not confirm the assumption.[11] Important in this regard, however, is Nelken's comment that in Italy, 'even quite minor cases go through a series of procedural hoops and are reviewed by a large number of judges, and there are two stages of appeal (the first stage being a retrial on the facts)'. Protracted criminal proceedings thus seem to be a feature of (in this case) the Italian legal culture (Nelken 2009: 291 and 302).

Much deeper analysis is necessary to explore the different legal notions and practices from a comparative perspective. However, even the data compiled in European statistics reveal that comparative research that aims to measure the impact of remand detention on the prison population as a whole is possible only to a limited extent. A statement such as the one by Vogler quoted above might be true but its veracity cannot be justified on the basis of isolated data. Nevertheless, the statistics do hint at differences in the use of remand detention throughout Europe. For example, even if allowance is made for different modes of categorization, the English rates indicate relatively sparing use of remand detention, particularly, if compared to the overall prisoner rates in England and Wales and their development over time (see in particular Hucklesby 2009: 3; Cavadino and Dignan

[9] *Monell and Morris v United Kingdom* App nos 9562/81 and 9818/82 (ECtHR, 2 March 1998), para 41 ff; an earlier decision was *Wemhoff v Germany* (1979–80) 1 EHRR 55, para 9.

[10] In the SPACE I statistics Germany and Sweden until recently provided data subdivided in the different categories. In both countries the share of remand prisoners in appeal procedures was very low (less than 1%; see SPACE I editions 2007 and earlier).

[11] *European Commission for the Efficiency of Justice (CEPEJ)* 2006: 104 and 2008: 159 and 277 (Table 157). The last report published in 2010 does not include data on the length of criminal proceedings.

2010: 244).[12] In this case, however, the political climate after the riots in English cities in August 2011 may change things. First data published suggest that judges in these cases have tended to order remand custody even for very young suspects, and to ignore concerns they might otherwise have had about the presumption of innocence.[13] All in all, the comparison allows one to explore the factors that enable some criminal justice systems to make more cautious use of remand detention than others.

## D. Cross-Border Aspects and the Problem of Foreigners in Remand Detention

Comparative work on remand detention is not only interesting for academic reasons but has also considerable practical value for European criminal policy: the cross-border or transnational component is particularly strong because of the considerable number of foreign remand detainees in European prisons (see also Melossi, this volume).

Remand prisons are particularly affected by high proportions of foreign inmates. Research from various countries reveals that foreign citizenship is often taken as an irrefutable indication of a risk of absconding. Alternative bail possibilities are often not deemed appropriate for non-nationals, so it seems to be thought indispensable to keep foreign suspects in remand detention, often for quite minor offences (van Kalmthout et al 2009b: 73 and Dünkel et al 2010b: 1102). Longitudinal analyses have demonstrated that in the past two decades the share of foreigners in prisons in some countries has increased significantly. According to the SPACE data this is true for Spain, Belgium, Portugal, Greece (with a dramatic increase only in the last decade, Pitsela 2010: 442), Italy (see for more details Melossi 2003) and Austria. In Austria the significant growth of the prison population between 1990 and 2004 can be explained exclusively by the growth of the foreign prison population (Pilgram and Hofinger 2007: 95 ff).

In 2009 the highest proportion of foreigners in remand institutions was to be found in Switzerland (almost 80 per cent), followed by Greece (63 per cent) and Austria (60 per cent).[14] In Spain and Belgium more than 50 per cent were foreign nationals. In Italy and Germany this proportion was 44 per cent, in Portugal about 36 per cent. Smaller percentages of foreign

[12] For more longitudinal analysis from different countries, see Morgenstern (2011c) and the country reports in van Kalmthout et al (2009a) as well as in Dünkel et al (2010a).

[13] Data from magistrates' courts were published in the *Guardian*, 18 August 2011, available online at www.guardian.co.uk/news/datablog/2011/aug/11/uk-riots-magistrates-court-list.

[14] All data are taken from SPACE I, except the Swiss figures (*Bundesamt für Statistik der Schweiz* available online at www.bfs.admin.ch/bfs/portal/de/index/themen/) and the Czech figures (Annual Report 2010, Prison Service of the Czech Republic available online at http://www.vscr.cz).

remand detainees could be found in the three legal systems of the UK (but showing an upward trend). In the Nordic states too, a relatively small proportion of prisoners are foreigners. Norway with 52 per cent is an exception (but with small absolute numbers, as in the other Nordic states). Throughout Central and Eastern Europe the percentage of foreigners in prisons is small[15]—the same applies for Turkey. The percentage of foreigners in remand institutions is usually a little higher but remains a single-digit figure (with the exception of Slovenia, with 17 per cent, and the Czech Republic, that recently reported 22 per cent).

## III. EUROPEAN STANDARDS AND INITIATIVES

### A. A European Definition for Remand Detention?

Recommendation (2006) 13 of the Committee of Ministers of the Council of Europe on the use of remand in custody, the conditions in which it takes place and the provision of safeguards against abuse offers the following definition in its first section:

> [1] 'Remand in custody' is any period of detention of a suspected offender ordered by a judicial authority and prior to conviction. It also includes any period of detention pursuant to rules relating to international judicial co-operation and extradition, subject to their specific requirements. It does not include the initial deprivation of liberty by a police or a law enforcement officer (or by anyone else so authorised to act) for the purposes of questioning.
>
> [2] 'Remand in custody' also includes any period of detention after conviction whenever persons awaiting either sentence or the confirmation of conviction or sentence continue to be treated as unconvicted persons.
>
> [3] 'Remand prisoners' are persons who have been remanded in custody and who are not already serving a prison sentence or are detained under any other instrument.

Rule 94 of the European Prison Rules (Recommendation (2006) 02) gives the following definition:

> 1. For the purposes of these Rules, untried prisoners are prisoners who have been remanded in custody by a judicial authority prior to trial, conviction or sentence.
>
> 2. A state may elect to regard prisoners who have been convicted and sentenced as untried prisoners if their appeals have not been disposed of finally.

[15] Estonia seems to be an exception, with 40% 'foreigners' in its prisons. This, however, can be explained by the fact that all Estonian citizens (usually those of Russian origin) who have not applied for an Estonian passport are counted as foreigners.

These definitions are relative or technical ones—a remand prisoner is a prisoner who is in a remand institution according to national law. A truly common definition of 'remand detention', in particular with regard to its scope, is thus not provided by the European instruments. European activities that try to overcome common problems with a common approach have to bear this in mind. It remains to be seen, however, whether this poses a practical problem for the envisaged intensified cooperation in that field, in particular within the EU (see below IIIE).

## B. The Impact of the European Convention on Human Rights

Several provisions of the ECHR safeguard the rights of remand prisoners. In addition to the above-mentioned Article 5(1)(c) that lists the grounds on which it is permissible to deprive a person of his or her liberty, Article 5(3) of the ECHR provides that everyone who is deprived of his liberty by arrest or detention shall be entitled to take proceedings by which the lawfulness of his detention shall be decided speedily by a court and his release ordered if the detention is not lawful. Unacceptable detention conditions may also violate Article 3 of the ECHR ('No one shall be subjected to torture or to inhuman or degrading treatment or punishment'), even where there is no evidence of a positive intention to humiliate or degrade the detainee (see above I). As mentioned before, the ECtHR does not interpret Article 6(2) of the ECHR in a way that encompasses the period of appeals proceedings, and thus limits its guarantees to the period until a first conviction/sentence has been pronounced. After this period, however, the fair-trial guarantees of Article 6(1) of the ECHR that include the right to a speedy trial apply.

Extensive jurisprudence of the European Court of Human Rights has shaped these guarantees over the decades. The case law has established that a decision to remand someone in custody cannot be based solely on the past record of the suspected offender or the fact that certain (serious) offences have allegedly been committed.[16] The requirement that the length of detention must be limited and the requirement of a speedy procedure in all detention cases is closely related to the presumption of innocence. According to the Court, the continuation of remand detention may never be misused as an anticipation of a custodial sentence and should (at least) be limited by the time the defendant would possibly spend in prison.[17] Detention cases therefore have to be reviewed constantly and a release has to be ordered as soon as the continuing detention ceases to be 'reasonable' (without translating this concept into a fixed maximum period). In many decisions

[16] Eg *Tomasi v France* (1993) 15 EHRR 1, para 89; *Jecius v Lithuania* (2002) 35 EHRR 16, para 94.

[17] Eg *Klamecki v Poland* (2004) 39 EHRR 7, para 122.

the Court has tried to establish criteria of reasonableness and argued inter alia that the needs or requirements of the inquiry in itself do not suffice.[18] Comprehensive analyses of this jurisprudence have been undertaken by Esser (2002) and Trechsel (2006).

Since a decision of the ECtHR is binding on the Member State that is a party to the case, it should have the power to change the actual practice and sometimes the law in the country concerned. Much could be said about how grudgingly decisions from Strasbourg are accepted and how effectively they are implemented. However, the jurisprudence of the Court often works more widely as a catalyst for improving human rights guarantees in national legislation and practices (Esser 2002: 89). It can also be seen as a protective factor against more punitive turns in penal policy and practice. Two examples may illustrate the impact of the Court's jurisprudence: in Germany, the law had to be changed in order to improve the ability of defence counsel to inspect the files and to challenge the remand detention order. This change was precipitated by a number of cases that the German government lost in Strasbourg.[19] In England and Wales the provisions for mandatory remand detention (or better: automatic denial of bail) for certain crimes had to be changed as a result of the *Caballero* case in 2000.[20]

The decisions of the ECtHR put additional pressure on national courts to avoid formalistic reasoning based on stereotypes when they consider the imposition or continuation of remand detention. Although in Germany the higher courts have set strict rules for the duration of remand detention, the ECtHR has found even more violations of Article 5(3) of the ECHR due to the excessive length of detention in some instances. With regard to Poland, such a violation was found in 67 cases between 2000 and 2007 alone. After the *Kudla* decision,[21] new legislation was enacted in order to speed up procedures.[22] Without suggesting a direct causal influence, it should be added that in both countries the numbers of remand detainees have decreased during the past 10 years, although the overall prisoner numbers (thus of the sentenced prisoners) increased until recently. At least in some European

[18] Eg *Letellier v France* (1992) 14 EHRR 83, para 35; *Kudła v Poland* App no 30210/96 (ECtHR, 26 October 2000), para 22.

[19] § 147(2) CCP (in force since 1 January 2010) was changed with reference to the case of *Mooren v Germany* App no 11364/03 (ECtHR, 13 December 2007); *Mooren v Germany* (2010) 50 EHRR 23. See also *Erdem v Germany* (2002) 35 EHRR 15 or *Lietzow v Germany* App no 24479/94 (ECtHR, 13 February 2001).

[20] *Caballero v United Kingdom* (2000) 30 EHRR 643, para 18 ff. Ashworth and Redmayne (2010: 238) raise doubts as to whether the changed law now is in conformity with Art 5 ECHR.

[21] *Kudła v Poland* App no 30210/96 (ECtHR, 26 October 2000).

[22] The problem has been noted in the Committee of Ministers Interim Resolution CM/ResDH(2007)75 concerning the judgments of the European Court of Human Rights in 44 cases against Poland relating to the excessive length of detention on remand adopted by the Committee of Ministers on 6 June 2007, at the 997th meeting of the Ministers' Deputies.

countries, Germany being one, remand detention today seems to be much less subject to punitive pressures than it had been previously.[23] This has several domestic reasons (eg the decline in overall crime rates and other topics high on the political agenda), but certainly the standards set by the ECtHR restricted the leeway of judges to impose remand detention and, more importantly, to allow it to continue for a long time. Moreover, the decisions of the Court provide moral support for a moderate penal policy.

## C. The Recommendations of the Council of Europe

The contradictory character of the procedure before the ECtHR (Articles 32–34 and 46 of the ECHR) limits the direct effect of its jurisprudence to the Member State that is a party to the case, thus hindering the direct transferability to all Member States' jurisdictions. Additionally, the Court was very reluctant to make clear rulings on the way remand detention was enforced. In *Peers v Greece* in 2001 the Court even stated that 'the Convention contains no Article providing for separate treatment for convicted and accused',[24] although this means falling short (Trechsel 2006: 181) of Article 10(2) of the International Covenant of Civil and Political Rights (ICCPR).[25] As a remedy for these shortcomings, a new recommendation was developed. Recommendation (2006) 13 aims to strengthen procedural safeguards, to set strict limits on the use of remand in custody; to encourage the use of alternative measures wherever possible etc. It requires judicial authority for the imposition and continued use of remand in custody and alternative measures. It also stipulates that persons remanded in custody should be held in conditions and subject to a regime appropriate to their legal status, which is explicitly based on the presumption of innocence; require the provision of suitable facilities and appropriate management for the holding of persons remanded in custody and to ensure the establishment of effective safeguards against possible breaches of the rules. More clearly than in the case law of the Court, it provides that the presumption of innocence is accompanied by a presumption in favour of liberty during criminal proceedings (No 3).

A direct impact of Recommendation (2006) 13 on national developments, however, is hard to detect. This is different for the 2006 European Prison Rules (EPR) which are widely recognised throughout Europe (see,

[23] See for other examples: Dünkel et al (2010b: 1080 ff) and for more details on the German and Polish cases see Morgenstern (2011a).

[24] *Peers v Greece* (2001) 33 EHRR 51, para 78.

[25] 'Accused persons shall, save in exceptional circumstances, be segregated from convicted persons and shall be subject to separate treatment appropriate to their status as unconvicted persons.' The Covenant is legally binding on all Member States of the Council of Europe.

especially: van Zyl Smit and Snacken 2009: 18 ff and 354 ff). EPR 18.8 stipulates that remand prisoners should be separated from sentenced prisoners. Special provisions for remand prisoners can be found in Part VII (EPR 94-101) of the Rules. EPR 101 is particularly interesting: 'If an untried prisoner requests to be allowed to follow the regime for sentenced prisoners, the prison authorities shall as far as possible accede to this request.' This rule is innovative because requests from untried prisoners to work or to participate in some form of therapy, etc are sometimes rejected on the basis that this would infringe the presumption of innocence.[26] Defence counsel even report that sometimes remand prisoners choose not to appeal, because they want to be transferred to a 'normal prison' (Paeffgen 1986: 286). EPR 101 therefore stipulates that the same opportunities should exist for sentenced prisoners and for remand prisoners. The implementation of this recommendation may prove difficult and probably it works best where remand and sentenced prisoners are accommodated in different wings of the same building, but the presumption of innocence may never serve as an excuse for not offering anything. It should be possible, however, for those who decide to appeal to choose whether they want to be transferred to a prison where they can start to serve their sentence. This possibility exists in some countries such as Poland, Lithuania and Switzerland. It is, however, problematic to make such a transfer compulsory, as is done in the Netherlands.[27]

## D. The Work of the CPT and the European Commissioner of Human Rights

As indicated before, the CPT Standards set out in the substantive sections of the Annual Reports of the CPT offer important guidelines for (prison) authorities. More directly, CPT visits can lead to changes in legislation or practice and have in fact done so. In Denmark, for example, solitary confinement that is ordered when there are reasons to believe that detention itself is insufficient to prevent an inmate from impeding the criminal process, has been much debated in recent years (Stoorgard 2009: 278). As a result of the critical reports submitted by the CPT after its visits in 2002 and 2008, the use and the length of solitary confinement were reduced (European Committee for the Prevention of Torture and Inhuman or Degrading Treatment or Punishment (CPT) 2008 and 2009). Equally, the European Commissioner for Human Rights has discussed the issue of remand detention in his reports on country visits. His role is restricted to

[26] For the (abated) discussion in Germany see eg Seebode (1985: 211).
[27] Van Kalmthout (2009: 708).

'thematic advice and awareness raising'. Yet, because he has unrestricted access to all institutions he wants to visit (like the CPT), his reports have also proven to be an important source of information. As a 'Human Rights Comment' on the former commissioner's website shows, remand detention in Europe is currently seen as an important and obviously worrisome topic.[28]

## E. The European Union and Remand Detention

In a speech delivered in March 2010, the European Commissioner for Justice, Fundamental Rights and Citizenship made very clear that the European Union must now be seen as a powerful player in the field of criminal justice in Europe. She pointed out that 'those who only want to rely on the old system point to the tools such as the Council of Europe conventions and the often archaic mutual legal assistance systems that we already have. I say that this is not enough. We must improve these tools.'[29] One tool that is important for our discussion is the Framework Decision on Supervision Measures as an Alternative to Provisional Detention.[30] Its working title was 'European Supervision Order (ESO)', which shall also be used here. Like several other Framework Decisions, it is based on the idea of mutual recognition of judicial decisions within the EU[31] and was drafted and adopted under the provisions in force before the Treaty of Lisbon became applicable. Even though the former three-pillar system has disappeared and the relevant provisions have been recast in Title V (Area of Freedom, Security and Justice), chapter 4 (Judicial Cooperation in Criminal Matters) of the Treaty of the Functioning of the European Union (TFEU), the prevailing principle remains the mutual recognition of judicial decisions (Article 82 TFEU). Framework Decisions already adopted have to be implemented in national law, in the case of the ESO by December 2012. The basic idea behind the ESO is to replace remand detention of foreign

[28] 'Excessive use of pre-trial detention runs against human rights', posted on 18 August 2011, available online at http://commissioner.cws.coe.int/tiki-view_blog.php?blogId=1&date_min=1312149600&date_max=1314827999.

[29] 'The Future of European Criminal Justice under the Lisbon Treaty', speech held at the European Law Academy in Trier, 12 March 2010 available online at ec.europa.eu/commission_2010-2014/reding/multimedia/speeches/index_de.

[30] Council Framework Decision 2009/829/JHA of 23 October 2009 on the application, between Member States of the European Union, of the principle of mutual recognition to decisions on supervision measures as an alternative to provisional detention OJ L294/20.

[31] The best-known Framework Decision is the European Arrest Warrant of 2002. It is of importance also for the subject discussed here because meanwhile a significant number of warrants are issued each year (Council of the European Union 2009: 8 ff). The existence of a functioning system for arrests of foreigners who leave the country in which they are prosecuted is also a strong counter-argument for the quasi-automatic remand detention of foreign suspects coming from other EU countries.

nationals coming from EU Member States other than the one in which they are prosecuted with so-called supervision measures. These may include of the obligation to inform the authorities of the monitoring country of any change of residence, prohibitions from entering certain locations, requirement to comply with certain restrictions for leaving the territory of the monitoring country, to report at specified times to a designated authority in the monitoring country or to refrain from contacting specific persons connected to the alleged crime.

Remand detention is considered to be of transnational importance because one of the four basic freedoms, the freedom of movement (Article 21 TFEU, formerly Article 18 Treaty of the European Union, TEU) may be affected by it. Because of the overrepresentation of foreigners in remand prisons discrimination against EU citizens on the basis of nationality (outlawed by Article 18 TFEU, formerly Article 12 TEU) also seems possible. The mechanism of the ESO provides that the competent authority of the EU country that issued the decision on supervision measures (instead of a remand detention order/arrest warrant) may forward this decision directly to the competent authority of the EU country that will carry out the monitoring tasks. Article 9(1) ESO requires that the suspect concerned must have consented to this procedure. The country to which a decision on supervision measures is forwarded must recognise this decision and take the necessary steps for monitoring the supervision measures within 20 days. The Framework Decision lists certain offences for which decisions on supervision measures must in all cases be recognised, without verifying the double criminality of the acts. However, these offences must be punishable by a custodial sentence or a measure involving deprivation of liberty for a maximum period of at least three years in the country that issued the decision on supervision measures.

The first draft for the ESO was issued in 2004, and the final adoption came as late as October 2009. This long delay suggests that some Member States have been somewhat reluctant to endorse it. One question was whether there was a need for such an instrument. The European Commission claimed there was;[32] critics doubted this.[33] Both sides in the debate expressed their views without sufficient empirical basis because the number of EU citizens in European prisons (or, more generally, the citizenship of foreign prisoners) is usually not included in comprehensive statistics. However, SPACE I now includes this question in the survey sent to Member States. The data published for 2009 show that in some countries,

[32] Commission communication of 29 August 2006 on a proposal for a council framework decision on the European supervision order in pre-trial procedures between Member States of the European Union COM (2006) 468 final.

[33] Eg the German *Bundesrat* (a legislative body representing the 16 Federal States), BR-Drs 654/1/06, Nr 6.

most foreigners in prisons come from other EU countries: 70 per cent of all foreigners in Belgian prisons, roughly 50 per cent in Hungary, Finland and the Czech Republic—in the latter three, however, the absolute numbers are very small. In France, Spain, the Netherlands or Germany, only one-third of all foreigners come from other EU countries; here, however, the absolute numbers are larger. This relates to the overall prison population. No comparative data are available for the percentage of EU citizens in remand imprisonment. According to a survey in Germany (data for 2008), roughly 15 per cent of all remand prisoners (1,800 individuals) were EU citizens (Morgenstern 2011b: 95) This is a considerable number and should be an incentive for national politicians seriously to consider alternative mechanisms, thus the European Supervision Order. It is also interesting to note that the attitude towards fellow countrymen imprisoned abroad seems to differ significantly within Europe. Scant attention is paid to their fate in Germany and data on their numbers and whereabouts are hard to find in official sources or the media. This may explain why a transnational mechanism that allows German citizens to await their trial without being detained abroad was not of much interest in Germany. In contrast, in the UK or the Netherlands, not only do the media seem to report more, but NGOs such as Prisoners Abroad[34] also provide services for such prisoners and their families.

Human rights concerns played an important part in bringing the ESO about. The Swedish government became involved in this question (and initiated the ESO) after a young Swede spent a long time in a Greek remand institution before he was finally transferred to Sweden to serve his sentence there. Several EU parliamentarians followed up on this and similar cases, and argued that such practices should not occur within the much-trumpeted 'common area of freedom, security and justice'.[35] The initiative therefore enjoyed widespread support and, unlike the European Arrest Warrant, was motivated by the wish to support individual suspects and safeguard their rights, rather than by a punitive, security-oriented motivation that looks for more effective cross-border prosecution.

Nevertheless, critics fear that the practical implementation of the ESO could undermine national procedural guarantees or that the judicial systems, in particular in the new Eastern or Central European EU Member States, will not be able to deal with the orders efficiently or in accordance with the rule of law. Some critics also allege that there could be net-widening, as countries could be compelled to implement orders imposed by other countries that they would not have been allowed to impose themselves.

[34] Different European NGOs are organised as Expert Group on Foreign Nationals under the umbrella of the CEP, www.cepprobation.org.

[35] European Parliament 'Debate on the future of the area of freedom, security and justice' [2004] OJ C116 E/9.

Thus, for example, German law allows supervision measures only as a substitute for remand detention, while others, such as England or Poland, have a graduated system that also allows supervision measures where remand detention would not be possible. This matter was raised in the advisory opinions given by various German professional associations in the context of the initiative (Morgenstern 2011b: 99). Without going into further details, it becomes clear that there may be a lack of the mutual trust that is necessary for mutual recognition. Practitioners active in the field of remand detention either do not know enough about the systems with which they are supposed to co-operate or they believe that they know enough to be of the opinion that they are inefficient or lack the necessary judicial guarantees. In the debates concerning the ESO, both prejudices could be observed for example in two expert meetings organised by the Commission in 2006 and 2009.[36] There must therefore be serious doubts about whether the ESO will work smoothly once it is implemented. It certainly will not solve the wider problem of foreigners in European prisons as a whole since most of them come from non-EU countries.

The EU Commission has published a Green Paper on detention about the interplay between detention conditions and mutual recognition instruments.[37] Green Papers seek to involve stakeholders, usually professional associations but also human rights organisations or other NGOs as well as scholars, who are asked to submit their comments on specific questions formulated by the Commission. The reactions to these calls are often meagre. This time, however, more than 60 responses from 17 states in 10 different languages were published on the Commission's website.[38] One issue that was raised in many different contributions was the concern that the EU could duplicate or, worse, water down what is already done by the Council of Europe, in particular by the CPT and the Court. Several responses suggested that the EU should rather strengthen these efforts than create own new mechanisms. Nevertheless, the ESO was generally endorsed. It should be noted in this context, that the Green Paper itself states (p 12) 'Given its substantial experience and work in this area, the Council of Europe has a leading role.'

## IV. CONCLUDING REMARKS

Because the legal concept and the scope of what is meant by 'remand detention' are not identical across Europe, comparative work (in particular

[36] Protocols of the meetings were published online but are no longer available on the Commission's website.

[37] Commission Green Paper 14 June 2011 on the application of EU criminal justice legislation in the field of detention COM(2011) 327 final.

[38] http://ec.europa.eu/justice/newsroom/criminal/opinion/110614_en.htm.

when using statistics) has to be done carefully. Nevertheless many European countries have similar problems: overcrowding often affects remand institutions. Excessively long terms of remand detention can be found in many countries. Serious problems arise with regard to foreigners, who are clearly overrepresented in many (western) European remand prisons. Mechanisms must be found to prevent foreigners from being detained on remand almost automatically. This, first of all, is a matter for national legislation and practice and must comprise judicial safeguards against detention not only in criminal but also in administrative procedures against (illegal) non-nationals. With regard to EU citizens, the EU Framework Decision on the European Supervision Order might be a remedy in many cases.

The jurisprudence of the European Court of Human Rights has set some important standards with regard to the grounds for and length of remand detention, and the accountability of the justice system. Otherwise things would be (even) worse in the Member States. Additional impact stems from the work of the CPT. Much remains to be done, however, to implement the European Prison Rules and the Recommendation with regard to the conditions under which remand detention is executed; in particular concerning overcrowding and meaningful activities during the day. The presumption of innocence should not serve as an excuse for not offering such activities.

Due to its nature as a 'provisional' procedure, remand detention is often neglected in penal and criminological research. However, it impacts heavily on the rights and lives of those affected, and on the sentencing decision in their individual cases. The attitude towards the presumption of innocence and the acceptance of remand detention only as a measure of last resort more generally influences the size of the prison population and may impact on the overall climate of penal policy. This makes it an important and worthwhile topic for European penology.

## REFERENCES


Aebi, M and Delgrande, N (2011) *Annual Penal Statistics (SPACE I). Survey 2009 (PC-CP [2011] 3)* (Strasbourg, Council of Europe).

Ashworth, A and Redmayne, M (2010) *The Criminal Process,* 4th edn (Oxford, Oxford University Press).

Cavadino, M and Dignan, J (2010) 'England/Wales', in F Dünkel, T Lappi-Seppälä, C Morgenstern and D van Zyl Smit (eds), *Kriminalität, Kriminalpolitik, strafrechtliche Sanktionspraxis und Gefangenenraten im europäischen Vergleich* (Mönchengladbach, Forum).

Commission Communication of 29 August 2006 on a proposal for a council framework decision on the European supervision order in pre-trial procedures between Member States of the European Union COM (2006) 468 final.

Commission Green Paper 14 June 2011 on the application of EU criminal justice legislation in the field of detention COM(2011) 327 final.

Council of the European Union (2009) *Evaluation report on the fourth round of mutual evaluations: The practical application of the European Arrest Warrant and corresponding surrender procedures between Member States. Report on Germany,* Doc. 7058/2/09 REV 2. (Brussels).

Darbyshire, P (2008) 'Criminal Procedure in England and Wales', in R Vogler and B Huber (eds), *Criminal Procedure in Europe* (Berlin, Duncker & Humblot).

Dünkel, F and Morgenstern, C (2010) 'Einführung', in F Dünkel, T Lappi-Seppälä, C Morgenstern and D van Zyl Smit (eds), *Kriminalität, Kriminalpolitik, strafrechtliche Sanktionspraxis und Gefangenenraten im europäischen Vergleich* (Mönchengladbach, Forum).

Dünkel, F, Lappi-Seppälä, T, Morgenstern, C and van Zyl Smit, D (eds) (2010a) *Kriminalität, Kriminalpolitik, strafrechtliche Sanktionspraxis und Gefangenenraten im europäischen Vergleich* (Mönchengladbach, Forum).

—— (2010b) 'Zusammenfassung und Schlussfolgerungen', in F Dünkel, T Lappi-Seppälä, C Morgenstern and D van Zyl Smit (eds), *Kriminalität, Kriminalpolitik, strafrechtliche Sanktionspraxis und Gefangenenraten im europäischen Vergleich* (Mönchengladbach, Forum).

Duff, RA (1986) *Trials and Punishment* (Cambridge, Cambridge University Press).

Esser, R (2002) *Auf dem Weg zu einem europäischen Strafverfahrensrecht* (Berlin, de Gruyter).

European Commission for the Efficiency of Justice (CEPEJ) (2008) *European Judicial Systems. Editions 2006 and 2008: Efficiency and quality of justice* (Strasbourg, Council of Europe).

European Committee for the Prevention of Torture and Inhuman or Degrading Treatment or Punishment (CPT) (2008) *Report to the Government of Denmark on the visit to Denmark from 11 to 20 February 2008 carried out by the European Committee for the Prevention of Torture and Inhuman or Degrading Treatment or Punishment* (CPT/Inf (2008) 26) (Strasbourg, Council of Europe).

—— (2009) *Response of the Danish Government to the report of the European Committee for the Prevention of Torture and Inhuman or Degrading Treatment or Punishment (CPT) on its visit to Denmark from 11 to 20 February 2008* (CPT/Inf (2009) 12) (Strasbourg, Council of Europe).

—— (2010) *The CPT standards—'Substantive' sections of the CPT's General Reports,* CPT/Inf/E (2002) 1, Rev. 2010 (Strasbourg, Council of Europe).

European Parliament 'Debate on the future of the area of freedom, security and justice' 13 October 2004 [2004] OJ C116 E/9.

Hammarberg, T (2008) *Memorandum by Thomas Hammarberg, Council of Europe Commissioner for Human Rights, following his visit to France from 21 to 23 May 2008,* CommDH(2008)34 (Strasbourg, Council of Europe).

Heinz, W (2010) *Das strafrechtliche Sanktionensystem und die strafrechtliche Sanktionierungspraxis in Deutschland 1882-2008.* Konstanzer Sanktioneninventar, available online at www.ki.uni-konstanz.de/kis/.

Hucklesby, A (2009) 'Keeping the Lid on the Prison Remand Population: The Experience in England and Wales' *Current Issues in Criminal Justice*, 21, 3–23.

Jones, C (1994) 'Schottland/Scotland', in F Dünkel and J Vagg (eds), *Waiting for Trial. International Perspectives on the Use of Pre-Trial Detention and the Rights and Living Conditions of Prisoners Waiting for Trial* (Freiburg, Max-Planck-Institut für ausländisches und internationales Strafrecht).

Kaiser, G (1996) *Kriminologie*, 3rd edn (Heidelberg, Müller).

Kaiser, G, Knapen, M and Morgenstern, C (eds) (2009a) *Pre-trial Detention in Europe* (Nijmegen, Wolf Legal Publishers).

Kaiser, G, Knapen, M and Morgenstern, C (2009b) 'Introductory Summary', in A van Kalmthout, M Knapen and C Morgenstern (eds), *Pre-trial Detention in Europe* (Nijmegen, Wolf Legal Publishers).

Kowalzyck, M (2008) *Untersuchungshaft, Untersuchungshaftvermeidung und geschlossene Unterbringung bei Jugendlichen in Mecklenburg-Vorpommern* (Mönchengladbach, Forum).

Melossi, D (2003) 'In a Peaceful Life: Migration and the Crime of Modernity in Europe/Italy' *Punishment & Society*, 5, 371–97.

Morgan, R (1994) 'England/Wales' in F Dünkel and J Vagg (eds), *Waiting for Trial. International Perspectives on the Use of Pre-Trial Detention and the Rights and Living Conditions of Prisoners Waiting for Trial* (Freiburg, Max-Planck-Institut für ausländisches und internationales Strafrecht).

Morgenstern, C (2011a) 'Die Stärkung prozessualer Garantien im Recht der Untersuchungshaft in Deutschland und Polen: Der Einfluss des Europäischen Gerichtshofs für Menschenrechte' *Zeitschrift für Internationale Strafrechtsdogmatik*, 11, 240–47.

—— (2011b) 'Von Straßburg nach Schwerin, von Brüssel nach Berlin: Jüngere Entwicklungen von Recht und Praxis der Untersuchungshaft in Deutschland und Europa' in R Egg and A Dessecker (eds), *Justizvollzug und Strafrechtsreform im Bundesstaat. Schriftenreihe Kriminologie und Praxis (KuP) 61* (Wiesbaden, Kriminologische Zentralstelle).

—— (2011c) 'Untersuchungshaft in Europa: Probleme im Rechts(tatsachen)vergleich' *Monatsschrift für Kriminologie und Strafrechtsreform*, 94, 452–73.

Nelken, D (2009) 'Comparative Criminal Justice. Beyond Ethnocentrism and Relativism' *European Journal of Criminology*, 6, 291–311.

Paeffgen, HU (1986) *Vorüberlegungen zu einer Dogmatik des Untersuchungshaftrechts* (Cologne, Heymanns).

Pilgram, A and Hofinger, V (2007) 'Austria', in A van Kalmthout, F van der Meulen and F Dünkel (eds), *Foreigners in European Prisons* (Nijmegen, Wolf Legal Publishers).

Pitsela, A (2010) 'Griechenland', in F Dünkel, T Lappi-Seppälä, C Morgenstern and D van Zyl Smit (eds), *Kriminalität, Kriminalpolitik, strafrechtliche Sanktionspraxis und Gefangenenraten im europäischen Vergleich* (Mönchengladbach, Forum).

Player, E, Roberts, J, Jacobson, J, Hough, M and Robottom, J (2010) 'Remanded in Custody. An Analysis of Recent Trends in England and Wales' *The Howard Journal of Criminal Justice*, 49, 231–51.

Pradel, J (1992) 'La preuve en procédure pénale comparée: Rapport général' *Revue internationale de droit pénal*, 63, 13–21.

Raes, A and Snacken, S (2004) 'The Future of Remand Custody and its Alternatives in Belgium' *The Howard Journal of Criminal Justice*, 43, 506–17.

Seebode, M (1985) *Der Vollzug der Untersuchungshaft* (Berlin, de Gruyter).

Stoorgard, A (2009) 'Denmark', in A van Kalmthout, M Knapen and C Morgenstern (eds), *Pre-trial Detention in Europe* (Nijmegen, Wolf Legal Publishers).

Stuckenberg, CF (1998) *Untersuchungen zur Unschuldsvermutung* (Berlin, de Gruyter).
Trechsel, S (2006) *Human Rights in Criminal Proceedings* (Oxford, Oxford University Press).
Van Kalmthout, A (2009) 'Netherlands', in A van Kalmthout, M Knapen and C Morgenstern (eds), *Pre-trial Detention in Europe* (Nijmegen, Wolf Legal Publishers).
van Zyl Smit, D and Snacken, S (2009) *Principles of European Prison Law and Policy. Penology and Human Rights* (Oxford, Oxford University Press).
Vogler, R (2008) 'Introduction', in R Vogler and B Huber (eds), *Criminal Procedure in Europe* (Berlin, Duncker & Humblot).

## EUROPEAN COURT OF HUMAN RIGHTS CASES

*Caballero v United Kingdom* 8 February 2000 (32819/96) (2000) 30 EHRR 643.
*Erdem v Germany* 5 July 2001 (38321/97) (2002) 35 EHRR 15.
*Jecius v Lithuania* 31 July 2000 (34578/97) (2002) 35 EHRR 16.
*Klamecki v Poland* 3 April 2003 (31583) (2004) 39 E.H.R.R. 7.
*Kudła v Poland* 26 October 2000 (30210/96).
*Letellier v France* 26 June 1991 (12369/86) (1992) 14 EHRR 83.
*Lietzow v Germany* 13 February 2001 (24479/94).
*Mooren v Germany* 13 December 2007 (11364/03).
*Mooren v Germany* [GC] 9 July 2009 (11364/03)(2010) 50 EHRR 23.
*Monell and Morris v United Kingdom* 2 March 1998 (9562/81 and 9818/82).
*Peers v Greece* 19 April 2001 (28524/95) (2001) 33 EHRR 51.
*Savenkovas v Lithuania* 11 November 2009 (871/02).
*Tomasi v France* 27 August 1992 (12850/87) (1993) 15 EHRR 1.
*Wemhoff v Germany* 27 June 1968 (2122/64) (1979–80) 1 EHRR 55.

## COUNCIL OF EUROPE INSTRUMENTS

Committee of Ministers Interim Resolution CM/ResDH(2007)75 concerning the judgments of the European Court of Human Rights in 44 cases against Poland relating to the excessive length of detention on remand adopted by the Committee of Ministers on 6 June 2007 at the 997th meeting of the Ministers' Deputies.
Recommendation (2006) 13 of the Committee of Ministers concerning the use of remand in custody, the conditions in which it takes place and the provision of safeguards against abuse adopted by the Committee of Ministers on 27 September 2006 at the 974th meeting of the Ministers' Deputies.

## EU LEGISLATION

Commission green paper 14 June 2011 on the application of EU criminal justice legislation in the field of detention COM(2011) 327 final.

Council framework decision 2009/829/JHA of 23 October 2009 on the application, between Member States of the European Union, of the principle of mutual recognition to decisions on supervision measures as an alternative to provisional detention OJ L294/20.

# 10

# *Prison Privatisation in Europe and Beyond: Changing States and Penal Rationalities*

ALISON LIEBLING*

PRISON PRIVATISATION IS one of the most significant, and yet undocumented 'patterns of penality' in contemporary criminal justice practice (Cavadino and Dignan 2006: 304). It is also one of the least visible, or researched.

This chapter arose out of a commentary on the original book proposal, requested of me by the publishers. I welcomed the well-crafted collection, but observed that a book on European penology would be incomplete without any mention of privatisation. Its omission was surprising, given the increasing prominence of private prison and security companies on the European stage, the shift to new managerialist discourse and practice in many European jurisdictions, and the implications of these developments, taken as a whole. It is also the case that little empirical or evaluation research is currently being conducted on this expanding dimension of penological practice among European scholars. Few papers on the subject of prison privatisation appear on the programme at the annual European Society of Criminology Conference, for example.

There are three problems with the state of research in the area of private-sector involvement in criminal justice work: (1) unclear procedures and protocols for securing access; (2) a distaste among many European penologists for privatisation, and so a lack of eagerness to enter the field; and (3) the creation of a self-organised 'knowledge base' by so-called 'experts' who are not research-based (that is, they are neither methodologically trained nor independent) but who work for the organisations concerned. These problems

* I am most grateful to Andrew Coyle, Tappio Lappi-Seppälä, Stephen Nathan, Ioan Durnescu, Dirk van Zyl Smit, Tom Daems, Brian Lawrence, Odd Lindberg and Finn Grav for informative conversations, and for alerting me to relevant materials during the writing of this chapter. I am also grateful to my colleagues, Ben Crewe, Susie Hulley and Clare McLean for their contributions to the ESRC-funded project on which I draw in the third part of this chapter. We are currently preparing more detailed publications on the results of this research.

result in a knowledge gap in this increasingly important field. Many of the available studies are either methodologically weak or sociologically 'thin'. There is a vast and informative critical literature consisting of detailed fact-gathering, monitoring and the reporting of abuses and other controversies in private prisons in many jurisdictions, but this material tends to be un-synthesised and is often overlooked by sociologically inclined scholars. Developments in the field are extensive and varied, but proceed without evaluation. So it is difficult to locate a considered body of evidence on the relative quality, culture or outcomes of public versus private-sector prisons.

I was invited to attempt to address the gap I identified. To do the task thoroughly would be impossible in a short, time-bound chapter, so instead I shall sketch out some important developments and argue primarily that scholarly attention should be paid to this rapidly evolving and complex field.[1] I shall focus my attention on countries I know a little about, but hope that this chapter might stimulate original research, some attempts to compile a more comprehensive account of current practice and policy development, as well as attempts to develop a more considered analysis of the significance of these trends, in the future. The research I have carried out for this chapter outside of the UK has mainly consisted of interrogating known individuals, scouring reports of activities, gathering relevant papers together, and absorbing information at relevant conferences and professional meetings.

## I. PRIVATISATION IN THE UNITED KINGDOM

The most important developments in the UK are as follows.

— The opening of three privately managed and nine DCMF[2] (privately owned and managed) prisons in England and Wales since 1991 (one of the former was returned to public ownership at the expiry of its first contract). These prisons are operated by three companies: G4S, Serco and Sodexo (formerly Kalyx). A 12th prison, consisting of a partnership between Serco and the third sector, opened early in 2012 (Belmarsh West). A 13th opened in Wolverhampton (Oakwood) in April 2012. This

[1] Which means paying substantially more attention than has previously been the case to matters beyond the remote and unsociologically posed question of cost (for two attempts to address the area of cost sociologically, see Cooper and Taylor 2005; and Armstrong 2007), or to official performance or 'black box' reconviction comparisons. A research agenda should include, for example, within prison establishments and between sectors: management competence and practices; staff cultures, professional practices, and self-legitimacy; prisoner evaluations; and a range of outcomes, from prisoner well-being and personal development in prison to post-release survival. Beyond individual institutions and jurisdictions, the most critical research questions relate to matters of 'exterior legitimacy', such as impact on imprisonment practices and policy-decisions (eg, the growing size of establishments and populations); probity and operating values of companies; and networking and influence.

[2] Design, construct, manage and finance.

brings the total number of privately operated prisons in England and Wales to 14, and the proportion of prisoners currently serving sentences in private prisons to 15.1 per cent (Prison Reform Trust 2012: 69).

— The continued operation of four secure training centres for 12–17-year-olds by two private companies (G4S and Serco).
— A fast-developing competition for existing public-sector prisons, and the transfer of the first existing public-sector prison (Birmingham) to private management (by G4S) from October 2011. Many more public-sector prisons are expected to be transferred from public to private hands in the near future. A competition for the 'next nine' prisons was announced in November 2011, to be decided in September 2012. An explicit attempt to attract a new and more diverse range of companies in to the competition has formed part of this round of bids. One of these prisons is currently in private hands, and so could be competed for by the public sector. The public sector were not allowed to bid for any of the newly built private prisons opened since 1991.
— The operation of privately contracted electronic monitoring schemes, escorts, court services, probation hostels, and police custody and 'back office' suites in the UK.
— The operation of an increasing number of immigration removal centres in England (and one in Scotland) by the same companies who are involved in the ownership and management of prisons, with GEO and GSL also managing two and one respectively.
— The opening of two private prisons in Scotland, in 1999 and 2008 respectively, but a reversal of the plan to procure a third after the minority SNP Government came to power in 2007. These prisons (Kilmarnock and Addiewell) are run by Serco and Sodexo respectively.
— In Northern Ireland, a significant Prison Service Review was published in 2011, which calls for modernisation of the three establishments currently operational there, with the intention that private-sector competition may be avoidable if the significant reform programme is delivered (Prison Review Team 2011). This 'internal' approach to reform, including improved cost control, using the threat of privatisation elsewhere to impose 'realism' on public-sector staff, was attempted in Scotland and Western Australia, before private-sector prisons were introduced.
— The lowering impact of competition on the pay, conditions, union and working arrangements of prison staff in both sectors (see for example Ludlow 2012). In response, lower staffing levels, higher turnover, fewer grades and more efficient working practices in the public sector are being introduced at all staffing levels, and form part of the requirement of the bidding process. Public-sector bids are now coming in at a lower cost than many private-sector bids.
— An increasing number of formal partnerships between private prison companies and the third or voluntary sector, as the emphasis shifts

from providing more decent and cost-effective prisons to, in addition, seeking better outcomes on release, eg, via untested 'payment by results' contracts. This development is 'changing the very nature of NGOs in society' (Nathan 2010: 1) as well as the professional identity and values base of the public sector. The increasing reliance on private companies to supply key goods and services in otherwise publicly run prisons raises many unresolved questions about 'what counts as punishment' (Armstrong 2007: 14; see also Moyle 2001).

These developments have coincided with increasing prison population size in all three jurisdictions in the UK, and with significant efforts being exerted to monitor and improve performance in all existing establishments, as well as lower costs *and* improve outcomes. They have also coincided with a shift towards 'firmer' penal ideologies (for example, involving a renewed emphasis on 'hard work and discipline', Home Office 2010) and towards 'firmer, more penal modes of immigration management and asylum policies' (Bosworth 2008: 204). The free market, deregulation and the 'war on terror' is forcing general populations to 'move' in unprecedented ways, generating huge numbers of 'displaced persons, economic, social and political migrants' (Nathan 2010: 3). These populations have become 'big business' for the private sector in many jurisdictions.

Whilst it is generally the case that pro-privatisation arguments tend to come from right of centre, and anti-privatisation arguments from left of centre ideological or political positions (if these terms and distinctions can still be said to hold meaning), the policy of increasing use of the private sector in criminal justice provision in England and Wales continued under 15 years of Labour Government rule. In England and Wales, it has been intensified under the Liberal-Conservative coalition Government since 2010.

## II. WIDER DEVELOPMENTS

Whilst England and Wales 'has the most privatised criminal justice system in Europe ... no other government in Europe has implemented a policy where the private sector finances, designs, builds and fully operates prisons' (POA Briefing Paper 2011: 5), there are significant steps being taken in this direction (that is, entrances being found into the criminal justice market), including:

— The extensive development of (more than 30) PPP (mixed management) prisons in France, also some areas of Germany (eg Lower Saxony and Hesse)[3], Belgium, Denmark, Spain, Hungary, Japan, and

[3] Despite some claims that Germany is a 'tortoise' (like Norway) when it comes to New Public Management; see Boin et al 2005; and later.

Chile: a model retaining state employment of officers, whilst the private sector builds the prison and employs staff delivering non-custodial services including transportation, work and vocational training. This model, about which operational and other concerns have been raised[4] (see Blanc et al 2009; Cour de compte 2006), is rapidly being exported beyond Europe.

— The establishment of 20 privately managed probation hostels in Sweden and extensive use of the private sector in probation in one German *Land*.
— The widespread operation (and marketing) of privately contracted electronic monitoring schemes, escorts, court services, and police custody suites, in many European jurisdictions, including Poland and suppliers of the technology establishing contracts in Denmark, Sweden, the Netherlands, Estonia, Russia, Belgium, Germany, Luxembourg, Austria, Switzerland, Italy, Serbia, Portugal, Spain and Israel (Nathan 2011).
— A fast-growing privately managed immigration detention and removal sector, (including escorting in two cases) in Denmark, Sweden, and Belgium, and a new contract for the housing of asylum-seekers in England and Wales. This is the fastest-growing part of the market. Even Scandinavian countries, persistently resistant to resort to 'the market', increasingly tend to distinguish between the principles underlying their penal systems, which include explicit attention to rehabilitation, and the emerging 'parallel' detention systems applicable to non-citizens (see Ugelvik 2012; Ugelvik 2013 forthcoming; Ugelvik and Ugelvik 2013 forthcoming).
— In the Netherlands, the Dutch subsidiary of British private security firm Securicor was awarded a contract to run detention facilities for offenders imprisoned for offences related to drug-trafficking in 2001 (Cavadino and Dignan 2006: 324). More recently, the Dutch Government 'has expressed the intention to prepare privatisation of some tasks of prisons' and is considering entering into PPP agreements 'to realise austerity', reduce labour costs, and increase labour flexibility (Nathan 2011).

The 'ideological groundwork for private prisons is being laid' in these countries (as well as 'in India, the Philippines, and elsewhere'): Nathan (2010: 4). According to Nathan (2009: 8), 'in Europe lawyers are working on ways to break down the constitutional barriers to full privatisation'.

Whilst immigration detention does not technically fall under the criminal justice umbrella, there is considerable overlap with prison ideology,

[4] Including lack of access to meaningful or reliable performance data, failure to lead to cost savings, and lack of control over market conditions.

practice and personnel (see eg Bosworth 2008; Simon 1998). It is significant that experience in handling foreign people in detention (who are increasingly 'aligned with terrorists, undocumented immigrants and criminals' (Bosworth 2008: 203)) is becoming one of the grounds on which the private sector claims expertise. The changing nature of the prisoner population from a largely domestic to a (in some establishments) predominantly foreign, and from (for example, in the UK) an Anglo-Christian to a multi-faith, mixed ethnicity population is de-skilling existing public-sector prison staff with significant implications for the criminal justice 'market-place'.[5] That there is a language of 'punishment services' and 'a criminal justice market place' is significant in itself.

But it is in Central and Eastern Europe (as well as beyond—for example, in Africa, Brazil, and South Korea), that the most significant and rapid penal developments are taking place. Private prisons are operational, and private companies are 'more than visible'—actively promoting their services in relation to custody and electronic monitoring in particular—in Romania, Bulgaria, and many other European countries struggling to improve their prison regime standards, but unwilling to stem prison population increases despite financial constraints. Romania is expecting to receive an influx of up to 11,000 transferred prisoners (the population is currently around 30,000) following Framework Decision 2008/909/JHA which deals with the transfer of prisoners between EU Member States. The mass export of populations without citizenship status to home countries is likely to create an urgent political need for prison places, without governments having the resources to meet this need.

There are many motives for governments seeking private-sector provision of 'punishment services', including a need to provide more prison places at lower cost (the alternatives are decarceration and diversion from criminal justice). Other attractions include speed of provision, the dismantling of powerful unions, a faith in competition as a mechanism for bringing about innovation, and a need to convince a sceptical public that criminal justice is effective at securing safety and public protection: a form of 'governing through crime' that modern governments have come to rely on (Simon 2007). Paradoxically, it is often losses or deficits in perceived legitimacy of existing prisons that lead to decisions to allow the private sector in (see Boin et al 2005).

Prison officer unions in many jurisdictions, some of which have resorted to strike activity when such reforms are proposed, are increasingly seen as obstructing much-needed reform and threatening the safety and well-being of prisoners in their charge, to promote their own self-interest. The

[5] For example, GEO advertise themselves as experts on the management of 'criminal and non-detained alien populations' (GEO 2012).

European Committee for the Prevention of Torture (CPT), for example, has criticised the Belgian prison service heavily in the wake of a number of suicides by prisoners during strikes of prison personnel (Daems, personal communication, 2012; and Council of Europe 2010). These developments illustrate the complexity of any choice made to invite private-sector competition into traditionally public-sector criminal justice systems, when their directors (and host governments) come up against intense financial and 'moral' pressure. Looked at as an accountability or human rights issue, the *empirical* questions become a compelling mixture of 'how to avoid censure by investigative bodies', and 'under what conditions or arrangements is the physical and psychological integrity of prisoners best secured'? The *moral* question of privatisation's legitimacy may remain unresolved, even if we had answers to these empirical questions (see Sparks 1994). Short-term improvement may be no indicator of the longer-term effects on prisoner numbers or well-being of extensive contracts with unpredictable global companies, whose identities, ownership and market strengths change.

One way of looking at these developments as a whole, despite the differences so far evident between wholesale prison privatisation in the UK and more limited public-private partnerships in the rest of Europe, is to see the common denominator as representing a reduction in the role of the State, and a growing role being played by economic rationalism in policy-making. These developments are together making inroads into some taken-for-granted inhibitions against private-sector involvement in 'punishment services'. This is the case in countries where private-sector involvement was unthinkable 20 years ago. I have found only one exception (Norway, not part of the European Union, but a Schengen state) where privatisation is not 'in the air', or under discussion, and so will describe some of its 'exceptional' qualities later. In Belgium, the decision to house some prisoners in a borrowed 'prison-with-capacity' in the Netherlands is also representative of the significant shifts in penal rationalities afoot in Europe. These departures from taken-for-granted penal principles in European countries (see Downes 1988 on the 'humane and enlightened Dutch system') may simply be illustrated by the growing role of the private sector in all things punishment-and-detention-related.

## III. INCENTIVES TO PRIVATISE: CONTROLLING COSTS, IMPROVING QUALITY AND MANAGING UNIONS

Public prisons in most European jurisdictions fall short of expressed standards and fail to achieve the kind of outcomes for offenders post-release that governments claim, or hope for. In the UK, considerable evidence of impoverished and damaging regimes, and resistant or indifferent staff, dilapidated buildings, weak or ineffective management, and a lack of ability to impact positively on these longstanding difficulties has been in the public domain for many years (see for example, Stern 1987; Fitzgerald and Sim 1980; Home Office 1979; Prison Service 1997; Home Office 1991; Ramsbotham 2003). This evidence has been repeatedly provided by both internal and external sources, and has persisted despite considerable improvements in some aspects of prison organisation, design and management. Some of these failures may of course be rooted in the concept of the prison per se (Coyle, personal communication), but others suggest deficiencies in vision, management, and organisation. A culture of failure, cynicism, inward-looking complacency, and staff-centred working practices, has been exposed in many Inspectorate Reports, major inquiries, and investigations (see, eg, Audit and Corporate Assurance 2011; and Justice Keith 2006). Prisons may have in-built tendencies towards destructive and negative cultures and practices, but here was an opportunity to experiment with a different provider. It could be established, after all, whether introducing a rival supplier of labour could undo or prevent some of these tendencies. Perhaps a public-sector bureaucracy had, or had produced, the *wrong* values: an unhealthy preoccupation with bureaucracy and hierarchy, no concept of 'the customer', a tolerance for (or indulgence of) underperforming staff, negative attitudes towards prisoners, and a lack of concern for outcomes, or sense of 'the public interest'. An impatience with public-sector prison management to bring about improvement (better 'value for money') coincided with a more widespread lack of faith in the public sector to do anything efficiently or well (see Hood 1991) and with broader powerful ideological currents (Windlesham 1993).

The onset of both managerialist approaches to public-sector management (and performance) in general and a turn to market-like mechanisms to support this agenda in particular, made the privatisation of prisons an appealing option (Windlesham 1993). Private-sector competition offered an opportunity to 'correct shameful practices' (Windlesham 1993: 276) and set out the terms of 'imprisonment service delivery', with private companies eager to enter this lucrative market. As critics have suggested, the fact that it is lucrative indicates something about the way the contracts have been drawn up (Coyle, personal communication). In England and Wales, a more 'dynamic', compliant, transparent, efficient and effective Prison Service was sought, with competition, innovation, and cross-fertilisation of good practice at the heart of the Conservative Government's decision to legislate accordingly. In the rest of Europe, new partnerships inspired by the same ideals, but somewhat more limited in their reach (so that to date the prison officer remains a public servant), began to form.

There are many untested assumptions in the above set of aspirations and developments—from the value of 'innovation' (is it a good in itself?), the working of new partnerships, and the standardisation of professional practices (to make them amenable to audit), to the concepts of 'quality', culture, and the packaging of prison regimes as 'services to be delivered'. These assumptions and developments are crying out for evaluation. The key argument of this chapter is that that there is little sociological-empirical research in this field on practices, quality, outcomes, accountability or management—perhaps surprising given the apparently 'experimental' basis on which private prisons were first introduced in the UK (Home Affairs Committee 1987; Ryan 1993). The main sources of evaluation are coming from private-sector organisations themselves (eg Serco has a 'research institute'), or from quasi-government or government sources (eg, the Home Affairs Committee 2001; or the National Audit Office 2003). The appearance in recent years of some scholarly analysis from business schools (appearing in finance journals) is both encouraging and troubling, as these studies work within a performance framework, rather than within any more critical sociological or penological framework. Very few 'in-prison' studies are available. Research is especially difficult to negotiate, organise, fund and publish in this area, either within particular establishments, or in relation to the lobbying, networking or other creative market activities of private companies, and their effects on policy decision-making (see Justice Policy Institute 2011).

## IV. RESULTS FROM A UK STUDY: STRIVING FOR PERSONAL DEVELOPMENT?

The author has, together with colleagues, been involved in the only independently funded evaluation of several specific privately managed establishments in England and Wales and in one Home Office funded evaluation of the first private prison in the UK, (see James et al 1997), as well as in several other studies including private prisons in them. Unusually in such evaluations, a detailed conceptual framework was employed based on the term 'moral performance' (see Liebling, assisted by Arnold 2004). Some of the key results from the more recent of these evaluations will be considered below. Other significant studies (eg conducted by colleagues in Australia) have had limited airing (one of the most comprehensive has been prohibited from publication), but developments there are also of interest as Australian states have been among the world leaders in models of privatisation, yet have made some reversals and modifications in recent years.

In this 30-month study conducted between 2007 and 2010 (see Liebling, Crewe and Hulley 2011; Crewe et al 2011), the authors found that comparing 'quality of life' between public- and private-sector prisons was both an informative exercise and highly complex. The authors selected four establishments thought to be operating towards the high official performance end of the quality spectrum (two each in both sectors), in order to explore differences in provision, culture, values and practices between the sectors. The research team selected establishments that could be matched on as many variables as possible, which meant restricting the study to adult male establishments and selecting a local and a training prison in each sector. The four original establishments in the study were: two local prisons—Forest Bank (private), matched with Bullingdon (public sector), and two Category B training prisons—Dovegate (private) and Garth (public). The research team took advice on which establishments to choose, and how comparable they were in size, function, cost and design. They all had modern buildings, as one of the key characteristics of private-sector competition until recently has been its operation in primarily new, purpose-built facilities.

The early findings from this study suggested that the two private prisons were not as competent or high-quality operationally (in terms of their 'moral performance') as expected. Although one potential research establishment had been ruled out (Altcourse, in Liverpool) on the grounds that it was the most expensive contract and therefore unrepresentative of the private sector, *prisoners* in the main research sites talked about Altcourse and one other private prison (Lowdham Grange, in Nottingham) so positively that we added them in to the study. Prisoners in our main study kept saying, 'Altcourse is really good. You should go and have a look at what's going on there.' So, in the interests of further learning, we did.

A third private-sector prison, Rye Hill, was added in to the study because it was going through a formal rectification process. It was officially 'in trouble', or performing badly, so in a series of events linked to our feedback meetings with the (then) oversight body, the Office for Contracted Prisons, we were invited to include Rye Hill in the research. This was an affirming message—that our methods for studying prison quality were considered reliable and objective by the field, and the findings were apparently useful to those seeking to improve their performance. It is significant, nonetheless, that most of the energy and interest encountered throughout and since the completion of this work has come from the private sector, who are strongly motivated (by profit, mainly) to improve performance and win further contracts. The public-sector Prison Service were less energetic or curious about our findings in this respect, until the competition for nine existing public-sector prisons was announced. At this point, the search for 'a convincing, empirically supported model', required by the bidding process, began. If the private sector is motivated primarily by profit, the public sector seems to be motivated by increasingly aggressive political demand. This can mean that, under unfavourable political conditions, private companies can use the contract to resist what they see as risky or unworkable political demands (for harsher and more restricted conditions, for example). An example is the resistance by the private sector to a politically motivated restriction in the public sector on the use of telephones in prisoners' cells. Private-sector prison directors were convinced of the positive impact of telephone access on suicide risk, and overall well-being. Public-sector officials were advised that telephones in cells would be regarded as 'indulgent'. Over time, the private-sector preference was accepted.

In the end, the design of the study was somewhat unbalanced, with two fairly well performing public-sector prisons, two matched private-sector prisons, and three additional private-sector prisons in it, two of which were exceptionally well organised at the time of our research. The authors had access to 'moral performance' data collected by the National Offender Management Service's Audit team for all other public-sector prisons, however, which suggested that few public-sector prisons performed as well as the two 'top-scoring' private-sector prisons. Importantly, one did: Grendon, the only exclusively therapeutic public-sector prison in England and Wales, surpassed both of the top-scoring private-sector prisons. This indicates that well-functioning therapeutic prison environments are evaluated highly positively by most prisoners, and that the public sector can manage prisons well.

The author and colleagues have spent much of their professional lives developing ways of conceptualising and measuring the quality of prison life (see, eg, Liebling, Crewe and Hulley 2011) so to apply these methods in the under-researched field of public/private-sector comparisons was a logical development. This use of detailed quality surveys in prisons has been a cumulative and developmental project, drawing on considerable structured conversation with staff and prisoners, and using an 'appreciative inquiry' method aimed at the identification and articulation of 'what matters most' (see further, Liebling, assisted by Arnold 2004; and Liebling 2012). 'What matters most' is operationalised using a set of survey statements about their quality of life, with which prisoners and staff agree or disagree on a five-point scale. These items are organised into a series of dimensions reflecting (we argue) an approximate test of the legitimacy of the inner life of a prison (for a review of work in this area, see further, Bottoms and Tankebe 2012). The dimensions are clustered into conceptual categories: 'harmony' dimensions, which are the mainly relational dimensions of prison life; 'security' dimensions, such as policing and safety; 'professionalism' dimensions, which relate mainly to the use of authority by staff, and which bind the relational and security dimensions together; 'conditions and family contact' dimensions; and 'well-being and development' dimensions (which can be regarded as 'intermediate outcomes' in the language of the prison's journey towards reducing reoffending; see NOMS 2010).

Table 10.1 sets out the dimensions used in the prisoner questionnaire.[6]

**Table 10.1: Revised Measuring the Quality of Prison Life (MQPL) dimensions**

| Harmony and Professionalism | Security, Conditions and Well-Being |
|---|---|
| **Harmony** | **Security** |
| — Entry into custody | — Policing and security |
| — Respect/courtesy | — Prisoner safety |
| — Staff-prisoner relationships | — [Prisoner adaptation] |
| — Humanity | — [Drugs and exploitation][7] |
| — Decency | **Conditions and family contact** |
| — Care for the vulnerable | — Regime decency |
| — Help and assistance | — Family contact |
| **Professionalism** | **Well-being and Development** |
| — Staff professionalism | — Personal development |
| — Bureaucratic legitimacy | — Personal autonomy |
| — Fairness | — Well-being |
| — Organisation and consistency | |

The following section draws on the quantitative findings only. Substantial qualitative data were also collected and have been (or will be) reported elsewhere (see, eg, Crewe et al 2011; Hulley et al 2012).

In the analysis of the survey results, a mean score above three is an overall positive evaluation by the prisoners, but the higher above three, the better. Anything below three is negative. Apparently small statistical differences are often highly significant, so that an apparently numerically small difference (.1) can reflect a considerable difference in the prisoner experience as well as being a statistically significant difference. Table 10.2 shows the range on those dimensions on which prisons varied most, from lowest to highest, in this seven prison study. The letter following each dimensions (eg, 'p') indicates the conceptual cluster to which each dimension belongs.

The dimensions which show the most significant variation between prisons include: 'staff professionalism'; 'organisation and consistency'; 'bureaucratic legitimacy'; 'staff-prisoner relationships'; and 'fairness' (see Table 10.2). Some of the scores on these dimensions tend to be very low in general—these are the important aspects of prison life and quality that prisons do not find it easy to deliver.

[6] A detailed account of their meaning and content, as well as the methods from which they were derived, can be found in Liebling, Crewe and Hulley 2011.

[7] The two dimensions in brackets are 'outcomes' of many of the other prison quality dimensions and so are treated somewhat differently in analyses of quality of life.

**Table 10.2: Revised MQPL dimensions showing the most variation between prisons**

| Dimension | Range | Variation |
|---|---|---|
| Staff professionalism (p) | 2.62–3.53 | .91 |
| Organisation and consistency) (p) | 2.23–3.08 | .85 |
| Staff-prisoner relationships (h) | 2.74–3.45 | .71 |
| Fairness (p) | 2.46–3.15 | .69 |
| Decency (h) | 2.72–3.38 | .66 |
| Help and assistance (h) | 2.74–3.37 | .63 |
| Bureaucratic legitimacy (p) | 2.35–3.97 | .62 |
| Well-being (w) | 2.57–3.19 | .62 |
| Personal development (w) | 2.69–3.28 | .59 |

The first headline finding from the study was that the differences within the private sector were so great that comparing public with private prisons was not straight-forward. Instead, the seven prisons in the study could be divided into four quality quadrants, from 'poor' to 'very good'. The private prisons were both at the bottom and at the top end of this quality spectrum (this has been found before: eg, National Audit Office 2003). So Dovegate and Rye Hill were both 'poor' private-sector prisons (see Table 10.3). The next quadrant is 'average'. Forest Bank (also a private prison) was average because, at the time the surveys were conducted, it looked like a 'typical' prison (that is, it was within an expected range). Bullingdon and Garth (both public-sector prisons) were both 'good' (that is, above average). Lowdham Grange and Altcourse, two of the new private-sector prisons added in to the study, were in the top quadrant: 'very good'. Prisoners were right: they were outstanding in all sorts of ways.

Table 10.3 shows that overall, very few of the 'dimensions that matter' made it over the threshold in 'poor' and 'average' prisons. Only 'respect/courtesy' and 'safety' were positively scored in Dovegate and Rye Hill. These prisons were not delivering many of the things that really matter to prisoners, on our prisoner-informed measures of prison quality. So 'respect/courtesy' was there, but at a very low level. 3.01 is a neutral, not positive, score. Prisoners were really talking about staff being polite (see further, Hulley et al 2011). In these slightly chaotic private prisons with inexperienced staff, custody officers were described as 'nice', and quite benign, but they were not delivering much that was of significance to prisoners. There was a low score, for example, on 'prisoner safety'. In Rye Hill, 'care for the vulnerable' appeared, which is a dimension about looking after prisoners at risk of bullying or suicide, but again at 3.01, barely above the threshold. In the analysis of the survey data, every dimension is scored positively,

**Table 10.3: Quality of life dimensions scoring positively in seven prisons**

| A – 'Poor' | | B – 'Average' | C – 'Good' | | D – 'Very Good' | |
|---|---|---|---|---|---|---|
| *Private Trainer* | *Private Trainer* | *Private Local* | *Public Local* | *Public Trainer* | *Private Trainer* | *Private Local* |
| *Dovegate* | *Rye Hill* | *Forest Bank* | *Bullingdon* | *Garth* | *Lowdham Grange* | *Altcourse* |
| Respect/ courtesy *3.01*<br>Prisoner safety *3.24* | Respect/ courtesy *3.07*<br>Care for the vulnerable *3.01*<br>Prisoner safety *3.32*<br>Drugs and exploitation *3.02* | Respect/ courtesy *3.18*<br>Staff-prisoner relationships *3.10*<br>Care for the vulnerable *3.10*<br>Staff professionalism *3.18*<br>Prisoner safety *3.32* | Respect/ courtesy *3.24*<br>Staff-prisoner relationships *3.15*<br>Care for the vulnerable *3.27*<br>Help and assistance *3.22*<br>Staff professionalism *3.24*<br>Policing and security *3.35*<br>Prisoner safety *3.46* | Respect/courtesy *3.29*<br>Staff-prisoner relationships *3.17*<br>Humanity *3.08*<br>Care for the vulnerable *3.15*<br>Help and assistance *3.05*<br>Staff professionalism *3.25*<br>Policing and security *3.26*<br>Prisoner safety *3.36*<br>Personal development *3.04*<br>Personal autonomy *3.04* | Entry into custody *3.21*<br>Respect/courtesy *3.47*<br>Staff-prisoner relationships *3.27*<br>Humanity *3.17*<br>Decency *3.30*<br>Care for the vulnerable *3.24*<br>Help and assistance *3.20*<br>Staff professionalism *3.27*<br>Policing and security *3.22*<br>Prisoner safety *3.57*<br>Drugs and exploitation *3.22*<br>Personal development *3.07*<br>Personal autonomy *3.14*<br>Well-being *3.19* | Entry into custody *3.10*<br>Respect/courtesy *3.48*<br>Staff-prisoner relationships *3.45*<br>Humanity *3.27*<br>Decency *3.38*<br>Care for the vulnerable *3.44*<br>Help and assistance *3.37*<br>Staff professionalism *3.53*<br>Fairness *3.15*<br>Organisation and consistency *3.08*<br>Policing and security *3.27*<br>Prisoner safety *3.48*<br>Personal development *3.28*<br>Personal autonomy *3.22*<br>Well-being *3.07* |

whichever way round the items are expressed, so a score above 3 on 'drugs and exploitation' means that prisoners are saying, 'Staff are in control here. They are doing everything they can to stop drugs coming in ... Prisoners are prevented from exploiting each other.' But these are the only positive scores of 21 dimensions that matter.

Moving to the next quality quadrant, in Forest Bank (private, average), the dimension, 'staff-prisoner relationships' appears, and also 'staff professionalism' for the first time. This is about 'staff confidence and competence in the use of authority' and includes items like: 'staff in this prison have enough experience and expertise to do things that I need them to do.' So this dimension is about staff being competent and engaging with prisoners in a way that exerts a certain amount of authority in the prison (the kind of 'unobtrusive professionalism' first talked about in a Control Review Committee Report arising from a series of major disturbances in British prisons; see Home Office 1984). The score on 'prisoner safety' is higher at Forest Bank than at either Dovegate or Rye Hill. There seems to be a cumulative or hierarchical effect appearing here: once a prison has accomplished 'respect', 'prisoner safety' and 'care for the vulnerable', these dimensions can be 'taken for granted' in the next quality column, usually at a higher level, and other dimensions build on those basic foundations.

In Bullingdon and Garth, the two good public-sector prisons, we see slightly higher scores on 'staff professionalism' and a new dimension, 'policing and security' appears for the first time. This means that prisoners are saying, 'staff are policing the wings ... This is a reasonably secure prison. Authority is flowing from the right place.' For the first time, in Garth, we see 'personal development'—a key dimension, to be considered further below.

In the two outstanding (and unusual) private-sector prisons, more dimensions-that-matter made it over the threshold: the scores for 'Staff professionalism' are higher than in the previous quality quadrants—'prisoner safety', 'policing and security', 'personal development' appear, and for the first time, 'well-being' appears. Well-being is, like other dimensions in the study, expressed 'appreciatively' but can be seen as the opposite of distress. Previous research has shown that the higher the levels of distress among prisoners, the more likely those prisons are to experience higher rates of suicide (see Liebling et al 2005). Prisons with lower levels of distress, or higher levels of well-being, tend to be prisons where prisoners feel treated respectfully, the prison feels safe, and prisoners are engaged in offending behaviour programmes, personal development projects, and so on (another defence of the therapeutic environment). We can see in these findings much support for the argument we have made elsewhere that prisons differ significantly, to the extent that some are 'more survivable' than others. That the private sector appear at both ends of a very varied quality spectrum is a significant finding in its own right.

Our interpretation of the findings shown in Table 10.3 is that, at their best, private prisons seem to be able to deliver regimes that are experienced by prisoners as constructive and facilitating their own personal development. This kind of regime seems to be harder to deliver in the public sector (although the better public-sector prisons come close, and Grendon does better than all other prisons). It is also the case, however, that badly functioning private prisons perform more badly in this respect than their public-sector comparators. There are two general conclusions that can be drawn from these findings. First, private prisons are a high-risk option: they are either very good or very bad. There is certainly no guarantee of satisfactory performance. Reasons for this extreme variation should be more systematically explored. We have some important clues in the higher turnover and poorer pay and conditions of prison staff, as well as in flatter management structures (see further, Crewe et al 2011). They have so far been new prisons, with largely inexperienced staff. These prisons are difficult to open and manage successfully. Secondly, few prisons, whatever their management arrangements, deliver 'a feeling of personal development', whatever their claims. Creating an environment in which individual prisoners can make 'progress' in areas that matter to them is difficult, and all other aspects of a prison's environment have to function well if this is to be a possibility.

These generally poor results raise significant questions about the so-called 'rehabilitation revolution' in England and Wales. Only in three out of seven prisons do prisoners describe the experience of imprisonment as allowing them to plan for their future, think about their personal development, or engage in offending behaviour courses, and so on. In the remainder, prisoners are preoccupied with daily survival and endurance.

'Personal development' is defined, based on what prisoners said, as 'an environment that helps prisoners with offending behaviour, preparation for release, and the development of their potential'. Where a prison is scoring reasonably high on personal development, it means that prisoners are agreeing, or strongly agreeing, with the following sorts of items: 'My needs are being addressed in this prison'; 'I am encouraged to work towards goals and targets' in this prison; 'I am being helped to lead a law-abiding life on release'; 'every effort is being made by this prison to stop offenders committing offences on release', and so on. Our working hypothesis in our current programme of research is that this dimension might work (at least somewhat) in the same 'predictive' way as the distress dimension did in the suicide prevention study, so that if prisoners are agreeing with all of these personal development items, they may stand more chance of doing better or surviving longer when they are released (there is some research evidence to support this hypothesis). In chaotic private prisons, like Rye Hill and Dovegate, prisoners remained in survival mode, so preoccupied with getting through the day, staying safe, and manoeuvring their way towards getting their basic entitlements, that they could not think about or plan for their futures. This is not a morally defensible state of affairs.

Why, then, is personal development the last dimension (of those that appear at all) to emerge in a study of prison quality? Basically, a prison has to be respectful, safe, and protective; staff have to be professional, delivering help and assistance to vulnerable individuals, doing policing and security well, and there has to be organisation and consistency (some people call these the 'hygiene dimensions' of organisational life) before it can be experienced as 'constructive' or future-oriented. These dimensions—the basic conditions of professional organisation—only appear in the very best prisons. It's only in these circumstances, with well-organised, professionally competent and well-managed staff, together with the requisite activities on offer, that prisoners can experience personal development. Too little authority—chaos and disorganisation—can be as damaging for prisoners as too much (see further, Crewe, Liebling and Hulley, under review).

Five key dimensions in our survey explained most of the variation in levels of personal development between prisons. These were: Humanity ('an environment characterised by kind regard and concern for the person'); Staff Professionalism ('staff confidence and competence in the use of authority'); Help and Assistance ('support and encouragement with problems, including drugs, healthcare and progression'); Organisation and Consistency ('the clarity, predictability and reliability of the prison'); and finally, Bureaucratic Legitimacy ('the transparency and responsivity of the prison system'). The term 'Bureaucratic Legitimacy' means that prisoners understand their sentence and know how to work their way through it; they understand the decision making process, and how to get on the right courses. Staff are able to translate some of these increasingly complex 'system-wide' processes of working one's way towards release into meaningful conversations with prisoners. This need for guidance is an increasingly pressing issue for prisoners serving newly complex, long and indeterminate sentences, so that inexperienced staff who do not yet know their way around the system, or the law, are regarded as adding to the pains and frustrations of imprisonment (see further Hulley et al 2012).

Even in the best private prisons we found one consistent area of weakness, related to the use of professional authority by staff. So in Lowdham Grange and Altcourse, the best private prisons in the study, the areas where these prisons did not outperform the better public-sector prisons was in 'policing and security', 'drugs and exploitation', and the use of authority. To abbreviate, what we found in the private sector, even at its best, was a slightly lax or permissive model of order, reminiscent of old-style maximum security or long-term dispersal prisons (see Sparks et al 1996; Liebling 2002; and Crewe, Liebling and Hulley, under review). Power was not always flowing in the right places, or in the right way. Because staff in private-sector prisons were inexperienced, fewer in number, and professionally less powerful than their public-sector colleagues, they disproportionately tended to work to a slightly naïve-permissive model of 'policing' where too much was tolerated, avoided or went unseen. This model can be (or has been) observed in some public-sector prisons too, but it is less likely (the opposite—the over-use of authority—is more common) and where it has been found in the past, it has tended to be deliberately cultivated, in the interests of humanity and rehabilitation, and therefore to be ideologically driven; see Crewe et al, submitted). In private prisons, prisoners disproportionately complain that staff do not use their authority properly, they are somewhat permissive, and that they 'don't know where the boundaries are' (see Crewe et al 2011).

One conclusion from this study is that there may be a hidden strength in the public sector which is not acknowledged in the debate about public-versus private-sector prisons but which is fundamental to the public-sector status and identity of prison officers: that when prison staff in the public sector 'get it right' (which they do not always), they *can* use their authority in a professional and competent way, and when they do, prisoners appreciate that. This may mean that prisoners have better and more constructive experiences in traditional-professional public-sector prisons than they do in slightly permissive and under-resourced private-sector prisons. To return to the argument this chapter opened with—there may be some strengths to practices and value bases that are linked, after all, to belonging in the public sector. Public-sector prison staff have a more highly developed form of competence in something beyond custodial goals (see Cowles and Dorman 2003): they understand and sign up to the use of authority when they join the Prison Service. This can be both a strength and a weakness, depending on how staff collectively approach the use of authority (and how they are managed) in individual establishments. These distinctions in the orientation of staff towards authority and purpose in the different sectors remain almost completely unexplored. Whilst there are important limits to the generalisability of our findings to other jurisdictions, similar trends have been reported in Scotland, Western Australia and some American private prisons (see Liebling et al 2007; Gaes et al 1998). Social theorists have identified significant differences between the value orientations of employees with long-term loyalties versus employees with the shorter-term horizons and interests required by the new private-sector economy (eg Sennett 1998).

Briefly stated, there are some over-simplified arguments in the public-private prisons debate, including assumptions by neo-liberals that 'private is better', and the assumption by social democrats that 'public is better'. It is evident from our own work, but also from the work of several generations of prison sociologists, that prisons are highly complex institutions, full of the flow of power. It is important in the debate not to overlook the professional authority work that traditional public-sector prison officers do, at their best. Perhaps some of their resistances to so-called 'reform' are in fact resistances to unworkable new models of the imprisonment task. Pubic-sector prison officers often get it wrong, and veer towards the heavy and oppressive use of authority, as argued above. It is often the case in almost all aspects of prison work, that the 'right place to be' on several dimensions (like trust, relationships and the use of power) is dangerously close to the 'wrong place to be' (see further, Liebling 2011) and that finding the right way to make a prison 'work' at all is an art requiring balance and skill (Liebling, Price and Shefer 2011). Prison work is a highly demanding and complex task requiring more than market forces to make it professional.

The author and colleagues have argued elsewhere that if we were dropped into a private-sector prison blindfold, and then took our blindfolds off, we would know that we were in a private prison in an instant, whether it was high- or low-performing. This is, we have argued, because private-sector prisons have a distinctive 'lightness' about them. Public-sector prisons, on the other hand, carry a distinctive 'heaviness'. Staff in private-sector prisons tend to stay a little too far back from the prisoners, slightly under-enforcing the rules, and they are more powerless, so that there is, at best, a kind of 'powerless-professional' culture or atmosphere in private-sector prisons (Crewe, Liebling and Hulley, under review). Public-sector prisons, on the other hand, tend towards the heavy/oppressive end of a 'use of authority' spectrum. The right place to be, the ideal model, would be in what we have called the 'present-light' quadrant, where staff use their authority wisely, professionally, and lightly. We have observed prison staff doing this in some places or at some times, where staff just unobtrusively, but in a very confident way, make sure that they are in charge. They develop relationships with prisoners, but these are relationships with power flowing through them. Public-sector staff seem more able and likely to do this than private-sector staff, but only when they are ably led, free from overcrowding, and with a clearly stated value-base underpinning all aspects of their work. Altcourse (in this study) was the closest we have seen in the private sector to that sort of traditional-professional model. It outperformed the public-sector prisons included in the study on regime provision, and prisoners' personal development. In terms of interior legitimacy alone, that establishment had much to commend it.

The most interesting questions remain unanswered: how common is this? How significant to its relatively high performance was its ex-public-sector director's experience?[8] How frequently do private-sector prisons resemble the 'under-resourced' and more permissive, risk-laden model? Are public-sector resourcing and staffing models moving in this direction?

[8] As cost-cutting increases in the public sector, senior managers taking early retirement packages, or being made 'surplus', sometimes quickly re-establish their financial position and professional identities in the private sector. This is true even of some of those who expressed opposition to private prisons whilst in public sector posts.

Most important, and most general for the purposes of this chapter, do all private-sector models take cost, and therefore staff expertise, down to what may in the end be counterproductive levels? How should the decision-making processes leading to privatisation be evaluated? Should governments be experimenting with lower numbers in disposals, rather than cheaper provision of services lying outside the competence of many of the private companies willing to take the business on? Or should governments be learning the lessons from both sectors, and seeking a combined, moderate form of penal provision drawing on the cultural and operational strengths found in each sector? How are private-sector interests shaping penal policy and practice? These and other related questions require independent empirical study.

Finally, I turn to a growing body of other studies, some recently published, some more dated, that provide important source material in this area, even if, as in many cases, their design or focus tends to be 'remote' or their data secondary.

## V. EVIDENCE FROM RELATED STUDIES

Apart from a handful of studies carried out at the earliest stages of public-private partnerships in France and Belgium (eg Beyens and Snacken 1996) describing intense lobbying by private companies, and some more recent official reports showing mixed performance among 'outsourced' and partnership services in France (eg, Blanc et al 2009; Cour des comptes 2006), most European commentators bemoan a 'lack of reliable data' (ibid) on the effectiveness or operation of delegated criminal justice work. Considerable US literature exists (also showing mixed results and insufficient qualitative insight; see, for example, Gaes et al 1998; Perrone and Pratt 2003; and especially Gaes 2012 for a significant recent review). Most focus on reconviction outcomes alone, without the kind of qualitative insight that would help explain any interesting differences. Cowles and Dorman 2003 in the US provide one important example of the problems in practice of merging private with public-sector goals and practices. One well-crafted review of four recent US studies found that 'private prison inmates had a greater hazard of recidivism in all eight models tested' (Spivak and Sharp 2008).

Some interesting empirical work has been carried out in Australia on the early experiences of privatisation (Moyle 1993, 1995), on the role market testing played in producing disorder and threats to safety in one Corrections Centre (Rynne et al 2008), on the effectiveness of privatisation in New South Wales (General Purpose Standing Committee 2009) and on longitudinal developments in the governance of prison privatisation over time in Victoria, where current practice includes the return of the provision of key correctional practices to the public sector (English and Baxter 2010; English 2007). Australia and New Zealand together probably have the most well-documented (as well as the most ambitious and volatile) privatisation narrative, with some reversals of privatisation decisions following poor practices and changing parties in power, and a recent move towards increasing use of public-private partnerships rather than wholesale privatisation in some Australianstates as a result of some controversies and default notices (for example, see Cavadino and Dignan 2006: 309–14; and English and Baxter 2010): a model that many other jurisdictions (including the UK) are keen to follow.

Public-private partnerships (PPPs) can vary quite considerably and can be a mixture of different models, ranging from the private-sector financing, designing, building and maintaining a facility, through to financing, designing, building, maintaining and operating a prison facility. This is done by the private sector forming consortiums made up of banks, architects and builders (and so on), who then bid for the work. Western Australia, for example, are currently building a new prison in Kalgoorlie, which is based on this model—where a consortium will provide the finances and will then design and construct a 350-bed multi-gender medium-security facility which, once built (in 2015), will (probably) be operated by public-sector prison staff. This results in the government not having to finance the build or 'worry about maintaining the facility', all of which is done by the private provider and a contract. The process of developing the contracts is 'fairly complicated' (Lawrence, personal communication 2011), but it reduces the risk to the government, and invariably 'the facilities provide better innovation, are built on time and on budget'.

Another example is where the private provider builds and operates the facility, and then there is the 'mix and match' model, where the government provides the facility, but a private provider operates the prison (Western Australia's first private prison, Acacia and their new Young Adults Facility operate according to this 'mixed economy' model):

> PPP's are now the preferred model when it comes to Government Capital Works projects in Australia and new prisons in Victoria and New Zealand are being built and operated using the PPP model.
>
> (Lawrence, personal communication 2011.)

The key to these ventures being successful, is 'well-constructed contracts' that are well managed:

> It is no use saving millions of dollars on the facility being privately built, maintained and operated, to then hand back all the savings due to poor delivery of the services.
>
> (Lawrence, personal communication 2011.)

So when governments (or agencies) construct and prepare these contracts, they increasingly develop benefits realisation plans, which 'identify key benefits which are then measured and enforced over the life of the contract'. PPPs appear to be 'the way of the future' (Lawrence, personal communication 2011). Expertise in the specification and contracting process, and then the arrangements for resourcing, monitoring and review, become key matters in the success or otherwise of these arrangements (see, for example, English 2007). Competence on the part of the contracted company also has to be assured. The complex questions of what a 'well constructed' contract looks like, and in whose interests it operates in practice, have never been adequately explored. There is substantial critique ('deep concerns') of the financial implications and operation of existing PPP contracts (see House of Commons Treasury Select Committee 2011: 3; and, eg Pollock 2005; Pollock and Price 2010), suggesting that an independent knowledge-base is long overdue.

Following a search of the available literature, the only jurisdiction to be defending, and seeking to improve, its public-sector provision (in the interests of solidarity, equality and culture) was Norway: an exceptional jurisdiction in many respects. As one scholar concluded, following a review of public-sector provision in Norway:

> In contrast to the demand for 'major surgery' in the public sector, which had spread through international organisations such as the OECD…the minority Labour Party government concluded that Norwegian public administration on the whole functioned well. Though there was room for improvement in quality as well as efficiency, the government saw a need for adjustments rather than fundamental changes in the administration's size, structure, and working methods. According to the government, increased privatisation in areas such as education and health would alter the solidarity and equality on which Norwegian society should be built … There was no indication that efficiency and productivity in the public sector were lower than in the private sector. To make this point clear, the report was given the sub-title, 'Community Foundation'.
>
> (Olsen 1996: 180–81.)

Three unexplored but apparently significant differences between prison operations in Norway and the UK are first, the more limited (less punitive) views held about the use and operational or political effectiveness of imprisonment in Norway; secondly, the apparently more 'mature' or cooperative working relationships with staff unions, and thirdly, the considerably longer period of training provided for new entrant officers (a fact that may be related to the first difference, in correctional ideology). Whether these differences of culture and practice make the attractions of private-sector competition less persuasive or necessary, or whether the pre-existing commitment to public-sector provision supports better practices, remains unknown.

Other Nordic countries also maintain an apparent immunity to private-sector engagement in criminal justice practices:

> There are no plans to introduce prison privatisation in Finland, not least because it would contradict paragraph 124 of the Finnish constitution that any 'task involving significant exercise of public powers can only be delegated to public authorities'.
>
> (Lappi-Seppälä 2012: 219.)

The Finnish constitutional committee has specified a number of criteria constituting such exercise, including 'substantial interference with fundamental rights', such as the 'right to use force' (Lappi-Seppälä, personal communication). But there have been discussions relating to the use of the private sector to supply electronic monitoring, work programmes and transportation, and one competition for catering services, to date, 'which the private sector lost' (Lappi-Seppälä, personal communication)

Finland has 13 closed and 18 open prisons, of small size, suggesting (as Cavadino and Dignan (2006) also found) that those jurisdictions not contemplating private-sector competition share some other important cultural and political characteristics: social democratic economies, strong welfare states, smaller prisons, and penal arrangements that tend not to be 'deep' and 'heavy', reflecting a distinct and limited ideology of prison use, and a recognition of the broader social and economic consequences. Such countries tend to express a view that 'good social development policy is the best criminal policy' (see Lappi-Seppälä 2009: 18 and passim). But even in traditionally co-operative Nordic countries, signs of punitiveness, and of dialogue about uses of the private sector in criminal justice, can be found. Sweden, like some of its neighbours (for example Denmark, Norway and the Netherlands), has increased its prison population in recent years, as well as introducing more punitive language and practices into its penal system and more politicised rhetoric about both criminal justice and immigration.

It is interesting to consider Norway's apparently unwavering commitment to its public sector, and its resistance to privatisation, as part of its approach to new public management, especially in light of its apparently more liberal and humane prisons, its low use of custody, and its better outcomes for prisoners (Norwegian Ministry of Justice and Police 2008; but see Dullam and Ugelvik 2011). One comparative study of confidence in government in Norway, Sweden and the United States, showed that Norway's citizens trusted government more than in Sweden (as well as in the US), a fact explained by its multi-party, flexible and responsive political system assimilating minority and shifting interests (Miller and Listhaug 1990). This may mean that governments in Norway 'govern less through crime' (see Simon 2007) and see prisons as the tragic institutions they are, rather than as sites in need of improvement for the building of public trust. Despite official reservations about the purposes of and limits to prison use, new public-sector prisons are built to very high standards (see, eg, coverage of its most recently opened Halden prison in *The Guardian*: Friday 18 May 2012).[9]

Further from Europe, Israel's Supreme Court has, uniquely, declared private prisons to be unconstitutional on the grounds that they contravene

[9] The level of trust in government in Norway has tragically been sorely tested in the wake of highly critical accounts of police responses to, and treatment of intelligence leading up to, the 22 July 2011 bombings of its Ministry of Justice building, killing eight, and the shooting of 69 young labour supporters on the Island of Utoya in the same incident hours later.

the Basic Law relating to Human Dignity and Liberty, reversing a decision to open its first private prison in 2004 on an 'improved English model' (Harding 2012). The profit motive was incompatible with 'the rights of prisoners' and the public interest. Other jurisdictions (eg Chile—the first Latin American country to allow privatisation, in 2002), whilst challenged by human rights scholars, as well as on performance to date (see Menendez 2011), have not shown such reservations. In Costa Rica, a constitutional challenge did not lead to any decision making private prisons unconstitutional, but in practice led to the transfer of an existing contract from private to public hands on the grounds of substantial potential cost savings if a larger prison was built. Other smaller jurisdictions (for example, the Dominican Republic) have turned down energetic offers from private-sector companies to build and operate new, large centralised prisons, and have instead developed their own 'new model prison' (and training school) project, a model that has attracted a UN award, as well as attention from other jurisdictions. Colombia has rejected the PPP model after doing some cost comparisons of its own. Left to their own devices, then, some counter-trends and alternative models are being found.

## VI. CONCLUSIONS

This chapter constitutes an argument for closer empirical attention to be paid to the rapidly increasing and differentiated role being played by the private sector in criminal justice provision in most European jurisdictions, sometimes at the thin end of the wedge (in public-private partnerships, or in electronic monitoring) but the companies involved are confident that, once they establish a foothold and some legitimacy, then the market in these countries will open up to them in unprecedented ways. Decisions tend to be taken rapidly, so a system can radically alter the extent to which penal services are provided by the private sector within a matter of months. Models assumed to be 'road-tested' or gaining apparent approval in European jurisdictions are exported elsewhere, with the apparent blessing of Europe. According to the findings of our study, some aspects of private-sector provision improve on longstanding and apparently intractable problems of culture, poor delivery, and an inward-looking emphasis on self-maintenance (on security and order) rather than on outward-looking models of prisoner change. These apparent 'successes' should not be ignored in critical sociological attempts to digest and make sense of contemporary penal change. There are dangers that as neo-liberalism and 'corporatisation' gain ground throughout Europe and beyond, and as right-wing governments win national elections, the increased punitiveness that accompanies these developments makes privatisation too attractive to resist. Private-sector activity in criminal justice is changing the shape of practice and policy, and undoing some longstanding commitments to state ownership and responsibility. It is, as argued at the outset, one of the most significant, and yet undocumented 'patterns of penality' (Cavadino and Dignan 2006: 304) in contemporary criminal justice practice. Its scope and nature should not remain invisible, or under-analysed.

## REFERENCES

Armstrong, A (2007) 'What Good are Markets in Punishment?' *Prison Service Journal,* 172, 12–16.

Audit and Corporate Assurance (2011) *An MQPL Survey at HMP Pentonville* (London, NOMS).

Beyens, K and Snacken, S (1996) 'Prison Privatization: An International Perspective' in R Matthews and P Francis (eds), *Prisons 2000* (Basingstoke, Palgrave Macmillan).

Blanc, P, Daude, C, Duprat-Briou, O and Rivosy, J (2009) *Rapport sur les modalités de partenariat entre l'administration pénitentiaire et le secteur privé* (Inspection générale des finances).

Boin, A, James, O and Lodge, M (2005) 'New Public Management and Political Control: Comparing three European correctional systems', Paper for the SCANCOR Workshop 'Autonomization of the State: From integrated administrative models to single purpose organizations' Stanford University 1–2 April 2005.

Bosworth, M (2008) 'Border Control and the Limits of the Sovereign State' *Social and Legal Studies*, 17, 199–215.

Bottoms, A and Tankebe, J (2012) 'Beyond Procedural Justice: a Dialogic Approach to Legitimacy in Criminal Justice' *The Journal of Criminal Law & Criminology*, 102, 119–70.

Cavadino, P and Dignan, M (2006) *Penal Systems: A Comparative Approach* (London, Sage).

Cooper, C and Taylor, P (2005) 'Independently Verified Reductionism: Prison Privatisation in Scotland' *Human relations*, 58, 497–522.

Council of Europe (2010) *Rapport au Gouvernement de la Belgique relatif à la visite effectuée en Belgique par le Comité européen pour la prévention de la torture et des peines ou traitements inhumains ou dégradants (CPT) du 28 septembre au 7 octobre 2009* (Strasbourg, Council of Europe).

Cour des comptes (2006) *Rapport public thématique: Garde et réinsertion—La gestion des prisons* (Paris, Cour des comptes).

Cowles EL and Dorman L (2003) 'Problems in Creating Boundaryless Treatment Regimens in Secure Correctional Environment: Private Sector-Public Agency Infrastructure Compatibility', *Prison Journal*, 83, 235–56

Crewe, B, Liebling, A and Hulley, S (2011) 'Staff Culture, the Use of Authority, and Prisoner Outcomes in Public and Private Prisons' *Australia and New Zealand Journal of Criminology*, 44, 94–115.

Crewe, B, Liebling, A and Hulley, S (under review) 'Heavy/Light, Absent/Present: Rethinking the "Weight" of Imprisonment'.

Downes, D (1988) *Contrasts in Tolerance: Post-War Penal Policy in the Netherlands and England and Wales* (Oxford, Clarendon Press).

Dullam, J and Ugelvik, T (eds) (2011) *Penal Exceptionalism? Nordic Prison Policy and Practice* (London, Routledge).

English, L (2007) 'Performance Audit of Australian Public private Partnerships: Legitimising Government Policies or Providing Independent Oversight?' *Financial Accountability and Management*, 23, 313–36.

English, L and Baxter, J (2010) 'The Changing Nature of Contracting and Trust in Public-Private Partnerships: The Case of Victorian PPP Prisons' *Abacus: A Journal of Accounting, Finance and Business Studies*, 46, 289–319.

Fitzgerald, M and Sim, J (1980) 'Legitimating the Prison Crisis: A Critical Review of the May Report' *The Howard Journal of Criminal Justice*, 19, 73–84.

Gaes, GG (2012) 'The Current Status of Prison Privatization Research on American Prisons', Available at: http://works.bepress.com/gerald_gaes/1.

Gaes, GG, Camp, SD and Saylor, WG (1998) 'The Performance of Privately Operated Prisons: A Review of Research', in D McDonald, E Fournier, M Russell-Einhornand S Crawford (eds), *Private Prisons in the United States: An Assessment of Current Practice* (Boston, MA, Abt Associates).

General Purpose Standing Committee (2009) 'The Privatisation of Prisons and Prison-Related Services', 3 General Purpose Standing Committee 21.

Gentleman, A (2012) 'Inside Halden, the Most Humane Prison in the World' *The Guardian*, Friday 18 May.

GEO (2012) GEO Group Annual Report 2012 www.geogroup.com/documents/2011-report.pdf.

Harding, R (2012) 'State Monopoly of "Permitted Violation of Human Rights": the Decision of the Supreme Court of Israel Prohibiting the Private Operation and Management of Prisons' *Punishment & Society*, 14, 131–46.

Home Affairs Committee (1987) *The Contract Provision of Prisons* (London, The Stationary Office).

—— (1997) *The Management of the Prison Service (Public and Private)* (London, The Stationary Office).

Home Office (1979) *Committee of Inquiry into the United Kingdom Prison Service (the May Inquiry)* Cmnd 7673 (London, HMSO).

—— (1984) *Managing the Long-Term Prison System (The Control Review Committee Report)* (London, HMSO).

—— (1991) *Custody, Care and Justice: The Way Ahead for the Prison Service in England and Wales* (London, HMSO).

—— (2010) *Breaking the Cycle: Effective Punishment, Rehabilitation and Sentencing of Offenders* (London, The Stationary Office).

Hood, C (1991) 'A Public Management for all Seasons?' *Public Administration*, 69, 3–19.

House of Commons Treasury Select Committee (2011) *Private Finance Initiative: Government, OBR and NAO Responses to the Seventeenth Report from the Committee*. Twenty-fifth Report of Session 2010–12 (London, House of Commons).

Hulley, S, Liebling, A, and Crewe, B (2012) 'Respect in Prisons: Prisoners' Experiences of Respect in Public and Private Sector Prisons' *Criminology and Criminal Justice*, 12, 3–23.

James, AK, Bottomley, AK, Liebling, A and Clare, E (1997) *Privatizing Prisons: Rhetoric and Reality* (London, Sage).

Justice Policy Institute (2011) *Gaming the System: How the Political Strategies of Private Prison Companies promote Ineffective Incarceration Policies* (Washington, Justice Policy Institute).

Keith, The Honorable Mr Justice (2006) *The Zahid Mubarak Inquiry* (London, The Stationary Office).

Lappi-Seppälä, T (2009) 'Imprisonment and Penal Policy in Finland', in P Wahlgren (ed), *Scandinavian Studies in Law* 54 (Stockholm, Stockholm Institute for Scandinavian Law).

—— (2012) 'Criminology, Crime and Criminal Justice in Finland' *European Journal of Criminology*, 9, 206–22.

Liebling, A (2002) 'A 'Liberal Regime within a Secure Perimeter'?: Dispersal Prisons and Penal Practice in the Late Twentieth Century', in A Bottoms and M Tonry (eds), *Ideology, Crime and Criminal Justice: A symposium in honour of Sir Leon Radzinowicz* (Cullompton, Willan Publishing).

—— (2005) 'Measuring Prisons and their Moral Performance', in S O'Toole and S Eyland (eds), *Corrections Criminology* (New South Wales, Hawkins Press).

—— (2011) 'Distinctions and Distinctiveness in the Work of Prison Officers: Legitimacy and Authority Revisited' *European Journal of Criminology*, 8, 484–99.

—— (2012 forthcoming) 'What is MQPL' *Prison Service Journal*.

Liebling, A, assisted by Arnold, H (2004) *Prisons and their Moral Performance: A Study of Values, Quality and Prison Life* (Oxford, Clarendon Press).

Liebling, A and Crewe, B (2012) 'Prisons Beyond The New Penology: The Shifting Moral Foundations of Prison Management', in J Simon and R Sparks (eds), *Handbook on Punishment and Society* (London, Sage).

Liebling, A, Hulley, S and Crewe, B (2011) 'Conceptualising and Measuring the Quality of Prison Life', in D Gadd, S Karstedt and S Messner (eds), *The Sage Handbook of Criminological Research Methods* (London, Sage).

Liebling, A, Price, D and Shefer, G (2011) *The Prison Officer*, 2nd edn (Cullompton, Willan Publishing).

Liebling, A, Durie, L, Stiles, A and Tait, S (2005) 'Revisiting Prison Suicide: The Role of Fairness and Distress' in A Liebling and S Maruna (eds), *The Effects of Imprisonment* (Cullompton, Willan Publishing).

Ludlow, A (2012) 'Contestability and Competition in Action: Restructuring the Prison Sector to Achieve Workforce and Industrial Change' *Public Law*, 3, 508–26.

Menendez, ME (2011) *Prison Privatization and Prison Labor: The Human Rights Implications* (San Francisco, International Human Rights Clinic).

Miller, AH and Listhaug, O (1990) 'Political Parties and Confidence in Government: A Comparison of Norway, Sweden and the Unites States' *British Journal of Political Science*, 29, 357–86.

Moyle, P (1993) 'Privatisation of Prisons in New South Wales and Queensland: A Review of Some Key Developments in Australia' *The Howard Journal of Criminal Justice*, 32, 231–50.

—— (1995) 'Private Prison Research in Queensland, Australia' *British Journal of Criminology*, 35, 34–62.

—— (2001) 'Separating the Allocation of Punishment from its Administration' *British Journal of Criminology*, 41, 77–100.
Nathan, S (2009) *Private Prisons in Europe: Some Recent Developments and Issues* (Luxembourg, EUROFEDOP).
—— (2010) 'The Politics of Privatised Immigration', Lecture given to the Programme for the Study of Migration, Geneva, March 2010.
—— (2011) 'Prison Privatisation: Some International Developments in a Time of So-Called Austerity', Paper presented at Trades Unions Working for Better Prison Services in Europe Conference, Athens, May 2011.
National Audit Office (2003) *The Operational Performance of PFI Prisons: Report by the Comptroller and Auditor General HC 700 Session 2002–2003* (London, Stationary Office).
Norwegian Ministry of Justice and the Police (2008) *Punishment That Works—Less Crime—a Safer Society. Report to the Storting on the Norwegian Correctional Services* (Oslo, Norwegian Ministry of Justice and the Police).
Olsen, JP (1996) 'Norway: Slow Learner—or Another Triumph of the Tortoise?' in JP Olsen and G Peters (eds), *Experimental Learning in Administrative reforms in Eight Democracies* (Oslo, Scandinavian University Press).
Perrone, D and Pratt, TC (2003) 'Comparing the Quality of Confinement and Cost-Effectiveness of Public Versus Private Prisons: What We Know, Why We Do Not Know More, and Where to Go from Here' *The Prison Journal*, 83, 301–22.
Pollock, AM (2005) *NHS Plc: The Privatisation of Our Health Care* (London, Verso Books).
Pollock, A and Price D (2010) 'The Private Finance Initiative: the Gift that Keeps on Taking' *British Medical Journal*, 341, 1280–81.
Prison Officers' Association (2011) *The Private Finance Initiative and the hidden cost of Prison Privatisation* (London, POA).
Prison Reform Trust (2011) *Bromley Briefing Prison Factfile 2011* (Prison Reform Trust), Available at www.prisonreformtrust.org.uk/Portals/0/Documents/Bromley%20Briefing%20December%202011.pdf.
Prison Review Team (2011) *Review of the Northern Ireland Prison Service: Conditions, management and oversight of all prisons* (Belfast, Northern Ireland Prison Service).
Prison Service (1997) *Prison Service Review* (London, Prison Service).
Ramsbotham, D (2003) *Prisongate: The Shocking State of Britain's Prisons and the Need for Visionary Change* (London, Simon & Schuster).
Ryan, M (1993) 'Evaluating and Responding to Private Prisons in the United Kingdom' *International Journal of the Sociology of Law*, 21, 319–33.
Rynne, J, Harding, R and Wortley, R (2008) 'Market Testing and Prison Riots: How Public Sector Commercialisation Contributed to a Prison Riot' *Criminology & Public Policy*, 7, 117–42.
Sennett, R (1998) *The Corrosion of Character: The Personal Consequences of Work in the New Capitalism* (New York, WW Norton and Co).
Simon, J (1998) 'Refugees in a Carceral Age: The Rebirth of Immigration Prisons in the United States' *Public Culture*, 10, 577–607.
—— (2007) *Governing through Crime: How the War on Crime Transformed American Democracy and Created a Culture of Fear* (Oxford, Oxford University Press).

Sparks, R, Bottoms, A and Hay, W (1996) *Prisons and the Problem of Order* (Oxford, Clarendon Press).
Spivak, AL and Sharp, SF (2008) 'Inmate Recidivism as a Measure of Private Prison Performance' *Crime and Delinquency*, 54, 482–508.
Stern, V (1987) *Bricks of Shame: Britain's Prisons* (London, Penguin Books).
Ugelvik, T (2012) 'Imprisoned on the Border: Subjects and Objects of the State in Two Norwegian Prisons', in B Hudson and S Ugelvik (eds), *Justice and Security in the 21st Century: Risks, Rights and the Rule of Law* (Abingdon, Routledge).
—— (forthcoming) 'Less eligibility resurrected? Immigration, exclusion and the Norwegian welfare state prison' in KF Aas and M Bosworth (eds), *Borders of Punishment* (Oxford, Oxford University Press).
Ugelvik, S and Ugelvik, T (forthcoming) 'Immigration Detention, Norway Style', *European Journal of Criminology*.
Windlesham, D (1993) *Responses to Crime Volume 2: Penal Policy in the Making* (Oxford, Clarendon Press).

# Part Three

# Nationally Based Perspectives

# 11

# *Can Prosecutors be too Independent? An Italian Case Study*

DAVID NELKEN

## I. INTRODUCTION

GUARANTEEING THE INDEPENDENCE of judges and prosecutors is a sensitive issue in many countries. But this aim can also form part of transnational efforts to standardise or raise standards for prosecutors and trial processes in Europe (Jehle et al 2008). What is not always clear however is the way such attempts to establish common standards relate to developments in different jurisdictions. Are we really dealing with 'varying structures, convergent trends' (Jehle 2000)? What importance should be given to local debates and 'palace battles' (Dezalay and Garth 2002) that seem to show persistent differences? How are international blueprints spread (Melossi et al 2011)? Who translates supposedly transnational standards into the vernacular—in what ways, and for what reasons? In what sense are the intermediaries who are involved in the making and spreading of such common standards representative of others in their legal cultures (Merry 2005)?

Asking such questions when we seek to bring about common standards will help us better understand whose standards we are spreading and the likely effects of doing so. This contribution is thus not intended primarily to offer new data about the realities of prosecutorial independence in Italy (but see Nelken and Zanier 2006). Nor does it try to show what can be 'learned' for immediate policy purposes from arrangements in foreign jurisdictions. The aim is rather to seek to grasp the distinctive ways in which allegedly commensurable ideas of independence and impartiality are disseminated between and within different legal cultures (Nelken and Feest 2001). The point being illustrated here is that, when we look at prosecutorial independence comparatively, we need to ask in what way this issue is salient—and is made salient—in different contexts (Nelken 2010).

Too often, attempts to compare prosecutorial systems assume that we *already* know what is salient locally, rather than seeking to uncover it. Some of those concerned to harmonise European prosecution systems for example take the main challenge to be that of helping prosecutors deal more efficiently with their increasing case-loads of conventional crime (Jehle et al 2008). They make little or no reference to controversies, on the one hand, about the need to increase the effectiveness of criminal sanctions against the powerful—including politicians, or, on the other, the need to avoid greater punitiveness against immigrants. Policy-oriented criminologists, for their part, present us with supposedly trans-cultural data about the existing level of independence of different judiciaries. But they beg many questions. For one such leading author, Italy's judiciary (presumably including the prosecution, since they are part of the same profession)[1] comes rather low down on the criterion of 'independence' being used, whereas the judges in the UK and the US by contrast, are seen as among the very highest (the UK gets a score of 6, the US 5.7, Italy only 4.4: see Van Dijk 2007: 376). But a lot here depends on what is taken to be 'independence'. Independence from whom? The government? The public? Their own professional interests? This indicator is based to some extent on the perceptions of businessmen as to which judiciaries are most independent of undue pressure of government, private persons or firms. But theirs is far from being the only relevant perspective, especially when it comes to issues of criminal justice.

It could instead be argued that Italian prosecutors enjoy an especially high level of independence (especially from government, politicians and business). Institutionally, Italian prosecutors benefit from greater safeguards for their independence than are found in many other places. They are considered part of the judiciary and are similarly constitutionally immovable from their posts. Because judges and prosecutors in Italy belong to the same professional category, they share the same career path and can switch functions. Prosecutors, like judges, are thus fully independent of any other constitutional power, as required by Article 112 of Italy's Constitution. Their promotion and pay are almost entirely tied only to seniority (even without the need of changing job), so as not to subject them to the dictates of politicians who it is feared might otherwise exercise a conditioning effect on their decision-making. Decisions over who gets senior administrative roles, internal discipline and so on are made by the judiciary's own elected judicial parliament. According to many observers, this independence helped

[1] It could be suggested that these relative judgements about judges were not supposed to apply to prosecutors. But this would be strange given that the author comes from a continental jurisdiction.

make possible the famous *Tangentopoli* investigations in the early 1990s that brought about the collapse of all the government parties by exposing the centralised organisation of corrupt exchanges between politicians and businessmen (Nelken 1996a).

By contrast, until very recently, judges in England were appointed by the government from successful middle-aged lawyers—on the advice of a senior judge who was also a government minister. Sensitive prosecution decisions are in the hands of another government minister and in a number of recent cases there have been real doubts about how far government interpretations of the national interest has been placed above the normal rules of criminal law. Turning to the US, there, many judges are elected by the citizenry, whilst, for many of those who are appointed, the ability to curry political favour and mix with the local elites is an essential part of the job. And prosecutors are regularly accused of arbitrariness in their too-zealous search for successful conviction outcomes (Davis 2007). Perhaps the relatively low score of Italian judges points to the political attacks to which judges in Italy are so exposed? But then their successful resistance to these attacks might equally be seen as proof of how independent they are. Of course there is always more that can be said. There are documented cases of some Italian judges who have indeed been found to be corrupt. And, as will be seen, it is said that the allegiance that many judges and prosecutors in Italy have to the quasi-political groupings who are their representatives in the higher council of judges (the *Consiglio Superiore della Magistratura*—or CSM) both helps safeguard their corporate 'autonomy' from the politicians, but also weakens their independence as individual actors.

How are we to get beyond such apparent incommensurability? Certainly, we have to place prosecutors in the larger context of their criminal justice system and developments in society and politics more generally. But we must also pay attention to the distinctive local ways of talking about and studying them. For example, in the Anglo–American literature, because the police are so influential, a longstanding concern in the comparative study of prosecutors has been the extent to which they are able to control the police so as to avoid them abusing their powers (Goldstein and Marcus 1977; Langbein and Weinreb 1978; Fionda 1995; Hodgson 2005). But, in Italy, the main debate about prosecutors is only indirectly concerned with their relationship with the police (who are seen, rightly or wrongly, as playing a much more subservient role than in Anglo-American cultures). Against a background of sharp struggle between judges and politicians, especially during the Berlusconi years, the issue was rather whether prosecutors' independence was at threat from others or whether, on the contrary, they were themselves abusing their powers in politically motivated prosecutions.

## II. THE NEED FOR REFLEXIVITY

This chapter focuses on the argument made by some leading authors in Italy that in many respects prosecutors there are *too* independent. This claim obliges us to think about whether independence has the same meaning and implications cross-nationally in different legal systems and legal cultures and whether it can—or should—be made to do so. What does it mean (locally) to say that prosecutors should be independent? Of/from what and whom? The police, the judges, the heads of prosecution offices, the minister of justice, politicians in general, parliament, or even the general public? In Italy, all these possible sources of constraint are matters of discussion (some more than others). How does independence relate to the responsibility of the category of judges/prosecutors as a group as compared to single judge/prosecutors? What of the careful distinction made in Italy—but not so often elsewhere—between *external autonomy* (independence of all prosecutors from outside conditioning) and *internal independence* (the independence of the single prosecutor from hierarchical control)? More specifically, what is prosecutorial independence for? Can it go too far? Can it come at the expense of accountability? Does guaranteeing independence serve—and should it serve—the same purposes for both judges and prosecutors, as has been laid down in Italy since 1945? This last issue has come to lie at the centre of almost daily political battles in Italy over the last 20 years.

If we are to make sense of this debate, we need to be critical about the sources of information about prosecutors that we draw on. In Italy most writing on the subject is doctrinal, written by and for lawyers and judges. Even if the number, level and length of such legal analyses is impressive, they have primarily normative and descriptive rather than explanatory aims. But empirical data is not entirely absent. Some information can be found in the Italian Ministry of Justice website. But most such data is created for bureaucratic rather than scientific purposes. More sociologically informed contributions do exist, some in papers written for special occasions in other languages to explain the Italian system to foreigners. But, as will be seen, many contributions to the debate are (deliberately) ideologically coloured by the values being prioritised. On the one hand, those with centre-right and 'liberal' sympathies stress the need for more democratic accountability, meritocracy and efficiency. On the other, writers with centre-left and 'solidaristic' sympathies stress their concern with freedom from political interference, the need for equality of all before the law, and the risks of growing punitiveness and scapegoating of immigrants. Such different ideological sympathies are well understood by Italian scholars—even when the authors concerned do not spell out their political commitments. But this may be much less obvious for scholars coming from abroad who seek to make use of the work for the purposes of comparison or harmonisation.

To illustrate these points I offer a close reading of texts produced by Giuseppe ('Beppe') Di Federico (especially Di Federico 1998) and others of his 'school', most of whom are associated with an important National Research Centre (CNR) on judicial systems attached to Bologna University.[2] I have chosen to concentrate here on the Di Federico 'school' because they produce the bulk of empirical work on actors in the criminal justice system, especially that published in English. In addition, their work is deliberately comparative, making extensive reference to how arrangements for prosecution in Italy compare to that elsewhere. For present purposes it is interesting to see how they criticise the Italian system in the name of international standards[3]—sometimes with special reference to what is taken to be the situation in more advanced democratic Anglo-American legal cultures. Likewise it is instructive to see how they seek to show why special conditions in Italy do not justify different arrangements. For them, Italy is a deviant case and has little to teach others.[4]

The work of the Di Federico school is considered in Italy to be the major centre-right contribution to the debate. Di Federico, and to a lesser extent some of his colleagues, such as Carlo Guarnieri, are also political actors at home and internationally in efforts to change the role and status of prosecutors. Di Federico, for example, was a member of the CSM, having been elected there as a lay representative of the centre-right parties[5] active in shaping and trying to take ahead many of the institutional reforms proposed by those highly critical of what they see as judicial interference with politics. Di Federico, himself, would be likely to consider criticism of such practical involvement as a way of avoiding the substance of his criticism of prosecutors' behaviour. 'Those that have raised doubts regarding prosecutors' conduct', he argues, 'have invariably been accused of conspiracy against

[2] *Centro Studi e Ricerche sull'Ordinamento giudiziario dell'Università di Bologna e l'Istituto di Ricerca sui Sistemi Giudiziari del CNR* (see eg Di Federico 1995, 2005, 2008; Di Federico and Sapignoli 2002; Fabri 1997; Fabri and Cavallini 2008; Guarnieri 1981, 1984, 1994; Guarnieri and Pederzoli 2002; Guarnieri and Zannotti 2006; Sapignoli 2009; Zannotti 1989).

[3] Di Federico refers to the Seventh, Eighth and Ninth United Nations Congresses on the Prevention of Crime and the Treatment of Offenders. The discussion guide of the Ninth UN Congress on the Prevention of Crime and the Treatment of Offenders (topic 3 on prosecution, items 76, 77, 78) inter alia stresses, on the one hand, that prosecutors be independent and on the other, that prosecutorial discretion be subject to the 'democratic requirement of accountability'. See also Kyprianou (2009), who cites the (somewhat bland) recommendations and resolutions of the Committee of Ministers at the Council of Europe, Rec (2000) 19, Rec (92) 17, Rec (95) 12.

[4] It should be noted however that Di Federico uses the term 'deviant' ambiguously, in the double sense of different and bad. But even 'best practice' is deviant in the first sense of that term.

[5] Even in retirement he continues to publish his criticisms of prosecutors in a house journal produced by Berlusconi's political party (see Di Federico 2009).

the constitutional principle of prosecutorial independence for devious, particularistic or political reasons' (Di Federico 1998: 378).

Di Federico's views are set out forthrightly in the abstract of his oft-cited paper published in the *British Journal of Criminology* in 1998. It is difficult, he tells us, to reconcile the need for both independence and accountability. But the Italian case is an object lesson in failing to reconcile these. 'By ignoring the need to render prosecutorial discretion accountable [Italy] has de facto delegated to a totally independent prosecutor the definition of a good part of its criminal policy' (Di Federico 1998: 371). As Fabri and Cavallini (of the Di Federico school) likewise stress, 'prosecutors in Italy enjoy the same guarantees of independence and autonomy that judges have and are not answerable to the Government or Parliament for their actions, even indirectly, for example through the Attorney General. They cannot be held liable for any decision taken' (Fabri and Cavallini 2008; translation: DN).

He explains that the independence of the prosecutors was originally justified as a reaction to the compliant role they had played in the fascist period. But increasingly it came to be seen as offering protection for them in their work in making up for what weak Italian governments were unwilling to tackle. In the 1970s (and in keeping with ideological battles of the time), part of the magistracy (the so-called *pretori di assalti* or 'attacking judges') basing themselves on article 3 of the Constitution sought to promote equality in Italian society by taking initiatives to have law respected with regard to safety at work, environmental crime and similar causes. They also won considerable support for the fight against terrorism. By the 1990s their target had changed to defending the principles of the Constitution (and the rule of law, so-called 'jurisdiction') by means of dealing with widespread political corruption, and threats from organised crime. Di Federico argues that their visible role as 'problem solvers' for a considerable part of the political, social and economic issues of the day in the last 30 years or so, be they safety in the work place, environmental pollution, tax evasion, bank frauds and similar economic crimes, terrorism, organised crime or corruption of public officials and politicians, have also elicited great attention and interest in many other countries, nourishing in many the conviction that the Italian model of prosecutorial independence and the exceptional measures adopted for its protection may be the effective answer to the plague of political and administrative corruption everywhere.

But, for him, the balance is a negative one. Comparing Italy to other systems leads him to argue that: 'In this panorama Italy stands as a deviant case: absolute priority is given to the value of independence. No relevance is accorded to the democratic value of accountability for the choices that prosecutors are in any case called upon to make in the crucial area of criminal policy.' For him the 'negative consequences' of such independence 'inevitably bear upon the effective and efficient performance of prosecutorial functions, protection of civil rights in actual criminal proceedings, indeed the proper functioning of the basic mechanisms of checks and balances typical of democratic systems for all decisions concerning the judicial sector' (Di Federico 1998: 378). An examination of his discussions of the recruitment and disciplining of prosecutors, the significance of obligatory prosecution in Italy, the independence of the single prosecutor within the prosecution office, and the place of prosecutors in the trial process, will establish why he thinks 'that there should be greater care in defining the meaning and implications of the concept of independence' when applying it to prosecutors as opposed to judges (ibid: 385). But it will also show how little he helps us understand the views of those who are reluctant to abandon this equivalence.

## III. RECRUITMENT AND CONTROLS

There is an obvious link between the independence of prosecutors and the way they are recruited. In Italy, as in most places that adhere to civil rather than common law systems, judges and prosecutors are neither appointed nor elected, but rather selected by public examination immediately after university. They therefore represent a wide range of the political spectrum: as compared to the methods used in common law countries, the methods of early recruitment of judicial personnel in continental legal systems could be said to produce a better pluralism of political identifications. But Di Federico stresses the less attractive aspects. Since the 1970s, he tells us, the recruitment and careers of judges and prosecutors have been modelled after that of the higher echelons of national public bureaucracies. In particular, judges and prosecutors are jointly recruited by means of recurrent public competitions based on examinations, written and oral, in which the theoretical knowledge of various branches of the law is verified. As a rule, participants in those competitions are young graduates in law without any professional experience. In any case, previous professional experience *per se* is not in any way taken into account in the process of selection. This characteristic of recruitment, he argues, is much stricter in Italy than in some other continental European countries, where a limited proportion of judges and prosecutors is recruited from among lawyers, law professors or other persons having previous professional experience in the application of the law. The only, extremely limited, exception in Italy is the appointment for 'exceptional merits' of university law professors and lawyers with 15 years of professional experience as judges of the Supreme Court of Cassation (Di Federico 2005: 128).

For Di Federico the weaknesses of this method of recruitment are compounded by the lack of proper monitoring and weak disciplinary structures later on. Newly recruited magistrates (the *uditori giudiziari*), he tells us, have to undergo a period of initial training for 'no less than eighteen months', including five months on-the-job training where they are actually carrying out a function. But although the period of training can be prolonged or the trainee dismissed, this virtually never happens. Two years after recruitment the trainee will become a magistrate. The next step after 11 years of service is that the magistrate changes his or her status to that of the Court of Appeal level. Again this is semi-automatic. Another seven years on and almost all judges reach the level of Supreme Court judges. Negative evaluations, he tells us, occur mainly when the candidate has received disciplinary sanctions, criminal sanctions, or is subject to disciplinary or criminal proceedings. But the disciplinary sanctions applied by the CSM are few and mild, and even if judges are blocked from promotion they are virtually never dismissed. In his view, because promotion in terms of 'status' and pay proceeds independently of the actual role that judges and prosecutors are fulfilling, it thus becomes little more than a formality. Seniority is the main criterion that dictates who go on to higher-level posts (eg at the Appeal and Supreme Court level). Allocation of such posts and those with organisational responsibility in the various tribunals and at the head of the hierarchies is decided in the main at the CSM, usually by agreements or contests involving the judge's representative groupings at their 'parliament' (ibid).

Di Federico criticises the fact that all professional evaluations are actually made by collegiate bodies composed exclusively or prevalently of magistrates elected by their colleagues. As he puts it, somewhat pointedly:

> in the course of the past thirty-five years Italian magistrates have progressively realized that their aspirations in those matters must of necessity be cultivated through personal ties with the decision makers and more particularly with their colleagues elected to the CSM as representatives of one of the four factions of the National Association of Italian Magistrates (ANM). For this very reason almost all magistrates become members both of the ANM and of one of its factions. To be a member in good standing of one of the factions of the ANM is often a decisive factor in obtaining the desired decisions.
>
> (Ibid: 156.)

Although there are frequent promises to reform the system from within (both by the CSM and the ANM), Di Federico is right that change has been slow to come. What he does not tell us is that in almost all other sectors of Italian life the principle of co-option, on the basis of proven loyalty to a given political or clan like network, prevails over competitive merit. Certainly this is well evidenced also in the academic world (Nelken 2009b).

## IV. INDEPENDENCE AND OBLIGATORY PROSECUTION

Arguably, the very essence of the prosecutor's role is to exercise discretion in choosing which of the cases put forward by the police should be sent further (and with what charges). Di Federico (1998: 371) calls prosecutors 'gatekeepers'. Sarzotti (2007) entitles his latest book about them *Selecting for Criminalization*. Almost everything else the prosecutor does also involves an element of discretion: for example, deciding whether there is enough evidence in a case, on what cases to work, when investigations should be initiated, whether and when to set wiretaps, what other actions should be taken with cases that are diverted or otherwise not taken further, and what criteria to use in reaching agreements to negotiate penalties for conviction without having a full trial. The same applies to the range of choices in organising prosecutors' offices, allocating cases, etc. There are also specific features of the crime threats that Italy has to handle—including political corruption or so-called 'external support' for organised crime groups which involve a particularly high level of discretionary interpretation of what the law requires and allows.

But how is that discretion to be governed? In return for their independence from political pressure, judges and prosecutors are supposed to refrain from making arbitrary decisions. Italy is one of the very few countries still to insist on an unmodified (and constitutionally embedded) principle of obligatory prosecution. All cases for which there is sufficient evidence must be prosecuted (failure to do so being itself an offence). But is this just a myth? Di Federico (1998: 385) certainly thinks so and speaks of the 'empirically false assumption that criminal prosecution should be mandatory'. In his view:

> a vast amount of unregulated, politically relevant decisions have been de facto forced into the hands of the members of a bureaucratically recruited corps, that of prosecutors. In the absence of any formal regulation of such wide-ranging discretionary power, any formal regulation being in contradiction to the constitutional provision of mandatory criminal prosecution, prosecutors are left to themselves in deciding how to use it from time to time and from case to case. The result is that such powers end up being used in a different way by the various prosecutors' offices and even by each prosecutor within an office. Paradoxically, therefore, such an extreme version of prosecutorial independence inevitably carries with it at the operational level the defeat of one of the ultimate goals it is intended to guarantee, ie the equality of all citizens before the criminal law.
>
> (Ibid.)

Prosecution in Italy, he argues:

> is de facto just as discretionary as in other countries (such as Germany as France), and perhaps more ... in Italy too discretion de facto permeates prosecutorial decisions throughout the process that prosecutors have to perform (in relation to, for

> example, relative priorities in pursuing cases simultaneously, part of the prosecutor's workload, the amount and nature of investigative resources to employ in each case, restriction placed on personal freedom and assets.
>
> (Ibid: 378.)

Moreover, in Italy there is:

> more ample, unrestricted use of prosecutorial discretion than in those democratic countries where the discretionary powers of prosecutors are in various ways exposed and restricted by open regulation, through decisions taken within the democratic process, of the priorities to be followed and by rendering, therefore, prosecutors accountable for their violations. In Italy, instead, when prosecutors' decisions are publicly criticized, as often happens, for being discriminatory or partisan, they are recurrently and successfully defended as the 'mere', 'unavoidable' application of the constitutional principle of mandatory prosecution.
>
> (Ibid.)

Di Federico finds it unacceptable that single prosecutors can start investigations on their own initiative and not 'pay for it' even when their accusations, as sometimes happens, turn out to be totally groundless at the trial level (ibid). Relying on his interviews carried out with defence lawyers, he even goes as far as affirming that prosecutors cover up decisions that are really motivated by personal ambitions or political orientation (ibid: 382). But he does not try to tell us how often this happens or what reliable methods exist for uncovering the real motives of decision.

Di Federico and his school are right that there is considerable variety in prosecution decision-making, although they underestimate the degree to which individual decisions are shaped by senior prosecutors as well as by organisational routines. In a small-scale project, Nelken and Zanier studied the differences between prosecution offices at Bologna, Ferrara, Padova, Torino, Florence and Catania—interviewing head and substitute prosecutors, judges, lawyers and court administrators. They found that the approaches taken in different offices depended greatly on the leadership role taken by the different head prosecutors, the relationship between them and the substitutes, and with other relevant legal actors. There were differences between the north and the south, and between different size offices. They argued, however, that these differences were not well captured by describing them as politicised choices but rather that they should be understood as varying ways to structure discretion, bearing in mind the sort of office concerned, the type of crimes being dealt with and other aspects of local legal culture (Nelken and Zanier 2006; Zanier 2009). In a narrower but excellently designed recent study, Sarzotti and his collaborators examined the differences between the prosecution offices in Turin (in the north) and Bari (in the south). They showed that Turin is dominated by a managerial or so-called 'efficientist' approach geared to getting through cases as soon as possible and making whatever choices are necessary to achieve this. By contrast, Bari has an internal legal culture that stands for a formalistic respect for the rules and a 'fatalistic' attitude to the rule of obligatoriness. It has far too many cases to handle and far too few personnel and resources. But instead of trying to take an 'efficientist' approach and standardise responses, it is reactive rather than proactive. Nonetheless, individual prosecutors, even in a laissez-faire type of organisation of this sort, do use their own initiative to try to deal with particularly serious kinds of cases (Sarzotti 2007). What Di Federico does not really examine, when criticising the lack of consistency, however, is how far such variation is avoidable (it is certainly a feature of common law jurisdictions), and whether or not it could be justifiable in terms of the different circumstances facing different prosecution offices.

## V. THE MEANING(S) OF DISCRETION

Few Anglo-American commentators, if any, would disagree with Di Federico that it is impossible to get rid of discretion simply by banning it. But they would be more likely than him to pose the problem as how best to 'structure' it (Davies 1969). In arguing that obligatory prosecution is only a 'myth' there is also a tendency to exaggerate what is included in the term. In Italy discretion is more easily given the meaning of 'unacceptable' arbitrariness, rather than the more neutral 'room for limited choice to be exercised with judgement' that is associated with it in English.[6] Di Federico and his followers use the term discretion as if it had the same meaning in Italy as in the Anglo-American world. But in practice, they are seeking to spread a new Anglo-American nuance (that treats all prosecutor decisions as involving policy choices), at the same time as they continue to criticise the current use of discretion by prosecutors as something that, in the Italian sense, is and will inevitably be subject to 'arbitrariness' unless regulated by others.

Fabri and Cavallini (2008: 115, translation: DN) tell us that

> the modalities of exercise of the power of public prosecution are extremely different, often deprived of adequate coordination and based on arbitrary decisions by individual prosecutors substitutes.

[6] On the other hand, there is less discussion of the problem of police discretion in Italy—because, formally speaking, they are seen as only employing executive power as compared to the jurisdictional functions of prosecutors and judges.

But important Italian jurists emphasise the fact that most of the various decisions that prosecutors have to make do not pose the issue of 'discretion' but merely show that careful use of legal judgment is required (and that is what they are trained and paid to do). For leading criminal procedure experts, such as Franco Cordero (2003), the 'principle of legality' does not require that all the crimes be prosecuted in the same way: the prosecutor is allowed to choose the when and the how. The central problem of deciding priorities—he calls it 'discretion over priorities'—is not real discretion of the sort that the rule of mandatory prosecution is trying to eliminate. Faced with more cases to handle than they can realistically get through, Italian prosecutors have to decide which cases on their desk they need to handle before others. Inevitably, those that are taken up last (or that are given least attention) are the ones at most risk of never making it to trial, because of the delays in working up the investigation and, more banally, because those dealt with last will be automatically timed out by the rules of prescription.

As a matter of practice these decisions are often regulated internally by prosecution offices, the best-known example being the instructions laid down by Gustavo Zagrebelsky, then chief prosecutor in Turin, regarding the order in which different cases should be handled. Similar criteria are used elsewhere.

For the most part, the priority depends on the seriousness of the offence and its social harm as measured by the penalties laid down, public security and the necessities of investigation. But decision-making remains controversial (Nelken and Zanier 2006; Zanier 2009). Not all prosecutors are convinced that the penalties laid down by the legislature are a fail-safe guide to 'seriousness', especially given the way the sanctions for white collar and environmental crime have been reduced over the past years, whereas those for street crimes and illegal immigration have increased. Likewise, there are sometimes conflicts between prosecution heads and their substitutes when for example the latter try to avoid dealing with minor cases (so-called 'bagatelle' offences), so that these end up falling foul of the rules of prescription. Paradoxically, this time pressure can mean that prosecutors are asked to deal with minor cases sooner than more serious ones—precisely to avoid them falling into prescription (because the cut-off time arrives earlier for less serious offences). Admittedly too, the discretion to do nothing (leaving cases in the files) is difficult to regulate in any system, except if it can be shown that it was done with the explicit intention of making them end with prescription ('putting cases in the cupboard').

But none of this shows the rule of obligatory prosecution to be only a myth. It is easy enough to find cases where a prosecution is brought in Italy in situations where it would not be done following the 'principle of opportunity'; especially, but not only in cases where the special circumstances of the offence or the offender would have discouraged prosecution (see Nelken

2002). And even a myth has functions, not least in acting as a regulatory ideal. The possibility of making reference to the rule of obligatory prosecution served to protect prosecutors in the *Tangentopoli* anti-corruption investigations when their investigations brought them up against leading politicians, including the Minister of Justice himself (Nelken 1996a). Crucially, for those who think differently from Di Federico, it has continued to play this role of serving as a shield against the claim that it would not be in the 'public interest' to continue with such prosecutions, making it easier than it would otherwise be to treat the powerful and less powerful alike.

## VI. INDEPENDENCE AND IMPARTIALITY

For Di Federico the CSM needs reforming so as to make it possible to strengthen the supervisory powers of the heads of prosecutors' offices. The judges, for their part, defend the role of the CSM as a distinct state organ counterbalanced against the others defined in the Constitution. And some respected legal commentators see the CSM as playing a genuine role in providing accountability. Vogliotti speaks of

> a complex normative stratification, a system which, while not perfect, however, provides some transparency, wide consultation and a network of reciprocal checks in which a fundamental role is played by the CSM, which—because of its mixed composition (two-thirds of its members are elected by the magistrates and one third by Parliament)—provides representatives of the sovereign, people of influence and control instruments for the administration of justice, while respecting the independence of the judiciary.
>
> (Vogliotti 2004, translation: DN.)

Di Federico also tells us little of efforts by chief prosecutors to stay in touch with local committees representing the public (Borgna and Maddalena 2003).

Politicians of the centre-right, led by Berlusconi himself, often make wild accusations against the so-called 'red judges' with communist ideas. But while some of the leading judges who were and are active in the fight against corruption are identified with the centre-left, many more are not. For example, the prosecutors of the *Mani Pulite* pool of prosecutors in Milan at the time of the *Tangentopoli* investigations had a variety of political sympathies. This is even more true of the battle against organised crime which has seen many centre and right wing judges play vital roles. *Magistratura Democratica*, the left-leaning representative group in the Italian judges' parliament, is certainly well organised, and produces by far the most sophisticated journal for judges. But its support amongst the judges in elections for the CSM has rarely gone beyond a third, and there have been long periods when it has been outmanoeuvred by the other groupings acting in concert. It is also important to distinguish between levels of prosecutors. The more senior members of the judiciary and senior prosecutors tend to be pro-government, even if not necessarily in favour of any particular government. The annual speeches of heads of prosecution offices reporting on the crime situation in their tribunal districts at the start of each legal year frequently seek to align themselves to governmental (and public) concerns to reduce crime (Sarzotti 2007).

On the other hand, acting in their corporate interest, the judiciary is regularly at loggerheads with the government. The ANM (the national association of judges) sometimes lobbies, protests and uses strikes against legal reforms and other legislation of which it disapproves. It normally accepts the right of the government to legislate, though its current secretary (a prosecutor) did claim in 2010 that the Berlusconi Government lacked the historical, political, cultural—and moral—legitimacy to introduce its far-reaching reforms of the legal system. Deep reciprocal suspicions and well-founded charges of mutual interference in each other's spheres remain. The battle continues between those politicians who claim legitimacy on the basis of parliamentary elections and those judges who see themselves as safeguarding respect for the Constitution. In these struggles each side sometimes uses the others' 'weapons' as part of their on-going battles: judges making appeals via the media; and politicians choosing to change legal rules or use the powers available to the Minister of Justice, such as disciplinary investigations (Nelken 1996b). Controversially, judges enjoy the right not only to express their political opinions, but also to become politicians and then afterwards return to their previous role (even if it is not that common in practice). Some prosecutors whose decisions have changed Italian history in fact have become politicians, most notably Antonio Di Pietro (who founded his own party) and Lugi De Magistris—whose investigation of the Minister of Justice in the second Prodi Government helped bring about its downfall.

Those who defend current arrangements say that a high level of independence (including promotion depending mainly on seniority) is necessary in order to be able to oppose pressures from the powerful by which decisions whether to prosecute might be conditioned by the implications for promotion. For them, what is unique in the experience of Italian prosecutors is their success, especially during the *Tangentopoli*, anti-corruption investigations of the early 1990s, in driving from power all the established political parties (Nelken 1996a). Even the lack of overall coordination between prosecutors played a part in maintaining the momentum of attack. But Di Federico denies any connection. It is not true, he says, 'that the more one reinforces the independence of public prosecutors at the expense of democratic accountability, the better it is for the proper functioning of prosecution in a democratic country, especially with curtailing political and administrative corruption' (Di Federico 1998: 372). He points out that such independence did not lead to similar results in the 1980s. But to this it could be replied that such independence may be necessary but not sufficient and that wider social and political changes are also relevant. What is more questionable is whether the same arrangements needed to protect prosecutors from political interference in such moments of 'emergency' are well calculated to structure 'ordinary administration'. Unfortunately, in Italy emergencies seem to be ongoing.

## VII. INDEPENDENCE IN THE TRIAL PROCESS

Because of the high stakes involved, most attention is usually given to judicial independence in relation to governments and politicians in general. But, as elsewhere, the issue of independence in Italy also relates to the way the prosecution stage shapes or is shaped by other stages of the criminal process. Prosecution decisions with respect to deciding to prosecute and sending the case on to trial are subject to control by two different kinds of judges (the so-called judges for the preliminary investigation and for preliminary trial). Drawing again on evidence from interviews with defence lawyers, Di Federico argues that the relationship between prosecutors and judges (who are part of the same profession) is too close for these controls to be effective. 'Our field research findings', he says, 'confirm the existence of informal ex-parte communications between prosecutors and judges with reference to decisions that the latter have to take on matters concerning the measures to be adopted during the investigative phase'. He also adduces 'documentary evidence' not only 'on the inclination of judges to satisfy the expectations of their "colleagues" acting as prosecutors during the investigative phase, but also to the effect that such a phenomenon is not de facto considered as a violation of judicial ethics like it is in other countries' (Di Federico 1998: 382).

As proof that 'these phenomena are frequent and widespread', he points to

> the exceptionally high rate with which judges decide in conformity with the requests of their 'colleagues' (prosecutors), both during the investigative phase (including those concerning the limitation of personal liberty of suspects, like preventive detention) and at the end of such a phase when they have to decide whether to terminate the case or send it for a full public trial. The second element is the fact that the overwhelming majority of our sample of 1,000 defence lawyers indicated both that ex parte informal communications on the substance of the cases at hand between prosecutors and judges do take place, to the exclusion of the defence, as a matter of daily occurrence, and that the decisions of judges during the investigative phase and at the end of it consist, with rare exceptions, in a passive, almost rubber-stamp acceptance of the requests formulated by their colleague-prosecutors.
>
> (Di Federico 1998: 382; see also Fabri and Cavallini 2008: 213 ff.)

On the other hand, we are not shown where and when judges in other systems exercise any more control over prosecutors at the investigative stage.[7] Both Vogliotti (2004) and Montana (2009), by contrast, stress how much prosecutors in Italy see themselves as acting judicially rather than as 'crime-fighters'. Likewise, in sending cases on to trial prosecutors seek to anticipate what the judge will consider as satisfactory evidence so it is hardly surprising that their decisions are largely vindicated. Such an approach can help them to temper the sort of populist 'moral panic' that can otherwise lead to sending ever greater numbers of relatively petty offenders to jail (Montana and Nelken 2010).[8,9]

Di Federico and his school have long insisted that necessary controls can (only) be achieved by separating the careers of judges and prosecutors. Currently there is only 'separation of functions', for example prosecutors and judges are not allowed to switch roles in the same tribunal district, and have to wait a certain number of years before changing roles, etc. They also support proposals for a separate High Council of prosecutors alongside the one for judges and that the authority of prosecutor heads over their substitutes should also be tightened up. Those resisting such changes fear that this could mean that prosecutors then receive instructions from the Minister of Justice or Parliament and would thus be subject to political control, especially in high profile cases. Di Federico replies that this sort of government control is not inevitable. In any case, countries like France or England and Wales have systems involving government control but no one questions their being democracies. And the fact that prosecutors were part of a united profession with judges under fascism did nothing to help them resist government pressure then.

The debate over the role and powers of prosecutors also needs to be contextualised in terms of the 1988 reform of criminal procedure that sought to move Italy towards the accusatorial model (Caianiello 2012). The Di Federico school rightly argue that the logic of this reform means that what happens at trial rather than beforehand should be decisive and that prosecutors should be put 'on the same level' as defence lawyers. The reform was significantly modified by the Constitutional Court over (reasonable?) fears about its implications for trials of organised criminals. Resistance is also attributed to the pre-existing legal culture in which prosecutors represent 'the state' helping judges search for the (inquisitorial) truth (Grande 2000; Montana 2012). Defence lawyers are strong supporters of the move

[7] See Tonry (ed) (2012) for some recent discussion of problems of holding prosecutors accountable.

[8] For the larger relevance of this to Italy's response to the so-called 'punitive turn', see Nelken (2000, 2009a).

[9] But in cases involving a genuine threat to the state, such as political terrorism, organised crime-fighters and political corruption, there is more unity of purpose between police and prosecutors.

to separate careers. But, in Italy, defence lawyers are arguably part of a fragmented and poorly disciplined profession having less loyalty to the court than is found in common law countries. Hence there are fears that they will not play their proper role in the accusatorial dialectic of parts. More generally, even those who see the logic of 'putting prosecutors in their place' so as to equalise their status to that of defence lawyers are reluctant to support it where it is proposed by governments whose main concern seems to be finding a way of blocking prosecutions against corrupt politicians.

## VIII. DISCUSSION

In this contribution I have suggested that the pervasive and persuasive criticisms of prosecutors put forward by the Di Federico school are as much concerned to bring about change than describe the different positions in the relevant debate. But, it may be asked, isn't a critical approach to be welcomed? Does it even matter that academic writings form part of larger political involvements? (Isn't this what is increasingly being asked of public intellectuals?) Certainly, the problem of 'bias'—if that is the right word—can equally be raised regarding those with centre-left sympathies committed to defending the many controversial aspects of current arrangements insofar as they see them as linked to maintaining the independence of the judiciary and the promotion of equality in and outside the law. Many on this side of the debate can be seen to have vested interests as members of the judiciary. And for some scholars on the centre-left, the Gramscian idea of the 'organic intellectual' can easily prioritise fidelity to a political cause above looking for inconvenient facts. Any discussion of their arguments would also be able to identify special pleading and a selective use or even disregard of empirical evidence. More importantly, the political divide does not necessarily dictate where people will stand on particular issues. Some of those on the centre-right are stalwart defenders of the magistracy in its present form—or would even like to reverse the 1988 reform (Travaglio 2011). Conversely, there are people on the centre-left who are as concerned as those on the centre-right with procedural criminal process protections for the accused (called in Italian *le garanzie*), and therefore with curbing the power of judges and prosecutors, even if their ideal society is one very different from that envisaged by those on the centre-right. Some of these writers also devote more attention than the Di Federico school to the problems of the Italian version of plea bargaining agreements.

Di Federico and his school are heavily involved in cross-European links with regards to training for judges and the curriculum of proposed schools for judges. But it is beyond the scope of this chapter to answer (as some have asked me to do) the blunt question of whether Di Federico and his colleagues have used or abused 'Europe' to further their own agenda.[10] Nor should it be forgotten that so far, their agenda has still not been achieved.

The question is rather how Europe's agenda in these matters is to be formulated—and what it can learn from the Italian case. This requires an appreciation of the academic debate over prosecutor independence and the way it is shaped by the political context. Can there be too much independence?[11] On the one hand, we have a key 'insider-outsider[12] writing for a wider audience and acting as a cultural mediator between the Italian reality and an idealised system of democratic prosecutorial accountability. Attacking what he sees as a misguided and exaggerated conception of independence as an alternative to accountability, Di Federico cites the famous and martyred judge Giovanni Falcone, arguing that

> Judicial policies cannot be left in the hands of the head of the [prosecutors'] offices, or worse in the hands of each member of the various offices, without any institutional control. Such a system does not favour the effectiveness of the judicial function in terms of a real, co-ordinated, generalised control of crime, nor is it conducive to equal protection of citizens under the law ... nor does it favour the image of justice, which ... [thus] appears to public opinion as a wild variable of the system.
>
> (Di Federico 1998: 380.)

By contrast, a leading judge of the left-leaning *Magistratura Democratica,* writing in Italian for readers of their influential professional journal, concludes his recent discussion of the topic as follows:

> a) The principle of obligatory prosecution assured, at least from the 1970s, that prosecution avoided being shaped by political influence, something which is unacceptable in a rule of law state,
>
> b) The diffuse ineffectiveness of the penal system is not caused by the rule of obligatory prosecution but by the disproportion between crimes and the means to deal with them, and in any case even a regime of obligatory prosecution can be organised in a rational way in accordance with the general interest,
>
> c) The excessive fibrillation of the political class as a result of the exercise of obligatory prosecution can be dealt with by *appropriate constitutional adjustments*

[10] Although in the case of prosecutors Di Federico presents the Italian case as deviant, he also criticises what he alleges to be the growing power and 'politicisation of the judiciary' worldwide. A New York University Press book on this topic (Tate and Valinder 1997) is the product of a conference organised by Di Federico, whose financial support for its publication is acknowledged in the preface.

[11] Likewise, if court cases in Italy for the ECHR often take too long, can they elsewhere be unreasonably short? (see Nelken 2004, 2008).

[12] See further Nelken (2000).

that do not damage the principle of obligatory prosecution. But, this being the case, we have to ask the question why change it?

(Pepino 2011, translation: DN.)

Di Federico and his school try to bring the Italian system into line with others in Europe or, even more, those in the Anglo-American world. But they are of course selective in what they take from other systems, and tell us little about their drawbacks. For example, further movement towards the accusatorial system is supposed to make prosecutors more independent of trial judges but it could also make them more rather than less conviction-minded. (Perhaps it is assumed this will be at the expense of ordinary criminals rather than politicians?) Many Italian judges, and their supporters, think that the current arrangements in Italy are worth defending in their own right. But, in any case, before yielding up what they consider their political independence, they would first like to see Italy's politicians develop an ethos of self-restraint, which would make it plausible to trust them as repositories of the general interest.

## REFERENCES


Borgna, P and Maddalena, M (2003) *Il Giudice e i suoi Limiti. Cittadini, Magistrati e Politica* (Bari, Laterza).

Caianiello, M (2012) 'The Italian Public Prosecutor: An Inquisitorial Figure in Adversarial Proceedings?', in E Luna and M Wade (eds), *The Prosecutor in Transnational Perspective* (Oxford, Oxford University Press).

Cordero, F (2003) *Procedura penale,* 7th edn (Milan, Giuffrè).

Davies, KC (1969) *Discretionary Justice. A Preliminary Inquiry* (Baton Rouge, Louisiana State University Press).

Davis, AJ (2007) *Arbitrary Justice. The Power of the American Prosecutor* (Oxford, Oxford University Press).

Dezalay, Y and Garth, B (2002) *The Internationalization of Palace Wars. Lawyers, Economists, and the Contest to Transform Latin American States* (Chicago, University of Chicago Press).

Di Federico, G (1995) 'Obbligatorietà dell'azione penale, coordinamento delle attività del pubblico ministero e loro rispondenza alle aspettative della comunità', *Archivio Penale*, 306.

—— (1998) 'Prosecutorial Independence and the Democratic Requirement of Accountability in Italy: Analysis of a Deviant Case in a Comparative Perspective', *British Journal of Criminology*, 38, 371–87.

—— (2005) 'Recruitment, Professional Evaluation, Career and Discipline of Judges and Prosecutors in Italy', in G Di Federico (ed), *Recruitment, Professional Evaluation and Career of Judges in Europe: Austria, France, Germany, Italy, The Netherlands and Spain* (Bologna, Lo Scarabeo).

—— (2008) 'Obbligatorietà dell'azione penale e indipendenza del pubblico ministero', *Osservatorio del processo penale*, 4–6, 1–13.

—— (2009) 'Divisione delle carriere: Può essere efficace senza modificare il principio di obbligatorietà dell' azione penale', *L'ircocervo*, 4.
—— and Sapignoli, M (2002) *Processo penale e diritti della difesa* (Roma, Carocci).
Fabri, M (1997) 'Discrezionalità e modalità di azione del pubblico ministero nel procedimento penale' *Polis*, XI, 171–92.
Fabri, M and Cavallini, D (2008) 'O ministério público em itália', in JP Dias and R Ghiringhelli de Azevedo (eds), *O Papel do Ministèro Público* (Coimbra, Almedina).
Fionda, J (1995) *Public Prosecutors and Discretion. A Comparative Study* (Oxford, Clarendon Press).
Goldstein, AS and Marcus, M (1977) 'The Myth of Judicial Supervision in Three "Inquisitorial" Systems: France, Italy, and Germany', *Yale Law Journal*, 87, 240–83.
Grande, E (2000) 'Italian Criminal Justice: Borrowing and Resistance', *American Journal of Comparative Law*, 48, 227–59.
Guarnieri, C (1981) *L'independenza della magistratura* (Padua, Cedam).
—— (1984) *Pubblico ministero e sistema politico* (Padua, Cedam).
—— (1994) 'Justice and Politics: the Italian Case in a Comparative Perspective', *Indiana International & Comparative Law Review*, 4, 241–57.
Guarnieri, C and Pederzoli, P (2002) *The Power of Judges. A Comparative Study of Courts and Democracy* (Oxford, Oxford University Press).
Guarnieri, C and Zannotti, F (eds) (2006) *Giusto processo?* (Padua, Cedam).
Hodgson, J (2005) *French Criminal Justice* (Oxford, Hart Publishing).
Jehle, J-M (2000) 'Prosecution in Europe: Varying structures, convergent trends', *European Journal on Criminal Policy and Research*, 8, 27–42.
Jehle, J-M, Smit, P and Zila J (2008) 'The Public Prosecutor as Key Player: Prosecutorial Case-Ending Decisions', *European Journal on Criminal Policy and Research*, 14, 161–79.
Kyprianou, D (2009) 'Adversarial vs Inquisitorial Prosecution Systems in Europe: Commonalities and Diversities', in K Jaishankar (ed), *International Perspectives on Crime and Justice* (Newcastle, Cambridge Scholars Press).
Langbein, JH and Weinreb, L (1978) 'Continental Criminal Procedure: Myth and Reality', *Yale Law Journal*, 87, 1549–69.
Merry, S (2005) *Human Rights and Gender Violence. Translating International Law into Local Justice* (Chicago, University of Chicago Press).
Melossi, D, Sparks, R and Sozzo, M (eds) (2011) *Travels of The Criminal Question* (Oxford, Hart Publishing).
Montana, R (2009) 'Paradigms of Judicial Supervision and Co-ordination Between Police and Prosecutors: The Italian Case in a Comparative Perspective', *European Journal of Crime, Criminal Law and Criminal Justice* 17, 309–33.
—— (2012) 'Adversarialism in Italy: Using the Concept of Legal Culture to Understand Resistance to Legal Modifications and its Consequences', *European Journal of Crime, Criminal Law and Criminal Justice*, 20, 99–120.
Montana, R and Nelken, D (2010) 'The Ambivalent Role of Italian Prosecutors and their Resistance to "Moral Panics" about Crime', in CJ Smith, SX Zhang and R Barbaret (eds), *Handbook of International Criminology* (London, Routledge).

Nelken, D (1996a) 'Judicial Politics and Corruption in Italy', in D Nelken and M Levi (eds), *The Corruption of Politics and the Politics of Corruption* (London, Blackwell).

—— (1996b) 'Stopping the Judges', in M Caciagli and D Kertzer (eds), *The Stalled Transition: Italian Politics 1996* (Boulder, Westview Press).

—— (ed) (1997) *Comparing Legal Cultures* (Aldershot, Dartmouth).

—— (2000) 'Telling Difference', in D Nelken (ed), *Contrasting Criminal Justice* (Aldershot, Ashgate).

—— (2002) 'Comparing Criminal Justice', in M Maguire, R Morgan and R Reiner (eds), *Oxford Handbook of Criminology*, 3rd edn (Oxford, Oxford University Press).

—— (2004) 'Using the Concept of Legal Culture', *Australian Journal of Legal Philosophy*, 29, 1–28.

—— (2008) 'Normalising Time: European integration and Court Delays in Italy', in H Petersen, H Krunke, A-L Kjær and M Rask Madsen (eds), *Paradoxes of European Integration* (Aldershot, Ashgate).

—— (2009a) 'Comparative Criminal Justice: Beyond Ethnocentricism and Relativism', *European Journal of Criminology*, 6, 291–311.

—— (2009b) 'Corruption as Governance', in F von Benda-Beckmann, K von Benda-Beckmann and J Eckert (eds), *Rules of Law and Laws of Ruling* (Aldershot, Ashgate).

—— (2010) *Comparative Criminal Justice. Making Sense of Difference* (London, Sage).

Nelken, D and Feest, J (2001) *Adapting Legal Cultures* (Oxford, Hart Publishing).

Nelken, D and Zanier, L (2006) 'Tra norme e prassi: durata del processo penale e strategie degli operatori del diritto', *Sociologia del Diritto*, 143–66.

Pepino, L (2011) 'Ancora sulla obbligatorità del azione penale', *Questione Giustizia*, 2, 110.

Sapignoli, M (2009) *Qualita della giustizia e independenza della magistratura nell'opinione dei magistrati italiani* (Padua, Cedam).

Sarzotti, C (2006) *Cultura giuridica e culture della pena* (Turin, L'Harmattan).

—— (2007) *Processi di selezione del crimine* (Milano, Giuffrè).

Tate, CN and Vallinder, T (1997) The Global Expansion of Judicial Power (New York, New York University Press).

Tonry, M (ed) (2012) *Prosecutors and Politics: A Comparative Perspective* (Chicago, University of Chicago Press).

Travaglio, M (2011) 'Un Programma per la giustizia penale' MicroMega, 7, 24.

Van Dijk, J (2007) *The World of Crime* (London, Sage).

Vogliotti, M (2004) 'Les relations police—parquet en Italie: un équilibre menacé?' *Droit et Société*, 58, 453–97.

Wade, M (2006) 'The Power To Decide—Prosecutorial Control, Diversion and Punishment in European Criminal Justice Systems Today', in J-M Jehle and M Wade (eds), *Coping with Overloaded Criminal Justice Systems: The Rise of Prosecutorial Power across Europe* (Berlin, Springer).

Zanier, ML (2009) *Tra il dire e il fare: Obbligatorietà dell'azione penale e comportamenti degli attori giuridici* (Macerata, EUM).

Zannotti, F (1989) *La magistratura: Un gruppo di pressione istituzionale* (Padua, Cedam).

COUNCIL OF EUROPE INSTRUMENTS

Recommendation Rec (92) 17 of the Committee of Ministers to member states concerning consistency in sentencing adopted by the Committee of Ministers on 19 October 1992 at the 482nd meeting of the Ministers' Deputies.

Recommendation Rec (95) 12 of the Committee of Ministers to member states on the management of criminal justice adopted by the Committee of Ministers on 11 September 1995 at the 543rd meeting of the Ministers' Deputies.

Recommendation Rec (2000) 19 of the Committee of Ministers to member states on the role of public prosecution in the criminal justice system adopted by the Committee of Ministers on 6 October 2000 at the 724th meeting of the Ministers' Deputies.

# 12

# *Truth in (the Implementation of) Sentencing: Belgium and Elsewhere*

KRISTEL BEYENS, SONJA SNACKEN AND
DIRK VAN ZYL SMIT

## I. INTRODUCTION

'TRUTH IN SENTENCING' is an apparently simple concept, with considerable rhetorical power, if only because it would be hard to support its opposite: 'dishonesty in sentencing'. On closer examination, however, the concept is more ambiguous than it might seem at first glance. As Freiberg and Moore (2009: 107) have pointed out, truth in sentencing originally referred to the difference between the sentence imposed by a court and the time actually served by the offender. Proponents of truth in sentencing therefore tended to attack early release of sentenced prisoners. Where they were successful, this is related in a number of jurisdictions to the restricted use, if not the outright abolition, of remission and parole (Freiberg 1992). It is worth noting, however, following Freiberg and Moore further, that truth in sentencing may also be a critique of the sentencing process itself, for it can also refer to the gap between statutory maximum penalties and the sentences imposed by the courts and to the idea that the nature and form of the sentence should be honest and transparent.

Truth in sentencing in its original sense is often seen as a policy concern that is typical of common law jurisdictions. Certainly, it has achieved much prominence and arguably had its greatest impact on penal policy in the United States of America, Australia, the United Kingdom and elsewhere in English-speaking world. However, as we will argue more fully below, using Belgium as a primary example, there are instances in European civil law jurisdictions too where truth in sentencing, in the sense of requiring that the sentences imposed by the judiciary be enforced (more) fully, has been a key factor both in arguments presented by the judiciary and in public debate, and has even influenced sentencing practice.

The other uses of the concept of truth in sentencing identified by Freiberg and Moore have had less political purchase in Europe. The second has had little relevance in the European context. It has played a limited role, in the case of life sentences, for example, where the courts or even the legislature have sometimes been criticised for setting minima that are too low to reflect the severity of a sentence of life imprisonment. However in most European jurisdictions, most sentences are determinate, and criticism on this ground is relatively muted. The third use of the concept has arisen in respect of the quality of the law governing sentencing and is developed in the European context as an element of the *Rechtsstaat*. As will become apparent, it has played a role, albeit a fairly technical one, in European debates.

The concept of truth in sentencing is a largely rhetorical idea, which is used more often in political than academic discourse. This may in part be because scholars in various European jurisdictions have developed theories about the relative autonomy of the various stages of the punishment process as a more nuanced way of understanding how the various state powers and actors that play a part in the overall process of defining, imposing and implementing sentences interact or should interact (Schüler-Springorum 1969; Müller-Dietz 1978; Dupont 1998; Feest 2006: 1; van Zyl Smit and Snacken 2009: 76–80). Following the constitutional principle of the separation of state powers, developed by Montesquieu as a means to achieve reciprocal control and balance between those powers, most European countries recognise that the legislature defines offences and sanctions in general, the judiciary applies this legislation in individual cases, but can also control the constitutionality of the legislation, and the executive implements the decisions of the courts within the legal framework governing the implementation of sentences.

One clear limit on the autonomy of the implementing authority, which is universally recognised in European legal doctrine, is that the implementing authority cannot continue to enforce a sentence beyond the limits of the sentence imposed (*M v Germany* 2009). More controversial, though, is the scope of the implementation power of the executive bodies within these limits, especially in view of the increasing individualisation of the implementation of sentences of imprisonment in Europe. This individualisation is present both in the external aspects of the implementation of a prison sentence, when a prisoner is released back into society by being granted temporary leave from prison or forms of early or conditional release, and in the internal aspects of the implementation of the sentence, relating to the modalities of the prison regime inside the walls. The theory of relative autonomy (for Belgium, see Dupont 1998) recognises the complexity of the various aims of punishment at these different stages of the criminal justice process. It emphasises that their importance may vary between the moment of imposing sentence and the implementation of the sentence. Sentencing is an important symbolic moment in which a judge publicly expresses the censure of a particular offence with due regard to the responsibility and guilt of the offender. Although the court may take the future of the offender into consideration when choosing between different penalties, the sentencing decision is primarily directed towards the past, namely the offence that has taken place (and usually the criminal record of the offender). The implementation of the prison sentence takes place during a more or less long period of time, during which the prisoner is subjected to a prison regime for 24 hours of the day. Even if society is temporarily protected by the incapacitation of the prisoner, the majority of prisoners will eventually be released into society. The implementation of the prison sentence must therefore necessarily also be oriented towards the future, and the prison regime must be organised accordingly. As a result, where the sentencing judge decides to take the offender out of society by imposing a term of imprisonment, the actors responsible for the implementation of this sanction must have due regard to the conditions for his reintegration into society. This theory of relative autonomy therefore allows an emphasis on special prevention through reintegration/resocialisation as a specific aim of the implementation of sentences and legitimises adaptations and relaxations of prison (and community penalty) regimes, and systems of temporary or early release from the restrictions that these sentences impose. It also results in the recognition of rights of both prisoners and those subject to community sentences that are independent of the aims that are given most prominence at the sentencing stage (van Zyl Smit and Snacken 2009: 80–84).

This relative autonomy of the implementation of sentences from their imposition, and the importance of preparation for reintegration into society as an aim of the implementation of prison sentences, are recognised explicitly in the constitution or penal legislation of several European countries (eg Germany, Spain, Italy, Belgium). It can be said also to be recognised implicitly by the existence of the possibility of (conditional) early release in all European countries (Tubex 2003) and its support by European standards (van Zyl Smit and Snacken 2009: ch 8). Because such decisions have important consequences for the rights and degrees of freedom enjoyed by offenders, many European countries have introduced judicial control over the executive bodies or have transferred some decisions to specialised judicial or multidisciplinary bodies (Tubex 2003; Padfield et al 2010).

It should immediately be recognised, however, that the theory of relative autonomy, while arguably intellectually coherent within its own set of assumptions, may not be persuasive to all. Both penal decision-makers and the general public may regard 'relative autonomy' as a weakening of the retributive, deterrent or incapacitatory effects that sentencers may have intended, and therefore simply ignore it, or deny or question its validity.

This chapter is concerned primarily with the first aspect of Freiberg and Moore's definition of truth in sentencing: that is, the gap between the sentence imposed and the sentence executed (Freiberg and Moore 2009).

It seeks to analyse the consequences of this gap at different levels. In particular, the chapter discusses the proposition that, if prison sentences are not, or are only partly, executed, the punitive element of the sentence is eroded. Underlying this proposition is the view that, as the function of the judiciary is to communicate the denunciation of the criminal conduct of the offender by imposing an appropriate punishment, it loses legitimacy in its own eyes and those of the public if such punishments are not (fully) implemented. Particular attention is paid to the different actors involved, who interact with each other: (1) the public, (2) politicians and other penal policy actors, (3) sentencing judges and (4) authorities responsible for implementation. The discussion takes place at two levels: 'practice' and 'rhetoric'. We argue that the rhetorical level has a significant symbolic element that has gained importance in late modern punishment and plays a vital role in the political discussion on truth in sentencing.

This chapter initially focuses on the example of Belgium in order to unravel and explain the complex interaction of different actors at various levels (discourse at the symbolic representational level versus practice). Such a specific focus is adopted in order to recognise the importance of a situated understanding of how 'truth in sentencing' plays itself out as an element in penal policy. However, in the subsequent section consideration is given to wider European developments in respect of the implementation of sentences and the early release from them, which may impact on the evolution of local policies and particularly on a narrow understanding of truth in sentencing. They may also serve as examples of how best to develop policy in this area.

## II. BELGIUM

Since the early 1990s, the Belgian prison system has been confronted with growing prison populations and prison overcrowding. Although a reductionist penal policy has been advocated by subsequent governments,[1] in practice, no real 'front door' policy to reduce the use of imprisonment by imposing fewer or shorter prison sentences was ever really established (Snacken and Beyens 2008). Penal policy in Belgium can be characterised as a policy of bifurcation, and although legislation has enlarged the possibilities for the application of non-custodial sanctions and measures, judges generally continue to view these as favours or warnings, which cannot fundamentally replace imprisonment as the standard reaction to crime (Snacken 2007). The increase of the prison population, due to more

[1] This policy emerges from the White Paper of 1996 of Minister De Clerck and subsequent policy papers (see Snacken 2007).

long-term prisoners, a steadily growing prison population under remand and more convicted and remand prisoners with a non-Belgian nationality, has led (despite expansion of the prison capacity) to untenable prison overcrowding. At short notice, the government fell back on the use of a 'back door' policy to relieve prison overcrowding. This back door policy was realised by an increasing use of provisional release of prisoners with sentences of up to three years, which has led to a great deal of discontent amongst the judiciary and the general public.

To understand the complex Belgian early release system, outlined in Figure 12.1, one has to distinguish between prisoners with a prison sentence of up to three years, on the one hand, and prisoners with a prison sentence of three years and more, on the other. This distinction between sentences of more than and less than three years has grown out of an evolving practice. The eligibility for provisional release has been increased over the last 20 years by the Minister of Justice through a series of Ministerial circular letters.[2] For convicted prisoners with a prison sentence of three years and more, there has always been a stricter policy. With the introduction of the Sentence Implementation Courts, the decision-making on their conditional release has been handed over to a judicial body, as is explained more fully below.

In the first group of prisoners with sentences of up to three years, those who are sentenced to a maximum of six months' imprisonment are immediately released; they are released after one month's detention if they are sentenced to a maximum of seven months' imprisonment; after two months' detention if they are sentenced to a maximum of eight months'

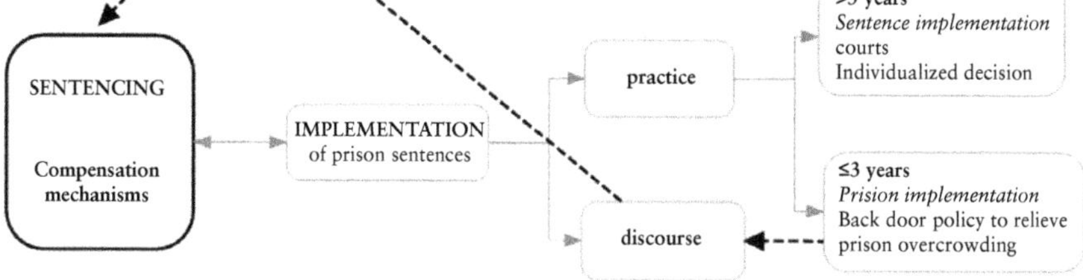


**Figure 12.1: The Belgian early release system**

[2] For a detailed account on the Belgian early release system, see Snacken et al (2010).

imprisonment; or after three months' detention if they are sentenced to a maximum of one year. In all these cases no risk assessment is carried out, and eligibility depends solely on time served. Prisoners sentenced to more than one year but with a maximum of three years' imprisonment may benefit from provisional release after having served a third of their sentence.[3] This system, however, may be described as a discretionary one, for the benefit of the measure is here subordinated to the additional prerequisite of absence of counter-indications. Such counter-indications relate to whether it is possible for the prisoner to provide for their material needs, to any possible serious risk they might represent for others' integrity and—especially for those sentenced for sexual abuse of minors—to the risk that they might harass their victims. In these cases, individual conditions or guidance can be imposed, if deemed necessary by the prison administration. The probation period for all provisional release is up to two years. In all these cases, and they have made up more than 80 per cent of all early releases in Belgium in recent years, it is the prison governor or the prison administration that takes the decision to release. In practice, under the pressure to relieve the worst of the prison overcrowding, prison governors and the administration tend to use it as a device to reduce the size of the prison population. And the more this form of early release has been used as a form of routinised, quasi-automatic early release, the more vehemently has it been attacked.

Prisoners sentenced to more than three years' imprisonment are released according to the Act of 17 May 2006 on the External Legal Position of the Sentenced Prisoner and the Rights of the Victims.[4] Here there are not only time conditions to be fulfilled (prisoners are eligible for release after one-third, for a first offender, and two-thirds for a 'legal recidivist'), but other conditions also need to be met before a prisoner is released on parole. These include having a 'reintegration plan' developed by the prisoner, with the help of the psycho-social service, and the absence of counter-indications. The decision is not taken by the prison administration, but since 1 February 2007,[5] by a multidisciplinary Sentence Implementation Court,[6] which is presided over by a professional judge, assisted by two 'lay judges', of whom one must be an expert on social reintegration and the other an expert on prison matters. This composition is supposed to make decision-making more independent and more closely based on expert knowledge, which in turn are supposed to increase the credibility of the early release system.

[3] Ministerial Circular No. 1771 of 17 January 2005.

[4] This Act was supposed to transfer the decision-making on all prison sentences to the implementation courts. However, the implementation of this aspect has been postponed for pragmatic reasons for sentences up to three years.

[5] A first transfer of the decision making to independent and multidisciplinary 'parole commissions' was introduced by the Acts of 5 and 18 March 1998.

[6] The so-called *Strafuitvoeringsrechtbank* or *Tribunal d'Application des Peines*.

There is thus a big difference in decision-making between the two groups: provisional release for shorter sentences of up to three years is merely used as a device to regulate the size of the prison population by the prison administration, while conditional release for long-term prisoners is an individualised, thoroughly prepared measure, backed by risk assessments of psychologists and guarantees of supervision and control by justice assistants.[7] Due to the complexities of the different forms of early release and the regulation of provisional release through ministerial circulars, which are not public and may therefore be regarded as, at best, a form of quasi-legislation, the public and even the judiciary has become steadily more confused between the two systems of conditional and provisional release, notwithstanding the differences of procedure and substance between them.

The implementation of prison sentences became even more complicated with the introduction of electronic monitoring as a modality of implementation of prison sentences since 2000. Electronic monitoring was, and still is, advocated at the political level as *the* solution for prison overcrowding. It was initially praised for its reintegrative and harm-reducing characteristics in comparison to imprisonment. Also in this regard there are different systems related to the length of the imposed sentence. Prison sentences of up to three years can be fully or partly converted into an electronic monitoring measure by the prison governor or the prison administration. Prisoners with a sentence of more than three years can be placed under electronic monitoring before their conditional release. In this instance the decision is taken by the Sentence Implementation Court.

The combination, since the 1980s, of the instrumentalisation and quasi-automatic use of provisional release with the expanding use of electronic monitoring as a modality of the implementation of prison sentences for prisoners sentenced to a maximum term of three years has led to the situation that a growing number of offenders sentenced to terms of imprisonment not exceeding three years do not have to serve a single day,[8] or only a very short period, in prison. This nourishes the idea amongst the judiciary, the media and members of the larger society that offenders can avoid their due punishment. However, the actual situation is much more complex than is supposed or depicted in the media. Research has indicated that the application of provisional release is not as automatic as is generally assumed, inter alia, for sex offenders who spend much longer periods in detention (Tubex and Strypstein 2005). Moreover, short 'sentences' have been reintroduced indirectly through the decision-making by investigation judges, who increasingly admit to applying remand custody as a 'short sharp shock' penalty, which they

[7] Justice assistants are the Belgian counterparts of probation officers.
[8] Although it is important to note that this is not always the case.

regard as necessary because short prison sentences are seldom implemented (Raes and Snacken 2004: 514). They feel less inhibited about remanding offenders in custody, or keeping them there, because they regard it as an 'advance instalment' of the sentence of imprisonment that will probably be imposed,[9] but which is likely not to be executed in prison. This can be regarded as a compensation mechanism in the pre-sentencing stage, and leads to a growing prison population on remand.[10]

To get the full picture it is also important to understand the complexities of the Belgian administrative rules on the execution of prison sentences: when someone is serving a long prison sentence, short sentences are brought into effect concurrently. There are also situations where short sentences are indeed executed because there are regulations specifically requiring that it be done. Short prison sentences of less than six months, for example, are actually executed when they are a substitute for a work penalty that has not or has only partly been executed. This is stated clearly in the Ministerial Circular Letter 1771 of 17 January 2005, and is done in order to enhance the credibility of the work penalty.

This last situation has two consequences. First, judges see the work penalty and its substitute sentence as a more credible sentencing option than a short prison sentence, because work penalties are actually implemented, and short prison sentences are not. With regard to fairness and consistency of the punishment scale, a work penalty becomes in this situation a 'harsher' penalty than a short prison sentence, a consequence which can be questioned. However, substitutive (short) prison sentences are almost automatically converted into house arrest with electronic monitoring, which leads to the situation that people who receive a work penalty can end up with a (short) period of electronic monitoring.

Beyens and Scheirs investigated the knowledge that the judiciary has of this implementation policy, and their reactions to it (Beyens 2009; Scheirs 2010). They did so by studying judges' accounts of their perception of the implementation of 'their' sentences. Many judges stated that they had a poor knowledge of the implementation of their sentences; they pointed to the lack of transparency of the implementation system, and would have liked to have had more feedback and knowledge of the implementation practice. It was interesting to note that several judges confused the two release systems (those for sentences above and below three years). They were not in favour of early release mechanisms in general, and thus did not support

[9] When someone has been placed in remand custody, judges are inclined to 'cover' this remand period with a prison sentence. Although this is not a legal mechanism, it is a widely accepted practice with sentencing judges (Snacken 1986; Beyens 2000; Raes and Snacken 2004).

[10] Belgium has one of the highest proportions of prisoners in remand custody in Europe: about 34.5%, on 1 September 2010 (Directorate General of the Prisons 2011).

the idea of relative autonomy of the implementation of sentences from their imposition. However, the research showed that judges were less negative towards the conversion of a prison sentence into electronic monitoring than they were towards the early release system. We noted a great deal of frustration and many complaints about the erosion of 'their' decisions, and claims that it led to a loss of proportionality and punitiveness. Judges were frustrated about their loss of authority and questioned the meaningfulness of their work. 'Does it make sense that we impose sentences?' is the base line question posed by many judges today.

Different coping strategies for dealing with what judges perceive as a loss of authority can be distinguished in their discourse. Although many judges are not very well acquainted with the different modalities of release, we see that they tend to anticipate possible release decisions in their sentencing. Certain sentencers admit openly that they anticipate the (non-) execution of prison sentences and that they pronounce longer sentences to be sure that the convicted person will spend at least a certain period in prison. Others reject this form of 'compensation' and state that they do not take into account potential changes to their decisions during the implementation phase.

However, it should be noted that we have strong indications that the accounts given by the judges in the interviews do not always reflect what is happening in practice. Their ambiguous attitudes could be explained by the pressure of the professional judicial culture to represent the judge as 'neutral' and 'impartial', and not being influenced by factors other than those that are relevant for the case (ie the characteristics of the offender and (the circumstances of) the offence). Compared to 30 years ago (Peeters 1988), or even 10 years ago (Beyens 2000), we see, however, a greater willingness to talk openly about compensatory mechanisms, which operate by imposing longer sentences to ensure that an offender will end up in prison (see Pieters 2010). And although the judicial discourse nourishes the broader discourse on impunity in society by stating publicly that compensation mechanisms operate, judges are also influenced by this general impunity discourse by the media and some policy makers.

An important aim of the introduction of the Sentence Implementation Courts was to give early release a judicial basis and to enhance its legitimacy. The research shows, however, that many sentencing judges are not yet very familiar with the functioning of this new judicial body (Beyens 2009; Scheirs 2010). Those who are familiar with it are positive about the fact that this new body decides about the implementation of their sentences, and are inclined to impose sentences of three years and longer if possible in order to bring them within the jurisdiction of the new body. Sometimes they even impose sentences with the symbolic period of 36 months and one day, or 37 months of imprisonment, to ensure that the release decision will be taken by the implementation court and not by the prison administration (see

Pieters 2010).[11] This leads to a 'punitive spiral', with longer sentences being imposed by the sentencing judges. This increases the overcrowding, which in turn increases the resort to provisional release. It also shows that sentencing judges have more confidence in these Sentence Implementation Courts, as they accept that such courts have greater legitimacy than the prison administration to make decisions in which they exercise a degree of 'relative autonomy'. Hence it could cautiously be stated that sentencing judges are not necessarily against 'relative autonomy' if decisions are taken by a body that they regard as 'appropriate'—ie by a judicial body of some kind.

There is an undeniable and important emotional/affective dimension in this debate, which is greedily picked up by the media, who spread the idea of impunity to the general public and the judiciary. Policy-makers worry about the widespread perception of impunity. Since 2008, White Papers on penal policy have made reference to the importance of a credible implementation system (Vandeurzen 2009; De Clerck 2010). The 'impunity discourse' has thus become an official, authoritative account of the functioning of the Belgian criminal justice system and has insidiously gained legitimacy. Moreover, the demand for truth in sentencing implementation has become a major concern for policy-makers and is the most important impetus for the expansion of prison capacity and the further implementation of electronic monitoring as a replacement for remand custody today. The discourse about the lack of punitiveness and credibility of the penal system obscures and even discredits the importance of early release as a potential vehicle for reintegration and crime prevention.

## III. THE WIDER EUROPEAN CONTEXT

The Belgian example illustrates the practical difficulties of dealing with radical claims for 'truth in sentencing' in a penal system in which the process of imposing sentences is public and ostensibly legitimate, while some of the processes relating to implementation and, in particular to release, are shrouded in uncertainty. There is an absence of a clear understanding of the different functions of the various institutions involved in the implementation process and a lack of clear ideological support for their activities. Can 'European penology' offer much by way of support?

[11] This perverse effect was anticipated by the Holsters Commission, which advised the Minister of Justice and the Parliament about the introduction of the Sentence Implementation Courts. The Commission proposed the abolition of the artificial distinction between sentences of up to and more than three years, and letting the president of the Sentence Implementation Court decide on all proposals for early release where a consensus had been reached between the prisoner, the public prosecutor and the local prison governor. This latter procedure would probably have included most of the shorter sentences (Snacken 2004).

In as much as European penology is reflected in the jurisprudence of the European Court of Human Rights (ECtHR) the answer, at first glance, is very disappointing. At least, where determinate sentences of imprisonment are involved, the ECtHR has resolutely held that the protections relating to preventing wrongful detention and ensuring fair trials contained in Articles 5 and 6 of the European Convention on Human Rights do not apply to routine measures designed to allow for release prior to the completion of the term of imprisonment.[12] In *Dybeku v Albania* (2007), for example, the ECtHR stated bluntly that 'the Convention does not guarantee, as such, a right to conditional release or to serve a prison sentence in accordance with a particular sentencing regime'.[13] What this means in practice is that, where determinate sentences are involved, the ECtHR consistently declines to review the procedural fairness of decisions to refuse early release,[14] or even the recall of someone who has been released conditionally, on grounds that they have allegedly infringed the conditions of their release.[15] The effect of this line of cases is to reinforce the impression that the initial sentencing decision to imprison is the most important taken in the course of the penal process and that the decisions relating to the implementation are not so important.

Fortunately, the jurisprudence of the ECtHR has more to offer to a debate about the limits of truth in sentencing than these cases would suggest. In cases of life imprisonment where the sentencing court makes clear that the sentence is to be divided into penal and incapacitatory parts, the ECtHR has specified that, after the minimum penal period has been served, decisions on further detention have to be taken by a court-like body that meets the procedural standards of Articles 5 and 6 of the European Convention on Human Rights.[16] These cases mostly involved the United Kingdom, where such a division was most clearly drawn. The result has been that the Parole Board, which in England decides on continued detention after the minimum period has been served, has been compelled to evolve from a body that merely advised the Minister, to a body that takes binding decisions after

[12] There may be exceptions for humanitarian reasons: for example, an illness that cannot be treated in prison may require release in terms of Article 3 of the European Convention on Human Rights, even before the fixed-term sentence has expired (*Mouisel v France* (2004) 38 EHRR 34).

[13] *Dybeku v Albania* App no 41153/06 (ECtHR, 18 December 2007), para 57. See also the earlier decisions of the European Commission for Human Rights in (*A v Austria* 1990) and in (*Savic v Slovakia* 1997).

[14] *Hudec v Slovakia* App no 4123/0224 (ECtHR, October 2006).

[15] *Ganusauskas v Lithuania* App no 47922/997 (ECtHR, September 1999).

[16] *Weeks v United Kingdom* (1988) 10 EHRR 293; *Thynne, Wilson and Gunnell v United Kingdom* (1991) 13 EHRR 666; *T v United Kingdom* (2000) 30 EHRR 121. These cases culminated in the decision of the Grand Chamber in *Stafford v United Kingdom* (2002) 35 EHRR 32.

following procedural due process. Similar developments have followed in other parts of the United Kingdom.

Although the Parole Board still has shortcomings,[17] this outcome has clearly strengthened its role vis-a-vis both the sentencing judges and the Minister who previously decided informally on the release of persons serving life sentences. The unreformed process was particularly murky, as Lord Mustill commented:

> The sentence of life imprisonment is also unique in that the words, which the judge is required to pronounce, do not mean what they say. Whilst in a very small minority of cases the prisoner is in the event confined for the rest of his natural life, this is not the usual or intended effect of a sentence of life imprisonment ... But although everyone knows what the words do not mean, nobody knows what they do mean, since the duration of the prisoner's detention depends on a series of recommendations ... and executive decisions.
>
> (*R v Secretary of State for the Home Department, Ex parte Doody* [1994] 1 AC 531, HL: paras 549H–550B.)

The impact of the reforms, driven by the ECtHR in this instance, has been that there is more truth in sentencing in the sense that the process of decision-making is clearer and more public than previously while at the same time some of the discretion to release prisoners before the end of their lives has been retained.

The ECtHR has commented favourably on the presence of such procedures in other countries too: see the case of *Léger v France*.[18] Moreover, the ECtHR has gone a long way towards finding that life sentences that do 'mean what they say', that is, are wholly irreducible in law and in fact, are inhuman and degrading and thus infringe Article 3 of the European Convention on Human Rights. In this regard the Court recognises the relative autonomy of the implementation of sentences and rejects a strict interpretation of the first criterion of the truth in sentencing dictum, as life sentences which were legitimate at the time of sentencing may become a form of inhuman and degrading punishment if fully implemented. However, it has hitherto declined to set any procedural standards that all decisions relating to the release of lifers must meet. In the leading case of *Kafkaris v Cyprus* the Grand Chamber of the ECtHR held that 'at the time the applicant committed the offence, the relevant Cypriot law taken as a whole was not formulated with sufficient precision as to enable the applicant to discern, even with appropriate advice, to a degree that was reasonable in

[17] The English courts have held that, contrary to what that ECtHR thinks, the Parole Board is not fully independent: *R (Brooke) v Parole Board* [2008] ECWA Civ 29; [2008] 1 WLR 1950 (discussed in Padfield 2010). A further major weakness is that, while it can order release, it cannot, unlike its German equivalent, the *Strafvollstreckungskammer*, order the prison authorities to make the necessary preparations for a prisoner's release (van Zyl Smit 2010).

[18] *Léger v France* (2009) 49 EHRR 41, GC.

the circumstances, the *scope of the penalty* of life imprisonment and the *manner of its execution*'.[19] This, the Grand Chamber ruled, meant that Article 7 of the European Convention on Human Rights had been infringed as the 'quality of the law' was inadequate.[20] The significance of this dictum is that the Grand Chamber has set a requirement that meets the objection of supporters of truth in sentencing who approach that concept broadly, that is, in terms of the third criterion specified by Freiberg and Moore and referred to in the Introduction above, namely, that the nature and form of the sentence should be honest and transparent.

Finally on the jurisprudence, it is worth noting the comments by Judge Costa in his dissenting opinion in *Léger v France* (2006). In this case Judge Costa argued that, if the purpose of national legislation

> was to increase the role of the courts in dealing with applications for release, it would be ludicrous for the European Court of Human Rights to fly in the face of this trend by refusing to review the relevance, adequacy and lack of arbitrariness of the grounds on which the appropriate courts' decisions were based.
>
> (*Léger v France* App no 19324/0211 (ECtHR, April 2006): partly dissenting opinion of judge Costa, para 9).[21]

If this approach were to be applied by the ECtHR in all cases in which questions about implementation of sentences are raised, a body of jurisprudence that brings the implementation of sentence within the requirements of the *Rechtsstaat* would soon emerge. This could offer an important response to the dogmatic supporters of 'truth in sentencing' who believe that procedural fairness can only be achieved by ensuring that all sentences of imprisonment are served by keeping the offender in prison for the full term.

It should be emphasised that European penology as a whole has gone much further in providing insights into how sentences should be implemented than the current line of European cases dealing with release from determinate sentences in particular may suggest. Snacken has argued that fundamental to European penal policy is a concern with ensuring that imprisonment be used as a last resort, and then only for as long as it

[19] *Kafkaris v Cyprus* (2009) 49 EHRR 35, para 150; emphasis added.

[20] Art 7 deals primarily with the prohibition of retrospective sentences. The Grand Chamber, however, went out of its way to emphasise that it was not concluding that Kafkaris's sentence had retrospectively become heavier. It had always been a life sentence and changes in the mode of its execution did not in the view of the Court amount to the imposition of a heavier penalty (*Kafkaris v Cyprus*: para 151). Instead, the Grand Chamber was concerned with the question it called, in its own quotation marks, the 'quality of the law'.

[21] Although this comment was made in a dissent, it is given further salience by the fact that *Léger*'s case was referred to the Grand Chamber of the ECtHR, only for the Court to decline to give a judgment following the death of both the applicant and his lawyer (*Léger v France* (2009, GC)).

is necessary (Snacken 2006).[22] Support for this argument can be found in a wide range of Recommendations of the Committee of Ministers of the Council of Europe,[23] and also in some judgments of the ECtHR[24] that have recognised in general terms the desirability of not imprisoning people unnecessarily.

Important for current purposes is that these Recommendations include detailed guidance on how sentences of imprisonment should be implemented that is related to this policy of using imprisonment as sparingly as possible. Most significant in this regard is undoubtedly the Recommendation No R (99) 22 concerning prison overcrowding and prison population inflation, which explicitly supports a reductionist penal policy.[25] As far as early release is concerned, the 2003 Recommendation of the Committee of Ministers on Conditional Release (Parole), spells out both the substantive case for early (conditional) release and the procedural standards that should be met in granting it. It is worth pausing briefly to consider both aspects. The general principle on the substance is contained in para 3:

> Conditional release should aim at assisting prisoners to make a transition from life in prison to a law-abiding life in the community through post-release conditions and supervision that promote this end and contribute to public safety and the reduction of crime in the community.

[22] See also van Zyl Smit and Snacken (2009); van Zyl Smit and Spencer (2010).

[23] Recommendation No R (80) 11 of the Committee of Ministers to Member States concerning Custody Pending Trial; Recommendation No R (87) 3 of the Committee of Ministers to Member States on the European Prison Rules; Recommendation. No R (92) 16 of the Committee of Ministers to Member States on the European Rules on Community Sanctions and Measures; Recommendation No R (92) 17 of the Committee of Ministers to Member States concerning Consistency in Sentencing; Recommendation No R (99) 22 concerning Prison Overcrowding and Prison Population Inflation; Recommendation Rec(2003)22 of the Committee of Ministers to Member States on Conditional Release (parole); Recommendation Rec(2003)23 of the Committee of Ministers to Member States on the Management by Prison Administrations of Life Sentence and other Long-term Prisoners; Recommendation Rec(2006)13 of the Committee of Ministers to Member States on the Use of Remand in Custody, the Conditions in which it Takes Place and the Provision of Safeguards against Abuse.

[24] See most recently the discussion of gross disproportionality in *Vinter and Others v United Kingdom* App nos 66069/09, 130/10 and 3896/10 (ECtHR, 17 January 2012) and the sources cited there.

[25] This Recommendation states that 'deprivation of liberty should be considered as a last resort; expansion of prison capacity does not generally offer a lasting solution to prison overcrowding and should hence be an exceptional measure; a coherent set of community sanctions and measures must be provided for, leaving room for graduation according to severity; public prosecutors and judges must be incited to apply them as much as possible; member states should consider the possibilities to decriminalise certain offences or to requalify them in order to avoid deprivation of liberty; the factors contributing to prison overcrowding and to prison population inflation must be analysed in order to conceive a coherent action; this analysis must include i.a. which offences produce long term prison sentences, priorities in the struggle against criminality, attitudes and concerns of the public and existing practices in sentencing'.

The Recommendation goes on to underline that:

> In order to reduce the harmful effects of imprisonment and to promote the resettlement of prisoners under conditions that seek to guarantee safety of the outside community, the law should make conditional release available to *all* sentenced prisoners, including life-sentence prisoners.
>
> (Para 4(a); emphasis added.)

These general principles in the Recommendation already support to a crucial extent the relative autonomy doctrine, for they emphasise the twin objectives of harm reduction and reintegration into the community which are unlikely to have been the primary objective at the sentencing stage. Further support is contained in the procedural safeguards in paragraphs 32 and 33 of the Recommendation. These provide that:

> 32. Decisions on granting, postponing or revoking conditional release, as well as on imposing or modifying conditions and measures attached to it, should be taken by authorities established by law in accordance with procedures covered by the following safeguards:
>     a. convicted persons should have the right to be heard in person and to be assisted according to the law;
>     b. the decision-making authority should give careful consideration to any elements, including statements, presented by convicted persons in support of their case;
>     c. convicted persons should have adequate access to their file;
>     d. decisions should state the underlying reasons and be notified in writing.
> 33. Convicted persons should be able to make a complaint to a higher independent and impartial decision-making authority established by law against the substance of the decision as well as against non-respect of the procedural guarantees.

Implicit in these detailed arrangements is the requirement for due process in all aspects of decision-making relating to conditional release. The authority that is needed to do this must inevitably provide some form of balance to that of the sentencing court. In other words, for procedural reasons too, it must be relatively autonomous from the sentencing court. This is important, for, in so far as such a body meets these standards, it has a basis for its own legitimacy which it can assert publicly in face of the criticism from the judges that 'their truth' should prevail by restricting early release decisions severely, if not outlawing them completely. It is also important for another reason. The relative autonomy of the authority that decides on release matters may be challenged, not only by the judiciary that may demand that its sentences be carried out (more or less) in full, but also by the executive which may demand that it be allowed to exercise an unfettered discretion in making decisions about various aspects of implementation, including those relating to release. In this regard the distinction which was drawn, as noted above, in the account of the relative autonomy doctrine between the external and internal aspects of implementation of sentences, has particular salience. What it recognises is that internal decisions, such as allowing a prisoner or someone subject to a community sanction to attend a particular training course, might play an important role in the external decision on whether or not to release such a person from prison or to change the conditions to which such a person is subject in the community.

Comparative insights can be useful too. Around Europe there are various models of structural arrangements that facilitate the recognition of the relative autonomy of the various components of the penal process within some form of overall (judicial) supervision that is separate from the initial sentencing decision-making. One of these is the combination of the direct involvement of a specialist arm of the judiciary in internal prison matters, with decision-making relating to release and to some aspects of sanctions that are implemented in the community. For example, the German *Strafvollstreckungkammern,* with their judges who are supposed to be experts in both the internal and external aspects of the implementation of sentencing, have close equivalents in the offices of the *juge de l'application des peines* (and for prisoners serving imprisonment of more than three years also the *tribunal de l'application des peines*) in France (Reuflet 2010), the *magistrato di sorveglianza* in Italy (Gualazzi and Mancuso 2010) and the *juez de vigilancia* in Spain (De la Cuesta and Blanco 2007). Although there are important variations between them, they have in common that they involve a member or members of the judiciary, often sitting as a specialist chamber of a court, who have a function in safeguarding prisoners' rights and ensuring that prison conditions meet minimum standards, while at the same time deciding on release of prisoners and on aspects of how their early release will be implemented.

National critics, who often tend to be harsher than outsiders, recognise the value of their expertise. However, they often doubt their independence, sometimes citing structural reasons which do not give them the independence from prison administrators which one would expect of the office of a judge (Dünkel 1997). Moreover, in France, for example, such judges cannot give binding instructions to the authorities in respect of prison conditions (Herzog-Evans 1997). Critics also argue on more sociological grounds that their constant involvement in prison matters leads to their being 'captured' by the priorities of penal administrators, on whom they may be dependent for information and access. This is a reason why some countries, such as Belgium, have opted for separate bodies for judicial review of decision making in internal versus external prison matters (complaint committees versus implementation courts). Nevertheless, they do provide a model for a relatively legitimate way of regulating both release decisions and some of the immediate factors that influence them. Broadly speaking, they meet the requirements which the Recommendation on conditional release, as well as other related recommendations of the Council of Europe, sets for the making of release decisions. The Belgian Sentence Implementation Court fits squarely in this tradition but, as described above, its actual limited implementation has meant that its legitimacy as an independent overseer of all early releases has been substantially restricted.

Comparative insights are not limited to what can be gained by comparing legal procedures. In Finland, for example, as Tapio Lappi-Seppälä has vividly described, a successful reductionist policy was implemented within a system in which sentencing was governed by what he calls 'humane neo-classicism' (Lappi-Seppälä 2007; 2010). However, this did not lead to calls for truth in sentencing in the sense of demands that imposed sentences be fully enforced. Instead, community sentences and early release mechanisms were used to reduce prison populations without much public opposition. Lappi-Seppälä suggests that what made it possible, and what distinguished the Finnish developments from those in the United Kingdom, was the dominance of experts in the process of shaping both the complex interlocking mechanisms of imposition and implementation of sentences, and of wider public opinion. The latter was possible because the media were much more respectful of expertise than is the case in the United Kingdom, where the media has shaped public opinion by appealing directly to arguments such as truth in sentencing, without calling on experts to put them into context.

The Finnish example has much to commend it as a strategy to be applied at national level across Europe, including of course in Belgium. Very often though, in Belgium as elsewhere, the problem is not a shortage of national penological expertise or its conversion into practical suggestions: in the Belgian case the reports of the Dupont and Holsters Commissions, which prepared the implementation of the Belgian legislation on the internal and external legal position of prisoners, are models of how European penological theory can be translated into sophisticated national policy documents based on humane reductionist principles (Dupont 1998; Commissie strafuitvoeringsrechtbanken, externe rechtspositie van gedetineerden en straftoemeting 2003). However, this does not guarantee their acceptance by a broader audience and unaltered translation into policy and practice. In Belgium, the non-execution of short prison sentences and the widespread application of provisional release were not introduced following a principled approach to the relative autonomy of the aims of punishment fostering reintegration at the level of implementation of sentences, but as purely pragmatic 'solutions' to the everlasting prison overcrowding. The example illustrates how isolated back door strategies may backfire in the absence of a coherent reductionist policy at all levels of the criminal justice system.

A related issue appears to be the question of how policies based on the principle of relative autonomy can be conveyed to key actors in the penal system such as the judiciary, as well as to the wider public, so that they can be applied without raising the fears that are embodied in the slogan, truth in sentencing. The Belgian example again shows that communication and information are important: sentencing judges who were more familiar with the implementation courts were also more favourably disposed to the principle of relative autonomy. However, being able or trying to explain the merits and rationales of the principle of relative autonomy in order to get it understood and/or accepted by a wider public or by the sentencing judges is only one part of the story. Discourses on punishment are embedded in cultures and emotions, and are dependent on how they are captured by the media. Sparks rightly points to the importance of 'the networks, forms and formats through which knowledge, understanding, commitment and belief are circulated and exchanged' in order to gain a 'situated understanding' of the complex interaction between practices and compensation mechanisms and narratives on these practices (Sparks 2001: 196). The expert narrative is thus only one voice in this complex setting. The Belgian case shows how other influential voices, such as those of policy makers and judges, may become dominant and give credibility to the construction of the problem of non-, or partial implementation of sentences and how they can overrule a more rational, expert-driven, logic.

## REFERENCES


Beyens, K and Scheirs, V (2009) 'Geruchten, frustraties en verdeeldheid. Belgische strafrechters over de strafuitvoering', *Proces*, 88, 16–34.

Beyens, K, Françoise, C and Scheirs, V (2010) 'Les juges Belges face à l'(in)exécution des peines', *Déviance et Société*, 34, 401–24.

Commissie strafuitvoeringsrechtbanken, externe rechtspositie van gedetineerden en straftoemeting (2003) *Eindverslag van de Commissie strafuitvoeringsrechtbanken, externe rechtspositie van gedetineerden en straftoemeting* (Brussels, Ministerie van Justitie).

De Clerck, S (2010) *Straf- en strafuitvoeringsbeleid. Overzicht en ontwikkeling* (Brussels, Kabinet Justitie).

De la Cuesta, J-L and Blanco, I (2007) 'Le système pénitentiaire espagnol', in JP Céré and C Japiassú (eds), *Les systèmes pénitentiaires dans le monde* (Paris, Dalloz).

Directorate General of the Prisons (2011) *Activiteitenverslag 2010* (Brussels, Federale Overheidsdienst Justitie).

Dünkel, F (1997) 'Judicial Control and Supervision', in Penal Reform International (ed), *Monitoring Prison Conditions in Europe* (Paris, Penal Reform International).

Dupont, L (1998) 'Proeve van een voorontwerp van beginselenwet gevangeniswezen en tenuitvoerleggng van vrijheidstraffen', in L Dupont (ed), *Op weg naar een beginselenwet gevangeniswezen* (Leuven, Universitaire Pers Leuven).

Feest, J (ed) (2006) *Kommentar zum Strafvollugsgesetz (AK-StVollzG)*, 5th edn (Neuwied, Luchterhand).

Freiberg, A and Moore, V (2009) 'Disbelieving Suspense: Suspended Sentences of Imprisonment and Public Confidence in the Criminal Justice System', *Australian and New Zealand Journal of Criminology*, 42, 101–22.

Gualazzi, A and Mancuso, C (2010) 'Italy', in N Padfield, D van Zyl Smit and F Dünkel (eds), *Release from Prison: European Policy and Practice* (Cullompton, Willan Publishing).
Herzog-Evans, M (1997) 'Judicial Oversight on Prison Sentences', in Penal Reform International (ed), *Monitoring Prison Conditions in Europe* (Paris, Penal Reform International).
Kress, K and Sluiter, G (2002) 'Enforcement', in A Cassese, P Gaeta and JRWD Jones (eds), *The Rome Statute of the International Criminal Court: A Commentary*, Vol II (Oxford, Oxford University Press).
Lappi-Seppälä, T (2007) 'Penal Policy in Scandinavia', in M Tonry (ed), *Crime, Punishment, and Politics in Comparative Perspective* (Chicago, University of Chicago Press).
—— (2010) 'Finland', in N Padfield, D van Zyl Smit and F Dünkel (eds), *Release from Prison: European Policy and Practice* (Cullompton, Willan Publishing).
Müller-Dietz, H (1978) *Strafvollzugsrecht*, 2nd edn (Berlin, Walter de Gruyter).
Padfield, N (2010) 'England and Wales', in N Padfield, D van Zyl Smit and F Dünkel (eds), *Release from Prison: European Policy and Practice* (Cullompton, Willan Publishing).
Peeters, E (1988) 'Een straftoemetingsonderzoek bij de correctionele rechter', *Panopticon*, 9, 39–62.
Poncela, P (2001) *Droit de la peine*, 2nd edn (Paris, Presses Universitaires de France).
Pieters, F (2010) 'Maar, wat als en mogelijkerwijze' in I Aertsen, K Beyens, T Daems and E Maes (eds), *Hoe punitief is België?* (Antwerp, Maklu).
Raes, A and Snacken, S (2004) 'The application of remand custody and its alternatives in Belgium' *The Howard Journal of Criminal Justice*, 43, 506–17.
Schüler-Springorum, H (1969) *Strafvollzug in Übergang* (Göttingen, Otto Schwartz).
Snacken, S (1986) *De korte gevangenisstraf. Een onderzoek naar toepassing en effectiviteit* (Antwerp, Kluwer).
—— (2004) 'De voorstellen van de subcommissie externe rechtspositie', in K Beyens, S De Valck, F Pieters and I Aertsen (eds), *De commissie Holsters buitenspel? De voorstellen van de commissie Strafuitvoeringsrechtbanken, externe rechtspositie van gedetineerden en straftoemeting* (Brussel, Politeia).
—— (2006) 'A Reductionist Penal Policy and European Human Rights Standards', *European Journal on Criminal Policy and Research*, 12, 143–64.
—— (2007) 'Penal policy and practice in Belgium', in M Tonry (ed) *Crime, Punishment and Politics in Comparative Perspective* (Chicago, University of Chicago Press).
Snacken, S and Beyens, K (2008) 'Tien jaar kwaliteitszorg in de strafuitvoering. "Sire we zijn ongerust"....', *Orde van de Dag*, 41, 103–22.
Snacken, S, Beyens, K and Beernaert, M-A (2010) 'Belgium', in N Padfield, D van Zyl Smit and F Dünkel (eds), *Release from Prison: European Policies and Practice* (Cullompton, Willan Publishing).
Sparks, R (2001) '"Bringin' it all back home": populism, media coverage and the dynamics of locality and globality in the politics of crime control', in K Stenson and RR Sullivan (eds), *Crime, Risk and Justice. The Politics of Crime Control in Liberal Democracies* (Cullompton, Willan Publishing).

Tubex, H, with the assistance of P Tournier (2003) *Study of Conditional Release (Parole) in the Member States. Analysis of Replies to the General Questionnaire* (Strasbourg, Council of Europe).
Vandeurzen, J (2009) *Beleidsverklaring van de Minister van Justitie* (Brussel, Kabinet Justitie).
Van Zyl Smit, D (2010) 'Release from Life Imprisonment: A Comparative Note on the Role of Pre-Release Decision Making in England and Germany', in M Groenhuijsen, T Kooijmans and T de Roos (eds), *Fervet Opus: Liber Amicorum Anton van Kalmthout* (Antwerp, Maklu).
Van Zyl Smit, D and Snacken, S (2009) *Principles of European Prison Law and Policy: Penology and Human Rights* (Oxford, Oxford University Press).
Van Zyl Smit, D and Spencer, JR (2010) 'The European Dimension to the Release of Sentenced Prisoners', in N Padfield, D van Zyl Smit and F Dünkel (eds), *Release from Prison: European Policy and Practice* (Cullompton, Willan Publishing).

## ENGLISH CASES

*R (Brooke) v Parole Board* [2008] ECWA Civ 29; [2008] 1 WLR 1950.
*R v Secretary of State for the Home Department, Ex parte Doody* [1994] 1 AC 531 (HL).

## EUROPEAN COMMISSION FOR HUMAN RIGHTS CASES

*A v Austria* 7 May 1990 (16266/90).
*Savic v Slovakia* 3 December 1997 (28409/95).

## EUROPEAN COURT OF HUMAN RIGHTS CASES

*Dybeku v Albania* 18 December 2007 (41153/06).
*Ganusauskas v Lithuania* 7 September 1999 (47922/99).
*Hudec v Slovakia* 24 October 2006 (4123/02).
*Kafkaris v Cyprus* [GC] 21 February 2008 (21906/04) (2009) 49 EHRR 35.
*Léger v France* 11 April 2006 (19324/02).
*Léger v France* [GC] 30 March 2009 (19324/02) (2009) 49 EHRR 41.
*M v Germany* (17 December 2009) (19359/04) (2010) 51 EHRR 41.
*Mouisel v France* (14 November 2002) (67263/01) (2004) 38 EHRR 34.
*Stafford v United Kingdom* [GC] 28 May 2002 (46295/99) (2002) 35 EHRR 32.
*T v United Kingdom* [GC] 16 December 1999 (24724/94) (2000) 30 EHRR 121.
*Thynne, Wilson and Gunnell v United Kingdom* 25 October 1990 (11787/85; 12009/86; 11978/86) (1991) 13 EHRR 666.
*Vinter and Others v United Kingdom* 17 January 2012 (66069/09 and 130/10 and 3896/10).
*Weeks v United Kingdom* 2 March 1987 (9787/82) (1988) 10 EHRR 293.

COUNCIL OF EUROPE INSTRUMENTS

Recommendation No. R (80) 11 of the Committee of Ministers to Member States concerning Custody Pending Trial adopted by the Committee of Ministers on 27 June 1980 at the 321st meeting of the Ministers' Deputies

Recommendation No. R (92) 16 of the Committee of Ministers to Member States on the European Rules on Community Sanctions and Measures adopted by the Committee of Ministers on 19 October 1992 at the 482nd meeting of the Ministers' Deputies

Recommendation No. R(99) 22 concerning Prison Overcrowding and Prison Population Inflation adopted by the Committee of Ministers on 30 September 1999 at the 681st meeting of the Ministers' Deputies

Recommendation No. R (92) 17 of the Committee of Ministers to Member States concerning Consistency in Sentencing adopted by the Committee of Ministers on 19 October 1992 at the 482nd meeting of the Ministers' Deputies

Recommendation Rec(2003)22 of the Committee of Ministers to Member States on Conditional Release (parole) adopted by the Committee of Ministers on 24 September 2003 at the 853rd meeting of the Ministers' Deputies

Recommendation Rec(2003)23 of the Committee of Ministers to Member States on the Management by Prison Administrations of Life Sentence and other Long-term Prisoners adopted by the Committee of Ministers on 9 October 2003 at the 855th meeting of the Ministers' Deputies

Recommendation No. R (87) 3 of the Committee of Ministers to Member States on the European Prison Rules adopted by the Committee of Ministers on 11 January 2006 at the 952nd meeting of the Ministers' Deputies

Recommendation Rec(2006)13 of the Committee of Ministers to Member States on the Use of Remand in Custody, the Conditions in which it Takes Place and the Provision of Safeguards against Abuse adopted by the Committee of Ministers on 27 September 2006 at the 974th meeting of the Ministers' Deputies

# 13

# *A Spanish Window on European Law and Policy on Employment Discrimination Based on Criminal Record*

ELENA LARRAURI AND JAMES B JACOBS*

## I. INTRODUCTION

IT IS A consistent conclusion of European and US empirical criminology that if ex-offenders cannot obtain legitimate employment, their risk of returning to criminal patterns of behaviour is higher (Sampson and Laub 1993; Uggen 2000; Farrall 2004; Richards and Jones 2004; Leverentz 2011). Employed ex-offenders will be less likely to reoffend, because employment provides income, a stake in staying out of trouble, a structured routine, pro-social work colleagues and associates, and self-esteem. Thus, policy-makers should presumptively support any policy that promotes ex-offender employment opportunities, and presumptively oppose any policy that impedes ex-offender employment opportunities.

Given the critical importance of legitimate employment for successful post-conviction and especially post-prison reintegration into mainstream society, it is surprising that conviction-based employment discrimination (CBED) is not a more salient penological topic in Europe.[1] Indeed, with the exception of one pioneer study (Damaska, 1968) and a contemporary

* The Spanish research has been done under a Research Project (DER 2009-08344 JURI: Género y Marginación: Victimización y Delincuencia) of the Ministry of Science and Innovation and the support of the Department of Universities of the Generalitat de Catalunya to the Research Group in Criminology (AGAUR 2009 SGR 1117). Thanks to Matti Joutsen and Dimitra Blitsa for helpful comments. We are extremely grateful to the senior National Conviction Register (NCR) official who patiently explained how the Spanish NCR works and provided relevant data on Criminal Conviction Certificates (CRC) requests. Thanks also to Kristel Beyens, Tom Daems, Frieder Dünkel, Krzysztof Krajewski, Sonja Snacken and Dirk van Zyl Smit for their helpful comments.

[1] The UK is a striking exception (Thomas 2007).

survey (Louks, Lyner and Sullivan 1998),[2] there has been no Europe-wide study of either de jure or de facto conviction-based employment discrimination. We are not aware of any European research that has sought to determine, as Pager (2003)[3] has in the US, the extent to which, if at all, ex-offenders face de facto employment discrimination from public and private employers.[4] Indeed, there is also inadequate research on national laws in Europe barring ex-offenders (de jure discrimination) from various occupations.

Perhaps European employers do not discriminate against job applicants or employees with criminal convictions?[5] If so, is that because European countries prevent employers from obtaining individual criminal history information, and/or provide powerful anti-discrimination remedies to ex-offenders who are discriminated against? Perhaps Europeans, including employers, believe that CBED is wrong or irrational, because a criminal conviction does not predict future misconduct on the job? However even if Europeans believe that prior convictions are predictive of future dishonesty, dangerousness and unreliability, perhaps they also support prohibiting CBED, in order to further goals perceived to be more important, like rehabilitation and social harmony? Finally, perhaps employers in Europe do discriminate on the basis of criminal record, but such discrimination is not well recognised?

This chapter seeks to address the relevance of a criminal record (CR) to employment opportunity in Europe. While we focus on Spain, the European country we know best, we believe the Spanish law and policy are similar to those in most, if not all, continental European countries.

[2] These authors tried to find out the EU policies that could affect the employment of people with a criminal record. Their main conclusions were: a) ex-offenders are not recognised as a stigmatised group in the EU; b) 'common to most countries (nine out of twelve) is a blanket ban on work for ex-offenders in the public sector or civil service'; c) most EU countries (with the exception of Ireland) have some means of purging criminal records; d) employer direct access to the national criminal register is not common, but providing individuals a right to obtain from the NCR their own criminal record, although discouraged by the European Council (Directive 11099/94), is common; e) in general, there is limited information (and much 'misinformation').

[3] Pager (2003) found that a criminal record reduces the chances of obtaining employment by almost 50%.

[4] To be sure, European ex-offenders have difficulty finding legitimate employment. However, in addition to employer discrimination, this is attributable to poor education, poor social skills and lack of work experience.

[5] In English, 'discriminate' can be used neutrally, as in 'We discriminate in favour of NYU graduates'. In Spanish and other European languages, however, 'discriminate' carries a connotation of being morally wrong. Thus, in the US, the law requires that certain employers may not hire (i.e. they must 'discriminate against') persons with certain criminal records. Obviously, the law does not regard such discrimination as morally wrong. In the text, we use 'discriminate' as it is used in the US.

In Spain, as in Europe generally, there is almost no academic work by criminal law or labour law scholars on CBED.[6] To the extent that academic lawyers attend to the topic (Grosso 1983; Harremanak 2001; Quintanilla 2001; Bueno Arus 2006; Conde 2006), they seem to assume that: 1) a conviction, especially if it involves a prison sentence, is an obstacle to employment and reintegration; 2) de jure CBED is limited to positions in the public administration; and 3) de facto CBED is extremely rare, even non-existent, because employers cannot obtain individual criminal history information from their national criminal registers (NCR).[7]

Although European employers have no direct access to conviction records, in fact, it is not true that European employers are unable to discover job applicants' criminal histories. Every country permits or does not forbid, at least some employers to ask job applicants to submit an official document attesting to a clean record or showing past convictions. For example, Spanish employers are not prohibited to ask job applicants to obtain a copy of their Criminal Record Certificate (CRC)[8] from the NCR and submit it with their employment application. Although it is widely believed that employers make such requests only rarely,[9] there are no empirical studies to confirm that impression.

## II. WHEN CONVICTION-BASED EMPLOYMENT DISCRIMINATION IS *REQUIRED*: DE JURE DISCRIMINATION

All European countries disqualify at least some categories of ex-offenders from some types of employment for some period of time after conviction.[10]

[6] Spanish criminal law scholars have produced only two academic works on criminal records. One is a doctoral dissertation on the regulation of criminal conviction records (Grosso 1983); the other is a book focusing on expungement policies (Bueno Arus 2006). Neither publication discusses CBED. For the most part, labour law scholars have also not dealt with this subject. However, a few scholars have touched on it (Goñi 1986; del Valle 1991; del Rey 1993; Fernandez 1996; Harremanak 2001; Quintanilla 2001; Goñi 2004; Tascón 2005; Alameda 2010) in the course of explaining an employee's right to privacy. In general, labour law academics just assume that the right to privacy protects job applicants from employers obtaining and considering past convictions, except for convictions directly related to the specific job requirements (see section IV).

[7] Unlike in the US, there are no private information vendors who collect and sell individual criminal history information (see Jacobs, 2006).

[8] A CRC is an official document issued by the NCR, that provides a complete record of every individual's convictions.

[9] We interviewed three senior officials responsible for employment assistance for incarcerated offenders, inmates of open prisons, and parolees. All three believe that a criminal conviction record is not a significant employment barrier, although they advise ex-offenders not to apply for positions in public administration and private security firms because a CRC is legally required.

[10] There are differences in detail, for example, regarding whether 1) 'administrative offences' (eg traffic violations) are recorded; 2) all, or just serious, criminal offences are recorded; 3) all convictions, or just those that have resulted in incarceration, are

The great comparative law scholar, Mirjan Damaska (1968), pointed out in a classic article published more than 40 years ago that European countries vary significantly with respect to which professions and occupations they place off-limits to ex-offenders, and for how long.

Ex-offenders are universally ineligible, at least for a certain period, to serve as judges, military officers, high-level executive branch officials or police officers of all ranks. This must reflect a European consensus that persons who hold positions of the highest trust and power should have and be seen to have impeccable honesty and integrity, and that ex-offenders, based solely on their prior criminal conduct, presumably lack those qualities of good character. By law, certain private-sector positions are also often closed to ex-offenders. Which private-sector jobs or occupational licences are off-limits to all/some convicted persons is usually explained by an egregious crime or scandal, rather than by focused consideration, logic or empirical data (Damaska 1968).[11]

Spain, like many European countries, requires a conviction-free record in order to work in the public administration as a teacher, university professor, medical doctor or civil servant. Additionally, there are laws requiring some government occupational licensing agencies to make a clean criminal record a prerequisite for obtaining a licence. For example, only individuals who have never been convicted of a crime (technically not having an unexpunged conviction) can be licensed as a commercial driver, a taxi driver (in some cities), operate a gambling enterprise, or manage a private school. Moreover, some professional organisations with authority to license and discipline members (for example, lawyers and notaries) require practitioners to have a clean criminal record. Spanish law also explicitly prohibits persons with an unexpunged conviction from working in a small number of private sector industries, businesses and jobs, for example, working for a private security firm or in a bingo parlour. Some laws and licences only render job applicants and employees ineligible if the sentencing judge explicitly included an employment disqualification; other positions are closed to individuals who have been convicted of any crime, or of an intentional crime, or of specified crimes. A few occupations are only open to persons with no previous administrative offences.[12]

covered; 4) when a conviction is removed from the NCR by expunction and/or when it is sealed. In Spain, 1) only criminal convictions are recorded; 2) a recent law (LO 2/2010) makes minor offences recordable after December 2011; 3) all penalties are recorded; and 4) criminal records are expunged five years after the sentence has been fully served.

[11] Grosso (1983) and Bueno Arus (2006) point out that there is no consistency with repect to which occupations require a criminal record certificate and which do not.

[12] Eg commercial drivers: Art 44 Ley 16/1987, de 30 de Julio, de ordenación de los transportes terrestres; private security: Art 8.2.b Ley 23/1992, de 30 de Julio, de Seguridad Privada.

These examples belie the widely held belief in Spain that a clean criminal record is not an occupational requirement, except to work in public administration. However, this apparent misconception can be somewhat reconciled by certain qualifications: first, for some positions (eg prison and police officers, firemen, Central Bank of Spain officials), administrative laws bar ex-offenders if they have any non-expunged convictions, but for other occupations (eg civil servant, university professor, judge) a previously convicted individual is disqualified only if the sentencing court explicitly imposed the occupational disqualification as part of the sentence.[13] Thus, a previously convicted Spanish citizen is not automatically disqualified from all public sector positions because many such disqualifications specifically apply only to persons who have not been *sentenced* to employment disqualification.[14]

Second, the impression that criminal records are not an occupational requirement may stem from the fact that the requirement to have a clean criminal record is *not effectively enforced,* in large part due to restrictions on access to individual criminal history information. In Spain, as in most European countries, the NCR's conviction records are available only to courts and certain law enforcement agencies (Jacobs and Larrauri 2012).[15] Some government agencies (eg the police) are explicitly authorised to obtain criminal record information directly from the NCR; that makes criminal background checking quite easy. For other positions (eg judges and lawyers), the government agency requires the job applicant herself to obtain and submit the CRC.[16] However, for many positions closed to ex-offenders (eg teachers and most civil servants), the agency merely asks the job applicant to sign a statement attesting that she has never been sentenced to an occupational disqualification.

Perhaps a third reason why Spanish criminal law scholars believe that ex-offenders seeking employment are not greatly hampered by CBED is the widely held view that ex-offenders rarely look to public administration for employment on account of inadequate educational credentials.[17]

[13] The recent and controversial conviction of Judge Baltasar Garzón provides a salient example. His sentence included an occupational disqualification for 11 years. See the Spanish Supreme Court decision STS 79/2012, 9 February.

[14] The sentence is a discretionary judicial sanction; the administrative law is a general, automatic consequence of the sentence. For a discussion of criminal sentences' collateral consequences, see Demleitner (1999).

[15] Real Decreto 95/2009 de 6 de febrero. For the history of this legislation, see Larrauri (2011).

[16] Spain, like most European countries, gives individuals the right to obtain a CRC from the NCR (see Real Decreto 95/2009 de 6 de febrero).

[17] In Spain 19.9% of the working population work in the public sector. Source: personal elaboration based on Encuesta de Población activa (Labour Force Population Survey) IV term 2011. Available at: www.ine.es/jaxi/tabla.do?per=03&type=db&divi=EPA&idtab=87&L=0.

Because law scholars assume that the vast majority of ex-offenders seek employment in occupations that do not disqualify ex-offenders (eg construction and hotels), they discount the significance of de jure CBED.

To determine the extent of de jure CBED, we obtained data about government agencies' CRC requests to the NCR. Because these data are not broken down according to reason for the agency's request,[18] we cannot reach definitive conclusions. However, and perhaps surprisingly, given prevailing impressions, 2010 data show 1.5 million CRC requests in only one year (see Table 13.1).

The government agencies' requests are the consequence of laws making a clean criminal record an employment or licence prerequisite. Most public agency requests for CRCs came from the police, army and private security companies which are legally prohibited from hiring persons with an unexpunged criminal conviction. Interestingly, of these government agency requests, 63.9 per cent are submitted on behalf of (non-EU) immigrants who need to demonstrate a clean record in order to obtain a work permit.[19] Table 13.1 shows that a prior criminal record has the biggest impact on non-EU immigrants. A conviction renders them ineligible

**Table 13.1: Requests to the NCR (2010)**

| **Requests to the NCR (2010)** | | | |
|---|---|---|---|
| Requests from private citizens | | 176,332 | 11.7% |
| Requests from government agencies in order to obtain: | | 1,335,834 | 88.3% |
| | Police jobs | 139,487 | 9.2% |
| | Enter the Army | 44,056 | 2.9% |
| | Firearms permit | 66,792 | 4.4% |
| | Nationality | 119,250 | 7.90% |
| | Residence/work permit | 966,249 | 63.9% |
| Total | | 1,512,166 | 100% |

[18] These data are not public. They were provided to us by a senior NCR official.

[19] Art 260 RD 557/2011. Oficinas de Extranjería (Delegación o Subdelegación del Gobierno) dependent from Secretaría de Estado de Inmigración y Emigración, Ministerio de Trabajo e Inmigración, y del Ministerio del Interior.

for work and residence permits,[20] and at a great disadvantage in seeking Spanish citizenship.[21]

In summary, criminal background checks in Spain, as in Europe generally, are legally required for a position in public administration. In addition, Spain and other European countries have laws barring some convicted offenders from a small number of private-sector occupations and professions. In recent years, some European countries have passed laws requiring criminal background checks for persons applying for jobs working with children or elderly persons (Thomas 2007; Boone 2011; Morgenstern 2011). Furthermore, a recent EU Directive[22] requires Member States to authorise sentencing judges, in cases of certain sex offences, to include an order prohibiting the convicted defendant from holding any position requiring close contact with children (Jacobs and Blitsa 2012).

## III. WHEN CONVICTION-BASED EMPLOYMENT DISCRIMINATION IS *PERMISSIBLE*: DE FACTO DISCRIMINATION

In Spain, as in other EU Member States, the vast majority of private-sector employers are neither required to nor prohibited from discriminating against job applicants (or current workers) on account of previous criminal convictions. It is therefore worth asking why employers would choose to discriminate against job applicants who have previously been convicted of crimes.

One possibility is that employers do not see their preference for employees with no criminal convictions as discrimination *against* those with prior convictions. They might argue that it is reasonable business practice to discriminate in favour of job applicants with good education, good qualifications, good prior experience, good personality and good indicia of personal integrity and reliability. Accordingly, selecting employees who excel in all those qualities does not constitute wrongful discrimination against job-seekers who have poor education, poor qualifications, no experience,

[20] Art 31 LO 4/2000, de 11 de enero y RD 2393/2004, de 30 de diciembre. An initial work and residence permit will not be issued to an individual with a criminal conviction. A conviction that occurs after the permit is granted is taken into account when the immigrant applies for a permit renewal. See for example STS 381/2010, sala de lo contencioso adminitrastivo secc 5ª, 12 febrero 2010.

[21] This policy reflects the view that immigrants who have committed criminal offences in Spain should not be permitted to remain in the country because they have demonstrated disrespect for Spanish law and pose a risk of future criminality. The law requires deportation of an individual who cannot renew his work and residence permit, but this is rarely enforced.

[22] Directive 2011/92/EU of the European Parliament and of the council of 13 December 2011 on combating the sexual abuse and sexual exploitation of children and child pornography. Art.10.1

an unpleasant personality and poor indicia of integrity and reliability. According to this logic, preferring employees with a clean criminal record is no different than universities selecting faculty who have a PhD degree from a prestigious university and strong recommendations from their supervisors; does that preference discriminate against applicants who do not have prestigious PhDs and positive recommendations?

A rational employer might also prefer to hire individuals without previous convictions because it wishes to minimise the risk of liability for injuries that an employee might inflict upon customers, clients, fellow employees and the business entity itself. Since, in Spain and Europe generally, employers are held strictly liable for harms caused by their employees,[23] they might have a financial incentive to screen out job applicants whom they believe pose a higher than average risk of acting violently or dishonestly.

Whether or not employers have good reason to discriminate against persons with prior criminal records, they rarely seek to obtain job applicants' conviction history. Obviously, if employers do not obtain criminal background information (or confirmation of the absence of prior criminal convictions), they cannot discriminate on the basis of past convictions. In an attempt to find empirical verification, we surveyed employers, workers and probationers and examined data from the NCR office.

In 2010, the NCR received 176,332 CRC requests from private individuals. A substantial (but unknown) number of these requests were presumably submitted in order to complete applications for jobs, and for licenses to operate certain businesses.[24]

While we were unable to conduct the kind of full-scale employer survey that has been done in the US and elsewhere,[25] we did send to 16 trade union workers a written questionnaire[26] asking if an employer had ever requested them to submit their CRC. Eight of these respondents answered negatively. Four of those who answered affirmatively had been asked to provide a CRC for jobs with state and local police, private security and a fire department. This is no surprise since the law disqualifies certain ex-offenders from serving in those positions. However, the four other affirmative responders said that a CRC had been requested for employment in office cleaning, domestic service, gardening and social services which provide personal care (one respondent said that the employer made the criminal record request orally).

23 Art 120.4 Spanish Criminal Code.

24 Other posible reasons unrelated to job requirements could be related to adoptions or in connection with firearms for hunting purposes.

25 In the UK, two-thirds of surveyed employers stated that they considered a job applicant's criminal record. In the US, half of employers check before hiring an applicant (Holzer et al 2007). In Australia, employers initiated 2.3 million criminal background checks in 2006–07 (Naylor, Patterson and Pittard 2008).

26 We are grateful to Luis Antonio Salvadores, a lawyer for the Comisiones Obreras trade union.

Obviously, much more empirical research is needed, but the fact that 50 per cent of our respondents reported that they or somebody they knew had been asked to submit their CRC, half of those (25 per cent) by private employers, casts some doubt on the widely held belief that Spanish private employers rarely consider job applicants' past convictions.

In another empirical foray, we surveyed 49 male probationers in Barcelona. Of this sample, 10.7 per cent had been asked by employers to submit a CRC.[27] Most of those requests involved applications for jobs (especially private security and commercial drivers) from which, by law, ex-offenders are barred. (Curiously, a TV reality show asked one of these probationer respondents to submit a CRC in order to be considered for an appearance on the show.)

NCR data (176,000 CRC requests by private individuals) and our own research cast doubt on the widely held belief that private employers rarely consider job applicants' past convictions. Still, it is puzzling why Spanish employers do not more frequently ask job applicants to submit a CRC. At this point we can only speculate. One possible explanation is that employers fill a large number of jobs with individuals whom they know personally or who have been recommended to them by family members or close friends.[28] Another possible explanation is that employers think, based upon an apparent consensus of scholarly opinion (see section IV) that, in the absence of a specific law requiring it, it is illegal to ask job applicants to submit a CRC. If this is the case, their belief is probably based on the fact that (1) employers cannot communicate directly with the NCR, (2) the NCR keeps criminal records confidential, and (3) the Spanish constitution explicitly includes a commitment to rehabilitation (Article 25.2 Spanish Constitution).[29]

## IV. WHEN CONVICTION-BASED EMPLOYMENT DISCRIMINATION IS *PROHIBITED*

If a country desired to increase ex-offenders' employment opportunities, it could prohibit CBED and punish violators civilly and/or criminally. Such a policy would equate CBED with racial, gender and religious employment discrimination. The enacting country would certainly not allow employers

[27] We interviewed personnel at four agencies that work on promoting offender reintegration and surveyed masters students who had applied for temporary jobs. All believe that employers only rarely ask job-seekers about past criminal convictions.

[28] There is no data for the whole population of people who got a job through friends and relatives. The Labour Force Population Survey 2009 refers to 47.92% of young people (16–34) who found their job through families or friends. Source: Personal elaboration based on Encuesta de Población activa (Labour Force population survey) module 2009. Available at: www.ine.es/jaxi/tabla.do?path=/t22/e308/meto_05/modulo/2009/l0/&file=01012.px&type=pcaxis&L=0.

[29] The Spanish Constitution (Art 25) provides that 'criminal punishments involving deprivation of freedom should aim towards rehabilitation and social integration'.

direct or indirect access to criminal record information; it would prohibit them from asking job applicants to reveal prior convictions. However, neither Spain nor any other European country has adopted that policy. European anti-discrimination laws do not prohibit CBED nor recognise offenders as a disadvantaged group entitled to special employment protection (Louks et al 1998).[30]

Spanish labour law prohibits employment discrimination based upon age, sex, national origin, marital status or political views;[31] criminal record is not mentioned. Arguably, this reflects a conscious decision not to treat CBED as immoral, irrational or unjustifiable. While the Penitentiary Law does state that CBED is unlawful,[32] it provides no remedy for an ex-offender who believes that she has been the victim of such discrimination, and has never been cited by a labour court.[33] In the absence of a specific labour law prohibition, Spanish private employers would seem free to engage in CBED.[34] This conclusion is strengthened by the fact that Spanish employers are not forbidden to require job applicants to submit their CRC with their job application.

Despite the fact that Spain's employment discrimination law does not protect ex-offenders, the majority of labour law scholars believe that it is illegal for private employers to ask job applicants to present a CRC.[35] They base this belief on a well-known Constitutional Court judgment[36] that declared that a criminal record subject's privacy right was infringed by

[30] See for example Council Directive 2000/78/EC of 27 November 2000 establishing a general framework for equal treatment in employment and occupation, Art 1: Purpose. 'The purpose of this Directive is to lay down a general framework for combating discrimination on the grounds of *religion or belief, disability, age or sexual orientation* as regards employment and occupation, with a view to putting into effect in the Member States the principle of equal treatment.'

[31] Estatuto de los Trabajadores, Art 4.2.

[32] Article 73.2 Ley Orgánica 1/1979 26 September, General Penitenciaria, states 'Conviction records can never be a basis for social or juridical discrimination.'

[33] There is no labour court judgment dealing with a challenge to an employer's requirement that a job applicant present a CRC. However, a few courts have referred to the Penitentiary Law provision. For example, in STSJ Andalucia (sala contencioso administrativa, sección 4, n. 349, 5 de marzo, 2010) the court said that a CR should not automatically foreclose renewal of a residence permit.

[34] However, the País Vasco ombudsman considered CBED to violate the Spanish Constitutional provision (Art 25.2) that states that rehabilitation is one goal of punishment (see Ararteko 1996). The ombudsman's recommendations have no binding force.

[35] A job applicant in Spain is not obliged to admit that she has a conviction record. Some labour law scholars believe that, if asked, a job applicant has the right to lie (Goñi 1986; Tascón 2005). It is not clear what this 'right to lie' means—presumably that she cannot be fired if the employer later discovers the lie. We have found only one judgment dealing with a worker who did not tell the employer about a previous sentence. The court concluded that the primary reason why the plaintiff was fired was for failing to appear at work (because he was in prison), not because he lied about a previous conviction (Tribunal Superior Justicia Comunidad Valenciana, 4 de Julio 1991).

[36] STC 22 July 1999, nº 144.

a government agency which, without affirmative authorisation, requested and received criminal record information from the NCR. From this judgment they infer that an official conviction record is 'private information' and thus that it is illegal for employers to ask prospective employees about prior convictions (for a discussion, see Jacobs and Larrauri 2012).

The labour law scholars draw further support for their belief that CBED is illegal from the Personal Data Protection Law that prohibits private individuals and entities from creating a register of criminal offenders or convictions. From this provision, they conclude that criminal records constitute protected personal data such as information about an individual's politics, trade union affiliation, religion, health and sex life (eg Goñi 1986; del Valle 1991; del Rey 1993; Fernandez 1996; Harremanak 2001; Goñi 2004; Tascón 2005; Alameda 2010). We do not think that a law prohibiting private parties from creating a database of convicted persons provides a persuasive argument for prohibiting an employer from asking a job applicant: 'Have you ever been convicted of a crime?' or 'Bring me your CRC'.[37]

Labour law scholars also argue that employers cannot ask for information about a job applicant's criminal convictions because information about 'moral character' is only rarely relevant to a job applicant's ability to perform the job for which she is applying. They reason that a conviction should only be a job disqualification when the offence is necessarily inconsistent with successfully performing a job's duties and responsibilities.[38] As a matter of policy, this opinion is also dubious. Many employers reasonably consider character relevant to every job that demands the employee to come to work when expected, stay until the end of the day and carry out duties conscientiously—in other words, every job. It is also important that employees abide by rules and comply with authority. These qualities of character are often as important, even more important, than particular skills.[39]

To conclude, Spain and the other European countries do not prohibit CBED as they prohibit race and gender discrimination. Moreover, their laws explicitly give individuals the right to obtain their CRC from the NCR.[40] If law-makers wanted to protect job-seekers from having to

[37] We agree with Del Rey (1993) that it is one thing to maintain a database of criminal offenders and a different thing to ask job applicants to submit proof that they have never been convicted. Beneyto, Herrero and Prados (2007) are the only Spanish authors who argue that asking *all* job applicants about prior convictions is not discriminatory.

[38] For example a person convicted of fraud could be denied a job as a cashier, but not a job as a gardener (Goñi 1986). However it is not clear how employers can assess the relevancy of convictions to particular jobs if they cannot ask the applicant or otherwise find out about that applicant's prior convictions.

[39] Admittedly, not all criminal records equally impeach good character (Henry and Jacobs 2007).

[40] Real Decreto 95/2009, de 6 de febrero.

produce their CRCs, they could have forbidden it.[41] They could also provide ex-offenders who are discriminated against in employment a civil remedy that would provide compensation and/or a hiring order. Moreover, with respect to any such CBED lawsuit, law-makers could make employers bear the burden of proving that the requested criminal record information is justified by business necessity. However, no European parliament has included ex-offenders in its anti-discrimination statutes,[42] and no such case has been reported by Spanish courts.

Of course, just because CBED is not prohibited, does not mean that it is standard practice. The extent of criminal background checks and CBED in Spain is not known. We also lack research on employers' attitudes towards hiring ex-offenders.[43] While CBED in Spain and other European countries is widely and uncritically accepted as appropriate for serving in the public administration, private sector employers are mostly not regulated with respect to discriminating on the basis of criminal record. The belief that criminal records are private information (Jacobs and Larrauri 2012) may well explain the general view that CBED is unlawful unless it is affirmatively authorised by legislation or a criminal sentence. However there is no specific legislation (or court judgments) to protect ex-offenders against employment discrimination.

## V. REFLECTIONS

CBED has not been much studied in Europe despite its likely (albeit unproven) importance for ex-offender re-entry. It is widely assumed that because European countries do not make individual criminal history information available to private and most public employers, employers do not obtain or consider prospective employees' prior convictions. That assumption may or may not be true. Certainly, employers could eventually request that job applicants obtain and present their criminal records (or lack thereof) with their employment application. How often employers make

[41] In Finland, only certain employees may request information on criminal records from the NCR. An individual must show 'need' to obtain his CRC from the NCR. With respect to employment, need exists only when the applicant is applying for certain occupations, such as those involving contact with children; information provided by Matti Joutsen (email communications, 28 June 2011).

[42] However, an employer cannot dismiss a worker just because she has a CR or because she has been sentenced. It is possible to dismiss a convicted person only for failure to attend work (see Art 54.2(a) Estatuto Trabajadores).

[43] Gutierrez and Sintas (1994) carried out the only research in Spain of which we are aware. They found that 25% of employers probably would not hire an ex-offender; this rises to 85% if the ex-offender is a recidivist. In the US, Holzer, Raphael and Stoll (2006) report that 60% of the employers are unwilling to hire ex-offenders.

such requests is unknown and deserves empirical research. Our preliminary research in Spain found that in 2010 there were 1.5 million requests to NCR.

CBED is a tough policy issue. First, it raises civil liberties concerns. Convicted criminals should not be punished, penalised or disadvantaged disproportionately to their just deserts. Lengthy or even lifetime exclusion from all legitimate employment would be a much more severe penalty than most defendants deserve. It would also be counterproductive from a societal point of view, because without opportunities for legitimate employment ex-offenders will gravitate back toward criminal activity.

The nub of the issue is whether an employment disqualification should be considered punishment. Arguably, a good character requirement for employment imposed by the discretionary licensing decisions of employers, governmental agencies and professional associations is not punishment any more than a PhD requirement for a faculty position punishes those without a PhD. An employment disqualification imposed by a general employment law is a closer question. Certainly, a law providing that the judge must include employment disqualification as part of the sentence should count as part of the punishment for the criminal offence.[44] Is it any different if the legislature imposes the same employment disqualification automatically?[45] Perhaps it could be argued that the automatic disqualification imposed by a general employment law is not intended to convey condemnation or impose a stigma, but to safeguard consumers or the general public from injuries that could be caused by unqualified/irresponsible persons working in sensitive occupations. However, that seems like a formalistic distinction, albeit one that many national courts accept to justify collateral consequences of a criminal sentence.

Employment discrimination against persons with prior convictions raises important social policy concerns. There is a strong societal interest in convicted persons successfully reintegrating into the societal mainstream. If convicted offenders are relegated to a criminal subculture and a future of repeated offending and punishment, society is harmed financially and physically. However, it is also true that employers have a legitimate interest in preferring reliable, honest and self-disciplined employees to employees who are unreliable, dishonest and dangerous. The dilemma cannot be made to disappear simply by insisting that a criminal conviction does not reflect character nor predict future misconduct. Reality does not confirm such wishful thinking. Empirical studies find different reoffending rates, depending upon the ex-offenders who are sampled and, of course, on the efficiency of the police. Admittedly, recidivism itself is in part a

[44] As suggested by von Hirsh and Wasik (1997).

[45] In the US literature, 'automatic disqualifications' are referred to as 'collateral consequences' of conviction (see Demleitner 1999 and Pinard 2010).

consequence of employment discrimination. There is certainly no reason to believe that recidivism rates are constant over time and place, or for all categories of ex-offenders. However, we are not aware of any recidivism study that finds that ex-offenders present no elevated risk of future offending.[46]

We think that a fully developed analysis of the justifiability of CBED should also consider the interests of job applicants who have never been convicted of a crime. When an ex-offender is not hired for a job, that position is filled by another person in need of work, perhaps severely in need. That never-convicted job-seeker might well feel, and with some justification, that his or her spotless criminal record should count as a plus on his or her curriculum vitae, in the same way that good educational credentials and good prior job experience should count favorably. If a spotless criminal record does not confer any advantage over a person with one or more criminal convictions, the resolve to avoid the temptations of crime might be weakened.[47]

Policy-making in this area is more complex than is often assumed. It touches on constitutional law, sentencing and criminal law, labour law, immigration and administrative law. Strong interests point in different directions and the most affected population are normally the most powerless (ex-offenders and immigrants). Perhaps that is why in Spain and the other European countries policy remains, to a large degree, under-researched and under-developed. This is unfortunate because it leads to many assumptions, eg that the vast majority of employers do not discriminate on the basis of criminal record. Acceptance of such assumptions obviates the need to explore policy options[48] for better regulating CBED.

[46] But see Kurlychek, Brame and Bushway (2007), who found that after seven years of crime-free (as measured by arrest-free) conduct, an ex-offender's risk of recidivating is similar to that of a person without any criminal record. Blumstein and Nakamura (2010) found that the hazard rate (probability of being rearrested) differs according to age and offence. But according to Blumstein only 30% of his sample of first-time arrestees actually reached the redemption point without another arrest (Alfred Blumstein, email communication 21 January 2012). More recently, Bushway, Nieuwbeerta and Blokland (2011) point out that the number of previous arrests affects 'time to redemption'. Maruna (2009) argues that CBED itself affects 'time to redemption'.

[47] There is lively debate about the effects of expungement policies (Funk and Polsby 1998) and policies forbidding public access to CR (Busway 2004; Holzer et al 2006; Freeman 2008; Stoll and Bushway 2008). The authors cited in the previous sentence believe that if US employers were denied access to job applicants' criminal records, they would be more likely to discriminate against minority applicants, especially blacks. Therefore blacks who have no criminal record would obtain fewer jobs.

[48] See eg Love and Chin (2010) on the need to inform the defendant about collateral consequences of conviction.

## REFERENCES


Alameda, MT (2010) 'La oportuna adopción de un acuerdo colectivo comunitario sobre protección de datos personales de los trabajadores', *Justicia laboral*, 41, 81–102.

Ararteko (1996) *Recomendación General.* 7.1. Necesidad de evitar el efecto discriminatorio de los antecedentes penales (unpublished manuscript).

Beneyto D, Herrero VM and Prados, JM (2007) *2000 Soluciones Laborales* (Valencia, CISS).

Blumstein, A and Nakamura, K (2009) 'Redemption in the Presence of Widespread Criminal Background Checks', *Criminology,* 47, 327–59.

—— (2010) '"Redemption" in an Era of Widespread Criminal Background Checks', *NIJ Journal*, 263, 10–17.

Boone, M (2011) 'Judicial Rehabilitation in the Netherlands: Balancing between safety and privacy', *European Journal of Probation*, 3, 63–78.

Bueno Arús F (2006) La Cancelación de Antecedentes Penales (Madrid, Thomson/ Civitas).

Bushway, SD (2004) 'Labor Market Effects of Permitting Employer Access to Criminal History Records', *Journal of Contemporary Criminal Justice*, 20, 276–91.

Bushway, SD and Sweeten, G (2007) 'Abolish Lifetime Bans For Ex-Felons', *Criminology & Public Policy*, 6, 697–706.

Bushway, SD, Nieuwbeerta, P and Blokland, A (2011) 'The Predictive Value of Criminal Background Checks: Do Age and Criminal History Affect Time to Redemption?', *Criminology,* 49, 27–60.

Conde, M (2006) *Derecho Penitenciario Vivido* (Granada, Comares).

Damaska, M (1968) 'Adverse Legal Consequences of Conviction and Their Removal: A Comparative Study (Part 2)', *The Journal of Criminal Law, Criminology and Police Science*, 59, 542–68.

Del Rey, S (1993) 'Tratamiento automatizado de datos de carácter personal y contrato de trabajo', *Relaciones Laborales, Sección Doctrina,* 2, 135–73.

Del Valle, JM (1991) 'El derecho a la intimidad del trabajador durante la relación de trabajo', *Actualidad Laboral, Sección Doctrina,* 3, 485–515.

Demleitner, NV (1999) 'Preventing Internal Exile: The Need For Restrictions On Collateral Sentencing Consequences', *Stanford Law and Policy Review*, 11, 153–71.

Farrall, S (2004) 'Social Capital And Offender Reintegration: Making Probation Desistance Focused', in S Maruna and R Immarigeon (eds), *After Crime and Punishment. Pathways to Offender Reintegration* (Cullompton, Willan Publishing).

Fernandez Villazón, LA (1996) 'Los derechos de los trabajadores frente al tratamiento de datos personales', *La Ley. Relaciones Laborales, Sección crónica internacional y comunitaria,* 22, 1178–1225.

Freeman, R (2008) 'Incarceration, Criminal Background Checks, and Employment in a Low(er) Crime Society', *Criminology & Public Policy*, 3, 405–11.

Funk, TM and Polsby, DD (1998) 'The Problem of Lemons and Why We Must Retain Juvenile Crime Records', *Cato Journal*, 18, 75–83.

Goñi, JL (1986) 'El respeto a la vida privada. A propósito del formulario MS1-02 del INI', *La Ley, Relaciones Laborales,* 2, 115–25.
—— (2004) 'Vulneración de derechos fundamentales en el trabajo mediante instrumentos informáticos, de comunicación y archivos de datos', *Justicia Laboral, Sección Doctrina,* 17, 13–53.
Grosso, M (1983) *Los Antecedentes Penales: Rehabilitación y Control Social* (Barcelona, Bosch).
Gutiérrez, A (2010) 'La Protección de datos personales como derecho fundamental del imputado, ¿también en el ámbito del proceso penal?', *La Ley,* 71, 1–10.
Gutierrez, J and Sintas, F (1994) 'Actitud de los empresarios hacia la integración laboral de personas que están o han estado sometidas a medidas privativas de libertad', *Anuario de Psicología Jurídica*, 4, 137–160.
Harremanak, L (2001) 'Medidas para fomentar el empleo de las personas que han sido privadas de libertad', *Revista de Relaciones Laborales,* 4, 1–33.
Henry, J and Jacobs, J (2007) 'Ban the Box to Promote Ex-Offender Employment', *Criminology & Public Policy*, 6, 755–62.
Holzer, HJ, Raphael, S and Stoll, MA (2006) 'Perceived Criminality, Criminal Background Checks, and the Racial Hiring Practices of Employers', *Journal of Law & Economics*, 49, 451–80.
—— (2007) 'The Effect of an Applicant's Criminal History on Employer Hiring Decisions and Screening Practices: evidence from Los Angeles', in S Bushway, MA Stoll, and DF Weiman (eds), *Barriers to Reentry?* (New York, Russell Sage Foundation).
Jacobs, JB (2006) 'Mass Incarceration and the Proliferation of Criminal Records', *St Thomas Law Review*, 3, 387–420.
Jacobs, JB and Blitsa, D (2012), 'US, EU & UK Employment Vetting as Strategy for Preventing Convicted Sex Offenders from Gaining Access to Children', *European Journal of Crime, Criminal Law and Criminal Justice*, 20, 265–96.
Jacobs, JB and Larrauri, E (2012) 'Are criminal convictions a public matter? The USA and Spain', *Punishment & Society*, 14, 3–28.
Kurlychek, M, Brame, R and Bushway, S (2007) 'Enduring Risk? Old Criminal Records and Predictions of Future Criminal Involvement', *Crime & Delinquency*, 53, 64–83.
Lam, H and Harcourt, M (2003) 'The Use of Criminal Record in Employment Decisions: The Rights of Ex-offenders, Employers and the Public', *Journal of Business Ethics*, 47, 237–52.
Larrauri, E (2011) 'Conviction Records in Spain: Obstacles to Reintegration of Offenders?', *European Journal of Probation*, 3, 50–62.
Leverentz, A (2011) 'Easing the Strains of Prisoner Reentry', *Offenders Programs Report*, 14, 65–80.
Louks, N, Lyner, O and Sullivan, T (1998) 'The Employment of People with Criminal Records in the European Union', *European Journal on Criminal Policy and Research*, 6, 195–210.
Love, CM (2005) *Relief from the Collateral Consequences of a Criminal Conviction: A State-by-State Resource Guide*. Open Society Institute, www.sentencingproject.org/doc/File/Collateral%20Consequences/execsumm.pdf.
—— (2011) 'Paying Their Debt to Society: Forgiveness, Redemption, and the Uniform Collateral Consequences of Conviction Act', *Howard Law Journal*, 3, 753–93.

Love, CM and Chin, JG (2010) '*Padilla v. Kentucky*: The Right to Counsel and the Collateral Consequences of Conviction', *Arizona Legal Studies*. Discussion Paper Nº 10–16.

Love, CM and Frazier, A (2006) *Certificates of Rehabilitation and Other Forms of relief from the Collateral Consequences of Conviction: A Survey of State Laws*. American Bar Association, http://meetings.abanet.org/webupload/commupload/CR203000/otherlinks_files/convictionsurvey.pdf.

Maruna, S (2009) '"Virtue's door unsealed is never sealed again": Redeeming Redemption and the Seven-Year Itch', in NA Frost, JD Freilich and TR Clear (eds), *Contemporary Issues in Criminal Justice Policy: Policy Proposals from the American Society of Criminology Conference* (Belmont, CA, Cengage/Wadsworth).

Morgenstern, C (2011) 'Judicial Rehabilitation in Germany—the Use of Criminal Records and the Removal of Recorded Convictions', *European Journal of Probation*, 3, 20–35.

Naylor, B, Paterson, M and Pittard, M (2008) 'In the Shadow of a Criminal Record: Proposing a Just Model of Criminal Record Employment Checks', *Melbourne University Law Review*, 32, 171–98.

Pager, D (2003) 'The Mark of a Criminal Record', *The American Journal of Sociology*, 108, 937–75.

Petersilia, J (2003) *When Prisoners Come Home: Parole and Prisoner Reentry* (New York, Oxford University Press).

Pinard, M (2006) 'An Integrated Perspective on the Collateral Consequences of Criminal Convictions and Reentry Issues Faced by Formerly Incarcerated Individuals', *Boston University Law Review*, 86, 623–90.

—— (2010) 'Collateral Consequences of Criminal Convictions: Confronting Issues of Race and Dignity', *New York University Law Review*, 85, 457–534.

Quintanilla, R (2001) 'El contrato de inserción', *Revista del Ministerio de Trabajo y Asuntos Sociales*, 33, 189–214.

Radice, J (2012) 'Administering Justice: Removing Statutory Barriers to Reentry', *University of Colorado Law Review*, 83, 715.

Richards, S and Jones R (2004) 'Beating the Perpetual Incarceration Machine: Overcoming Structural Impediments to Re-entry', in S Maruna and R Immarigeon (eds), *After Crime and Punishment. Pathways to Offender Reintegration* (Cullompton, Willan Publishing).

Rodriguez, M and Emsellem, M (2011) '65 Million "Need Not Apply": The Case For Reforming Background Checks For Employment' *The National Employment Law Project*, New York, www.nelp.org/page/-/SCLP/2011/65_Million_Need_Not_Apply.pdf?nocdn=1.

Roldan, H (2010) 'El uso de la libertad condicional y su influencia en el tamaño de la población reclusa en España', *RECPC*, 12-04, www.criminologia.net/reic.html.

Sampson, R and Laub, J (1993) *Crime in the Making. Pathways and Turning Points Through Life* (Cambridge, MA, Harvard University Press).

Stoll, MA and Bushway, SD (2008) 'The Effects of Criminal Background Checks on Hiring Ex-Offenders', *Criminology & Public Policy*, 7, 371–404.

Tascón, R (2005) 'El tratamiento por la empresa de los datos personales de los trabajadores ¿un problema resuelto o caído en el olvido?', *Aranzadi Social*, 16, 1403–40.

Thacher, D (2008) 'The Rise of Criminal Background Screening in Rental Housing', *Law and Social Inquiry*, 33, 5–30.
Thomas, T (2007) *Criminal Records* (New York, Palgrave Macmillan).
Travis, J (2002) 'Invisible Punishment: An Instrument of Social Exclusion', in M Mauer and M Chesney-Lind (eds), *The Collateral Consequences of Mass Imprisonment* (New York, The New Press).
—— (2005) *But They All Come Back. Facing the Challenges of Prisoner Reentry* (Washington, The Urban Institute Press).
Uggen, C (2000) 'Work as a Turning Point in the Life Course of Criminals: A Duration Model of Age, Employment, and Recidivism', *American Sociological Review*, 65, 529–46.
Von Hirsch, A and Wasik, M (1997) 'Civil Disqualifications Attending Conviction: A suggested conceptual framework', *Cambridge Law Journal*, 56, 599–626.

## EU INSTRUMENTS AND LEGISLATION

Council directive 2000/78/EC of 27 November 2000 establishing a general framework for equal treatment in employment and occupation, [2000] OJ L303/16.
Directive 2011/92/EU of the European Parliment and of the Council of 13 December 2011 on combating the sexual abuse and sexual exploitation of children and child pornography.

## NATIONAL CASE LAW

Sentencia del Tribunal Supremo (STS) nº 79, 9 February 2012.
STS nº 381, sala de lo contencioso adminitrativo secc 5a, 12 February 2010.
Sentencia del Tribunal Superior de Justicia (STSJ) Andalucia (sala contencioso administrative, sección 4, n. 349, 5 March 2010.
Sentencia del Tribunal Superior Justicia (STSJ) Comunidad Valenciana, 4 July 1991.
Sentencia del Tribunal Constitucional (STC) no. 144, 22 July 1999.

# 14

# *Penal Developments in Poland: New or Old Punitiveness?*

KRZYSZTOF KRAJEWSKI

## I. INTRODUCTION

The processes of integration, approximation and unification of laws taking place within European structures such as the European Union and the Council of Europe has resulted in the creation of a vast body of rules and standards subjecting the penal systems of European countries to various supra-national constraints. As a consequence, European countries are supposed to adhere to the same core values and ideas regarding the administration of criminal justice. These values and ideas are embodied not only in the European Convention of Human Rights and the jurisprudence of the European Court of Human Rights, but also in many other recommendations and standards prepared under the auspices of the Council of Europe and the EU (van Zyl Smit and Snacken 2009).

Notwithstanding that, for many years, all these rules, regulations and jurisprudence have had a significant influence over the penal law and criminal justice systems of European countries, it is equally true that huge differences remain, and that the way Council of Europe Member States implement these standards differs substantially. It is enough to point out that—theoretically—criminal justice systems not only in Western European countries or in Central Europe but also in Russia are supposed to be bound by a similar set of core values, standards and regulations, that should result in those systems operating in a similar way (at a very general level). Nevertheless, this is not necessarily so, and differences in that respect remain huge. Such differences become even more conspicuous when one considers not only the standards and rules regarding the functioning of the criminal justice system, but also outcomes in the shape of sentencing policies implemented in the Member States. Here vast differences prevail; differences not only between states, but also between the larger regions.

One of the most conspicuous among such regional differences is that with regard to criminal policies implemented in Western Europe (or the 'old'

EU Member States), and countries of Central and Eastern Europe which formerly belonged to the Soviet bloc but subsequently joined the EU (the 'new' EU Member States). It is of course easy also to point out substantial differences in criminal policies within Western Europe. But they usually become less significant, when contrasted with 'post-communist' ones. With minor exceptions, more than 20 years after the fall of the Iron Curtain, Europe remains clearly divided by two pretty different 'penal climates' prevailing in the western and the eastern parts of the continent. This division continues despite intensive implementation of the above-mentioned European standards and rules that have been adopted by the new Member States since they became members of the Council of Europe, and later on joined the EU. The fall of the communist system and the 'return' of the Central and Eastern European countries to 'Europe' resulted in expectations and hopes that within the foreseeable future, differences regarding punitiveness of sentencing policies would diminish, as Central and Eastern Europe would evolve—even if only slowly—in the direction of Western Europe. Moreover, it was often assumed that bridging this particular gap between the two parts of the continent would be easier than in the areas of economy, wealth and quality of life. Unfortunately, it does not appear to have happened. Differences regarding 'penal climates' persist and seem to be very resistant to change.

## II. DEVELOPMENT OF PENAL POLICY IN POLAND SINCE 1989

One of the most conspicuous examples of these problems is to be found in the penal policies implemented since 1989 in Poland, although this country only exemplifies similar problems encountered by other countries in Central and Eastern Europe. During the last 20 years Polish criminologists, penal reformers and policy-makers have had to face two kinds of problems: those resulting from 'turbulence' accompanying political, economic and social transformation from a totalitarian system and centrally planned economy to liberal democracy and market economy, and those resulting from the communist past of the country, which had been under Soviet domination since 1945. During the entire post-war period, penal policy in Poland was extremely punitive and harsh. This may be illustrated by the developments regarding the standard quantitative measure of punitiveness of the criminal justice system, namely the imprisonment rate. Throughout the entire period 1956–89 (Figure 14.1), this rate remained very high by western standards.

For example during the years 1970–80, the rate amounted on average to 259 per 100,000 inhabitants, and in 1972 reached an absolute record level of 347 per 100,000. It is important to underline that this was not primarily the direct result of political repression. Even after 1956, when Stalinist terror ended, there were still always political prisoners in Poland, but they

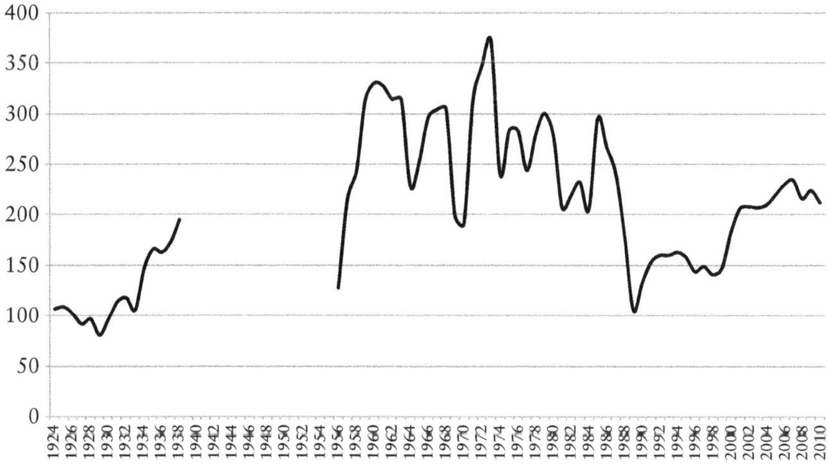


**Figure 14.1: Imprisonment rate in Poland 1924–2010**
Source: (Melezini 2003: 309) for the years 1924–38, and Statistical Yearbooks of the Polish Main Statistical Office 1956–2010.

constituted only a small fraction of the prison population. Therefore, the high imprisonment rate resulted largely from a tough approach to 'ordinary criminals'.

It is also interesting to note that under communism the imprisonment rate remained very unstable: throughout the entire period it was characterised by various radical switches. This may be seen by lows in 1956, 1964, 1969, 1970, 1974, 1977, 1982 and finally 1989, accompanied by highs in 1960, 1968, 1973, 1979, 1985. This pattern resulted from regular amnesties, which were used mainly to deal with the problem of prison overcrowding (Greenberg 1980). But the impact of each consecutive amnesty was always quickly nullified, usually after three to four years, as 'replacement inmates' were quickly found and the prison population returned to its previous level. Moreover, after every amnesty, it took less and less time for the criminal justice system to achieve this result. The last such amnesty came into effect in autumn 1989, after the first post-war non-communist government took office, and brought the imprisonment rate to a historical low of 106. It was assumed that this would be the last amnesty and that in the future the prison population would be kept at a reasonable level by means of rational and stable sentencing policies, and not by extraordinary measures.

For some time it appeared as if under the new circumstances the new system had tried to keep that promise. Despite some increase during the first half of the 1990s, imprisonment rates in that period remained substantially lower than under the communist regime. And in the years 1995–99 they even decreased a little further. This was probably the only period during which reforms of sentencing policies and changes in the attitudes of the judges contributed to changes in imprisonment rates (as opposed to the 1989–94 period, when the drop in the imprisonment rate resulted mainly from the long-lasting effects of the amnesty bill of 1989). Unfortunately, around 1999 all this changed, as the imprisonment rate started to grow rapidly again. During the past decade it has returned to a very high level, reaching its peak value of 234 in 2007. Although it still remains somewhat lower than in the 'worst' years during the 1960s and 1970s, it is very close to the rate under communism at the end of the 1980s. This means that all efforts undertaken during the 1990s under the motto of a return to a European 'penal climate' in fact had no lasting results.

It is interesting to note that Poland's high imprisonment rate does not seem to be the product of a long punitive tradition. Data for the brief period of Poland's independence between the two World Wars indicate that despite significant growth, especially during the 1930s, imprisonment rates during that period were much lower than under the communist regime. As a matter of fact, they were similar to those during the 1990s. For the period 1925–38 the average imprisonment rate amounted to 117, while during the years 1990–99 it was only slightly higher, at 135 per 100,000. This raises the question of whether developments during the last 20 years and the 'punitive turn' of the last decade result from the communist heritage, or whether they constitute an exemplification of some sort of 'new punitiveness' known in many western countries?

One of the standard explanations of the growth of imprisonment rate in post-communist countries like Poland refers to the growth of crime which has taken place since 1990. According to this account, the increasing number of inmates in prisons merely reflects the fact of more offences being committed by a greater number of offenders, which resulted in more persons being convicted by the courts. It is true that since 1989 the number of registered offences in Poland, and in all other countries of the region, went up sharply. In Poland this growth became especially conspicuous during the second half of the 1990s, with the crime rate peaking in the years 2003 and 2004 (Figure 14.2).

The registered offences rate in those two years was approximately 2.6 times higher than in 1989. Detailed discussion of the reasons for this growth is beyond the scope of this chapter (for more detail, see Krajewski 2004). One part of the story no doubt is a real growth of crime, as Poland joined the club of 'high crime societies' amid other political, economic and social transformations (Garland 2000). But another important factor is that in 'socialist countries' the number of registered offences was kept artificially low (Jasiński 1996). Changing patterns of reporting and registering offences after 1989 contributed, probably decisively, to the growth in the number of the registered offences. Changes in legislation and in the scope of criminalisation constituted additional factors.

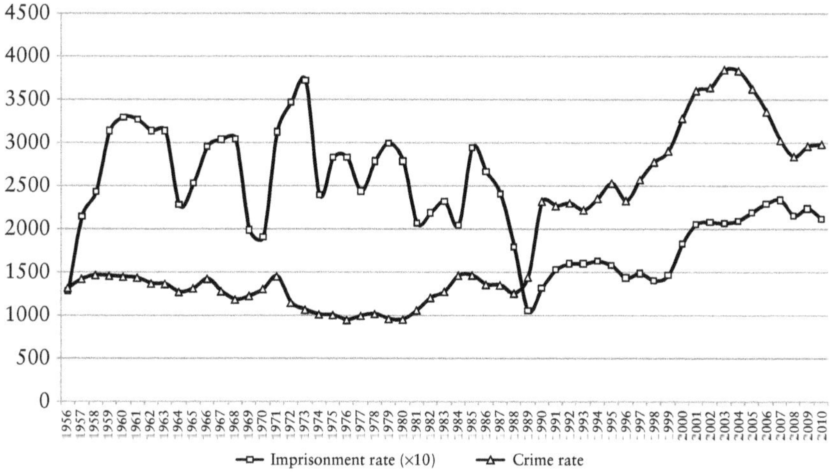


**Figure 14.2: Crime rate and imprisonment rate in Poland 1956–2010**
Source: Statistical Yearbooks of the Polish Main Statistical Office 1956–2010.

But this development was not necessarily followed by the imprisonment rate. What is most interesting is the fact that the relationship between them reversed completely after 1989. Before 1989, an extremely high imprisonment rate was accompanied by a relatively low (but probably quite artificial) registered offence rate; after that date the registered offence rate went up substantially while the imprisonment rate went down. The inversion of the relationship between crime rate and imprisonment rate during and after the communist period indicates that there was in fact a serious attempt to change penal policy. Without it, the growth in crime after 1989 would have resulted in an exorbitant increase of the prison population. But this effort was obviously not substantial enough to influence the imprisonment rate significantly and to have a lasting effect.

Furthermore, it is interesting to note that during the last 20 years, but especially during the last decade, the number of convictions was growing much faster than the number of persons imprisoned (Figure 14.3).

This suggests that the growth of the prison population was not a consequence of the growth in crime resulting in courts sentencing more offenders to immediate imprisonment. In other words, the number of offences and the number of convictions were both growing, but this did not necessarily involve a substantially increased use of custodial sanctions. Polish courts were obviously processing more offenders, but most of them were dealt with by means of non-custodial sanctions. This suggests that the growth of the prison population probably resulted mainly from the increasingly punitive way the criminal justice system has been treating the minority of offenders being sent to prison.

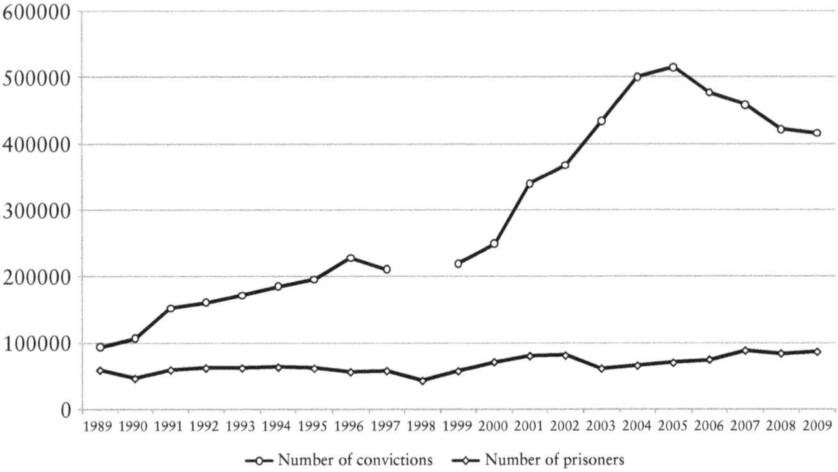


**Figure 14.3: Convictions and prison population in Poland 1989–2009**
Source: Statistical Yearbooks of the Polish Main Statistical Office 1989–2010.

This is confirmed by the data regarding the structure of the sanctions imposed by the Polish courts (Figure 14.4).

During the past two decades the proportion of custodial sentences has constantly decreased, while the proportion of non-custodial sanctions, especially of suspended sentences, has increased. Especially during the 1990s, one may observe a continuous decline in the proportion of immediate imprisonment (from about 26 per cent in 1989 to 12.2 per cent in 1997), and a substantial growth of the proportion of fining (from 19.2 per cent

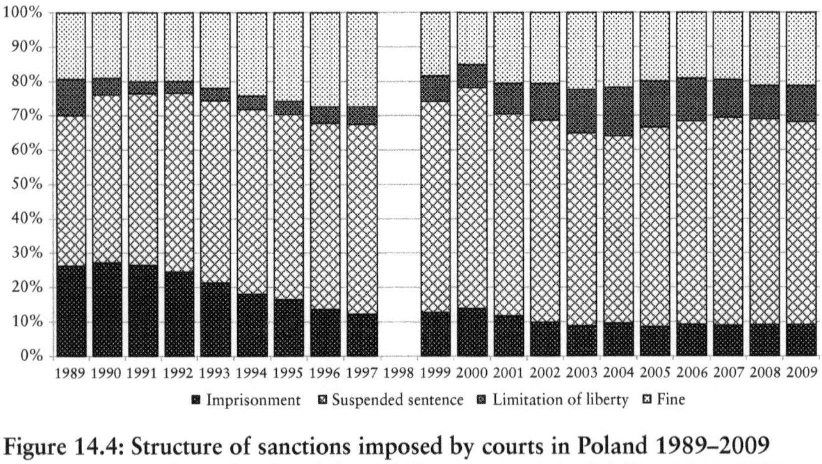


**Figure 14.4: Structure of sanctions imposed by courts in Poland 1989–2009**
Source: Statistical Yearbooks of the Polish Main Statistical Office 1989–2009.

in 1989 to 27.4 per cent in 1997). However, this was accompanied by a decline in the proportion of limitation of liberty, a community service type of sanction (from 10.6 per cent in 1989 to 5.2 per cent in 1997). Therefore, despite some positive tendencies, the use of alternatives to imprisonment such as community service remained very unsatisfactory. This meant a constant growth of the role of the suspended sentence (from 43 per cent in 1989 to 54 per cent in 1997).

After 1 September 1998, the date of entry into force of the new Penal Code, these tendencies became even more visible. Despite attempts to increase the use of fines by introducing the day fine system, the reverse occurred in practice. And this could not be balanced by some successes in stimulating the use of community service. Combined with a further decline in the use of immediate imprisonment, all this meant that the principal sanction under the Polish criminal justice system became the simple suspended sentence (60 per cent of all sanctions in 2007), imposed usually without any supervision or similar measures.[1] The fact that the Polish criminal justice system favours a widespread application of the suspended sentence suggests that in general this system may not necessarily be so terribly punitive. This means that the extremely high imprisonment rate must result not from a frequent use of imprisonment, but from patterns of use of custodial sanctions: they must be getting longer.

Detailed statistical data regarding this issue are not available for the entire period in question. But in 2000 the average time spent in prison by Polish inmates amounted to 9.3 months (Tournier 2001). By 2007 it had increased by more than one fifth, to 11.4 months (Aebi et al 2011). Interestingly enough, this probably resulted not from radical changes in sentencing patterns, but from more restrictive policies on conditional release. Conditional release in Poland is decided by the court, but on application either from the prison administration or from an inmate. An inmate's application always requires that an opinion must be provided to the court by the prison administration. In principle, conditional release is possible after half of the sentence has been served. These rules have not been changed since 1998. The government could not influence court decisions directly. Since 1999, however, the Ministry of Justice has tried by means of various guidelines to influence the prison administration to implement much more restrictive policies on conditional release. As a consequence the prison administration became much more reluctant to initiate conditional release procedures. Moreover, it has become much more reluctant to provide a positive opinion as required by the law if the application for conditional release is being

[1] Suspended sentences may be accompanied by various obligations imposed by the court, by a supervision by a probation officer, or both. However, for instance in the year 2006 only 24.9% of all suspended sentences were accompanied by any kind of obligation, and only 27% were accompanied by supervision.

initiated by the inmate. All of this probably had an impact on patterns of court decisions, although the final outcome resulted not from changes in judges' attitudes, but from courts' decisions being 'structured' by the new policies of the prison administration. Nevertheless, during the period 1990–98, on average 70 to 80 per cent of the motions for conditional release were granted by the courts. But from around 1996 this percentage started to decline, in 1999 falling below the 50 per cent mark for the first time, and during the past decade it has remained below 40 per cent (Stańdo-Kawecka and Krajewski 2010: 737–39). This confirms that the growth of the prison population in Poland during the past decade is not primarily the result of changes in sentencing patterns by the courts, but of changes in patterns of conditional release, resulting in prisoners staying longer behind bars than during the preceding decade.

Of course, analysing punitiveness of any criminal justice system exclusively by using data regarding imprisonment rates may be misleading. One cannot and should not forget that since 1989 enormous efforts have been made to change the Polish penal system. Radical prison reform started already in 1990 and changed penitentiaries and their staff beyond recognition. Some say that the prison reform was one of the most successful of its kind during the early stage of the transformation (Jasiński 1995). Moreover, Poland ratified the ECHR quite early, and became a full member of the human rights protection system within the Council of Europe. As a result, other Council of Europe instruments also played a significant role in the process of reforming penal law during the 1990s—a process that was finalised in 1997 by the adoption of the new Penal Code, the Code of Criminal Procedure, and the Code for the Implementation of Sentences. All this means that these days the Polish criminal justice system is quite different from what it was before 1989. However, the problem of the large prison population persists.

While discussing how the punitiveness of the criminal justice systems can be measured Tonry (2007b: 7–13) points to qualitative indicators of punitiveness, such as the use of capital punishment, the existence of mandatory minimum sentence laws and laws increasing sentence length, the use of pre-trial detention, the availability and use of prison alternatives, juveniles tried in adult courts and weakened procedural protection enactments. On many of those indicators Poland does not score too badly. This may change somewhat perceptions about the 'penal climate' in the country. Capital punishment was abolished formally by the new Penal Code in 1997, but this was preceded by an informal moratorium on executions that had been in force since 1988 (the year of the last execution), followed by a formal moratorium imposed by Parliament in 1995. The general statutory minimum prison sentence in Poland is one month. There are many offences in which this minimum is higher, and for felonies this minimum is generally three years (with some of the most serious felonies carrying higher statutory minima, such as eight years for murder, and 12 years for some aggravated forms of murder). But judges may disregard these minima by applying provisions on extraordinary mitigation of punishment (which is not uncommon). One should not forget also that apart from the possibility of imposing either a life sentence or 25 years' imprisonment for some of the most serious offences, the general upper limit for imprisonment is 15 years. Although, especially during the last decade, the Penal Code was amended several times in order to increase some statutory minima and maxima (for example in case of some types of murder, rape, and sexual offences against minors), judges still enjoy quite broad discretionary sentencing powers. Despite the fact that some research results show that Polish public prosecutors and judges are not necessarily very liberal in their views on sentencing policies, the average imprisonment sentence imposed by Polish courts tends more towards the minimum statutory limit than to the maximum (Melezini 2003). There is no significant problem of juveniles being sent for trial in adult courts. Polish juvenile law provides an almost purely care-oriented system for offenders under 17, and cases of juveniles being tried in adult courts are quite exceptional (Krajewski 2006).

What seems to constitute a problem is pre-trial detention. It is broadly considered to be used too often (which means that courts too readily accept the prosecutor's applications in such cases), and to last too long. Poland was notorious in recent years for losing a huge number of pre-trial detention related cases in the European Court of Human Rights (Morgenstern 2009). This results mainly from the fact that delay constitutes one of the most serious problems of the Polish criminal justice system. Several recent attempts to reform the functioning of the courts have failed to improve the situation. The fact that it takes a very long time from the initiation of investigation to the final valid conviction contributes significantly to the duration of preliminary detention during investigation and trial, and constitutes an important factor influencing the imprisonment rate. However, the impact of that factor may have diminished in recent years, as in 2010 detainees constituted 11.1 per cent of the prison population. But 10 years earlier, in the peak year of 2000, they constituted 31.2 per cent, and in the years 2001–07 this proportion on average amounted to 20 per cent of the prison population.

## III. POLAND AGAINST THE EUROPEAN BACKGROUND

It is important to underline that in respect to all the problems that we have mentioned above Poland is by no means an exception in Central and Eastern Europe. However, it may well be argued that it represents the most conspicuous example of regional problems. All countries of 'real socialism' were notorious for extraordinarily high imprisonment rates. As a matter of

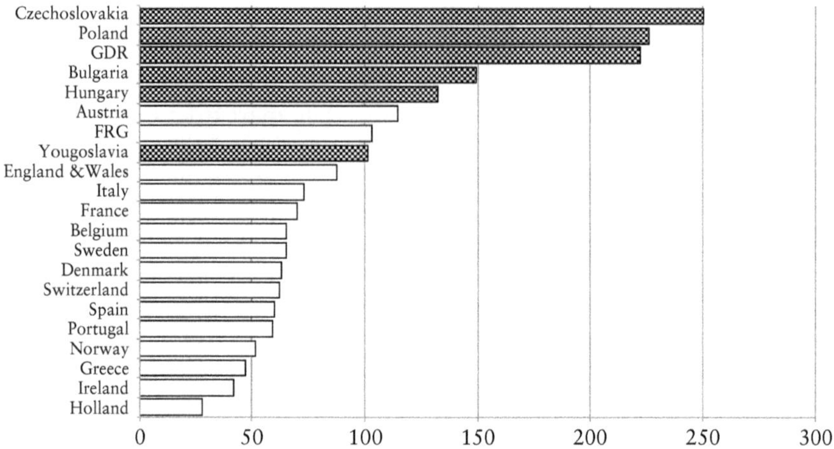


**Figure 14.5: Imprisonment rate in European countries (1983)**
Source: Jasiński (1986)

fact in 1983 no western country, including even the US, had an imprisonment rate above the level of the lowest from among the 'socialist brotherhood' (Figure 14.5).

Interestingly enough, despite the fact that during the 1990s not only Poland, but all the other countries of Central and Eastern Europe tried to reduce their prison populations, it did not change in any significant way the European ranking in that respect (Figure 14.6).

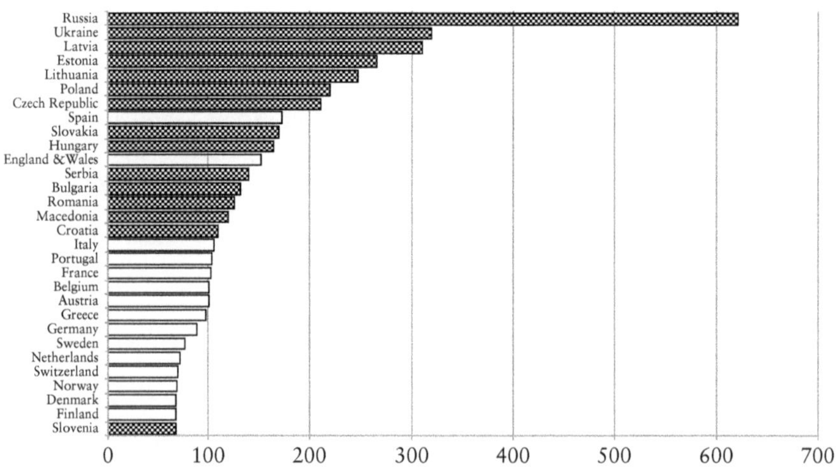


**Figure 14.6: Imprisonment rate in European countries 2009**
Source: Aebi and Delgrande (2011).

In 2009 the highest European imprisonment rates were found in broadly the same countries as in 1983. The ranking was slightly different only because Russia and the newly independent former Soviet republics started to publish data on imprisonment and immediately took the European lead. All this happened despite the fact that some western countries (notably, England and Wales, and Spain, but also Italy, Portugal and France) joined the club of high imprisonment rate countries (with rates exceeding 100 per 100,000 of population). Nevertheless, Europe remains in that respect quite visibly divided along the previous lines. This time it is not necessarily a political divide of the 'iron curtain', but a 'penal divide' between the two, to a large extent different, 'penal climates'. There is only one significant difference. The line dividing Europe has moved slightly eastwards, from the Elbe to the Oder, since those German federal states that constituted the former GDR adopted western sentencing policies.

This may be additionally illustrated by the data regarding tendencies in imprisonment rate in both parts of Europe during the last 20 years (Figure 14.7).

No western country matched developments in Poland. There were some increases in England and Wales, the Netherlands, Spain, and to a certain extent in Italy, but Polish growth was much more substantial, apart from the fact that imprisonment rate remained much higher. In most western countries imprisonment rates remained more or less stable, albeit with some fluctuations.

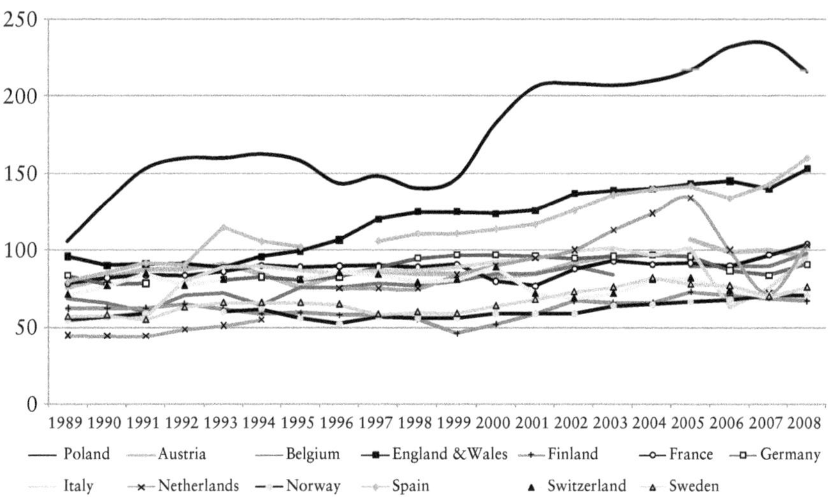


**Figure 14.7: Imprisonment rate in Poland as compared with Western Europe 1989–2008**

Source: Killias et al (2003); Aebi et al (2006); Aebi et al (2011).

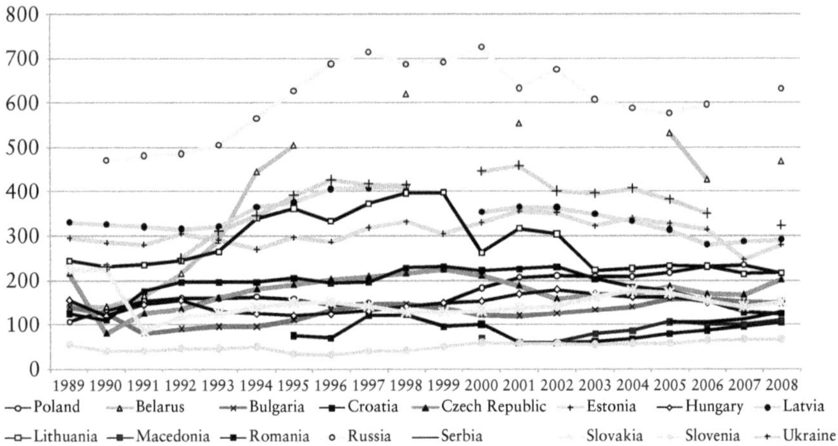


**Figure 14.8: Imprisonment rate in Poland as compared with Central and Eastern Europe 1989–2008**
Source: Killias et al (2003); Aebi et al (2006); Aebi et al (2011).

A comparison of Polish developments with other countries of the region, however, leads to substantially different results (Figure 14.8).

Here one can recognise four clusters. The first consists of Russia and Belarus, both notorious for their very high imprisonment rates. The second is constituted by the newly independent former Soviet republics, regardless of whether they belong to the EU (Estonia, Latvia, and Lithuania) or not (Ukraine). For most of the period they also had very high imprisonment rates, which were closer to Russian rates than to those in other parts of Europe. At the same time some of them, notably Estonia and Lithuania, made significant efforts to reduce their prison populations. Lithuania in particular had some lasting success in this area, as for several years its imprisonment rate has been closer to the Polish rate than to the Russian one. The third category is constituted by all other countries of the region (Bulgaria, Czech Republic, Hungary, Poland, Romania and Slovakia). There are some substantial differences between them (in 2008 the Czech Republic had an imprisonment rate of 208, while Romania's was 123). Nevertheless, none of those countries has currently, or had during the past decade, a rate below 100. The fourth cluster constitutes a more complicated case, having somewhat blurred borders. Undoubtedly Slovenia, as a champion of penal moderation in Europe over the past 20 years, belongs to this cluster. But it is interesting to note also that other countries of the former Yugoslavia (like Croatia, Macedonia and even Serbia) have for some time during the past decade had imprisonment rates lower than the rest of post-communist Europe, sometimes below the 100 mark. However, they were never as low as the Slovenian imprisonment rates, and in recent years it was possible to observe some growth tendency. This may mean that despite the turbulent recent history of the Western Balkans, the 'penal climate' there is still somewhat differently shaped by the heritage of the earlier Yugoslav model, rather than by the orthodoxy prevailing in the Soviet bloc proper.

It is interesting to note that most Central and Eastern European countries that have very high imprisonment rates do not score necessarily very high on the frequency of the use of imprisonment (Figure 14.9). In other words a high imprisonment rate usually does not coincide with a high proportion of immediate imprisonment sentences.

Amazingly enough, the 'champion' of frequent use of immediate imprisonment is Slovenia, the country that at the same time has Europe's lowest imprisonment rate! Other 'champions' with regard to the proportion of immediate prison sentences are Latvia, Lithuania and Romania. The first two have very high imprisonment rates, but the last one has not. Furthermore the Czech Republic, Poland and Slovakia, which have equally high imprisonment rates, impose this sanction with a frequency that is clearly below the European average of 22 per cent of immediate prison sentences in 2006. This confirms the assumption—indicated already in the case of Poland—that a crucial factor contributing to high imprisonment rates is not necessarily the frequency with which custodial sanctions are used, but their duration. Data regarding the average length of imposed unsuspended imprisonment in European countries, although available for a few countries only, seem to confirm this (Figure 14.10).

Most Central and Eastern European countries score very high on the length of time spent by inmates in prison. In Western Europe, with some notable exceptions (Spain and Portugal), this duration is usually shorter. The correlation with the imprisonment rate in these countries is not perfect, but both rankings are strikingly similar.

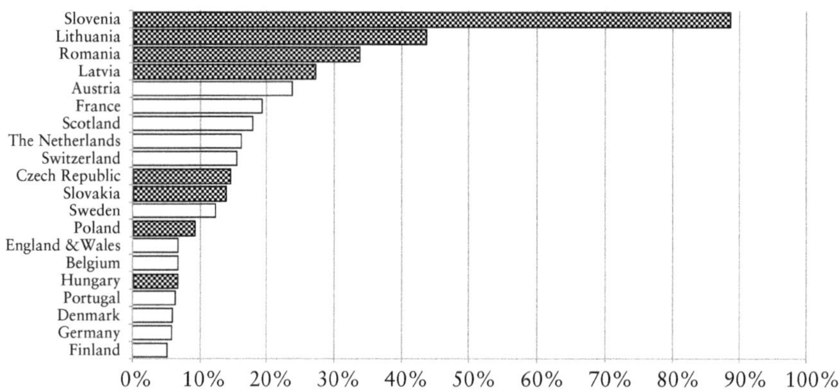


**Figure 14.9: Imprisonment in structure of sanctions in European countries 2006**
Source: Aebi et al (2011).

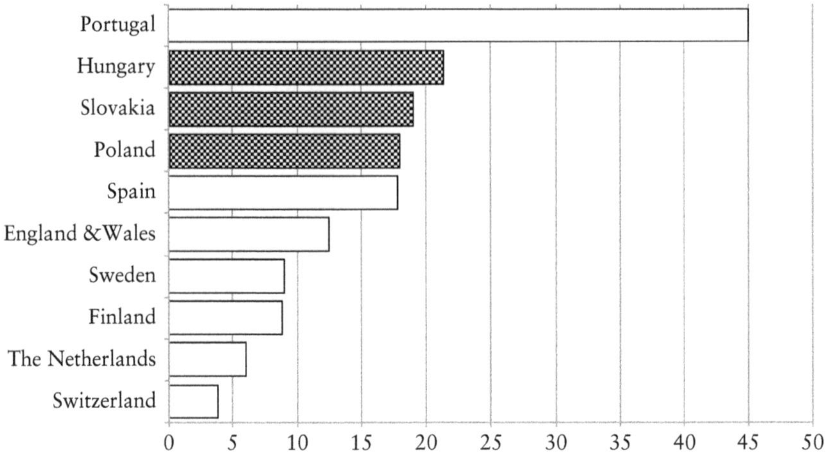


**Figure 14.10: Average length of imprisonment in months in European countries 2006**
Source: Aebi et al (2011).

A further set of data suggests that there is yet another important difference between Western and Central and Eastern European countries with regard to their sentencing patterns. It relates to the use of alternatives to imprisonment. Data on the frequency with which two other types of sanctions are used produce an almost absolutely unified ranking pattern of European countries. Let us first look at suspended custodial sanctions (Figure 14.11).

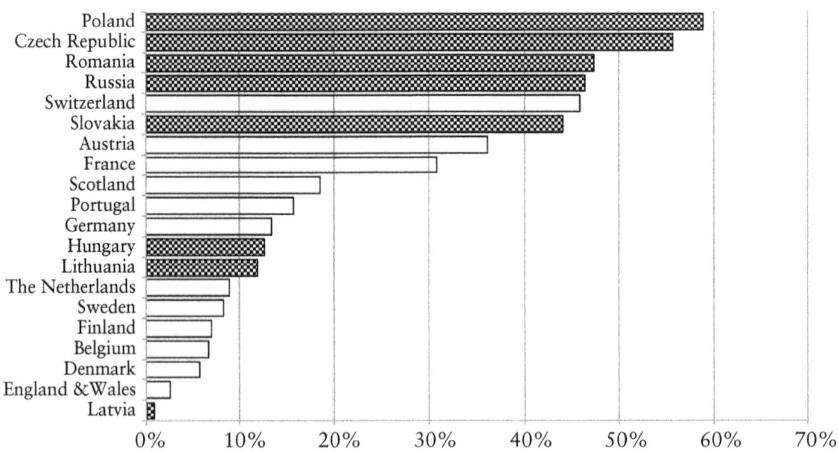


**Figure 14.11: Suspended sentence in structure of sanctions in European countries 2006**
Source: Aebi et al (2011).

It has already been mentioned that Poland very often, and in recent years increasingly so, uses suspended sentences. But this is characteristic not only for Poland. In all countries of the region this is the most often used type of sanction, constituting between 44 per cent (Slovakia) and 58.9 per cent (Poland) of all sanctions imposed. The European mean for 2006 in that respect amounted to 25 per cent, and only in Hungary, Latvia and Lithuania were the percentages below that. This indicates that most countries of the region, apart from putting their offenders behind bars for a rather long time (resulting in high imprisonment rates), have serious problems with alternatives to imprisonment, or more accurately, with their more sophisticated forms. This can be seen clearly in the situation regarding the use of fines (Figure 14.12).

The ranking here is the opposite of the situation regarding suspended sentences. Central and Eastern European Countries use this sanction very seldom, with Hungary and Lithuania being somewhat different, but still well below the European mean of 38 per cent in 2006.[2]

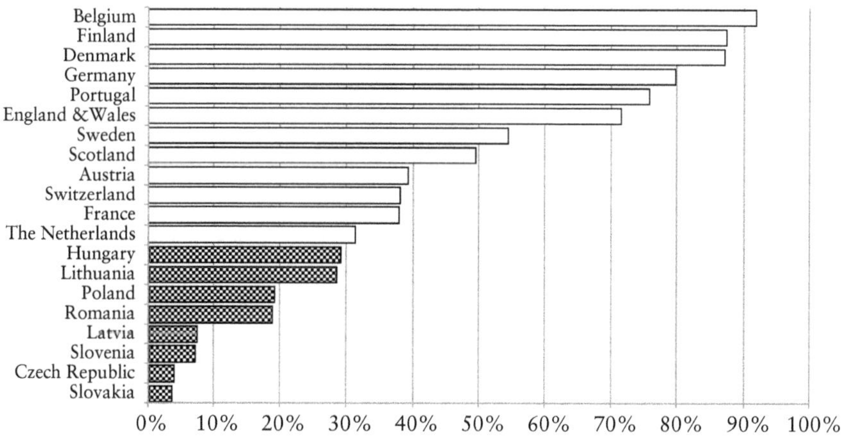


**Figure 14.12: Proportion of fines in structure of sanctions in European countries 2006**
Source: Aebi et al (2011).

[2] Of course the proportion of fines imposed in any country may differ, depending on the way sanctions for petty offences—dealt usually exclusively with fines—are registered. In some countries (Poland belongs to this category) such petty offences of administrative character, although tried by courts, are recorded in separate statistics, and not included in the 'regular' statistical data on sanctions imposed by the courts. This seems to be the case also in some other Central and Eastern European countries, and may distort the general picture. Nevertheless, it seems that the observation that countries of the region are reluctant to expand the use of fines into the area of offences other than petty ones remains valid.

## IV. EXPLAINING THE HIGH IMPRISONMENT RATE IN POLAND

As Tonry (2007a: vii) observes: 'penal policies and imprisonment patterns result from policy decisions. What we don't know is why particular policies emerge in particular places.' There is a large literature that attempts to explain differences in punishment patterns between various countries of the industrialised west. But little attention has been paid so far to the particularities of conditions in post-communist countries in transition, and their obviously persistent patterns of punitive sentencing policies and high imprisonment rates. There is no doubt that high imprisonment rates throughout Central and Eastern Europe during the communist era resulted from the totalitarian and authoritarian character of Soviet imposed communism. The problem is why, despite all the profound political, economic and social changes of the last 20 years, including accession to the EU, imprisonment rates that are excessively high by western standards persist throughout the region. In other words: what particular circumstances related to the region influence policy decisions in newly democratic states produce punitive crime control policies?

In an attempt to explain differences in crime control policies, Tonry provides a list of factors that may influence policies in this area (Tonry 2007b). First, he mentions several conditions and circumstances which he considers to be 'non-factors'. Those are: rising crime rates, rapid social and economic change, postmodernist angst, harsher public attitudes, cynical politicians, penal populism and ethnic tensions. The reason for them to be treated as 'non-factors' is that nowadays they are present throughout the world. But the problem may be whether they are present everywhere with the same intensity and have a similar impact. It seems that some of them may be of special significance in the countries of Central and Eastern Europe, like Poland. For instance, under the communist regime, Poland was certainly a 'low crime society'. Of course, this was probably somewhat artificial and resulted mainly from the earlier-mentioned fact that under communism the crime rate was usually manipulated by the authorities and kept artificially low for propagandistic reasons (Jasiński 1996). But the reality is that crime under communism was something quite different than it is nowadays. After 1989 it was not only the rate of registered offences that started to grow very quickly. The change of crime patterns in Poland and other countries of the region during the 1990s went well beyond what was experienced in the western world, not because of its scale but because of its rapidity. In the West, evolution towards 'high crime societies' started during the 1960s or even the 1950s, and it took a long time. This made gradual adjustment possible. Poland joined the club as a consequence of a more revolutionary change, which took place within a couple of years, and its impact has to be assessed against the background of the earlier low crime rates.[3] Additionally, one should not forget that after 1989, patterns of crime also changed profoundly. These included inter alia the appearance of previously unheard of forms of crime, such as serious violent offences with the use of firearms, organised crime, serious economic crime, drug offences etc.

The same applies to the scale of political, economic and social changes in the region. The change from authoritarian communism to liberal democracy, and from a centrally planned economy to a market economy, went further than any comparable social change during the second half of the twentieth century in the West. 'Real socialism' was able to provide social and physical security for most members of society. It is true that, as compared with the West, this security was guaranteed at an extremely low level. But still it was some sort of security. The fact that this was accompanied by a complete lack of freedom was not necessarily the greatest problem for all. The ascent of freedom was accompanied by the disappearance of this total, overwhelming security. This must have had a significant impact on all kinds of fears, well beyond postmodernist angst experienced in western societies, and may have resulted in much greater insecurities and harsher public attitudes towards social problems, including crime.

Finally, Poland and many other new democracies had no lasting democratic traditions, lacked an established system of political parties and had weak political elites. The middle class was also weak, and this could not be compensated for by the traditionally influential educated groups, or intelligentsia, who during the last 20 years have experienced a demise of their role in the region. Under such circumstances cynical politicians engaging in penal populism (or populism of many other sorts) seem to constitute a much bigger problem than elsewhere. It was probably only ethnic tensions that did not play such a significant role in the region.[4]

Tonry also provides a list of 'risk factors' that increase the probability of harsh penal policies developing in a country, as well as 'protective factors' (constituting usually opposites of risk factors), that decrease the probability of such developments (Tonry 2007b). It may be interesting to consider some of these factors in a more detailed way in the Polish and Central and Eastern European context. An important factor here seems to be the

[3] However, one has to remember that even now, after the period of substantial growth of crime, Central and Eastern European countries usually have registered offences rates below the average for Western Europe. This does not necessarily mean that there is less crime in those countries than in the West, however. Victimisation research results suggest that it is the rather lower reporting rate in Central and Eastern Europe which contributes to this (van Dijk et al 2007: 109–13).

[4] This was certainly the case at least in Poland, being ethnically a pretty homogeneous country, but not necessarily in Slovakia, Hungary and Bulgaria, where for example there are significant Roma minorities.

political culture of a country. Majoritarian democracies with a two-party political system (like in the US or UK) may contribute to rather harsher penal policies, while consensual democracies with multi-party political and corporatist systems (as exemplified primarily by Scandinavian countries) may encourage milder penal policies (Lappi-Seppälä 2011: 318–20).

It is not easy to answer questions regarding the character of political systems in Central and Eastern European countries: they are not characterised by a very clear political debate, due to the lack of an established system of political parties. But in principle all of them have multiparty political systems, which require political coalitions to form a government. As a matter of fact none of the Polish governments in the past 20 years was a single-party government; the current Hungarian government is probably the only single-party government in the region during the past 20 years. In principle this should encourage consensus-oriented political systems and a greater readiness for compromise, but it is not necessarily so. For example, the political system in Poland is dominated by various deep conflicts, one of them being the sharp conflict between post-communists and political parties which emerged from various dissident and opposition movements. This creates constant and very intensive political battles going far beyond traditional left-right controversies. In the region, accusations of treason levied at political opponents, the complete denial of political opponents' legitimacy and even their right to function in public life, are everyday occurrences rather than exceptions. Because of such extremely violent language being used in public discourse, compromise is quite uncommon and most political parties indicate in their programmes that they will not under any circumstances enter a coalition with a particular party or parties. This contributes to the political culture being highly conflictual. To what extent this high level of conflict influences penal policies is not clear. But at least in Poland public and parliamentary debates, even on trivial penal policy issues, seem to be especially heated, making rational discourse and rational decision-making much more difficult.[5]

As another risk factor, Tonry mentions politicisation of the criminal justice system, including the impact of election results on penal policy and decisions in individual cases (Tonry 2007b). There is no doubt that the criminal justice system in Poland (and other countries of the region) is supposed to be organised according to European standards and to be politically independent. Both public prosecutors and judges are career professionals appointed on merit by means of special selection procedures that are

[5] A good example may constitute the debate in the Polish parliament in April 2011 on some modest changes in the drug legislation in the direction of a very limited depenalisation of personal drug possession. During the parliamentary debate the Minister of Justice was accused by a former Deputy Minister of Justice from the largest opposition party of supporting the draft bill because of his involvement in the drug mafia.

protected from direct political influence. This should constitute one of the most important safeguards not only against criminal justice-related abuses, but also against administrative excesses, as career professionals are expected to define their roles primarily in terms of specific expertise isolated from emotions surrounding crime. But realities may be somewhat different. Under the communist system criminal justice was considered to be something of special importance for the communist party. For this reason the selection of cadres took place primarily according to one criterion: political loyalty. This applied first of all to public prosecutors, but to a lesser extent to judges, who even at that time were nominally independent. Moreover, the public prosecution system was organised according to Soviet principles. It was rigidly hierarchical and totally controlled by the communist party. This created a particularly docile mentality based on constantly attempting to second-guess the wishes of the superiors. After 1989 in Poland there was no general purge of the public prosecution system (the same applied to the judiciary). Only those prosecutors (but not judges), who behaved in an especially flagrant way (usually meaning persecuting dissidents) were dismissed. This meant that the old 'professional ideology' was largely retained and came to be transmitted to the younger generation. An additional problem was that since 1989 the Minister of Justice was at the same time Public Prosecutor General. This resulted in an enormous politicisation of the entire public prosecution system. Under these circumstances, the old prosecutorial mentality from communist times proved to be extremely useful. Situations in which the Minister of Justice intervened in individual cases or instructed prosecutors even at the lowest level were 'normal'. Especially during the years 2005 to 2007, when the Law and Justice Party, headed by the Kaczyński twins, was in power, the public prosecution system functioned as a political tool in the hands of the government. Only recently, in an attempt to isolate the public prosecution system from direct political interference, was it separated from the Ministry of Justice (Krajewski 2012).

One of the crucial factors influencing crime control policies may be the mass media. Recent experience in Europe indicates that very similar offences may be reported in a completely different way, which may have a crucial impact on social reactions and reactions by the criminal justice system (Green 2008). The media in countries such as Poland underwent an enormous change, from the 'good news media' they were before 1989 to the 'bad news media' they are now (Los 2002). Privatisation and challenges resulting from the market economy changed them enormously. It is also very problematic that the public media are often very politicised and after every election come under the control of the winning political party. This makes good, independent journalism rather rare, and there is no good counterbalance to low-quality private media. Under such circumstances incompetent and sensationalist reporting on crime predominates. And this must have an impact on the public (see eg Chiricos et al 1997). This also makes life very difficult, even for those politicians who are competent in matters of criminal justice and are reform-minded. As they are at the same time constantly watching public opinion polls, in problematic situations they prefer to avoid any controversial decisions, because they fear being attacked in the media. Moreover, in many situations they tend to support senseless solutions only because they think that in that way they may score a few points with the media and the public.[6]

Finally it is necessary to mention one more risk factor of enormous importance, namely populist conceptions of democracy. They are very common these days throughout the world, and have a significant impact on the criminal justice system (Pratt 2007). It is also true that current penal developments cannot be explained exclusively by the fact that politicians exploit crime issues for electoral purposes (Daems 2008: 97–98). But again, it seems that the problem may be of special importance in Central and Eastern Europe. This is due to a number of circumstances. The main one is again the lack of an established system of political parties that have a longer tradition and the absence of clear electoral views among the population. As a consequence the electoral behaviour of voters is very unstable and many people often change the parties for which they vote. Because of this, political campaigns are often reduced to 'beauty contests', with demagoguery as the prevalent electoral strategy. The lack of political sophistication of the population means also that it is very difficult to run campaigns based exclusively on the merits. Campaigns and political programmes centre around emotional issues and symbols, and constitute auctions in populist ideas. Under such circumstances any rational public discourse on the criminal justice system and crime control policies—but also any other policy issue—is usually extremely difficult, even impossible. For example in Poland, the unusual political career of the Law and Justice Party of the Kaczyński twins, who for several years remained completely marginalised politically, began in 1999 when the late president Lech Kaczyński became Minister of Justice. He immediately started a vigorous public 'law and order' campaign on a scale previously unknown, and in that way won huge public support. He also started to attempt to implement various ideas

[6] A good example of such an approach is the public reaction of Poland's current prime minister, Donald Tusk, on two different occasions regarding problematic criminal phenomena. The first one in 2009 regarded the case of a sexual offender who for many years raped his daughter and had two children with her. As this case produced—understandably—public outrage, the prime minister publicly denied that the perpetrator was a human being, and spoke in favour of 'castration' of such offenders. In 2010, responding to media hysteria, he proposed tough measures against shops selling so-called 'legal highs', which resulted in immediate closure of all of them. 'Legal highs' no doubt had become a serious problem in Poland, but the proposed radical measures were of dubious legal character, and recently were put into question by the administrative courts.

about penal policies, usually based on an absolutely uncritical view of the American experience. There is no doubt that the 'punitive turn' in Poland and the growth of the imprisonment rate coincided with his time in office as a Minister of Justice. But it proved also to be extremely effective for electoral purposes. For many years, Law and Justice remained a single-issue party, a party that was 'tough on crime'. This constituted a crucial factor in its electoral success in 2005.

According to Tonry, one of the important protective factors against excess in penal policies may be the role and influence of experts (Tonry 2007b). Isolation of law-making and law enforcement—at least to a certain extent—from emotions surrounding political debates and the crucial role played during such debates by independent experts, usually provides important protection against penal populism's impact on policy decisions. Indeed, it was probably an important factor shaping penal reform in Central and Eastern Europe, especially in Poland, during the 1990s and contributing to a somewhat milder 'penal climate' at that time. The change of situation in that respect at the beginning of the past decade could contribute decisively to the onset of the 'punitive turn'. Criminal justice reforms during the 1990s were visibly dominated by academic experts. Although even at that time, there was specific 'crime talk' in the media and in the public discourse, it was of a different character to that during the recent decade. New penal codes were drafted almost exclusively by experts, both from academia and practice. Politicians had relatively little say in that process. Also the media were not greatly interested. This meant that new penal legislation based on liberal principles was adopted in a relatively consensual way. It was only after it had entered into force that the media and some politicians 'realised' that it had a 'liberal and lenient' character, leading to an unprecedented campaign of accusations and a flood of proposals to amend it. Since that time experts, especially academic ones, have lost almost all influence over legislation in the area of criminal justice. During the Law and Justice government of 2005–07, most such experts were in fact completely excluded from any participation in the legislative process. Most legislative projects originated from political circles or obscure internal experts in the Ministry of Justice, and very often the only possible reaction of academics to them was the raising of a sceptical eyebrow.

It seems that many of the factors considered by Tonry to be significant for criminal policy decisions find confirmation in other research results (Lappi-Seppälä 2008; 2011). Such variables as political culture, welfare and trust, as well as public sentiments, fears and attitudes prevailing in a country, correlate quite strongly with punitiveness of the criminal justice system as measured by imprisonment rates. Unfortunately not all the tools for measuring these correlations are available for Central and Eastern European countries. For example, according to Lappi-Seppälä there is generally a high correlation between the imprisonment rate and variables characterising the political system such as the consensus-conflict index or corporatism index. But those indexes are not available for Central and Eastern European countries. For other variables, however, there seem to be clear patterns, which may explain the high imprisonment rates in Central and Eastern Europe. For example, most countries of the region score quite badly on income distribution fairness, as measured by the GINI index, and on the level of social protection as measured by indicators of public expenditure on welfare, which correlate strongly with imprisonment rates (Lappi-Seppälä 2008: 351–59). This shows that the relatively successful market reforms in some of those countries—Poland being one such example—were based on neoliberal schemes and were not accompanied by the development of effective protection for the 'losers' in the transformation process. This had profound social consequences, including a negative impact on penal policies.

These features have been accompanied by remarkably low scores for the countries of the region—again, especially Poland—on measures of trust and social capital, such as trust in people, trust in the police, or general trust in justice (Lappi-Seppälä 2011: 311–16). This has obvious consequences for social solidarity, collective responsibility and individualism. It may be a paradox, but in this context it is interesting to note that 'Solidarity' (*Solidarność*), the independent trade union created in 1980 in Gdańsk, was *the* dominant concept in Poland in the past 30 years. It became a symbol of opposition against Soviet domination and communist rule. It was supposed also to symbolise social cohesiveness and unity. It is true that in nineteenth-century Polish society, as in many other nations that had been under foreign rule for a long time, particular forms of social cohesiveness and social bonds were created that were necessary for survival under such circumstances. In Poland this included a specific form of staunch but very conservative Catholicism. In consequence, Polish society has been characterised until today by relatively strong family bonds and various other forms of local solidarity. On the other hand, these traditional social relations were severely damaged by 45 years of communist rule. Additionally, 20 years of transformation with strong liberal overtones indubitably contributed to increased atomisation and individualism, especially among the younger generation. Certainly, countries of the region are not as individualistic as most Anglo-Saxon countries are. But it may be true that they are heading in a similar direction.

Political legitimacy is another complicated factor among those analysed by Lappi-Seppälä. It is certainly true that communist authorities lacked political legitimacy among the vast majority of the population. And this may have been one of the reasons they implemented punitive crime control policies, which were not intended primarily to control crime but, first and foremost, were designed to increase the legitimacy of the authorities among the wider population. This illustrates clearly the proposition shared by Nietzsche and Durkheim that 'strong political regimes have no need to rely upon intensely punitive sanctions' (Garland 1996: 445). But it is equally true that societies of the region, which were often dominated by foreign powers and foreign states, generally do not fully trust authority of any kind. This may be especially true in Poland, which is often considered to be a pretty unruly society. Are current political regimes in the region equally weak, and do they lack legitimacy to such an extent that they have to resort to a similar type of policies? Here we may face a paradox. Post-communist and liberal parties in Poland have never indulged in very explicit 'law and order' rhetoric. It was the traditional national-catholic right that has done so, campaigning on tough crime control policies. At the same time this traditional right has always sought to deny any political legitimacy to post-communists and liberals, even if they were democratically elected. Their eventual electoral successes were always blamed on a misguided electorate acting under duress and on the consequences of a 'false consciousness'. Under this onslaught, left-wing, liberal political options, including a liberal approach to crime control, may have lost a substantial part of their legitimacy with the electorate.

Finally, it is necessary to mention that disintegration of social welfare, social trust, and social solidarity in Central and Eastern Europe is usually accompanied by strong feelings of insecurity, high punitivity scores and low social tolerance (Krajewski 2009), which again correlate usually with punitive crime control policies. In sum, it seems that the transformation process in Central and Eastern Europe is accompanied by a very conspicuous presence of several factors associated with punitive crime control policies. The question remains whether this situation constitutes an inheritance of the past, including the communist one, or whether it is the product of the transformation process, or both. Nevertheless, it seems that the post-communist condition in Central and Eastern Europe is somewhat different from the postmodern condition in the West, and many problems that are present in contemporary societies are aggravated in the region by specific conditions resulting from rapid transformation.

This may be well illustrated by the example of another explanatory model of factors influencing punitiveness of crime control policies (see Cavadino and Dignan 2006). They relate penal tendencies, including high imprisonment rates, to political economy. According to their typology it is the neo-liberal type of society, exemplified by countries such as the US, England and Wales, New Zealand or South Africa, which tends to produce very high imprisonment rates. Does it make any sense to attempt to apply this typology to countries like Poland? Or to formulate it differently, does it mean that high imprisonment rates in Central and Eastern Europe may be connected somehow to the neo-liberal type of social and economic order prevailing in the region? Certainly, the liberal or neo-liberal free market ideology had a significant impact on transition processes, at least in some of the Central and Eastern European countries. Poland is certainly one of them. This resulted in huge income differences in formerly egalitarian societies, which in addition had earlier been used to an egalitarian ideology. It resulted also in growing individualism and atomisation of society. Combined with the collapse and disintegration of the generous (although extremely wasteful) communist welfare system and withdrawal of the state from many areas of social policy, the result was a tendency for various forms of social exclusion to grow. The consequence was the creation of a relatively large group of losers who did not benefit from the transformation process—people excluded from the benefits of the transformation enjoyed by other parts of the population. This group has been the main target of the Polish right-wing parties in recent years. What makes this hugely paradoxical is that the political right is very conservative in ideological terms, but quite 'socialist' and egalitarian in terms of economic and social policies. At the same time it indulges constantly in 'tough on crime' rhetoric. It is nominally the 'post-communist left' that is much more liberal and free market oriented, and at the same time more reasonable on crime issues.

Additionally, a very important factor, at least in Poland, is that the political right in Poland often seems to adore absolutely uncritically everything American, including American penal policies. This creates a specific ideological mixture that is difficult to categorise clearly. It may be true that Poland has a lot in common with the neo-liberal social model and its consequences for penal policies. Consequently, it may be true that specific factors contributing to the high imprisonment rate under communism were very quickly—after a brief transitional period—substituted with the new ones, this time related to a neo-liberal ideology. But one has to be cautious with such analogies. Neither Poland nor other countries of the region may be referred to as neo-liberal societies in the same mould as the US. This would be a great exaggeration, even if some consequences of the economic and social transition in the region produced effects similar to the de-industrialisation experienced in the UK under Margaret Thatcher. One has to be also very cautious about treating Poland or other countries of the region as examples of 'penal states' (Wacquant 2009), where harsh criminal justice constitutes a substitute for social justice. It seems that Cavadino's and Dignan's typology cannot and should not be applied directly to Central and Eastern Europe. It should be supplemented with an additional type: post-communist societies in transition that have many specific features of their own that contribute to harsh criminal justice systems and high imprisonment rates.

## VI. CONCLUSION

Penal developments in developed countries over the last 20 years are often referred to as a 'punitive turn' (Pratt 2007) or the 'new punitiveness' (Pratt et al 2005). The question is to what extent explanations of this phenomenon provided in the literature may apply to Poland and other countries of Central and Eastern Europe, which these days usually have more punitive crime control policies than the West. Some of the contemporary features of these societies discussed above may explain part of the story, as certain factors made responsible for punitive crime control policies may be present in the region with special intensity. The question is whether there are some other features that may provide additional explanations for the phenomenon of high imprisonment rates? In other words, the question is whether what is going on in the region may be explained primarily as 'new punitiveness' stimulated by similar factors to those in the West, which are only aggravated by certain local particularities?

The answer to this question depends on one crucial issue. Penal developments in western countries since the Second World War are often referred to as a crisis of penal modernism (Garland 2001: 53–73). Penal modernism was characterised by moderate penal policies implemented in the US and Western Europe during the 1950s and 1960s, involving inclusive methods of crime control based on strategies such as rehabilitation of offenders, decarceration, and the search for alternatives to imprisonment. It resulted in penal policies becoming less punitive and more closely connected to social welfare policies. What happened during the last 20–30 years, and referred to as 'punitive turn', is the abandonment of such an approach and a return to repression-based, exclusionary crime control policies. Of course, it is true that the main examples of such policies are to be found in the US. And it is equally true that generalisations of certain (often anecdotal) evidence confirming such developments in countries like the US, the UK, Australia and New Zealand are to be treated with due caution. The tendency to treat transformations in the penal systems of the US or the UK as if they were paradigmatic of western systems as a whole is certainly wrong (Daems 2008: 47). The same applies to claims that also in Europe the welfare state is being substituted by a penal state. But this does not change the fact that also in continental Europe some increases in the punitivity of criminal justice systems can be observed in recent years.

To what extent have similar developments taken place also in Central and Eastern Europe? In particular, to what extent was penal modernism a factor contributing to crime control policies in these countries after the Second World War? The answer seems to be rather negative. Officially the Soviet Union and the other countries of 'real socialism' were supposed to be ideal welfare states, 'workers' paradises'. Under such circumstances, there was no place for acceptance of the thesis that crime has social roots, which constituted the fundament of modern penality (see Radzinowicz and King 1977: 69). As a consequence, countries of Central and Eastern Europe governed by communists and dominated by the Soviet Union, were for several years effectively cut off from the mainstream of penological discourse of the post-war period, with significant consequences for their penal law and criminal justice systems. Even if certain modern penological ideas were known and discussed, and there were some attempts to implement them in practice, political realities were such that criminal justice systems in the region were governed primarily by punitive Soviet orthodoxy. Offenders were treated simply as bad people deserving harsh punishment. This was an approach equivalent to that underlying the contemporary 'punitive turn' and the phenomenon of the penal state. As a matter of fact, countries of 'real socialism', and particularly the Soviet Union with its Gulags, may be considered to be model 'penal states' based on widespread repression not only of political dissent but also of ordinary crime.

The collapse of the communist system created expectations that this would change. Unfortunately, such did not prove to be the case. Despite attempts to change the situation, which under better conditions prevailing during the 1990s achieved some results, Poland, like other countries of the region, seems somehow to remain confined to the old-style model of punitive crime control policies. But this is hardly a punitive turn, or a new punitiveness resulting from the ascent of neo-liberal ideology. It is primarily an inheritance of the communist way of thinking about criminal justice, prevalent also among politicians who otherwise reject everything even slightly connected to communism. Zimring et al (2001) note that 'public attitudes are both a cause and an effect of the politics of criminal justice' (ibid: 161). Some 45 years of punitive communist crime control have decisively influenced attitudes and ideas about crime control that are still prevalent today among the population and the ruling elites. This is consistent with Garland's claim that 'penal institutions are thus "cause" as well as "effect" with regard to culture' (Garland 1990: 249). In other words, communist penal practices created a specific 'culture of control' that seems to have survived well beyond the communist system and still makes a crucial contribution to current crime control policies. These practices may be influenced and reinforced by many other factors. But the main reason for punitive crime control policies in Poland and other countries of Central and Eastern Europe seems to be a continuation of the old-style punitiveness inherited from the communist past, and not a 'new punitiveness' that is an expression of a postmodern penality.

## REFERENCES

Aebi, MF and Delgrande, N (2011) *Council of Europe Annual Penal Statistics—SPACE I Survey 2009* (Strasbourg, Council of Europe).

Aebi, MF, Aromaa, K, Aubusson de Cavarlay, B, Barclay, G, Gruszczyńska, B, von Hofer, H, Hysi, V, Jehle, J-M, Killias, M, Smit, P and Tavares, C (2006) *European Sourcebook of Crime and Criminal Justice Statistics—2006*, 3rd edn (The Hague, Boom Juridische uitgevers).

Aebi, MF, Aubusson de Cavarlay, B, Barclay, G, Gruszczyñska, B, Harrendorf, S, Heiskanen, M, Hysi, V, Jaquier, V, Jehle, J-M, Killias, M, Shostko, O, Smit, P and Þórisdóttir, R (2011) *European Sourcebook of Crime and Criminal Justice Statistics—2010*, 4th edn (The Hague, Boom Juridische uitgevers).

Cavadino, M and Dignan, J (2006) *Penal Systems. A Comparative Approach* (London, Sage).

Chiricos, T, Eschholz, S and Gertz, M (1997) 'Crime, news and fear of crime: Towards an identification of audience effects', *Social Problems*, 44, 342–57.

Daems, T (2008) *Making Sense of Penal Change* (Oxford, Oxford University Press).

Garland, D (1990) *Punishment and Modern Society. A Study in Social Theory* (Oxford, Oxford University Press).

—— (1996) 'The Limits of the Sovereign State. Strategies of Crime Control in Contemporary Society', *British Journal of Criminology*, 36, 445–71.

—— (2000) 'The Culture of High Crime Societies', *British Journal of Criminology*, 40, 347–75.

—— (2001) *The Culture of Control. Crime and Social Order in Contemporary Society* (Oxford, Oxford University Press).

Green, D (2008) *When Children Kill Children: Penal Populism and Political Culture* (Oxford, Oxford University Press).

Greenberg, DF (1980) 'Penal Sanctions in Poland: A Test of Alternative Models', *Social Problems*, 28, 194–204.

Jasiński, J (1984) 'Punitiveness of Penal Systems' (Polish) *Państwo i Prawo (State and Law)*, 39(6), 52–66.

—— (1995) 'Prison System and Prisoners', in J Jasiński and A Siemaszko (eds), *Crime Control in Poland. Polish Report for the Ninth United Nations Congress on the Prevention of Crime and the Treatment of Offenders* (Warsaw, Oficyna Wydawnicza).

—— (1996) 'Crime in Central and East European Countries', *European Journal on Criminal Policy and Research*, 5, 40–50.

Killias, M, Barclay, G, Smit, P, Aebi MF, Tavares, C, Aubusson de Cavarlay, B, Jehle, J-M, von Hofer, H, Gruszczyńska, B, Hysi, V and Aromaa, K (2003) *European Sourcebook of Crime and Criminal Justice Statistics—2003*, 2nd edn (The Hague, Boom Juridische uitgevers).

Krajewski, K (2004) 'Crime and Criminal Justice in Poland', *European Journal of Criminology*, 1, 377–407.

—— (2006) 'The Juvenile Justice System in Poland', in EL Jensen and J Jepsen (eds) *Juvenile Law Violators, Human Rights, and the Development of New Juvenile Justice Systems* (Oxford, Hart Publishing).

—— (2009) 'Punitive Attitudes in Poland—The Development in the Last Years', *European Journal on Criminal Policy and Research*, 15, 103–20.

Krajewski, K (2012) 'Prosecution and Prosecutors in Poland: In Quest of Independence', in M Tonry (ed) *Prosecutors and Politics. A Comparative Perspective. Crime and Justice. A Review of Research (Volume 41)* (Chicago, University of Chicago Press).

Lappi-Seppälä, T (2008) 'Trust, Welfare, and Political Culture: Explaining Differences in National Penal Policies', in M Tonry (ed), *Crime and Justice. A Review of Research (Volume 37)* (Chicago, University of Chicago Press).

—— (2011) 'Explaining Imprisonment in Europe', *European Journal of Criminology*, 8, 303–28.

Los, M (2002) 'Post-communist fear of crime and the commercialization of security', *Theoretical Criminology*, 6, 165–88.

Melezini, D (2003) *Punitivity of the Criminal Justice System in Poland in 20th Century* (Polish) (Białystok, Temida2).

Morgenstern, C (2009) 'Poland', in A van Kalmthout, MM Knapen and C Morgenstern (eds), *Pre-trial Detention in the European Union* (Nijmegen, Wolf Legal Publishers).

Pratt, J (2007) *Penal Populism* (London, Routledge).

Pratt, J, Brown, D, Brown, M, Hallsworth, S and Morrison, W (eds) (2005) *The New Punitiveness. Trends, theories, perspectives* (Cullompton, Willan Publishing).

Radzinowicz, L and King, J (1977) *The Growth of Crime. The International Experience* (New York, Basic Books).

Stańdo-Kawecka, B and Krajewski, K (2010) 'Polen', in F Dünkel, T Lappi-Seppälä, C Morgenstern and D van Zyl Smit (eds), *Kriminalität, Kriminalpolitik, strafrechtliche Sanktionspraxis und Gefangenenraten im europäischen Vergleich* (Mönchengladbach, Forum Verlag Godesberg).

Tonry, M (2007a) 'Preface', in M Tonry (ed), *Crime, Punishment and Politics in Comparative Perspective. Crime and Justice. A Review of Research (Volume 36)* (Chicago, University of Chicago Press).

—— (2007b) 'Determinants of Penal Policies', in M Tonry (ed), *Crime, Punishment and Politics in Comparative Perspective. Crime and Justice. A Review of Research (Volume 36)* (Chicago, University of Chicago Press).

Tournier, PV (2001) *Council of Europe Annual Penal Statistics—SPACE I. Survey 2000* (Strasbourg, Council of Europe).

van Dijk, J, van Kesteren, J and Smit, P (2007) *Criminal Victimization in International Perspective. Key findings from the 2004–2005 ICVS and EU ICS* (The Hague, Boom Juridische uitgevers).

van Zyl Smit, D and Snacken, S (2009) *Principles of European Prison Law and Policy* (Oxford, Oxford University Press).

Wacquant, L (2009) *Punishing the Poor. The Neoliberal Government of Social Insecurity* (Durham, Duke University Press).

Zimring, FE, Hawkins, G and Kamin, S (2001) *Punishment and Democracy. Three Strikes and You're Out in California* (New York, Oxford University Press).

# 15

# *Reversing the Punitive Turn: The Case of the Netherlands*

RENÉ VAN SWAANINGEN

## I. INTRODUCTION

This chapter is a search for answers to a phenomenon that we do not yet fully understand. In the international penological literature of the 1970s and 1980s, the Netherlands was often put forward as an archetypical non-punitive country, for it demonstrated how a highly industrialised and densely populated society could do with very little prisons. But, by that time a process of recarceration, involving an unprecedented growth of the Dutch prison system, had already started. When David Downes and I analysed this period of penal expansionism and new punitiveness for our chapter in a book on *Crime and Justice in the Netherlands*, we were not optimistic about the future. We even gave our chapter 'The Road to Dystopia?' as a title—although we did put a question mark behind that rather apocalyptic title (Downes and van Swaaningen 2007). In one of our conversations Downes argued: 'Once a punitive turn is taken, there is hardly ever a way back.' But all of a sudden, in 2005, the Dutch prison population did start to decrease again. And, moreover, there are no clear indications why. In fact, the political developments of the early 2000s, with a strong rise of the neo-nationalist populist Right—for whom 'getting tough' in the fight against crime was a key issue in the electoral campaigns—as one of the clearest examples, plead completely against it.

In my search for reasons for the declining imprisonment rates, I decided to trace back the reasons that have been identified earlier as the major motors behind penal expansionism and punitiveness, and then have a look at what happened to these factors after 2005. In the debate on punitiveness, imprisonment rates play an important role. In this chapter, I will argue that we need a more socio-cultural approach to punitiveness and, indeed, to *non*-punitiveness. We must understand their characteristics and the factors that are commonly used to explain them if we are to answer the question whether punitive turns can be reversed. The role expert knowledge plays in policy debates and the *kind* of expertise that is used receives special attention in this respect. Although the Dutch case is taken as an example here, it is analysed from an international comparative perspective. First, we will deal with the debate on punitiveness. Then we will move on to more empirical questions about the punitive turn of 1975–2005 and of the declining prison population after 2005. We will deal both with factors that are internal to the penal system and with external, societal factors. Lastly, we will argue in more normative terms about punitiveness: what is wrong with it anyway, and what is the most convincing argument to reverse the punitive turn?

## II. THE DEBATE ON PUNITIVENESS

The most commonly used indicator of punitiveness is the imprisonment rate. From this perspective, the United States of America currently is, despite a slight decline over the last two years, still by far the most punitive country in the world, with 730 detainees per 100,000 inhabitants in 2010. If we exclude some very small countries in the Caribbean and some African countries with figures that are too unreliable, it is followed by the Russian Federation, with 534 prisoners per 100,000.[1] In Europe, Russia and the other ex-Soviet states have the highest prison populations per 100,000 inhabitants (ranging from 439 to 220), followed by a number of ex-Warsaw Pact countries (from 230 to 150). In Western Europe, England and Wales (154), Spain (152) and Scotland (151) stand out. Analyses of the 'penal nightmare' in the United States in particular offer quite convincing support for the idea that high imprisonment rates are indeed a reasonably good indicator of punitiveness (Garland 2001).

But, is the opposite also true? Are low imprisonment rates an indicator of non-punitiveness? The world's lowest imprisonment rates are found in countries as different as Liechtenstein (19), Commoros (19), Timor Leste (20), the Faroe Islands (23) and Congo Brazzaville (26). These countries are either very small, rather isolated islands or they are basically failed states that are too poor and disorganised to build any prisons. Low imprisonment rates are thus not really the best indicators of non-punitiveness. In Europe, the lowest rates are also found in very small and isolated countries. Leaving these aside (eg Andorra, Iceland, Liechtenstein or Monaco), and countries where low imprisonment rates are unlikely to reflect a peaceful society (such

[1] The imprisonment rates mentioned in this chapter are all derived from the World Prison Brief, available online at www.prisonstudies.org/info/worldbrief, accessed on 15 August 2012. They were downloaded in December 2011. More detailed figures about the Dutch prison system are accounted for separately.

as Bosnia or Kosovo, that suffered from civil wars relatively recently), the lowest rates are found in Finland (59), Slovenia (64) and Norway (73).

With its 58 prisoners per 100,000 inhabitants, Japan is often presented as a non-punitive country as well. It is striking that analyses of some large countries with still lower rates, such as India (31), are by and large absent in the international penological literature. Japan is put forward because it is, like the Netherlands once was, a highly industrialised and densely populated country that nonetheless maintains relatively low imprisonment rates. Yet, Japan's 'punitiveness score' is quite high: similar to that of the United Kingdom, that has a much higher imprisonment rate (Cavadino and Dignan 2006: 30). Moreover, Japan's penal system can be characterised as an 'iron fist in a velvet glove', because the low imprisonment rates coincide with harsh prison conditions and intensive and tight, often quite punitive social control outside prison walls (Cavadino and Dignan 2006: 171; Miyazawa 2008).

Such odd statistical data have led Roger Matthews (2005) to conclude that the whole notion of punitiveness is a myth. First because, Matthews argues, the concept is so badly defined that we can hardly grasp what it actually entails. Second, it gives a too one-dimensional picture of penal developments; in reality there are always oppositional currents—non-punitive reactions to crime and 'improvements' within the penal system occur at the same time. Third, Matthews argues, the public concern about crime and 'lenient sanctioning' is in the literature on punitiveness too easily dismissed as 'penal populism', whereas the professional elites are nearly always seen to be right. These arguments certainly make some sense, but Matthews' conclusion that imprisonment rates are thus not a good indicator of punitiveness seems a bit bold.

With respect to the first objection, Matthews disregards literature on the empirical operationalisation of punitiveness—eg in the International Crime Victims Survey (ICVS) or the works of the Finnish criminologist Tapio Lappi Seppälä (2006, 2008). With respect to Matthews' second point, we can just as easily argue that exceptions indeed *confirm* the rule. Of course penal developments never go in just one direction, but with hindsight we can always distinguish main currents from the exceptions. Although it may be true, as Matthews argues, that a punitive public opinion is all too often discarded in penology, his third point leaves the fact untouched that there is quite some empirical support for the idea that emotions play a larger role in the political arena. Moreover, there is ample evidence that these political actors conceptualise public opinion rather loosely and creatively, and *think* 'the public' demands tougher sentencing, whereas in reality the population is much more nuanced (eg Roberts 2003; Ruiter et al 2011). But, most of all, Matthews' thesis disregards the conclusion of quantitative criminologists like Lappi Seppälä (2008) that imprisonment rates mostly correlate *quite well* with other indicators of punitiveness, such as the trust in fellow-citizens and in government, the amount of welfare expenditure, whether a country has a multi-party consensual political system or a polarised two-party system, whether there is an independent legal system or an elected judiciary, whether or not well-trained professionals are operating the criminal justice system and, last but not least, whether there is balanced media reporting or rather a sensationalist press.

If we speak about 'punitiveness' there is obviously much more at stake than just figures. Countries that apply torture or capital punishment may have low imprisonment rates, but can hardly be called 'non-punitive'. Therefore we need to deal with punitiveness as a socio-cultural phenomenon. Punitiveness entails both quantitative and qualitative elements (*cf* Pratt et al 2005). In a socio-cultural sense, we can speak of a punitive penal system if, for example, imprisonment is seen as the obvious, proper reaction to crime, the expressive value of punishment is stressed ('getting tough'), mere deprivation of liberty is seen as insufficient punishment and life in prison needs to be made extra-unpleasant ('no frills'), and if ideals of rehabilitation are replaced by a focus on (selective) incapacitation.

Turning these aspects of punitiveness around would imply that non-punitiveness includes attempts to bring imprisonment rates down, improve the quality of the penal system, reaffirm imprisonment as a 'last resort' and non-custodial measures as the first option, raise attention for the undesirable side-effects of imprisonment, reaffirm that mere deprivation of liberty is the punishment and that no extra suffering behind prison walls is needed, and reaffirm the 'rehabilitation for all' ideal. This comes close to the 'Dutch model' in the period of sustained reduction of imprisonment rates between 1947 and 1974. Imprisonment rates went down to as low as 18 per 100,000 inhabitants in 1973, and remained quite low until the mid-1980s. Dutch prisons, with their strong focus on rehabilitation and prisoners' rights, 'relaxed' inmate–staff relations and very few prison riots, were considered the 'least bad' prisons in the world (eg Downes 1988; Vagg 1994).

## III. THE PUNITIVE TURN

In the following period, from 1975 to 2005, the Netherlands became a classic case of penal expansionism. From one of the lowest imprisonment rates in Western Europe, the Netherlands suddenly rose to one of the highest rates (after Britain and Spain). Comparing the 18 prisoners per 100,000 of the population in 1973 to the 134 that were behind bars on any given day in 2005, we can conclude that the Netherlands locked up more than seven times as many people as 30 years before. That is one of the steepest rates of increase in the world. Moreover, there was a simultaneous, and equally impressive expansion of non-custodial sentences, diversions from the penal process and very intrusive 'preventative' measures (uit Beijerse and van Swaaningen 2007; van Swaaningen 2008). The steepest increase in non-custodial sentences coincided with penal expansionism, and there is no evidence that they have actually replaced any prison sentences—hence the conclusion of Jolande uit Beijerse and I (2007) that any further development of 'alternatives to prison' should be preceded by a moratorium on prison construction, and that an active search for alternatives should precede a decision about the imposition of custodial sentences. The new Dutch punitiveness is furthermore shown in the selective incapacitation of specific 'problematic groups' (most notably habitual offenders); austere, cheaply built prisons, far away from the larger cities from which most of the prisoners and their families come; a shift of focus in penal policy from rehabilitation to the protection of society and 'expressive sanctioning'; several violations of penal principles; and penal crises with respect to fire hazards and prison staff who have been silenced because they criticised the official policy line of the Minister of Justice (Downes and van Swaaningen 2007). The radical shift in Dutch penal politics was clearly visible from the early 1980s onwards, but it was picked up remarkably late in the international penological literature. In their book *Penal Systems: A comparative approach,* Michael Cavadino and James Dignan (2006) 'finally' conclude in their chapter on the Netherlands, that 'a beacon of tolerance was dimmed'.

In our study 'The Road to Dystopia?' David Downes and I concluded that the development of crime figures and imprisonment figures in the Netherlands have often gone in opposite directions (Downes and van Swaaningen 2007). When registered crime increased, imprisonment rates dropped. When registered crime rates increased more strongly, there was just a slow increase of imprisonment rates. And the enormous expansion of the prison system only started when registered crime rates stabilised! There obviously is a time-lag between the decision to build more prisons and the moment the new prisons are ready, but not 15–20 years! The thesis that 'we imprison more people because crime has increased' is an explanation with considerable appeal to common sense, but it is difficult to say what these figures actually measure: registration effects, police priorities, new criminalisation or an actual number of wrongdoings. And, because there is so little evidence of a direct correlation between registered crime and imprisonment rates, these two developments require different explanations.

In our study we also examined some other often-mentioned explanations for the expansion of the Dutch prison system. Drugs offences were a major driving force in this respect. It was explicitly argued in the 1985 White Paper *Society and Crime* that the Netherlands had become a major European 'narco-state', with a 'mafia' that controlled the real estate sector and the sex industry in several cities, and that—among other things—stiffer penalties were needed in order to counter this new tendency of organised crime. The same 1985 White Paper argued that the decline of informal social control from the 1960s onwards needed to be compensated by an increase in penal control and local governance of crime and insecurity. This is called the 'depillarisation theory': with the near demise of the traditional denominational pillars of society after the secularisation process of the 1960s, policing and punishment were seen as one of the few remaining mechanisms of social control. There is also a more economic, social policy version of this theory: with the severe budget cuts in welfare provision in the early 1980s, we ended up in a situation in which we were unable to solve social problems by social policy, and everything was referred to the police and the criminal justice system. This latter variety has more support in penological literature: countries that spend little money on welfare generally have high imprisonment rates, and those countries that are the most generous in welfare expenditure generally have lower imprisonment rates (eg Beckett and Western 2001; Downes and Hansen 2006).

By and large, we accepted the argument that imprisonment rates had risen because crime had become more serious and more violent, but we doubted whether that was really such an important part of the explanation. Lastly, we examined the growing importance of the victim in penal procedures and of 'fear of crime' in local security policies. The introduction of victim surveys in the early 1980s definitely marks a shift in media and political attention from the offender to the damage he has done. It has also resulted in some changes in court. Next to the traditional vision of administrating justice, in which the guilt of the offender is the key question, judges now also have to take the victim's interests into account. A victim's need for social recognition and for disapproval of the act committed against him may imply a reaffirmation of the Durkheimian function of punishment (Boutellier 2000), but it does not necessarily lead to increased punitiveness. The increased focus on restorative justice or mediation is a very different reaction to this same phenomenon.

With respect to the role drugs play in penological developments in the Netherlands we primarily have to point to the fact that the traditional 'harm reduction' approach with a focus on public health was gradually changed to a merely penal approach in the 1990s—though the prosecution of drug users who do not cause any nuisance remains exceptional. Some 20 per cent of all prisoners are convicted for drugs offences, and an unknown number for drug-related offences. Legalisation of drugs or a regulated distribution through, for example apothecaries, would probably have made expansion of the prison system unnecessary.

Whilst David Downes and I focused on sociological developments that had led to an increase in imprisonment, Miranda Boone and Martin Moerings (2007) analysed reasons for penal expansion that were more internal to the penal system. They concluded, for example, that accused persons were remanded in custody more often than before, and that the main rationale for it was the protection of society against junkies, beggars and petty violent offenders. They also saw that mentally disturbed offenders awaiting a place in a penal-psychiatric ('TBS') clinic led to extra pressure on the prison system. The fact that juvenile offenders, who are increasingly tried as adults, were locked up more frequently was also an important reason for the expansion of the prison system. And, albeit to a lesser extent, the increased use of detention for foreigners without valid travel documents, who cannot be deported, also put more pressure on the penal system. Boone and Moerings concluded that Dutch society was no longer able to solve social problems by social means, and that penalisation thus was a loincloth of a supposedly civilised society.

## IV. THE ROLE OF POLITICAL WILL, PENAL EXPERTS AND ACTIVISTS

If there is a moral and political will to bring imprisonment rates down, it has often proved possible to do so. But, why would we actually *not* want to lock up all these 'evildoers'? John Braithwaite and Philip Pettit argue in their book *Not Just Deserts* that

> it is good when societies feel uncomfortable about punishment. Just as it is healthy for citizens to be uncomfortable rather than morally smug about the rightness of killing others in war, so too with punishing criminals ... A society which feels morally comfortable about sending thousands of terrified young men and women to institutions in which they are bashed, raped, and brutalized, stripped of human dignity, denied freedom of speech and movement, has a doubtful commitment to freedom.
>
> (Braithwaite Pettit 1990: 6.)

In other words: putting 'limits to pain' in prison is a sign of civilisation. Civilised societies simply do not torture or inflict other forms of inhuman and degrading treatment upon other people.

The period of decarceration in the Netherlands emerged from the experience of the Second World War, when the elites—who generally do not end up in prison, but who were locked up under the Nazi rule—felt so ashamed of the appalling prison conditions they encountered that they felt the need to change these radically, if society was to overcome the barbarism of the Nazi wartime and establish a civilised society. In Spain, the humanisation of the prison system was also felt to be a necessary step in the transition to democracy after the death of the dictator Franco in 1975 (van Swaaningen 1997: 152–55). And the Finnish politics of decarceration started with the acknowledgement in 1976 that Finland's high imprisonment rate (when compared to neighbouring Scandinavian countries) was a disgrace (Lappi Seppälä 2006, 2008). Nils Christie (1993: ch 4) attributes Scandinavia's low incarceration rates to the joint moral community that shapes criminal justice policy in these countries. And Jeffrey Meyer and Pat O'Malley (2005: 205) argue that the Canadian decision in 2001 to follow a more penal reductionist policy started with the rhetorical, yet pivotal question: 'we either go the American way ... or develop meaningful, lasting alternatives'. In the 1980s, the Solicitor General of the Dutch Supreme Court, Jan Remmelink, characterised sentencing as a worrisome process and penal policy as a politics of bad conscience (de Haan 1990). In fact, having a high imprisonment rate was seen as something deeply problematic up till the late 1990s, both for economic reasons and as an indicator of our level of civilisation. Still in 1997, a report from the WODC, the research centre of the Dutch Ministry of Justice, that sought to analyse and explain the rising imprisonment rates between 1985 and 1995, started by arguing that we should seek to stop the 'unrestrained expansion' of the prison system over the investigated period of time (Grapendaal et al 1997: 6). The researchers argued explicitly for reductionist strategies that counter the most important causes of the increase. According to them, neither legal changes, nor an increased willingness to report delinquency to the police, nor the expansion of the capacity of the police and the prosecution service could be held responsible for the increase in sentencing. Basically, they blamed it on a more punitive attitude within the prosecution service, the judiciary, the legislature, the police and the prison service (Grapendaal et al 1997: 59).

With hindsight this seems to have been the last outburst of a genuine belief on the part of politicians and policy-makers in the desirability and possibility of reducing imprisonment rates. Most of today's politicians merely take the populist stance that 'the citizen is always right', presupposing that the public wants stiffer penalties, and ignore any challenges to that supposition. With an uneasy feeling I look at the eagerness with which Dutch policy-makers currently try to copy UK and US policy—from zero tolerance to ASBOs (Koemans 2011). It is quite telling in this respect that in 2010 the Dutch Ministry of Justice was renamed the Ministry of *Security* and Justice: with security mentioned first. There is, moreover, very little opposition to this punitive turn. At the political level nearly all parties, from Labour to the extreme right, seem to agree that we are still too lenient and need more overt sanctions. The once influential Dutch League for Penal Reform, the Coornhert Liga, has ceased to exist. A coherent penal philosophy is currently notable by its absence. When studying policy documents of the last 25 years, in order to find out what reasons officials gave for the continuous expansion of the penal system, we are struck by the *lack* of arguments. Basically, we only see two official storylines: one is the alleged 'public outcry' over penal leniency (that functions as a mantra, which is not examined seriously); and the other is the 'rising crime rates' (in fact crime rates have been fairly stable since the 1990s and declining since 2002).

The influence that law- and policy-makers actually have on the development of prison rates is not always so clear. In their study on overcrowding in Belgian prisons, Kristel Beyens, Sonja Snacken and Christian Eliaerts contend:

> Decreasing prison populations were sometimes the result of legislative reforms ... sometimes of an increased scepticism towards deprivation of liberty without any legislative reform ... and we also see many initiatives aimed at bringing down prison populations ... that remained without result.
>
> (Beyens, Snacken and Eliaerts 1993: 277, translation: RvS.)

Michael Tonry (2001) indicates how important it nonetheless is to study, in addition to socio-cultural and political developments, also the more concrete level of legislation and policymaking. While answering the question why American incarceration rates are so exceptionally high, Tonry points at legislative reforms and policies such as the war on drugs, the introduction of mandatory and indeterminate sentencing, 'three strikes and you're out' laws, and a strong penalisation of a breach of parole.[2] In his book *Downsizing Prisons,* Michael Jacobson (2005) proposes to reverse these reforms. Jacobson offers very practical policy solutions and strategies for awaking from the American 'penal nightmare'. These include changing how parole and probation agencies operate, significantly reducing punitive sentencing and 'technical' parole violations, and supporting drug-treatment programmes. As former Commissioner of the New York City Departments of Correction and Probation, Jacobson (2005: 223) presents himself explicitly as a practitioner who 'would contend that pragmatic strategies are even likely to assist, and perhaps contribute to forming and expanding, the strength of anti-incarceration social movements by rendering those movements' goals more attainable.' Yet, at the same time Jacobson is very normative as well, when he ends his book with the plea: 'Present policies have produced more harm than good, and it is time to stop. It's time to stop.'

From the work of Tapio Lappi-Seppälä (2006) we can also conclude that legislation and policy are indeed important factors in bringing imprisonment rates down—and indeed up—in a country that is most often put forward as an example over the last decade of a non-punitive society: Finland. In the Finnish case, the largest reductionist effects were achieved by: (1) reducing the penalties for theft in 1972 and again in 1991, (2) restricting the use of preventive detention in 1973, (3) the introduction of day-fines and conditional sentences in 1977, (4) the reduction of the term of parole in 1989, and (5) the introduction of the community service order as an alternative to custody in 1992 and 1995. The increase of Finnish imprisonment rates after 2000 have mainly been caused by: (1) increased

[2] It is worth mentioning that in the Netherlands the political right (particularly the extreme right) has proposed to introduce precisely these law reforms in the Netherlands.

penalties for assault, (2) a stronger penalisation of drug use and trafficking, and (3) of sex offences and domestic violence.

Michael Cavadino and James Dignan (2006: 151) characterise Finland as the 'most expert-orientated among the Scandinavian countries.' Though it cannot be proven that this correlates directly with Finland's low prison population, there are good reasons for considering the role of penal experts. Internationally, penal experts and penal reform movements play a key role as a political avant-garde for reductionist agendas (Bondeson 2005; van Swaaningen 1997: ch 7). The period of decarceration in the Netherlands confirms this thesis. It started with the Fick Committee, which set the guidelines for a new, humane prison system in 1947, and the Utrecht School of the 1950s, which was a main supporter of rehabilitation. It continued in the 1970s with the prisoners' rights movement, by abolitionists who engaged in penal pressure groups and legal reform in the 1970s and 1980s, and by the establishment of strongly expert-led policy-making in that same era. Nils Christie (1993: 41) has argued, however, that the proverbial 'Dutch tolerance' has always been a 'tolerance from above', led by professional elites who were far more 'tolerant' than the general public. This would make the moderate Dutch penal climate vulnerable, Christie argued. Unfortunately, with hindsight we have to agree that Christie was right on this point.

David Downes and I have also demonstrated how a strongly moralistic anti-crime and anti-leniency tone of the 1990 White Paper *Law in Motion* was merged with a managerial discourse on increasing the 'efficacy of the penal chain' (Downes and van Swaaningen 2007). A punitive populism came to dominate the politics of crime control from the late 1990s onwards, when the 'avant-garde' role was taken over by the populist (or extreme) right, which focused strongly on the threat that 'foreigners' in general and Islamic terrorists in particular posed to Dutch society. On a more direct policy level we see how a 'what works?' approach, with its discourse on 'evidence-based' 'best practices', replaces the social commitment of a previous generation of lawyers and criminologists. The discrediting of the reductionist penal philosophy coincided with the emergence of a different type of 'penal expert': the statistician, the risk-analyst, the manager, the psychiatrist and the psychologist. These new experts seldom comment on the punitive turn. They do not have the broad intellectual agenda of the preceding generation; they are hired for concrete advice in a concrete case and stick to that. Moreover, they have to obey the new managerial culture in which 'targets', 'output financing' and 'planning and control' are the buzzwords.

In a similar line, David Downes (2008: 1) asks: 'Would practitioners have the same freedom of manoeuvre and senior civil servant backing today as David Faulkner [a senior civil servant in the British penal administration with a reductionist agenda] and his team managed in the 1980s? I fear not.' Looking at the fact that, despite critical remarks of the British Justice

Secretary, Kenneth Clarke, about the 'astonishing number' of prisoners in England and Wales, the extremely high costs of the prison system and the fact that so many people become addicted to drugs while they are in prison, British imprisonment rates keep growing (from 141 in 2004 to 154 in 2011), we fear Downes is right.[3] Analyses of the Spanish prison system (with the second highest numbers in Western Europe, without having particularly high victimisation rates or levels of public punitiveness) point, in addition to the fact that penalties have become more severe and new criminalisation has taken place and also to the declining influence of professional elites on policy-makers, as a reason why the Spanish rates have been increasing, from 138 in 2004 to 152 in 2011 (Cid and Larrauri 2009).

## V. A PUNITIVE TURN REVERSED?

With 134 prisoners per 100,000 inhabitants in 2005, the Netherlands approached the West European peak—after Britain and Spain. But, while the imprisonment rates in these latter two countries continued to rise, the Dutch imprisonment rates went down—after 30 years of increase. With an imprisonment rate of 87 in 2011, the Netherlands is back at the level of the late 1990s. A recent trend analysis by the Ministry of Justice's research unit, WODC, expects imprisonment rates to decline even further, albeit not at the same pace as from 2005 to 2010 (Sonnenschein et al 2011). Eight prisons are being closed, and one has been rented out to Belgium, which suffers structurally from overcrowding. The closure of six more juvenile institutions is proposed. No penal expert had predicted this. There were no remarkable changes in the socio-cultural fabric of the country that would explain it, there was definitely no revival of reductionist politics, and neither was there any clear decriminalisation nor other policy initiative that would have any depenalising effect. The only thing we can say is that punitive turns can be reversed—if we take imprisonment rates as an indicator of punitiveness at least.

It actually took a couple of years before the first analyses of the decreasing number of prisoners emerged. The most often heard explanation was the seemingly obvious idea that imprisonment rates went down because registered crime rates were going down. This seemed all too simple. If we conclude that crime rates had hardly any correlation with the expansion of the prison system, why would they determine a decrease? Moreover, registered crime rates had dropped in most West European countries, whereas a decrease in imprisonment rates did not took place in these other countries.

[3] 'Minister wil beleid omgooien. Londen: sluit veroordeelden niet zo vaak op', *NRC Handelsblad* 30 June 2010.

Let us have a somewhat closer look at the decreasing crime rates in the Netherlands.

In 2009, the legal economist Ben Vollaard, the police official Peter Versteegh and the statistician Jan van den Brakel published a report on what they called the most promising explanations of the decline in the crime rate since 2002. First, they observed a spectacular decrease in the most serious forms of violent crime. On an aggregated level this resulted in shorter penalties, despite higher penalties for serious crime as such. Secondly, they concluded that the number of persons addicted to hard drugs had decreased by two-thirds. Since this group is held responsible for a large proportion of common street crime, their decreasing number contributes significantly to the average decrease of crime. Moreover, the introduction of a new measure that aims to get habitual offenders (about 90 per cent of whom are drug addicts) off the street for two years, regardless of the kind of offence they have committed (the so-called ISD measure), is seen to have had a major effect on the decrease of street crime. Other reasons for the declining crime rates that Vollaard, Versteegh and van den Brakel (2009) came up with are the decreasing number of young people in society, more effective, targeted policing, better prevention measures and lower prices for stolen goods.

As we saw when we were analysing the rise of imprisonment rates, the effect of the (this time decreasing) *seriousness* of the committed offences seems to have had the largest impact. But, one has to dig pretty deep into the figures in order to understand the relation with declining imprisonment rates. Offences registered as 'violent crime' actually rose, from 91,738 in 2000 to 111,888 in 2007. Yet, because the violent crimes that are brought to court are far less serious, penalties are lower. A similar story can be told with respect to drug offences. Infractions of the Opium Act increased from 7,474 in 2000 to 15,675 in 2007, but this increase was by and large due to an increased penalisation of soft drugs (ie cannabis derivates), for which lower penalties are meted out.[4] There certainly is an incapacitating effect of the ISD measure for habitual offenders, but it should not be overestimated. On any given day there are only 700 offenders in the ISD institutions—which is not a lot, on a prison capacity of approximately 12,000—and, incapacitation only has a temporary effect. Moreover, although rehabilitation is also an official goal of the ISD measure, its focus on incapacitation makes it predominantly a punitive measure (Struijk 2011).

[4] These figures are derived from Statistics Netherlands CBS's 'Statline', available online at www.cbs.nl/nl-NL/menu/themas/veiligheid-recht/nieuws/default.htm and the co-production Crime and Law Enforcement from the CBS and the WODC (see Kalidien and de Heer-de Lange 2011). Because the figures provided in this chapter are merely intended to illustrate a certain trend, we will deal with the figures globally in order not to be distracted from the general line of argumentation by complex statistical details.

A second reason for the decreasing imprisonment rates that is often mentioned is the increased use of non-custodial sanctions and electronic monitoring. It is true that the number of non-custodial sanctions for adults continued to increase when imprisonment rates were going down: in 2002, 20,949 non-custodial sanctions were imposed on adults, in 2007, 37,663, which is about the same number as the number of prisoners per year.[5] But, the number of non-custodial sanctions had risen most strongly during the period of penal expansionism, and from 2008 onwards the number of non-custodial sanctions actually declined slightly. We can also doubt whether the wider application of non-custodial sanctions is at all a symbol of a less punitive penal climate, if we observe that they involve an increasing number of conditions—including a plan to introduce plainly stigmatising fluorescent smocks bearing the text 'I work for society'—and these conditions become ever more strictly applied.

These most heard explanations are not fully convincing. We will need to dig a bit deeper. For this reason, I have examined to what extent the policy mechanisms and the mechanisms that are internal to the system, which have driven up the prison capacity in the past, now contribute to the decrease. It should be stressed that most of these are tentative explanations that to a large degree are still hypothetical. More research is needed to see how much sense they make. Let us start with some changes within the penal system.

The biannual statistical report, *Crime and Law Enforcement,* shows, for example, that far fewer unconditional prison sentences have been imposed for property crimes—which make up a large part of the judicial caseload. We can also observe that offenders are less often remanded in custody than in the early 2000s. And, fear of crime—which correlates more strongly with imprisonment rates than crime rates—is traditionally low in the Netherlands, and shows a downward trend since 1999, which continues even more steeply in the post-2005 period of decarceration (Kalidien and de Heer 2011).

Next, there are some policy changes that are worth examining in more depth. In 2005, the so-called 'prosecutorial settlement' (*OM afdoening*) has been introduced. This allows a public prosecutor to settle a case without bringing it to court. In order not to violate the habeas corpus principle (ie the offender's right to be heard by a judge), this pragmatic policy to solve court delays is limited to non-custodial settlements. Only after the intervention of a judge, can such settlements be converted into a custodial sanction. It is quite likely that this will have some effect on the volume of custodial sentences as well—although we can also observe that, compared to other West European countries, the chance of receiving a custodial sanction for

[5] For juvenile delinquents, some five times as many non-custodial sanctions (23,583) are meted out as prison sentences.

very minor offences is still relatively high in the Netherlands (Kalidien and de Heer 2011). Though quantitatively less important, there are two other policy measures that may have had a decarcerating effect. First, we have to point out the measure that was taken to shorten the waiting lists for offenders sentenced both to imprisonment and psychiatric treatment and who are awaiting a place in a penitentiary psychiatric ('TBS') clinic in prison: the so-called 'Fokkens regulation' made it possible to transfer these offenders after one third of their prison sentence to a TBS clinic. We have seen above, that the waiting list for TBS patients was one of the factors that put pressure on the prison system.[6] And secondly, we can point to the general pardon for some 27,000 asylum-seekers in 2007, amongst whom a substantial number were awaiting deportation in remand centres.[7]

Also on the sociological level, there are some further hypotheses that are worth investigating. First, we have to admit that we simply built too many prisons. Prognostic studies were based on trend analyses that started from the premises that crime would continue to increase, while registered crime had long stabilised.[8] Although it does not explain why imprisonment rates went down, it reveals the (costly) belief in punitive 'solutions'—and obviously the fact that so many prisons are closed or remain half-empty. Secondly, the judiciary seems to be more open to expert critiques of punitiveness than politicians or prosecutors. Various judges, including members of the Supreme Court (*Hoge Raad*) and the President of the Council for the Administration of Justice (*Raad voor de Rechtspraak*), have criticised the practice of bringing often very minor offences to court. Whether this has had any actual effect on sentencing still needs to be examined. We also have to acknowledge that, despite all the criticism of a declining quality of penitentiary regimes, Dutch prisons are still preferred by a large majority of inmates, in contrast to, for example, British prisons (Kruttschnitt and Dirkzwager 2011). Even under the strictest regimes in the Netherlands, prison staff try to achieve as humane conditions as possible. The possibly mitigating role of such 'street level bureaucrats' is worthwhile examining as well.

Another factor that is worth examining is whether more critical media attention to miscarriages of justice, prison guards who speak out about worsening conditions, reports about fire risks in penitentiary facilities and so on have 'disturbed' the generally held idea that imprisonment is a solution to

[6] The 'Fokkens regulation' was abolished in 2010 by then new government.

[7] Again, things can change very rapidly here as well: the 2010 right-wing minority government, that was supported by the populist right-wing anti-immigration and anti-Islam party PVV, propose to penalise residence in the Netherlands without valid documents. This is likely to result once more in rising prison rates.

[8] Albeit very implicitly, this seems to be acknowledged in the Ministry of Justice's 2011 trend analysis, in which a new way of prognosticating the demand for penitentiary capacity is proposed (Sonnenschein et al 2011).

crime. We have seen that at a macro-level, nuanced media attention to crime and insecurity correlates with low imprisonment rates. Tapio Lappi-Seppälä (2006, 2008) has explained the low Finnish imprisonment rates partly by the general absence of any tabloids in Finland, and the fact that the largest newspaper is a quality paper and that 90 per cent of all newspapers are still sold on the basis of subscription—ie there is no need for sensationalism to attract readers. Up until the late 1980s the situation in the Netherlands was not very different. The mediatisation of crime and insecurity, what we came to call 'crime infotainment', only emerged after commercial television entered the media landscape in the 1990s. Particularly in the early 2000s, in the period of political turmoil following the murder of the anti-Islam politician Pim Fortuyn and film director Theo van Gogh, columnists who oversimplified complex social phenomena became more influential than serious journalists, and a blunt political incorrectness became fashionable also in the serious press (van Swaaningen 2005). Over the last couple of years this seems to have changed again: during the banking and economic crises of 2008 and 2011 critical journalism came back *en vogue*. In politics, we can observe a similar development: in the early 2000s, law and order was a major electoral theme, but in the most recent electoral campaigns crime and insecurity have played a far less prominent role: far below the economy and healthcare. Moreover, the main political supporter of punitiveness, the neo-nationalist, populist right, is for the first time since 2001 losing ground. If crime news gets less prominence, the pressure for a punitive display of political muscle may decrease as well.

Can we say that the Netherlands has become less punitive, as imprisonment rates have gone down since 2005? There are too many other factors at stake to answer this question affirmatively. First, the percentage of offenders who actually receive a custodial sentence in the Netherlands is, in comparison with other European countries, quite high (Kalidien and de Heer 2011). On the political right there is a continuous pressure to use the present excess prison capacity to 'finally start punishing properly'. Successive governments have proposed very punitive measures—eg ASBOs, increasing the maximum length of imprisonment, custodial consequences for a breach of parole, non-custodial sanctions to be replaced by custodial ones if they are not carried out properly. Some other punitive measures have already been introduced—such as the super-max EBI prison, the watered-down 'three strikes' ISD measure, or the 'long stay' (read: till death) regime in penitentiary psychiatric TBS clinics. Moreover, imprisonment rates remain heavily ethnically biased. At present, 28 per cent of the Dutch prison population are foreign nationals (mainly Eastern Europeans and Africans), and it is overwhelmingly non-white—since most of the second-generation migrants and people from the former colonies have Dutch nationality. If we take custodial and non-custodial sanctions together, the overall level of punishment is still increasing. And, last but not least, extremely intrusive measures have been introduced under the banner of crime prevention. This has led sociologist Willem Schinkel (2011) to conclude that we are currently experiencing 'prepression': allegedly preventive measures have been given a sometimes extremely repressive edge. The old saying that one way of abolishing prisons is to turn society into a prison could well be on its way to being implemented in the Netherlands.

More than anything else, the Dutch case seems to reaffirm the Foucauldian story of a 'penal-welfare complex' in which welfare provisions serve to discipline the population. It is also reminiscent of Stan Cohen's (1979) notion of a 'punitive city'. Perhaps the prison population has merely decreased because we have creatively transformed policing and community safety politics into the main strategies of crime control? The buzzwords of 'broken windows' and 'zero-tolerance policing' have indeed reshaped the notion of social crime prevention in a rather exclusive, repressive direction (Koemans 2011). The merger of prevention and repression Willem Schinkel (2011) identified in Dutch local safety politics is strongly oriented towards the so-called 'pre-crimes' of the 'underclasses' (immigrants, homeless people, drug addicts, prostitutes), which makes the thesis of an urban revanchism that has gained a foothold in politics quite plausible (van Swaaningen 2008). The general policy line of 'persuading' 'outsiders' to adopt a 'decent' life-style, that sociologists Godfried Engbersen, Erik Snel and Afke Weltevrede (2005) have coined as 'social recapture' (*sociale herovering*), and the policy shift from 'crime' to 'anti-social behaviour' and 'pre-crime' means that we cannot consider the Dutch case as a true example that a punitive turn has been reversed. It is rather a case in which welfare provisions have been actively deployed in the fight against nuisance and insecurity.

## VI. COUNTERING PUNITIVENESS

WODC, the Dutch Ministry of Justice's research department, expects imprisonment rates to drop even further (Sonnenschein et al 2011). Yet, there is little reason to sit back quietly and rejoice. Because the decline in imprisonment rates just 'happened', without any plan or political decision, it can also turn around again 'just like that'. Moreover, we have seen that punitive elements have permeated into society at large. In order to argue against punitiveness, our focus may have to shift from prison to the 'penal-welfare complex' and its 'prepressive' measures and projects in society at large. Not just in prison, but also in society at large, it is, to use Braithwaite and Pettit's (1990) words once more, socially healthy to feel uncomfortable about punitive answers to social questions. Ian Loader's (2010) plea for 'penal moderation' can easily be translated to the 'punitive city' as well. Also here, the excess in punitiveness is to be met by restraint, parsimony and dignity, as Loader proposes. We expect too much of punishment, and insufficiently acknowledge the negative side-effects, whether in prison or in society.

One of the problems indicated above is the lack of a critical counter-current in the Dutch debate about crime and insecurity. Over the last couple of years we can, however, observe some careful changes in this respect. We have already hinted at the idea that journalism seems to have become a bit more serious and more critical again.[9] But there are many more signs that the counter-effects of punitiveness are again being taken more seriously. Some examples: the Dutch ombudsman warned in his annual report of 2008 that the current tendency to treat all citizens as potential lawbreakers alienates 98 per cent of all people of good will from the state (Nationale Ombudsman 2008). The arguments with which the ombudsman supported this warning have been picked up widely by the media and have indeed caused some public shock among rather large segments of society, who simply did not realise how harshly and with what indifference many state officials treat their citizens. It has been argued above that the government's claim that punitiveness is just a response to the public outcry for law and order remains an unjustified claim. Serious research into this question most often shows that if 'ordinary people' are given all the details about a particular case, they would punish only marginally more harshly than the allegedly far too liberal judges (Ruiter et al 2011). And there is much more support for the thesis that the people are not as punitive as is often claimed. Every two years the Dutch Social and Cultural Planning Bureau sends out a long questionnaire to 2000 citizens: they are interviewed about their wishes and their actual expectations for the future of society. The 2004 report showed a huge disparity between the two: people would like a more communitarian society with more solidarity, but they feared that society would become still more competitive and that the social climate would continue to toughen. Most interviewees pointed to the growing competitiveness of society, decreasing informal social control and globalisation as the major causes of crime and insecurity, but—and here is the pivot—*because* decreasing competitiveness, reinforcing informal social control and pushing back globalisation were seen to be impossible, further infringements on people's civil liberties, more surveillance and security and indeed stiffer penalties were seen to be indispensable. This can hardly be interpreted as a desire for punitiveness, although the pessimism about the possibilities to change social conditions can have punitive consequences.

The Social and Cultural Planning Bureau has also made a list of best practices in crime prevention and sanctioning (van Noije and Wittebrood

[9] A personal anecdote in this respect: 10 years ago even quality newspapers were reluctant to publish critical contributions of criminologists, whereas today these same critics are actually invited to contribute to the public debate; not only by (these) newspapers, but also by radio and television stations.

2008). This very widely publicised report could, despite all the positivistic connotations connected to the 'what works' movement, be used to serve a reductionist agenda, for it manifestly shows that expressive sanctions 'do not work', and that the plain presence of the police on the streets and social interventions like educational support and social skills training have much more positive effects on recidivism rates. I do not want to go into all the methodological pitfalls of the 'what works' approach here, but use it just as an example of how the tendency of 'acting out' with very expressive forms of punishment may be countered by arguments for a rational, evidence-based politics. It is also worthwhile to simply point at negative effects of punitiveness, such as the overburdened criminal justice system, the high costs of a largely ineffective penal system, the fact that non-custodial sanctions and crime prevention were originally meant to bring imprisonment rates down, and the undesirable effects of defiance and secondary deviance or a hardening social climate. For many journalists this turns out to be 'news'. 'Positive news', about declining crime rates, safer cities and non-punitive reactions to crime and insecurity, such as street coaches or 'safe houses' (*veiligheidshuizen*), is also picked up quite frequently by the media. What may be obvious for criminologists is not so obvious to the average citizen, journalist or politician, and thus to 'keep stating the obvious' is a good strategy for public criminology (Loader and Sparks 2011).

But, raised as I am in the penal abolitionist tradition in criminology, I feel we also need a 'utopian' replacement discourse to visualise the possibility of other, non-punitive answers to crime and insecurity (Bianchi and van Swaaningen 1986). If that is lacking, punitiveness is taken to be self-evident. Penal abolitionists have stressed both the critical and the utopian components, and in the 1970s and 1980s were able to get some public support for some of their goals (van Swaaningen 1997; Ruggiero 2010). Perhaps the term 'abolitionism' is not best suited to public criminology today, for it focuses too much on the negative (abolition) rather than the positive (social solutions to social problems), and it is surrounded by too many absolutist claims. But, abolitionism does provide us with some useful lessons. First, abolitionists have stressed that the need for utopias and for starting with the deconstruction of 'crime' as a meaningful category and of 'punishment' as a serious solution. With their normative style of argumentation they have shown that the penal discourse is often too technical to win the 'hearts and minds'. Instead, they have often tried to counter penal populism with an alternative morality.

Nils Christie famously started his book, *Limits to Pain,* with the following contention:

> Moralism in our areas has for some years been an attitude or even a term associated with protagonists for law and order and severe penal sanctions, while their

opponents were seen as floating in a sort of value-free vacuum. Let it therefore be completely clear that I am also a moralist. Worse: I am a moral imperialist.

(Christie 1981: 10.)

Christie's beautiful phrase, 'Sorrow is inevitable, but not hell created by man' is also well worth remembering. Christie's Dutch fellow-abolitionist Herman Bianchi (1994) was never tired of revealing, in the name of Justice with a capital 'J', the barbaric nature of locking people up in cages that was reminiscent of the times of slavery and corporal punishment. And there are also some good examples of how 'radicals' have directly influenced policy—eg Louk Hulsman's participation in many governmental committees, both in the Netherlands and in the Council of Europe (van Swaaningen and Blad 2011). I miss these voices. I have always been taken by the way Stan Cohen (1985) has reminded us, in his characteristic probing way, that it makes more sense to cautiously reaffirm one's own beliefs and values than becoming a detached critic. For me, that is the present-day value of abolitionism.

Will such a public criminology have any effect? Will it awake people from their punitive dream—or better: their punitive nightmare? Obviously we do not know, but that does not seem to be the most important question. The main issue here is that democracy simply demands opposition and that our ideas on punishment are imbedded in our commitment to social welfare, democracy and human rights (Snacken and Dumortier 2011). The classical role of intellectuals is to demonstrate that change starts with imagination. It is time to pick up that old message again. I do not think any reader seriously expected to find 'the answer' to punitiveness in this chapter. I do hope, however, to have pointed at some useful factors that determine both punitive turns and penal reductionism. It is to be hoped this will also help to avoid the grim pessimism that characterises most of the literature on punitiveness. We have made the mistake of surrendering to the idea that 'nothing works' once: let us not make that mistake again, for it makes (and has made) any critique impotent. It is still worth while to stress that, if we want, things can be changed, that policies can be oriented at penal reduction again. There are no simple solutions, but neither is punitiveness a mere 'plague from above' we simply have to endure; it ain't necessarily so ...

## REFERENCES

Beckett, K and Western, B (2001) 'Governing social marginality: welfare, incarceration and the transformation of state policy', *Punishment & Society*, 3, 43–59.

Beijerse, J uit and van Swaaningen, R (2007) 'Non-Custodial Sanctions', in M Boone and M Moerings (eds), *Dutch Prisons* (The Hague, Boom Juridische uitgevers).

Beyens, K, Snacken, S and Eliaerts, C (1993) *Barstende muren. Overbevolkte gevangenissen: omvang, oorzaken en mogelijke oplossingen* (Antwerp, Kluwer).

Bianchi, H (1994) *Justice as Sanctuary. Toward a new system of crime control* (Bloomington, Indiana University Press).

Bianchi, H and Swaaningen, R van (eds) (1986) *Abolitionism. Towards a non-repressive approach to crime* (Amsterdam, Free University Press).

Bondeson, U (2005) 'Levels of Punitiveness in Scandinavia: Description and Explanations', in J Pratt, D Brown, M Brown, S Hallsworth and W Morrison (eds), *The New Punitiveness. Trends, theories, perspectives* (Cullompton, Willan Publishing).

Boone, M and Moerings, M (2007) 'Growing Prison Rates', in M Boone and M Moerings (eds), *Dutch Prisons* (The Hague, Boom Juridische uitgevers).

Boutellier, H (2000) *Crime and Morality: The significance of Criminal Justice in Post-Modern Culture* (Dordrecht, Kluwer).

Braithwaite, J and Pettit, P (1990) *Not Just Deserts. A Republican Theory of Criminal Justice* (Oxford, Clarendon Press).

Cavadino, M and Dignan, J (2006) *Penal Systems. A Comparative Approach* (London, Sage).

Christie, N (1981) *Limits to Pain* (Oxford, Martin Robertson).

—— (1993) *Crime Control as Industry. Towards gulags Western style?* (London, Routledge).

Cid, J and Larrauri, E (2009) 'Development of Crime, Social Change, Mass Media, Crime Policy, Sanctioning Practice and their Impact on Prison Population Rates', *Sistema penal & violência: Revista Eletrônica da Faculdade de Direito PUCRS*, 1, 1–21.

Cohen, S (1979) 'The Punitive City: Notes on the Dispersal of Social Control', *Contemporary Crises*, 3, 339–63.

—— (1985) *Visions of Social Control: Crime, Punishment and Classification* (Cambridge, Polity Press).

de Haan, W (1990) *The Politics of Redress. Crime, Punishment and Penal Abolition* (London, Unwin Hyman).

Downes, D (1988) *Contrasts in Tolerance. Post-war penal policy in The Netherlands and England and Wales* (Oxford, Clarendon Press).

—— (2008) 'Commission on English Prisons Today: Response to Ian Loader: The Political Art of Penal Moderation', www.howardleague.org/fileadmin/howard_league/user/pdf/Commission/Penal_moderation_-_David_Downes.pdf.

Downes, D and Hansen, K (2006) *Welfare and Punishment. The Relationship Between Welfare Spending and Imprisonment* (London, Crime and Society Foundation).

Downes, D and Swaaningen, R van (2007) 'The Road to Dystopia? Changes in the Penal Climate of the Netherlands', in M Tonry and C Bijleveld (eds), *Crime and Justice in the Netherlands (Volume 35)* (Chicago, University of Chicago Press).

Engbersen, G, Snel, E and Weltevrede, A (2005) *Sociale Herovering in Amsterdam en Rotterdam: één verhaal over twee wijken* (Amsterdam, Amsterdam University Press).

Garland, D (ed) (2001) *Mass Imprisonment. Social Causes and Consequences* (London, Sage).

Grapendaal, M, Groen, P and Heide, W van der (1997) *Duur en volume. Ontwikkeling van de onvoorwaardelijke vrijheidsstraf tussen 1985 en 1995: feiten en verklaringen* (The Hague, WODC).

Jacobson, M (2005) *Downsizing Prisons. How to Reduce Crime and End Mass Incarceration* (New York, New York University Press).

Kalidien, SN and Heer-de Lange, NE de (eds) (2011) *Criminaliteit en rechtshandhaving 2010: Ontwikkelingen en samenhangen* (The Hague, Boom Juridische uitgevers).

Koemans, M (2011) *The War on Antisocial Behaviour. Rationales Underlying Antisocial Behaviour Policies. Comparing British and Dutch Discourse Analyses* (Leiden, Meijers Research Institute and Graduate School of the Leiden Law School).

Kruttschnitt, C and Dirkzwager, A (2011) 'Are there still *Contrasts in Tolerance*? Imprisonment in the Netherlands and England 20 years later', *Punishment & Society*, 13, 283–306.

Lappi-Seppälä, T (2006) 'Penal Policy and Prisoner Rates in Scandinavia. Cross-comparative perspectives in penal severity' (Helsinki, National Research Institute of Legal Policy).

—— (2008) 'Trust, Welfare, and Political Culture: Explaining Differences in National Penal Policies', in M Tonry (ed), *Crime and Justice: A Review of Research (Volume 37)* (Chicago, University of Chicago Press).

Loader, I (2010) 'For Penal Moderation: Notes Towards a Public Philosophy of Punishment', *Theoretical Criminology*, 14, 349–67.

Loader, I and Sparks, R (2011) *Public Criminology?* (London, Routledge).

Matthews, R (2005) 'The Myth of Punitiveness' *Theoretical Criminology*, 9, 175–201.

Meyer, J and O'Malley, P (2005) 'Missing the Punitive Turn? Canadian Criminal Justice, "Balance", and Penal Modernism', in J Pratt, D Brown, M Brown, S Hallsworth and W Morrison (eds), *The New Punitiveness. Trends, theories, perspectives* (Cullompton, Willan Publishing).

Miyazawa, S (2008) 'The Politics of Increasing Punitiveness and the Rising Populism in Japanese Criminal Justice Policy', *Punishment & Society*, 10, 47–77.

Nationale Ombudsman (2008) *De burger in de ketens. Verslag van de Nationale ombudsman over 2008* (The Hague, De Nationale Ombudsman).

Noije, L van and Wittebrood, K (2008) *Sociale veiligheid ontsleuteld. Veronderstelde en werkelijke effecten van veiligheidsbeleid* (The Hague, Sociaal en Cultureel Planbureau).

Pratt, J, Brown, D, Brown, M, Hallsworth, S and Morrison, W (eds) (2005) *The New Punitiveness: Trends, theories, perspectives* (Cullompton, Willan Publishing).

Roberts, JV, Stalans, LJ, Indermauer, D and Hough, M (2003) *Penal Populism and Public Opinion. Lessons from Five Countries* (Oxford, Oxford University Press).

Ruggiero, V (2010) *Penal Abolitionism* (Oxford, Oxford University Press).

Ruiter, S, Tolsma, J, de Hoon, M, Elffers, H and Laan, P van der (2011) *De burger als rechter. Een onderzoek naar geprefereerde sancties voor misdrijven in Nederland* (The Hague, Boom Lemma).

Schinkel, W (2011) 'Prepression: The actuarial Archive and New Technologies of Security', *Theoretical Criminology*, 15, 365–80.

Snacken, S and Dumortier, E (eds) (2011) *Resisting Punitiveness in Europe? Welfare, Human Rights and Democracy* (London, Routledge).
Sonnenschein, A, Braak, S van den, Moolenaar, D and Smit, P (2011) *Trendwatch. Introductie en eerste resultaten van een instrument ter verbetering van justitiële capaciteitsramingen* (The Hague, WODC).
Struijk, S (2011) *De ISD in perspectief. Een studie naar de ISD-maatregel in het licht van het Nederlands strafrechtelijk sanctiestelsel ter bestrijding van recidive en criminele overlast* (Nijmegen, Wolf Legal Publishers).
Tonry, M (2001) 'Why are U.S. Incarceration Rates so High?', in M Tonry (ed), *Penal Reform in Overcrowded Times* (Oxford, Oxford University Press).
Vagg, J (1994) *Prison Systems. A comparative study on accountability in England, France, Germany and the Netherlands* (Oxford, Oxford University Press).
van Swaaningen, R (1997) *Critical Criminology—Visions from Europe* (London, Sage).
—— (2005) 'Public Safety and the Management of Fear', *Theoretical Criminology*, 9, 289–305.
—— (2008) 'Sweeping the Street: Civil Society and Community Safety in Rotterdam', in J Shapland (ed), *Justice, Community and Civil Society. A contested terrain across Europe* (Cullompton, Willan Publishing).
van Swaaningen, R and Blad, JR (eds) (2011) *De ontmaskering van het strafrechtelijk discours. Een bloemlezing uit het werk van Louk Hulsman* (The Hague, Boom Lemma).
van Swaaningen, R and uit Beijerse, J (2012) 'Bars in your Head: Electronic Monitoring in the Netherlands', in M Nellis, R Bas, K Beyens and D Kaminski (eds), *Electronically Monitored Punishment: international and critical perspectives* (London, Routledge).
Vollaard, B, Versteegh, P and Brakel, J van (2009) *Veel belovende verklaringen voor de daling van de criminaliteit na 2002* (Apeldoorn, Politie & Wetenschap).

# *Index*

Page numbers in **bold** indicate reference to a table. Page numbers in *italics* indicate text within a figure.

www.ingramcontent.com/pod-product-compliance
Ingram Content Group UK Ltd.
Pitfield, Milton Keynes, MK11 3LW, UK
UKHW020132290926
15471UKWH00003B/442

9 781509 914500